How to Raise

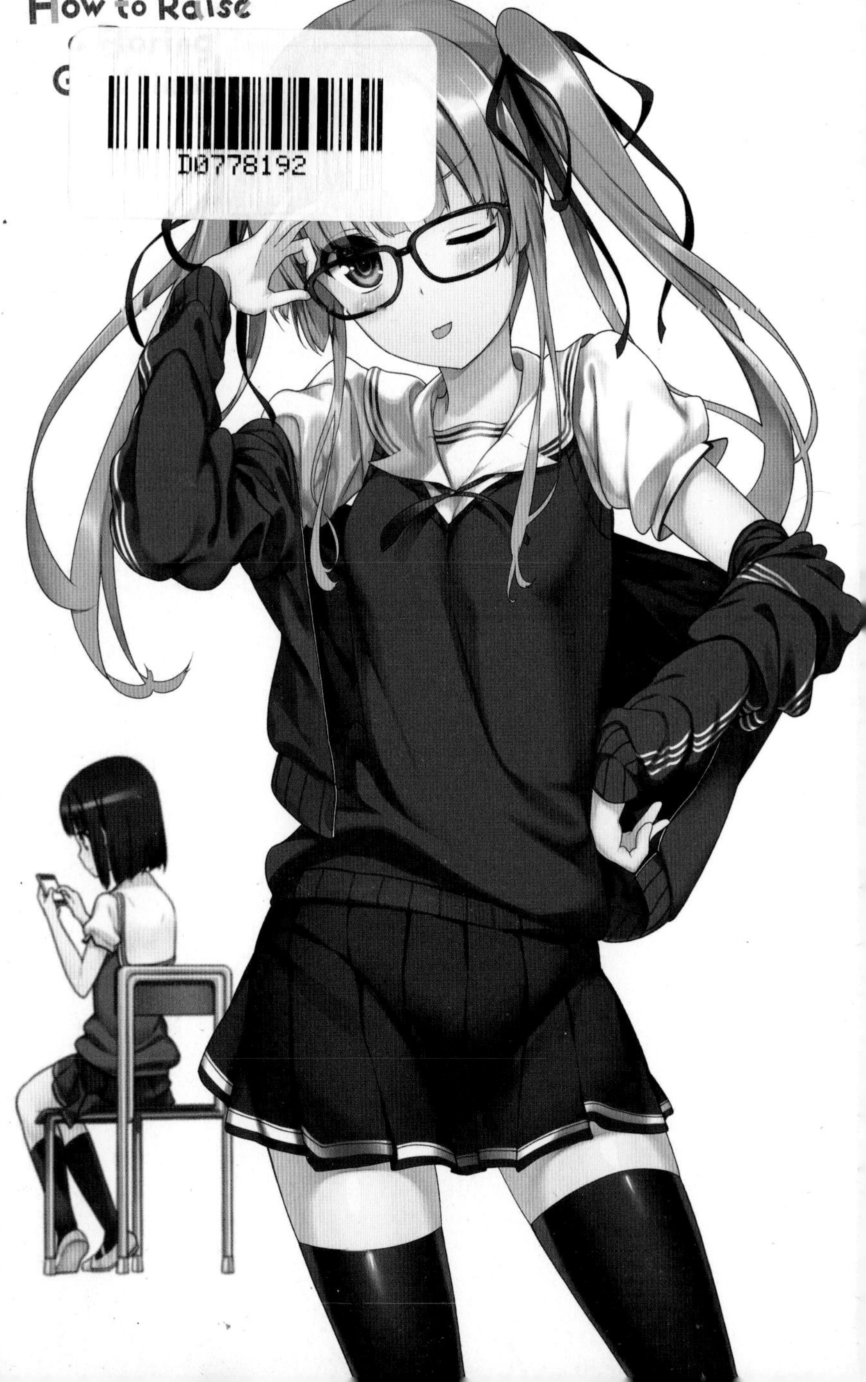

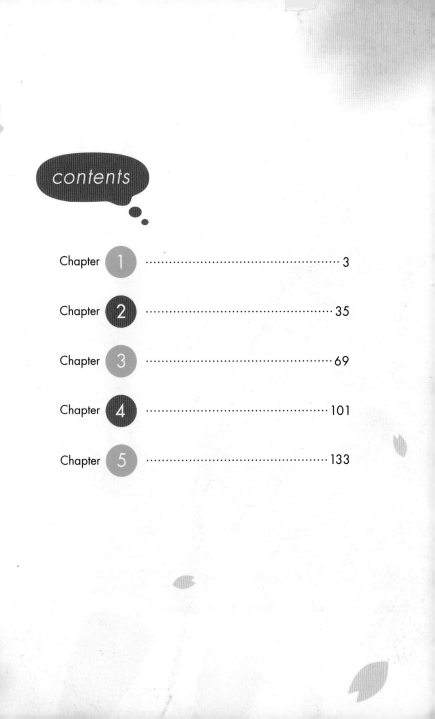

contents

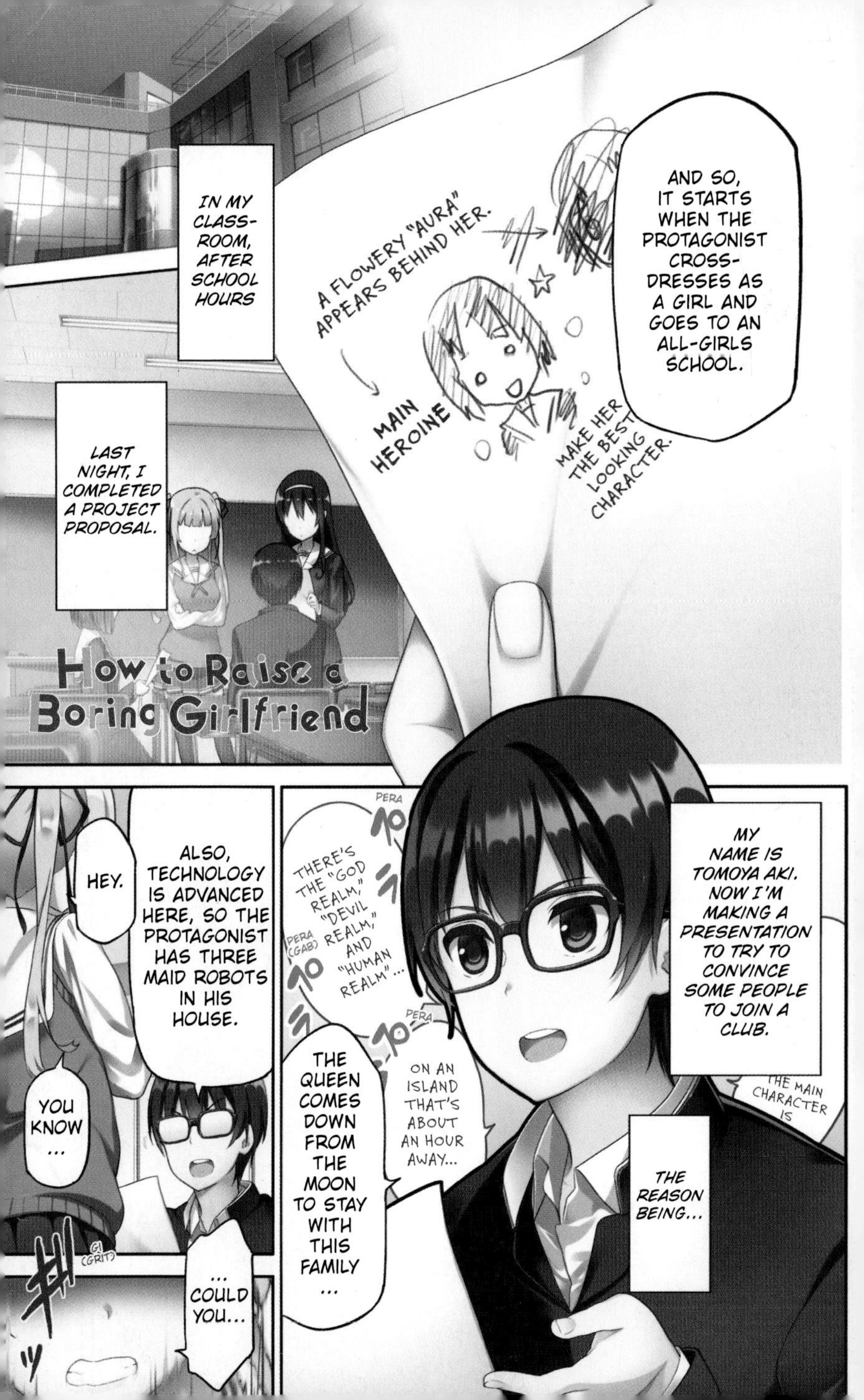
AND SO, IT STARTS WHEN THE PROTAGONIST CROSS-DRESSES AS A GIRL AND GOES TO AN ALL-GIRLS SCHOOL.
A FLOWERY "AURA" APPEARS BEHIND HER.
MAIN HEROINE
MAKE HER THE BEST LOOKING CHARACTER.
IN MY CLASS-ROOM, AFTER SCHOOL HOURS
LAST NIGHT, I COMPLETED A PROJECT PROPOSAL.
How to Raise a Boring Girlfriend
MY NAME IS TOMOYA AKI. NOW I'M MAKING A PRESENTATION TO TRY TO CONVINCE SOME PEOPLE TO JOIN A CLUB.
THE MAIN CHARACTER IS
THE REASON BEING...
PERA
THERE'S THE "GOD REALM," "DEVIL REALM," AND "HUMAN REALM"...
PERA (GAB)
PERA
ON AN ISLAND THAT'S ABOUT AN HOUR AWAY...
THE QUEEN COMES DOWN FROM THE MOON TO STAY WITH THIS FAMILY...
ALSO, TECHNOLOGY IS ADVANCED HERE, SO THE PROTAGONIST HAS THREE MAID ROBOTS IN HIS HOUSE.
HEY.
YOU KNOW...
GI (GRIT)
... COULD YOU...

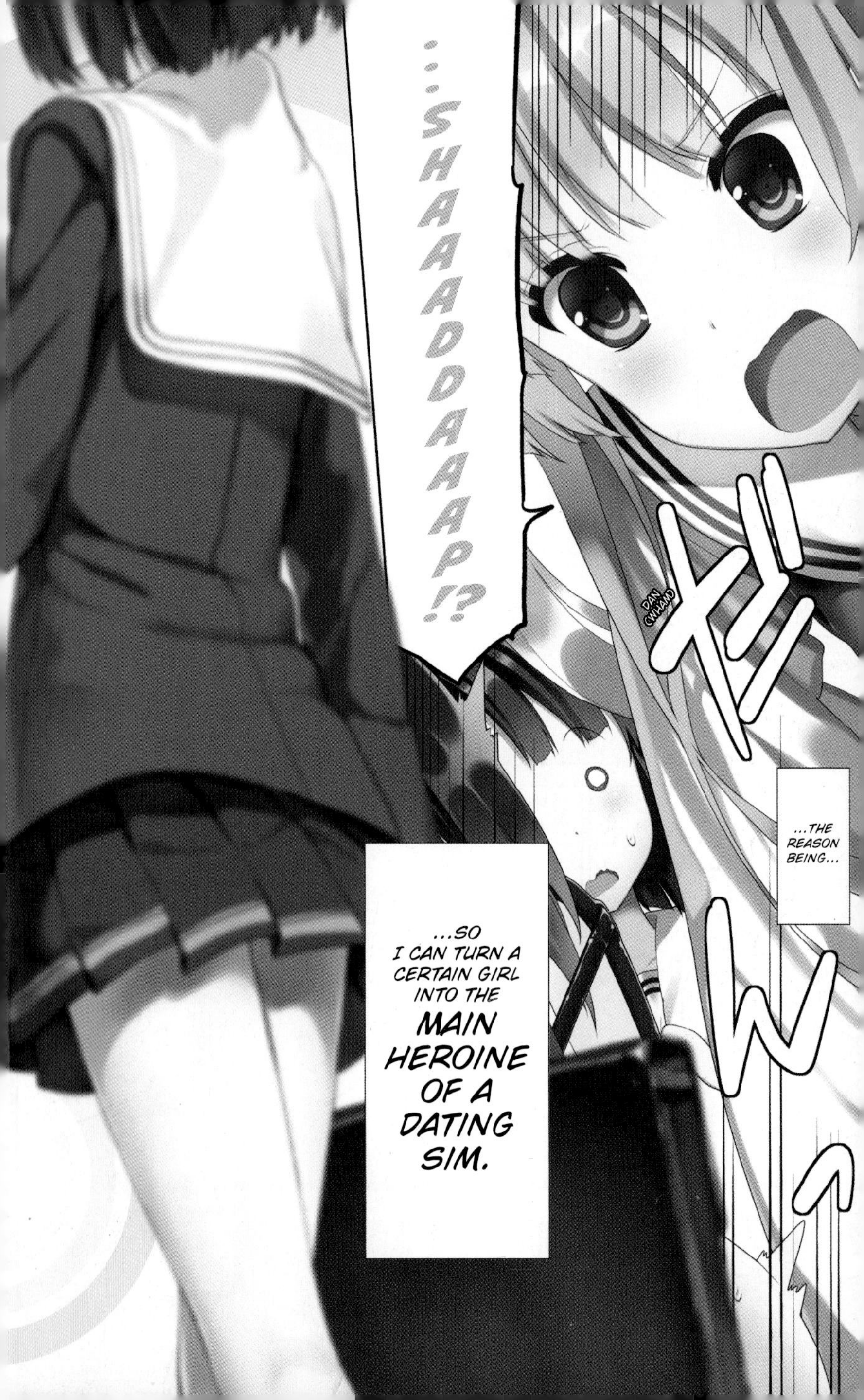
...SHAAADDAAAP!?
DAN CWHAM
...THE REASON BEING...
...SO I CAN TURN A CERTAIN GIRL INTO THE MAIN HEROINE OF A DATING SIM.

How to Raise a Boring Girlfriend

CHAPTER 1

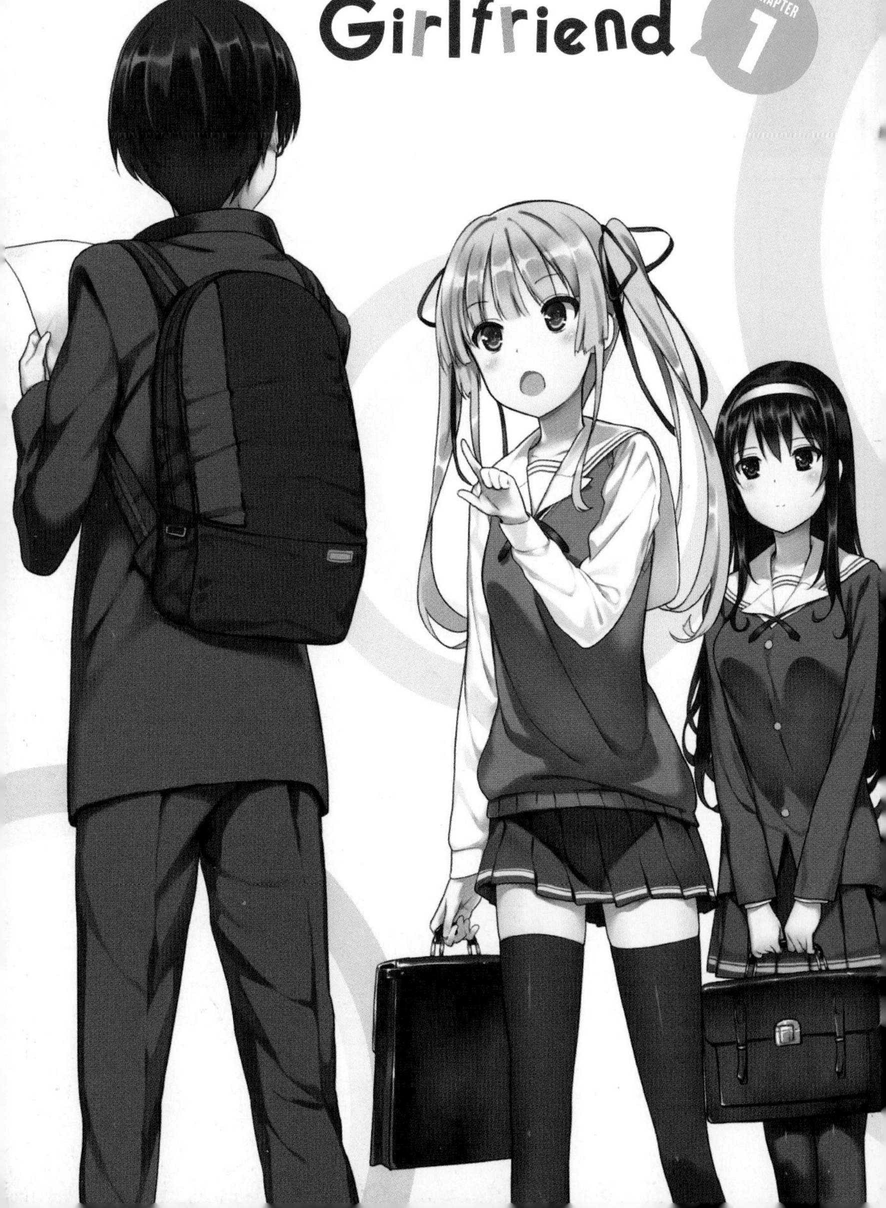

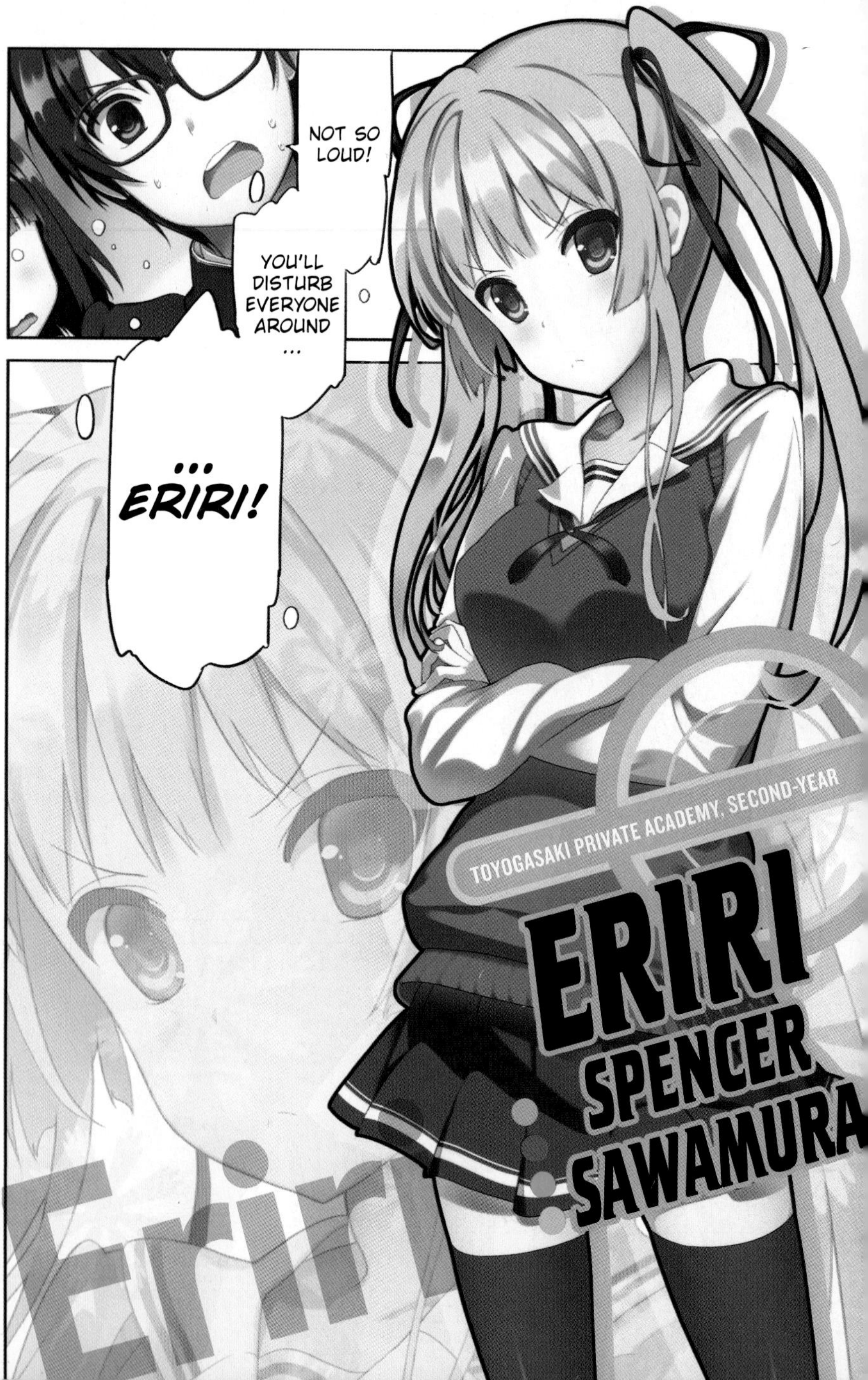
NOT SO LOUD!
YOU'LL DISTURB EVERYONE AROUND ...
... ERIRI!
TOYOGASAKI PRIVATE ACADEMY, SECOND-YEAR
ERIRI SPENCER SAWAMURA
Eriri

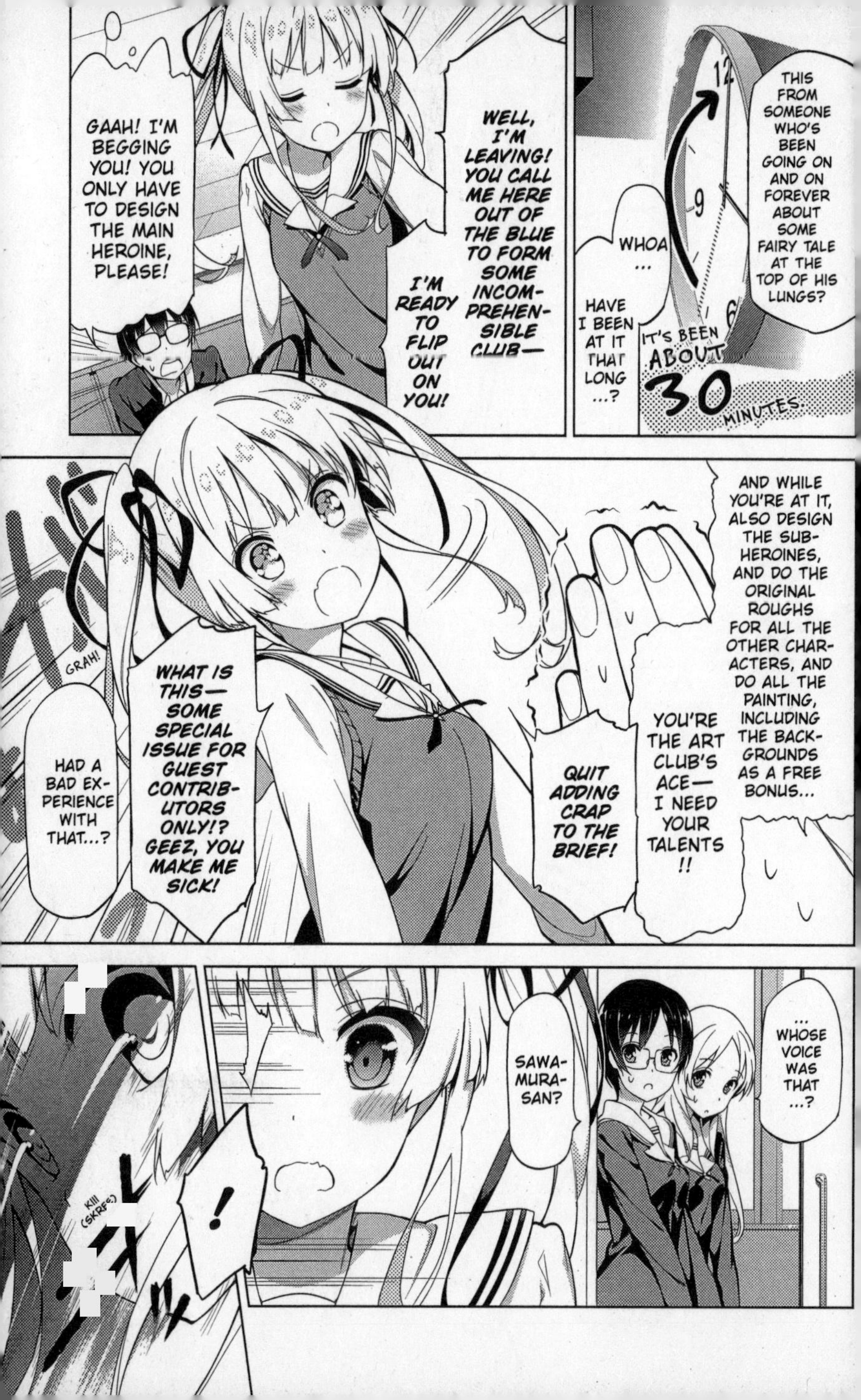
THIS FROM SOMEONE WHO'S BEEN GOING ON AND ON FOREVER ABOUT SOME FAIRY TALE AT THE TOP OF HIS LUNGS?
WHOA...
HAVE I BEEN AT IT THAT LONG...?
IT'S BEEN ABOUT 30 MINUTES.
WELL, I'M LEAVING! YOU CALL ME HERE OUT OF THE BLUE TO FORM SOME INCOMPREHENSIBLE CLUB—
I'M READY TO FLIP OUT ON YOU!
GAAH! I'M BEGGING YOU! YOU ONLY HAVE TO DESIGN THE MAIN HEROINE, PLEASE!
AND WHILE YOU'RE AT IT, ALSO DESIGN THE SUB-HEROINES, AND DO THE ORIGINAL ROUGHS FOR ALL THE OTHER CHARACTERS, AND DO ALL THE PAINTING, INCLUDING THE BACKGROUNDS AS A FREE BONUS...
YOU'RE THE ART CLUB'S ACE— I NEED YOUR TALENTS!!
QUIT ADDING CRAP TO THE BRIEF!
WHAT IS THIS— SOME SPECIAL ISSUE FOR GUEST CONTRIBUTORS ONLY!? GEEZ, YOU MAKE ME SICK!
GRAH!
HAD A BAD EXPERIENCE WITH THAT...?
...WHOSE VOICE WAS THAT...?
SAWAMURA-SAN?
!
KIII (SKREE)

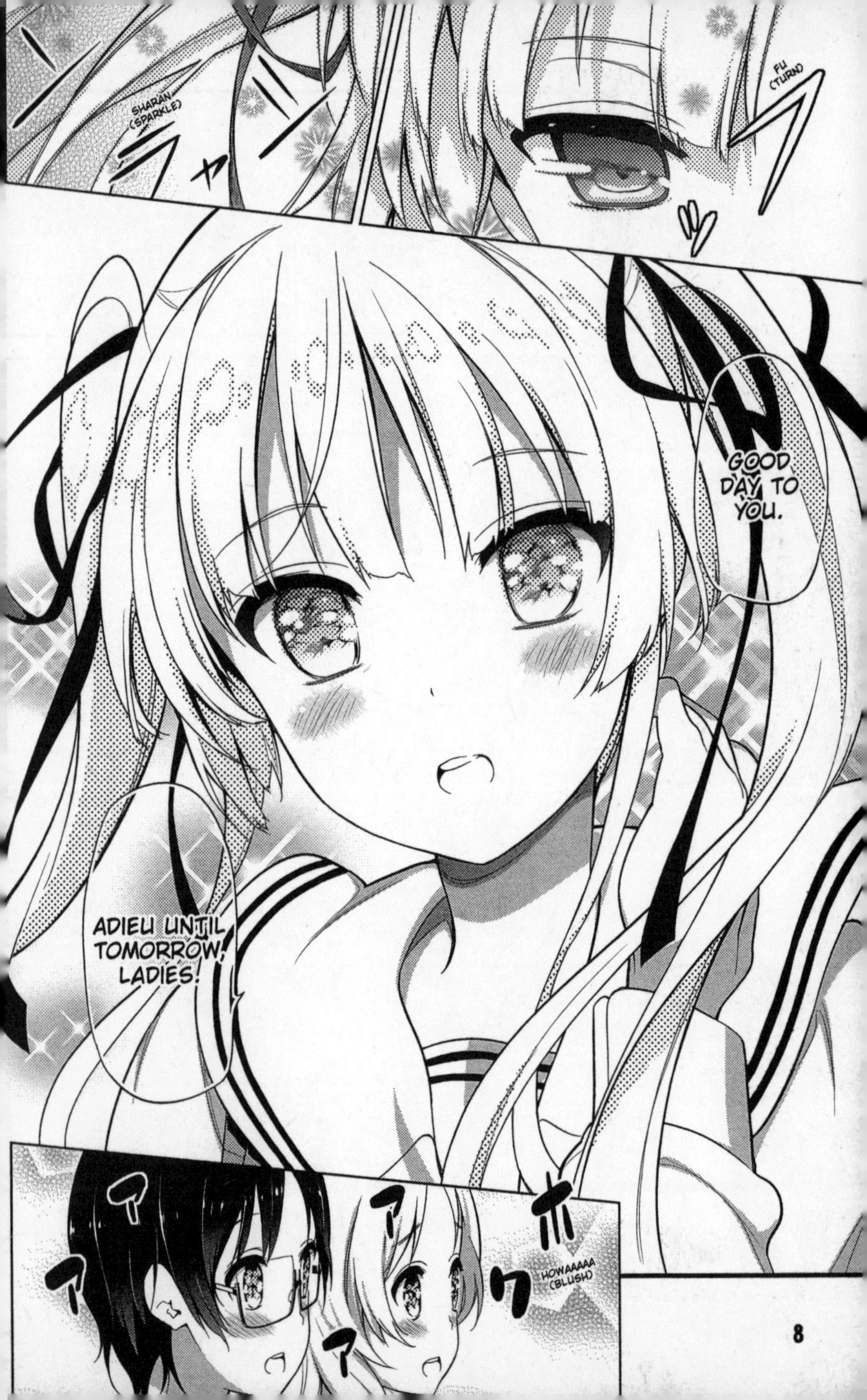
FU (TURN)
SHARAN (SPARKLE)
GOOD DAY TO YOU.
ADIEU UNTIL TOMORROW, LADIES!
HOWAAAAA (BLUSH)

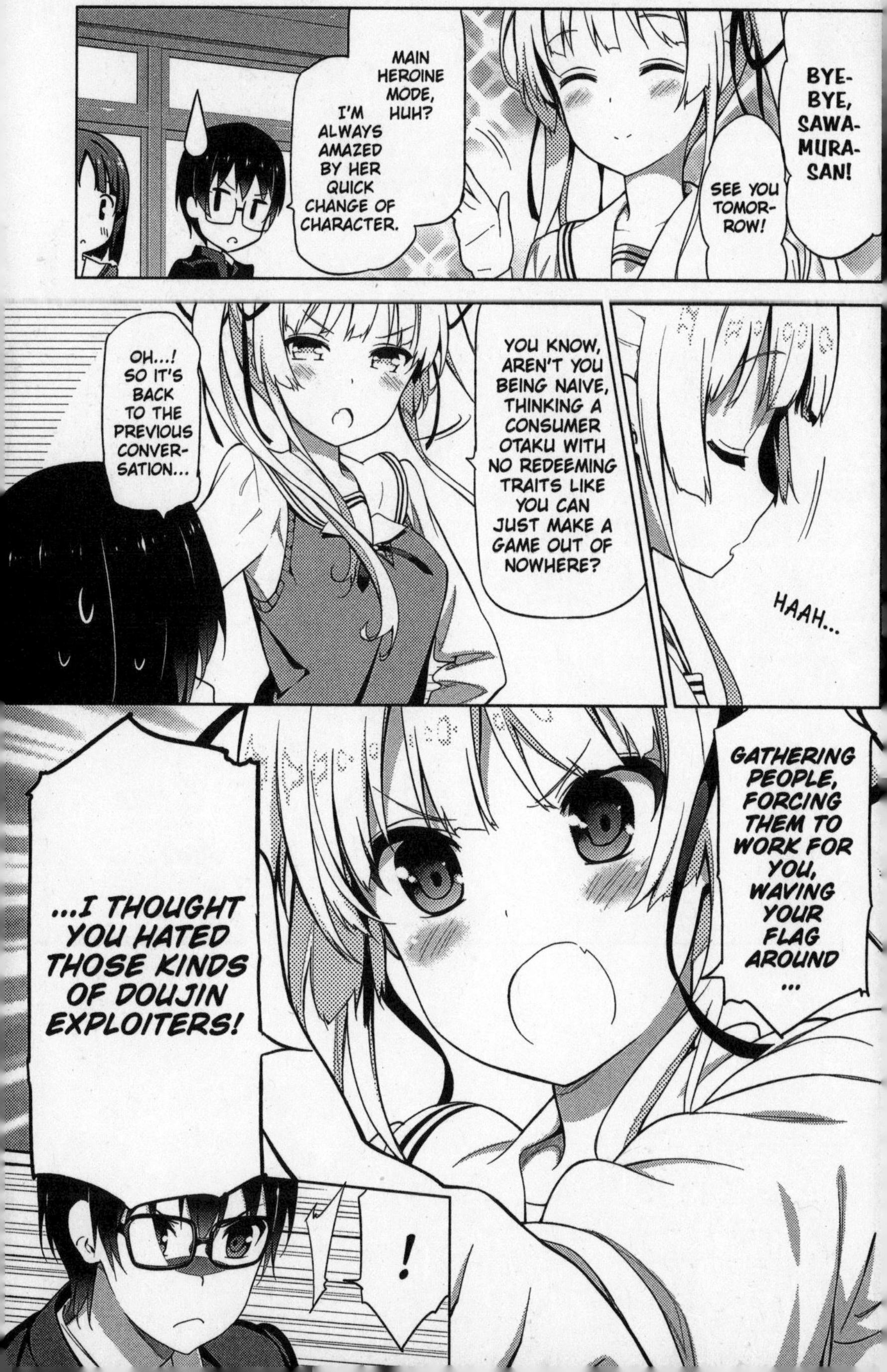
BYE-BYE, SAWAMURA-SAN!
SEE YOU TOMORROW!
MAIN HEROINE MODE, HUH?
I'M ALWAYS AMAZED BY HER QUICK CHANGE OF CHARACTER.
HAAH...
YOU KNOW, AREN'T YOU BEING NAIVE, THINKING A CONSUMER OTAKU WITH NO REDEEMING TRAITS LIKE YOU CAN JUST MAKE A GAME OUT OF NOWHERE?
OH...! SO IT'S BACK TO THE PREVIOUS CONVERSATION...
GATHERING PEOPLE, FORCING THEM TO WORK FOR YOU, WAVING YOUR FLAG AROUND...
...I THOUGHT YOU HATED THOSE KINDS OF DOUJIN EXPLOITERS!
!

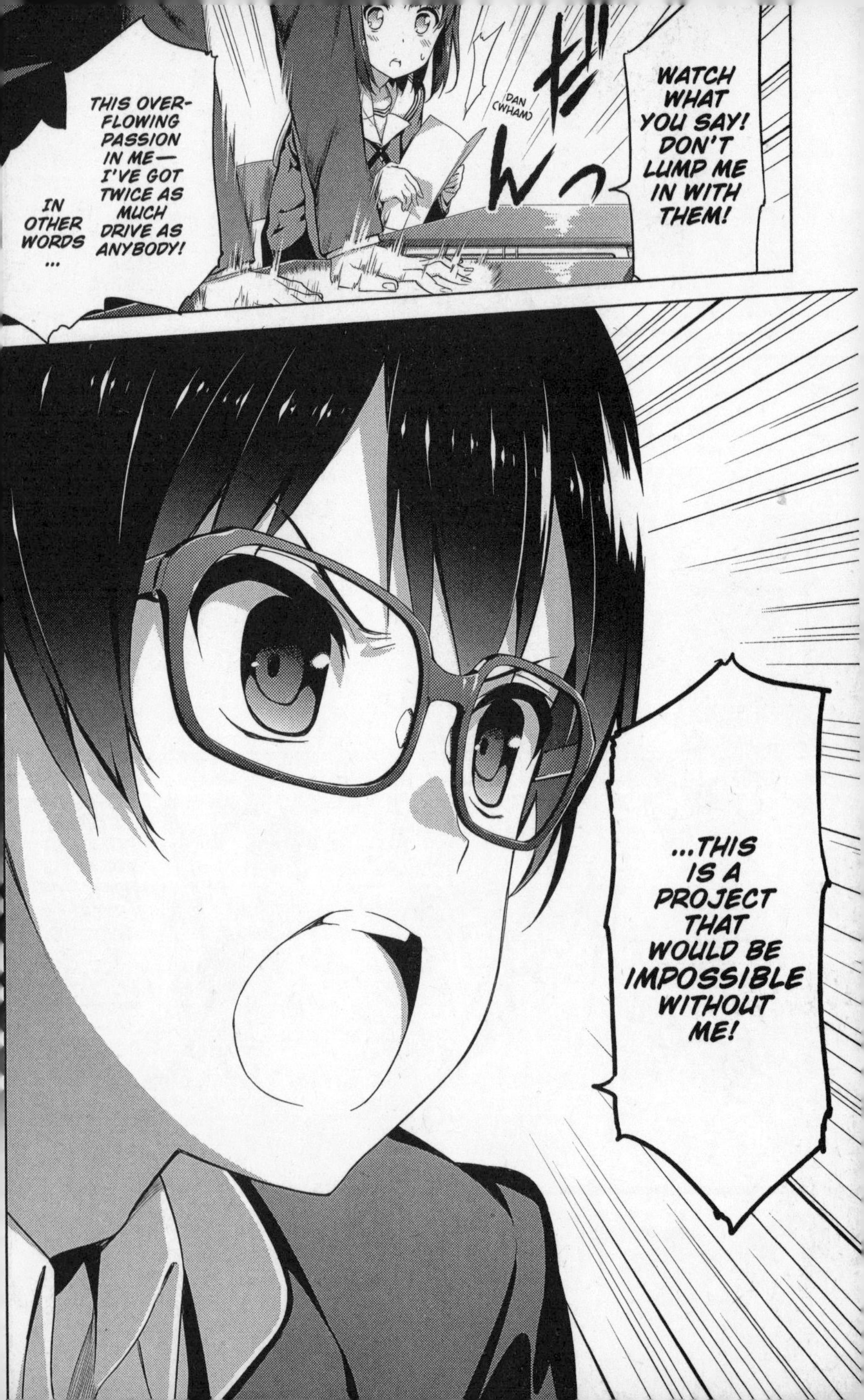
WATCH WHAT YOU SAY! DON'T LUMP ME IN WITH THEM!
DAN (WHAM)
THIS OVER-FLOWING PASSION IN ME— I'VE GOT TWICE AS MUCH DRIVE AS ANYBODY!
IN OTHER WORDS ...
...THIS IS A PROJECT THAT WOULD BE IMPOSSIBLE WITHOUT ME!

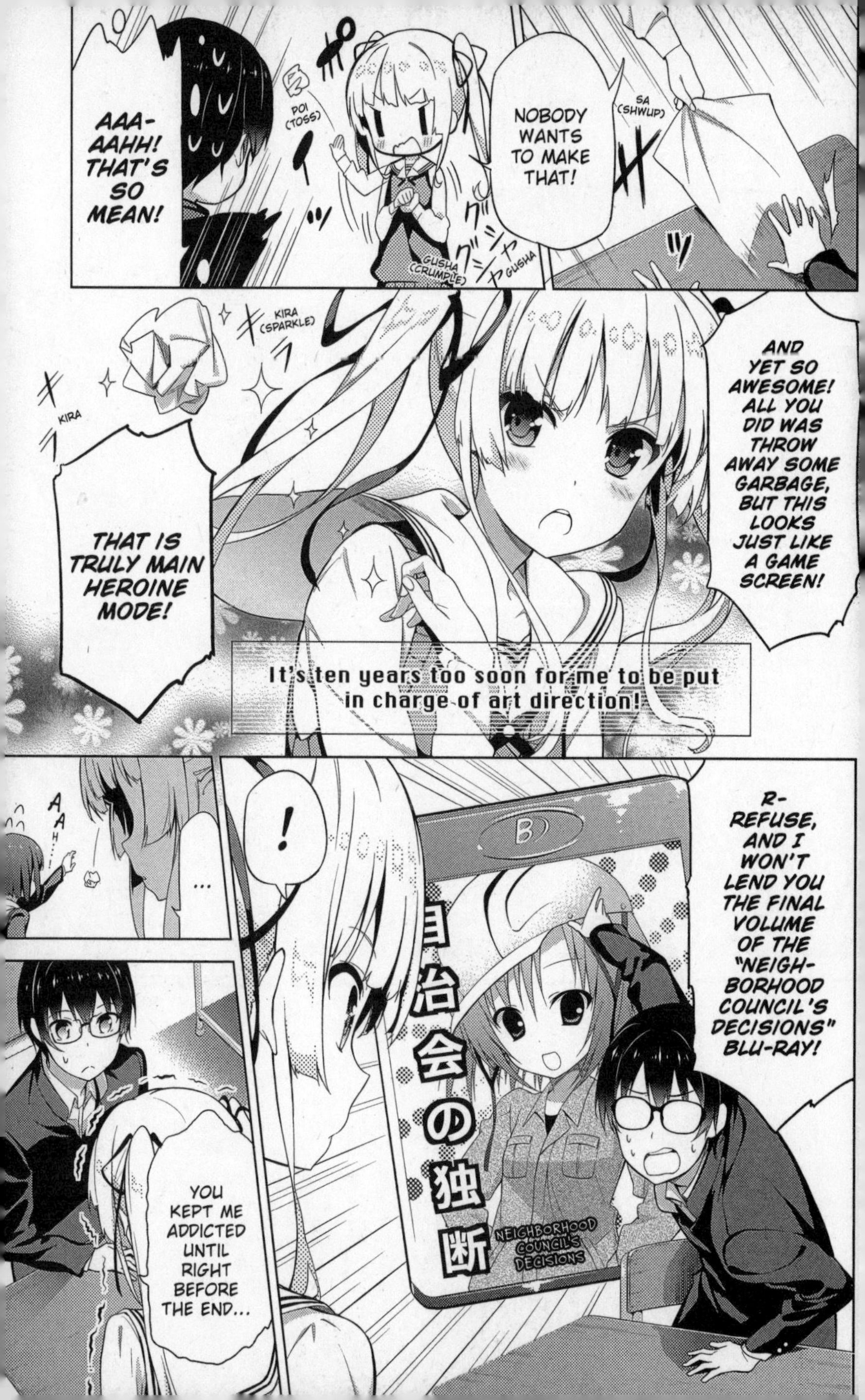
SA (SHWUP)
NOBODY WANTS TO MAKE THAT!
POI (TOSS)
GUSHA (CRUMPLE)
GUSHA
AAA-AAHH! THAT'S SO MEAN!
AND YET SO AWESOME! ALL YOU DID WAS THROW AWAY SOME GARBAGE, BUT THIS LOOKS JUST LIKE A GAME SCREEN!
KIRA (SPARKLE)
KIRA
THAT IS TRULY MAIN HEROINE MODE!
It's ten years too soon for me to be put in charge of art direction!
R-REFUSE, AND I WON'T LEND YOU THE FINAL VOLUME OF THE "NEIGHBORHOOD COUNCIL'S DECISIONS" BLU-RAY!
自治会の独断
NEIGHBORHOOD COUNCIL'S DECISIONS
!
AAH...!
...
YOU KEPT ME ADDICTED UNTIL RIGHT BEFORE THE END...

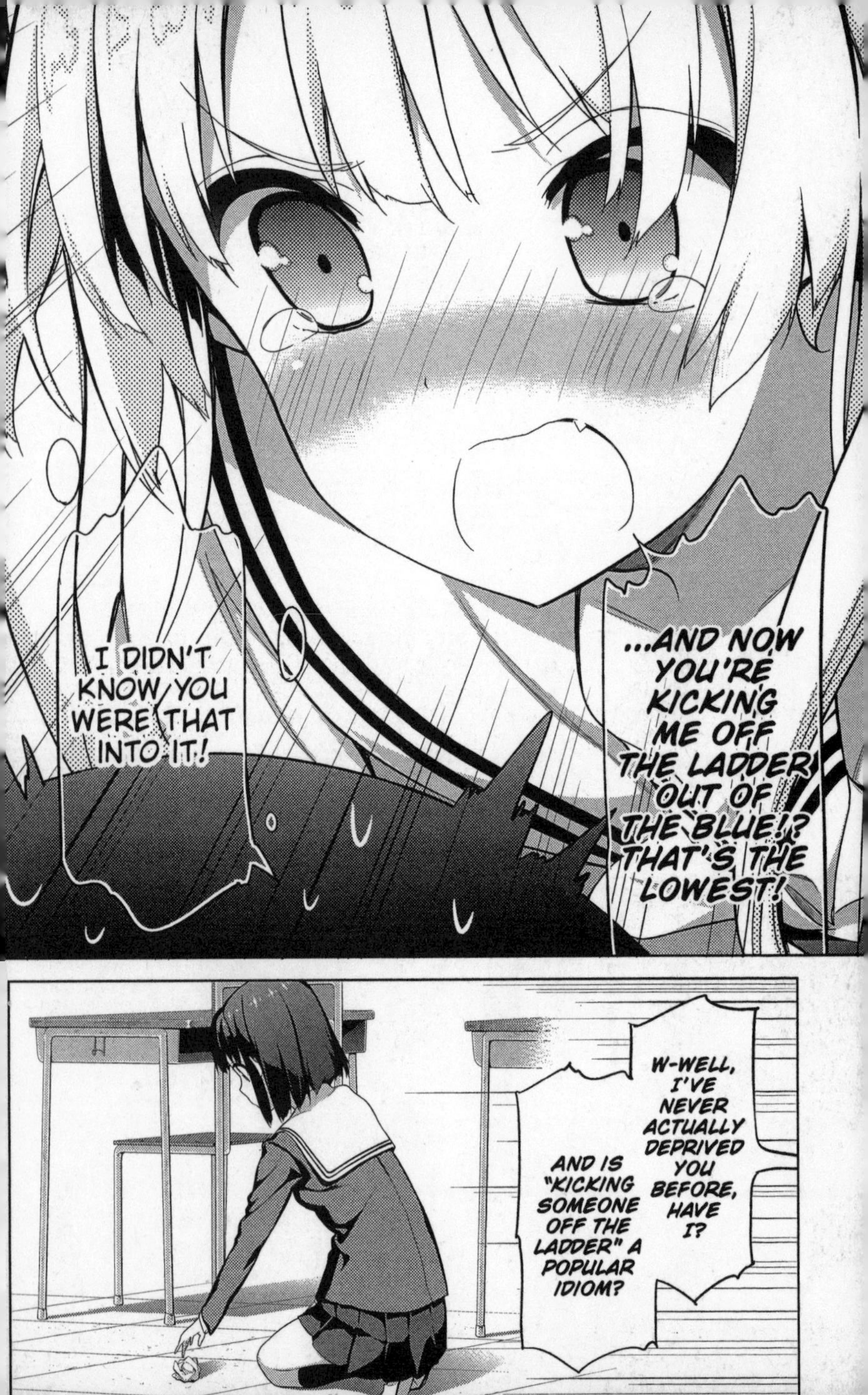
...AND NOW YOU'RE KICKING ME OFF THE LADDER OUT OF THE BLUE!? THAT'S THE LOWEST!
I DIDN'T KNOW YOU WERE THAT INTO IT!
W-WELL, I'VE NEVER ACTUALLY DEPRIVED YOU BEFORE, HAVE I?
AND IS "KICKING SOMEONE OFF THE LADDER" A POPULAR IDIOM?

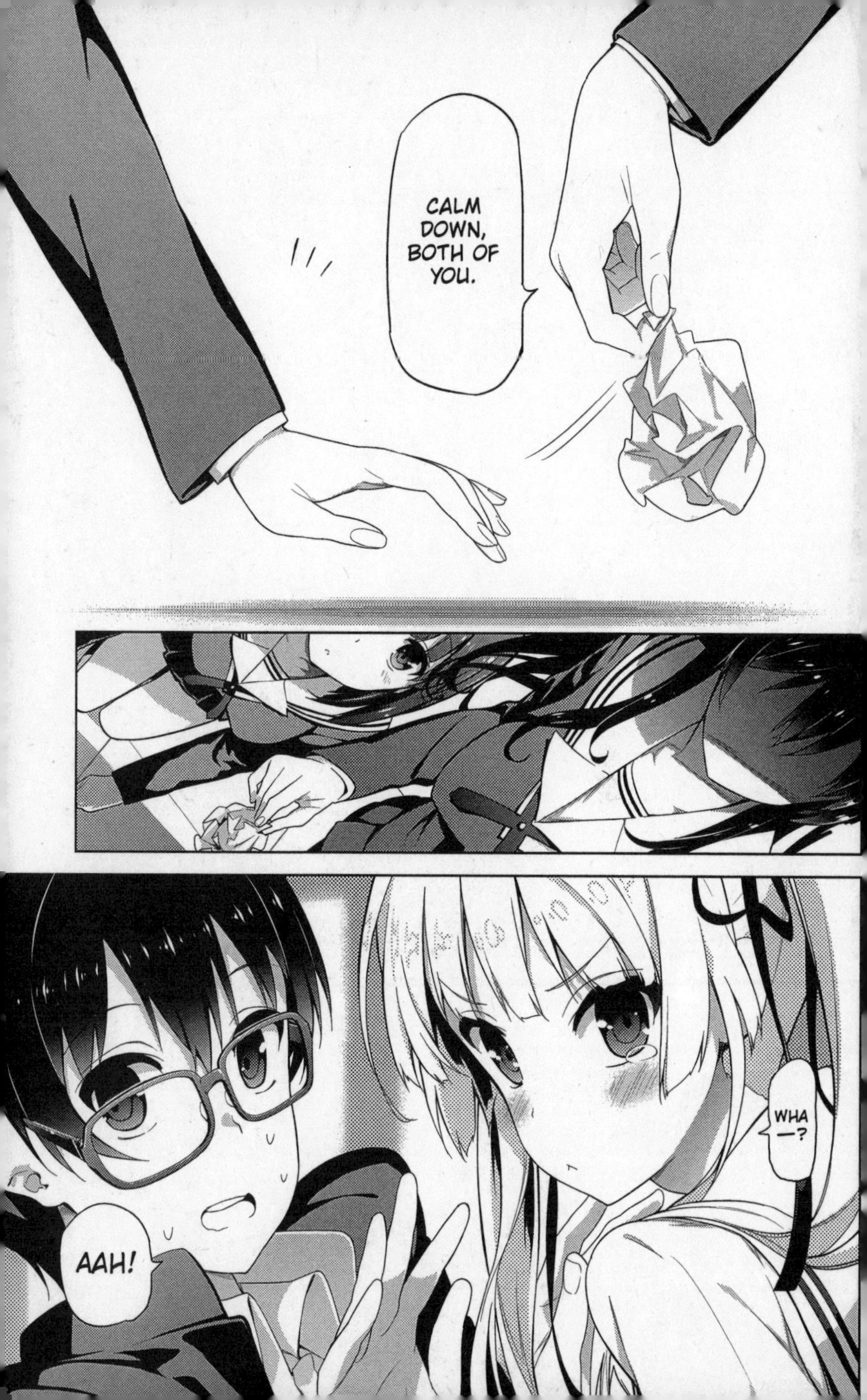
CALM DOWN, BOTH OF YOU.
WHA —?
AAH!

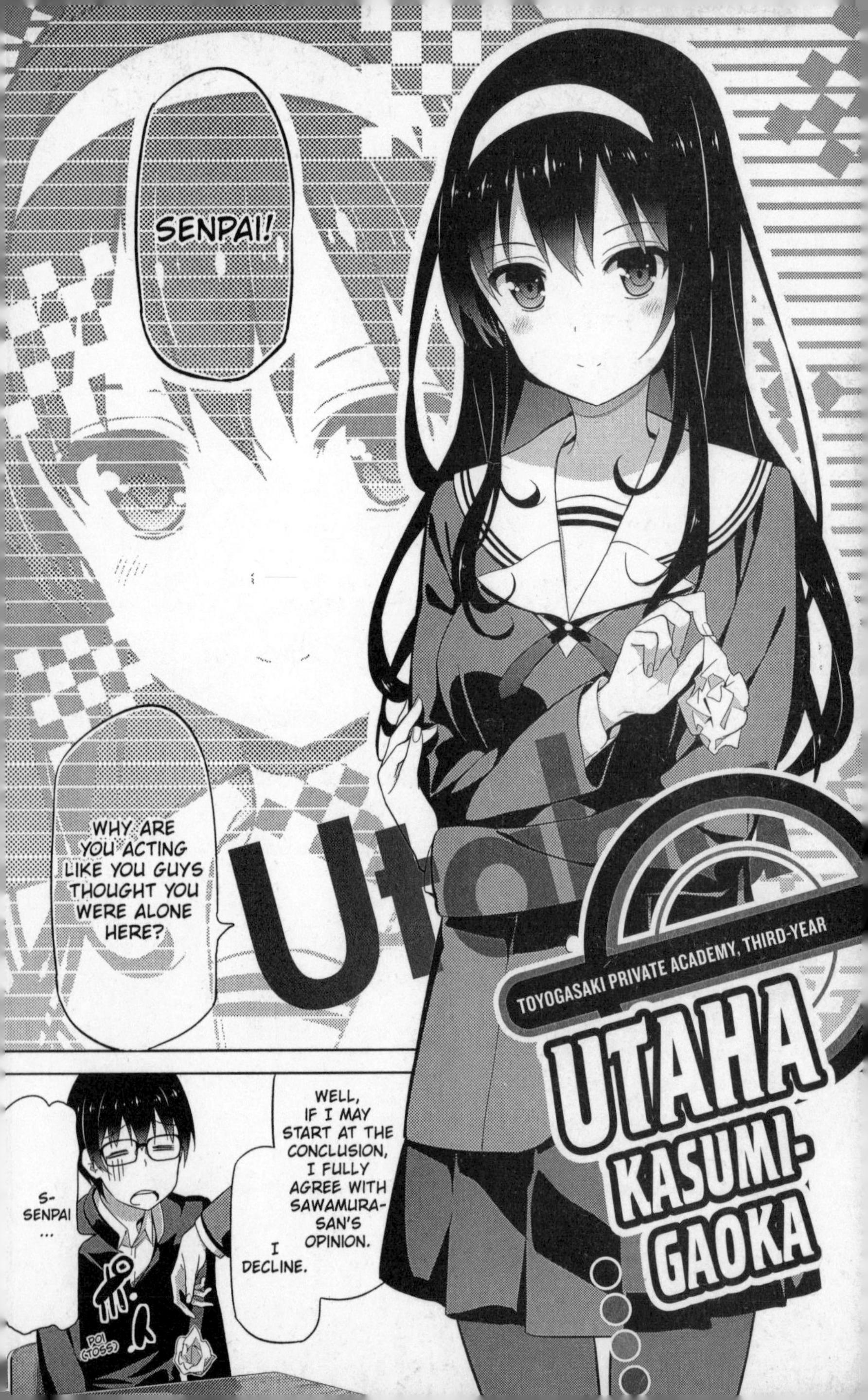
SENPAI!
WHY ARE YOU ACTING LIKE YOU GUYS THOUGHT YOU WERE ALONE HERE?
TOYOGASAKI PRIVATE ACADEMY, THIRD-YEAR
UTAHA KASUMI-GAOKA
WELL, IF I MAY START AT THE CONCLUSION, I FULLY AGREE WITH SAWAMURA-SAN'S OPINION.
I DECLINE.
S-SENPAI ...
POI (TOSS)

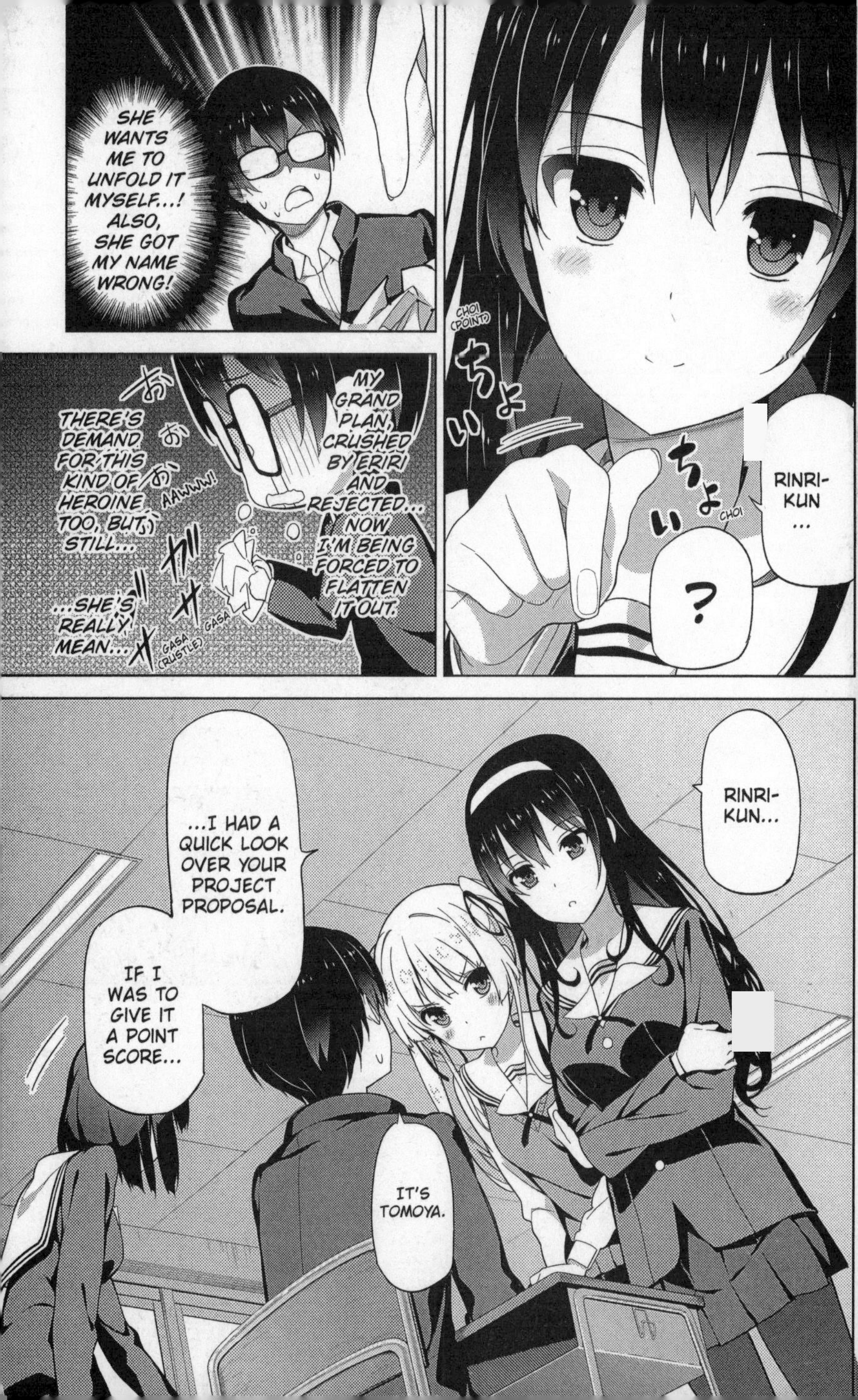
RINRI-KUN ...
ちょい
CHOI
?
ちょい
CHOI (POINT)
SHE WANTS ME TO UNFOLD IT MYSELF...! ALSO, SHE GOT MY NAME WRONG!
MY GRAND PLAN, CRUSHED BY ERIRI AND REJECTED... NOW I'M BEING FORCED TO FLATTEN IT OUT.
おおお
AAWWW!
THERE'S DEMAND FOR THIS KIND OF HEROINE TOO, BUT, STILL...
ガサ
GASA
ガサ
GASA (RUSTLE)
...SHE'S REALLY MEAN...
RINRI-KUN...
...I HAD A QUICK LOOK OVER YOUR PROJECT PROPOSAL.
IF I WAS TO GIVE IT A POINT SCORE...
IT'S TOMOYA.

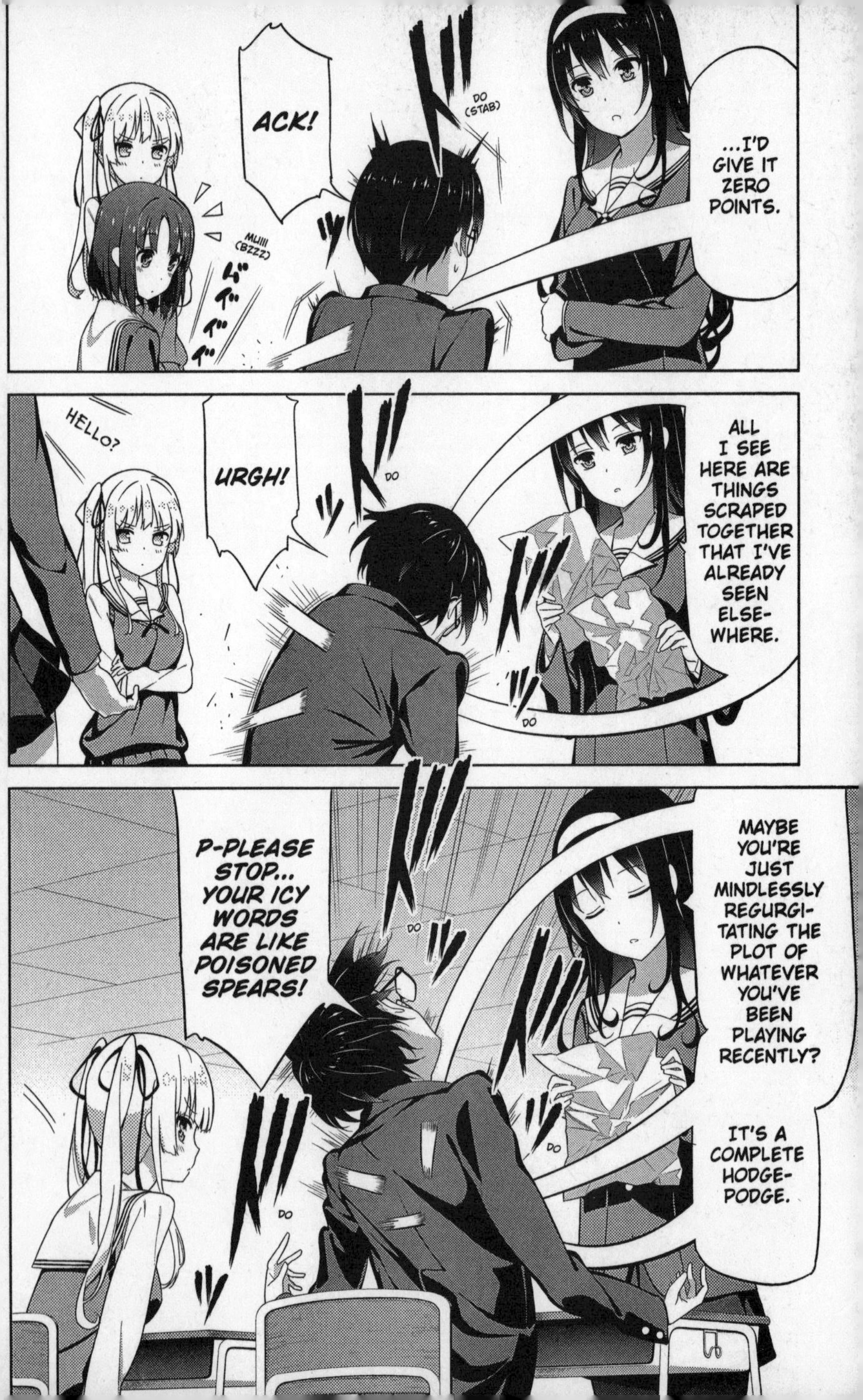
...I'D GIVE IT ZERO POINTS.
DO (STAB)
ACK!
MUIII (BZZZ)
ALL I SEE HERE ARE THINGS SCRAPED TOGETHER THAT I'VE ALREADY SEEN ELSE-WHERE.
DO
DO
URGH!
HELLO?
MAYBE YOU'RE JUST MINDLESSLY REGURGI-TATING THE PLOT OF WHATEVER YOU'VE BEEN PLAYING RECENTLY?
IT'S A COMPLETE HODGE-PODGE.
DO
DO
DO
P-PLEASE STOP... YOUR ICY WORDS ARE LIKE POISONED SPEARS!

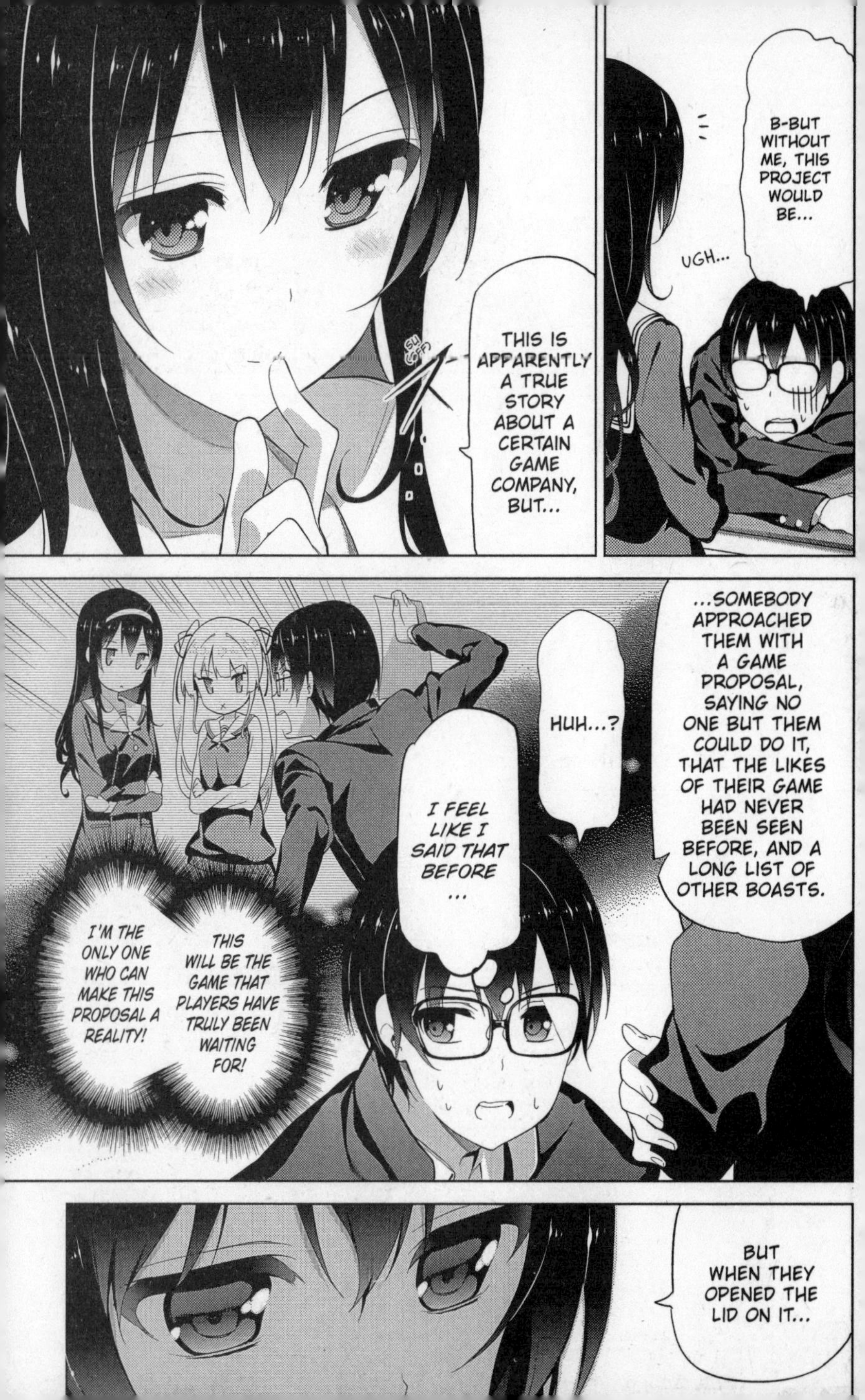
B-BUT WITHOUT ME, THIS PROJECT WOULD BE...
UGH...
THIS IS APPARENTLY A TRUE STORY ABOUT A CERTAIN GAME COMPANY, BUT...
...SOMEBODY APPROACHED THEM WITH A GAME PROPOSAL, SAYING NO ONE BUT THEM COULD DO IT, THAT THE LIKES OF THEIR GAME HAD NEVER BEEN SEEN BEFORE, AND A LONG LIST OF OTHER BOASTS.
HUH...?
I FEEL LIKE I SAID THAT BEFORE ...
THIS WILL BE THE GAME THAT PLAYERS HAVE TRULY BEEN WAITING FOR!
I'M THE ONLY ONE WHO CAN MAKE THIS PROPOSAL A REALITY!
BUT WHEN THEY OPENED THE LID ON IT...

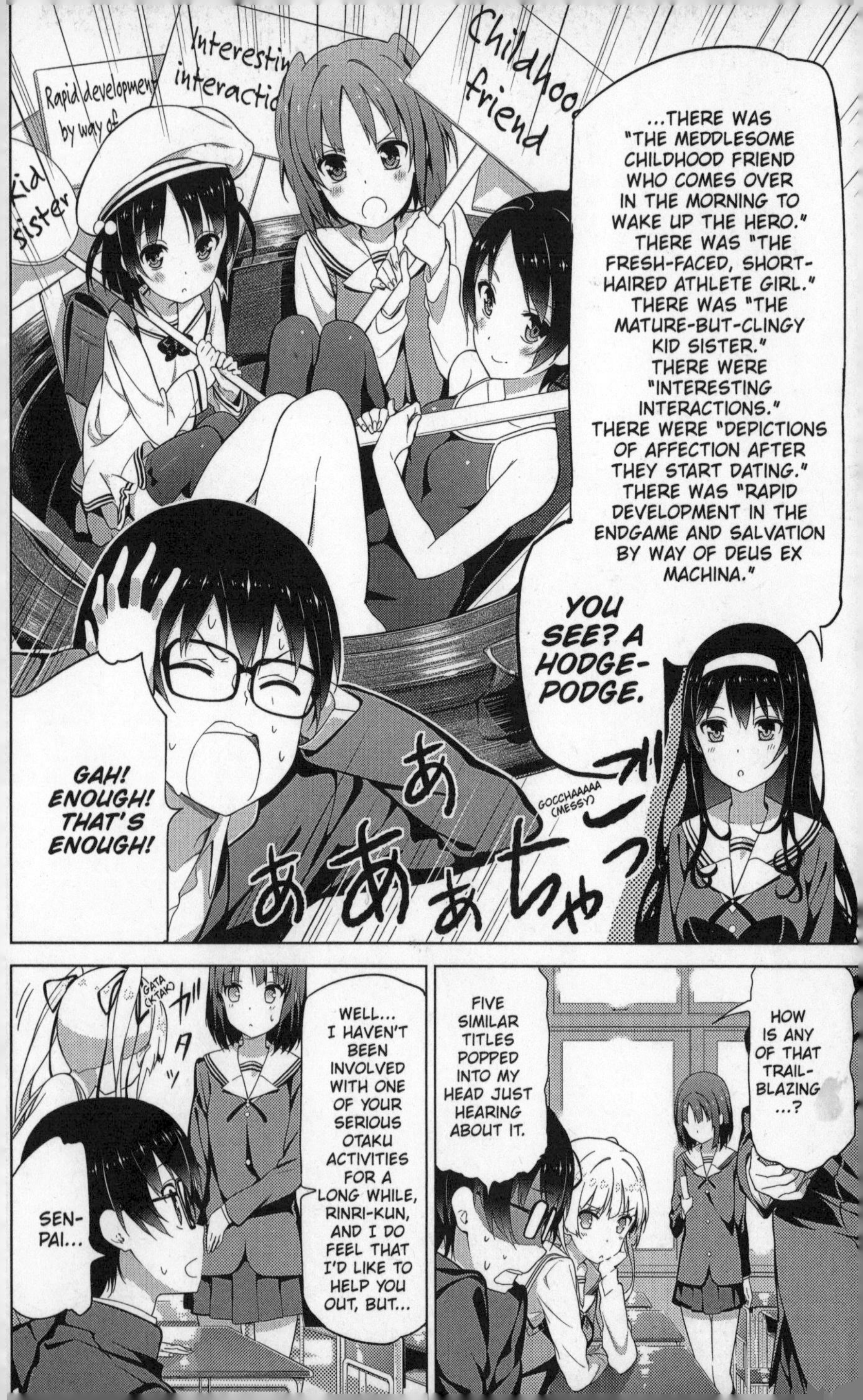
Childhoo
friend
Interestin
interactio
Rapid developmen
by way of
Kid sister
...THERE WAS "THE MEDDLESOME CHILDHOOD FRIEND WHO COMES OVER IN THE MORNING TO WAKE UP THE HERO." THERE WAS "THE FRESH-FACED, SHORT-HAIRED ATHLETE GIRL." THERE WAS "THE MATURE-BUT-CLINGY KID SISTER." THERE WERE "INTERESTING INTERACTIONS." THERE WERE "DEPICTIONS OF AFFECTION AFTER THEY START DATING." THERE WAS "RAPID DEVELOPMENT IN THE ENDGAME AND SALVATION BY WAY OF DEUS EX MACHINA."
YOU SEE? A HODGE-PODGE.
ゴッ
GOCCHAAAAA (MESSY)
あああぁちゃっ
GAH! ENOUGH! THAT'S ENOUGH!
HOW IS ANY OF THAT TRAIL-BLAZING ...?
FIVE SIMILAR TITLES POPPED INTO MY HEAD JUST HEARING ABOUT IT.
WELL... I HAVEN'T BEEN INVOLVED WITH ONE OF YOUR SERIOUS OTAKU ACTIVITIES FOR A LONG WHILE, RINRI-KUN, AND I DO FEEL THAT I'D LIKE TO HELP YOU OUT, BUT...
ガタッ
GATA (KTAK)
SEN-PAI...

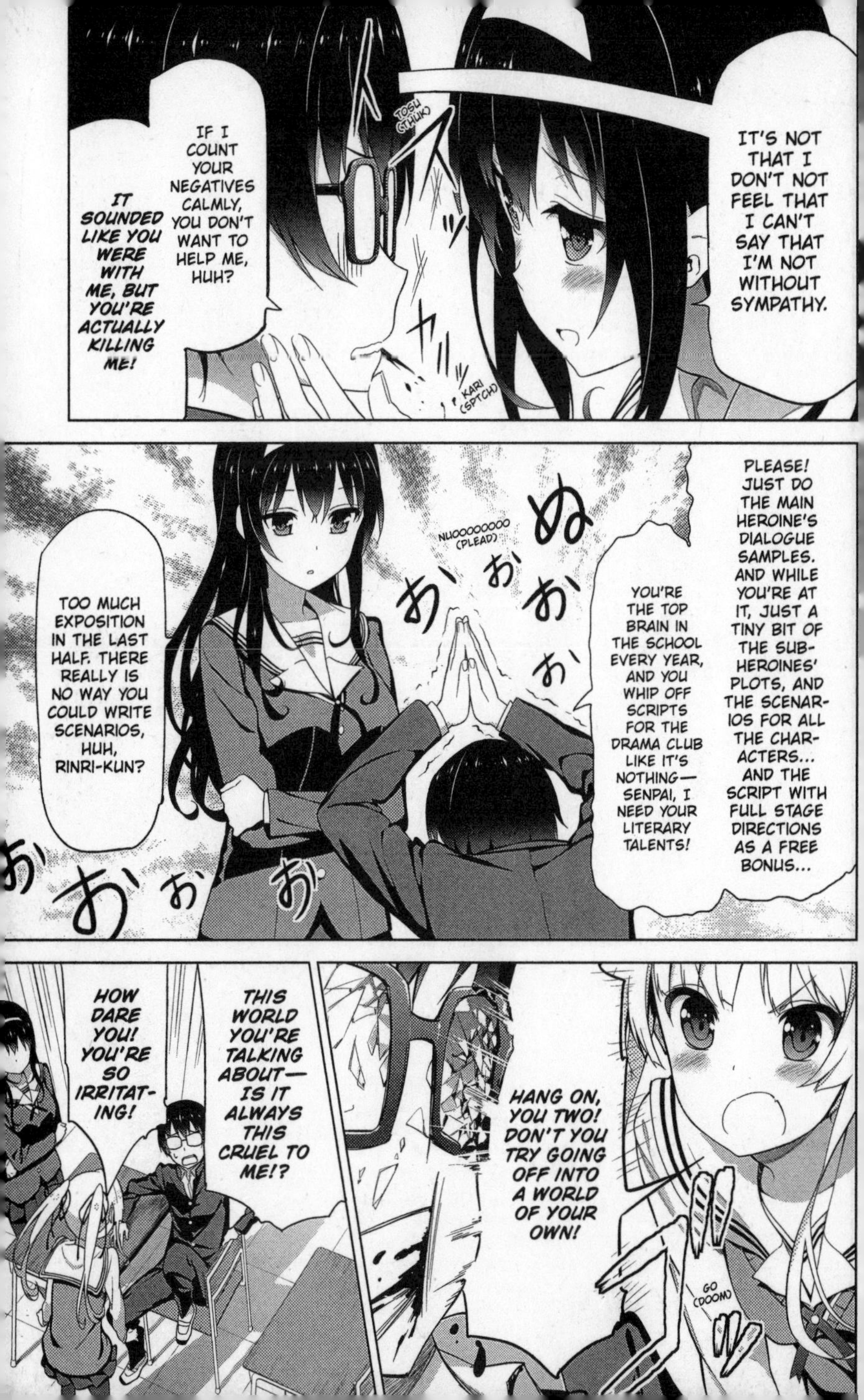
IT'S NOT THAT I DON'T NOT FEEL THAT I CAN'T SAY THAT I'M NOT WITHOUT SYMPATHY.
TOSU (THUK)
KARI (SPTCH)
IF I COUNT YOUR NEGATIVES CALMLY, YOU DON'T WANT TO HELP ME, HUH?
IT SOUNDED LIKE YOU WERE WITH ME, BUT YOU'RE ACTUALLY KILLING ME!
PLEASE! JUST DO THE MAIN HEROINE'S DIALOGUE SAMPLES. AND WHILE YOU'RE AT IT, JUST A TINY BIT OF THE SUB-HEROINES' PLOTS, AND THE SCENARIOS FOR ALL THE CHARACTERS... AND THE SCRIPT WITH FULL STAGE DIRECTIONS AS A FREE BONUS...
YOU'RE THE TOP BRAIN IN THE SCHOOL EVERY YEAR, AND YOU WHIP OFF SCRIPTS FOR THE DRAMA CLUB LIKE IT'S NOTHING— SENPAI, I NEED YOUR LITERARY TALENTS!
NUOOOOOOOO (PLEAD)
TOO MUCH EXPOSITION IN THE LAST HALF. THERE REALLY IS NO WAY YOU COULD WRITE SCENARIOS, HUH, RINRI-KUN?
HANG ON, YOU TWO! DON'T YOU TRY GOING OFF INTO A WORLD OF YOUR OWN!
GO (DOOM)
THIS WORLD YOU'RE TALKING ABOUT— IS IT ALWAYS THIS CRUEL TO ME!?
HOW DARE YOU! YOU'RE SO IRRITATING!

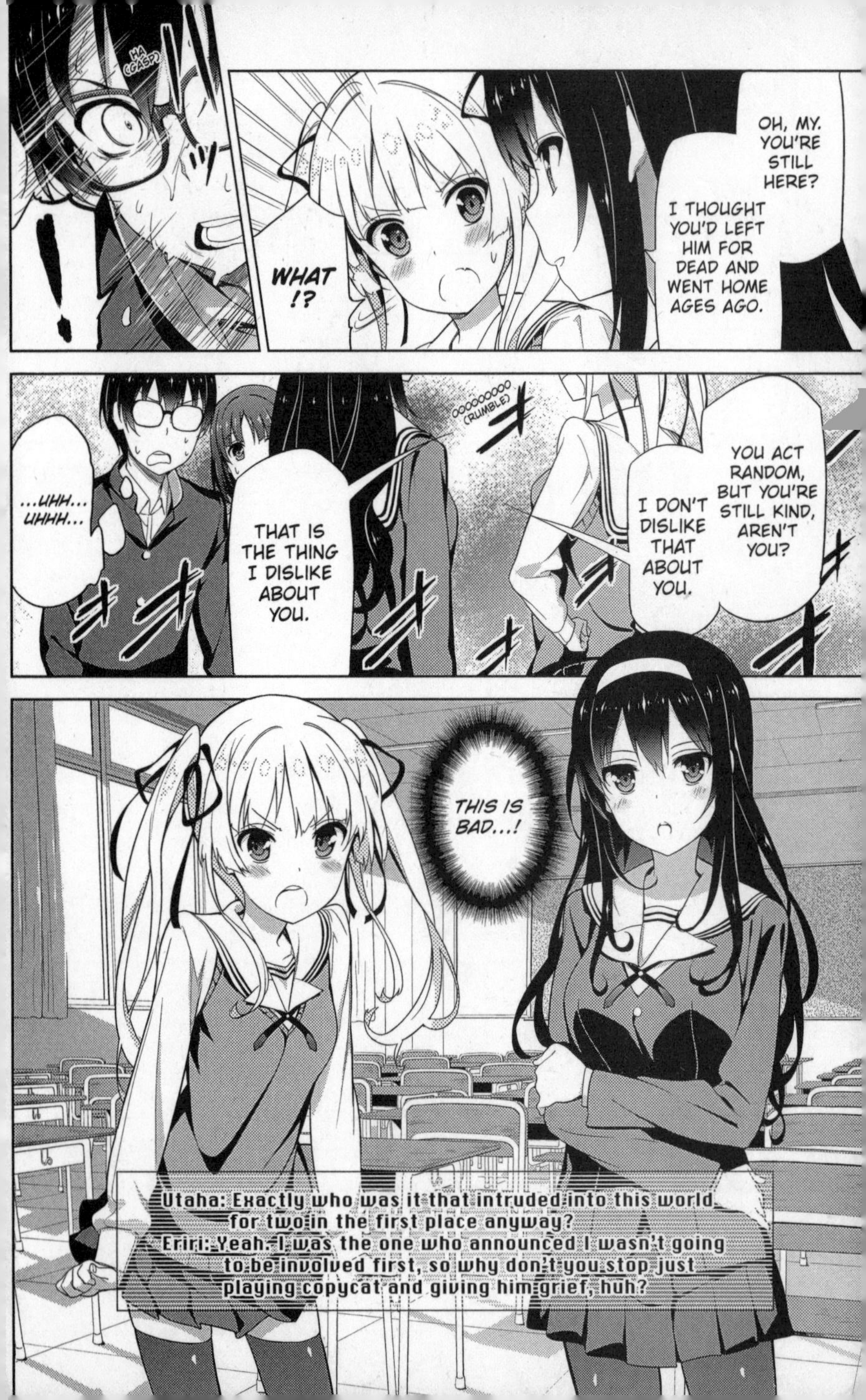
OH, MY. YOU'RE STILL HERE?
I THOUGHT YOU'D LEFT HIM FOR DEAD AND WENT HOME AGES AGO.
WHAT !?
HA (GASP)
YOU ACT RANDOM, BUT YOU'RE STILL KIND, AREN'T YOU?
I DON'T DISLIKE THAT ABOUT YOU.
OOOOOOOOO (RUMBLE)
THAT IS THE THING I DISLIKE ABOUT YOU.
...UHH... UHHH...
THIS IS BAD...!
Utaha: Exactly who was it that intruded into this world for two in the first place anyway?
Eriri: Yeah. I was the one who announced I wasn't going to be involved first, so why don't you stop just playing copycat and giving him grief, huh?

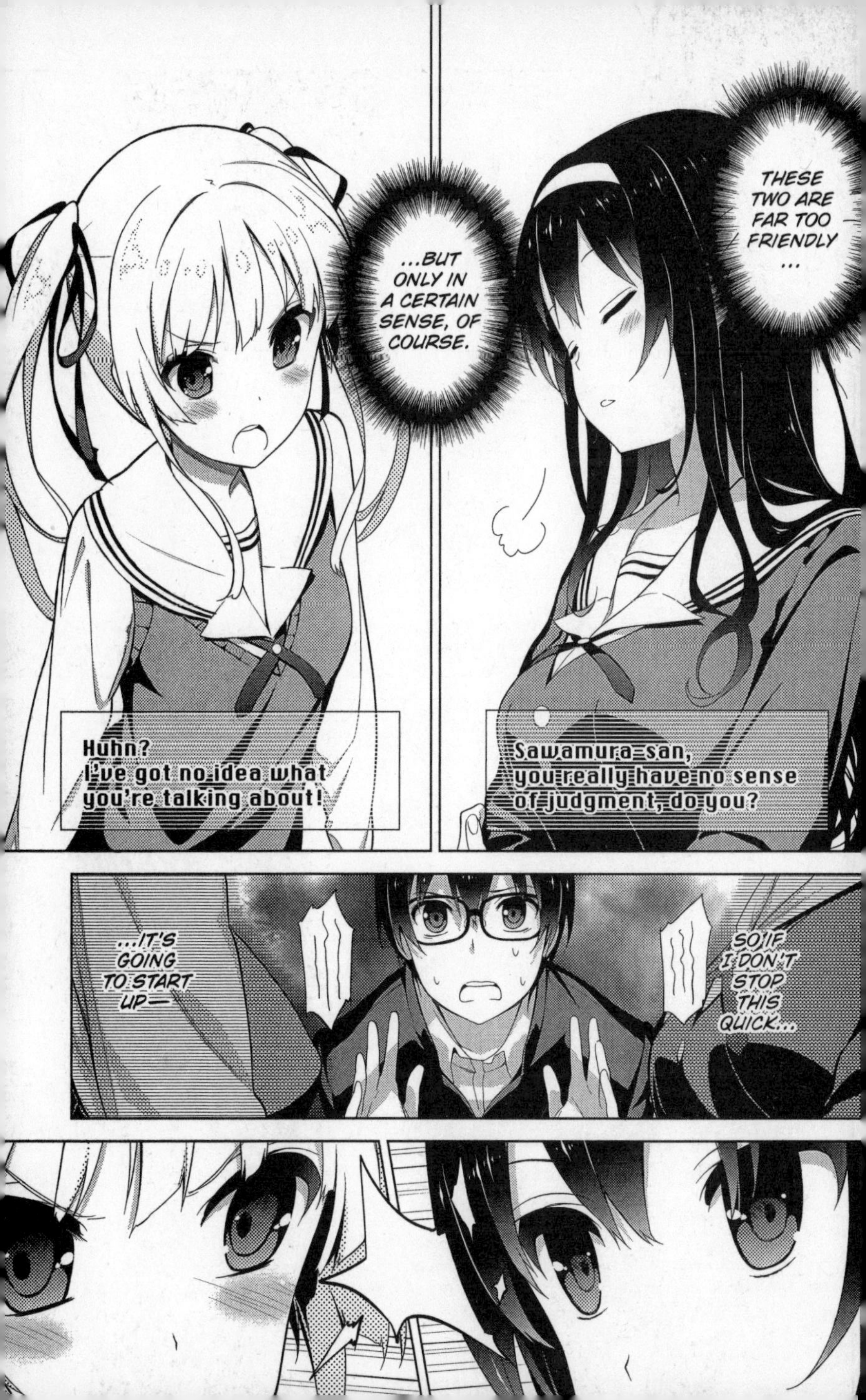
THESE TWO ARE FAR TOO FRIENDLY ...
...BUT ONLY IN A CERTAIN SENSE, OF COURSE.
Sawamura-san, you really have no sense of judgment, do you?
Huhn? I've got no idea what you're talking about!
SO IF I DON'T STOP THIS QUICK...
...IT'S GOING TO START UP—

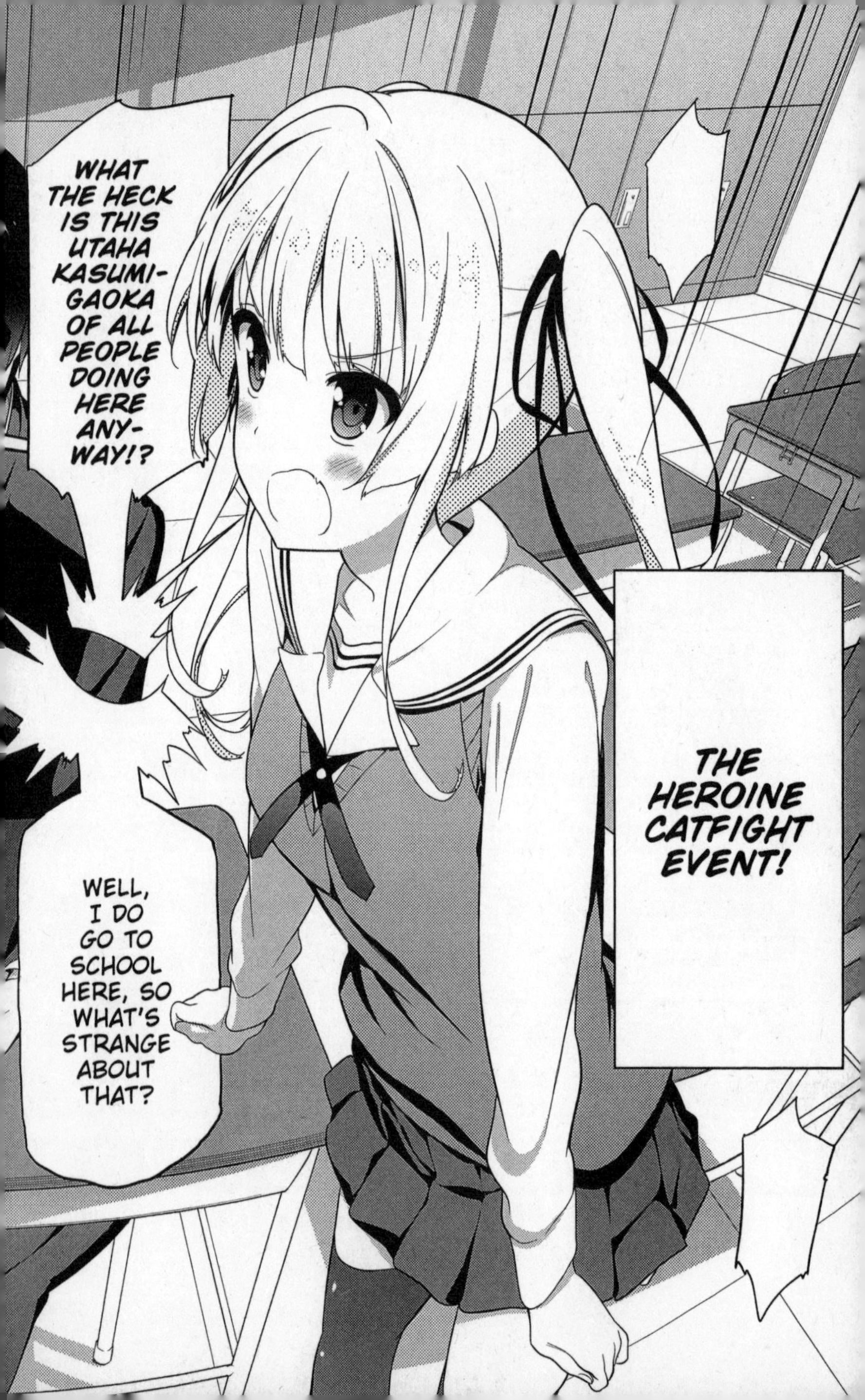
WHAT THE HECK IS THIS UTAHA KASUMI-GAOKA OF ALL PEOPLE DOING HERE ANY-WAY!?
THE HEROINE CATFIGHT EVENT!
WELL, I DO GO TO SCHOOL HERE, SO WHAT'S STRANGE ABOUT THAT?

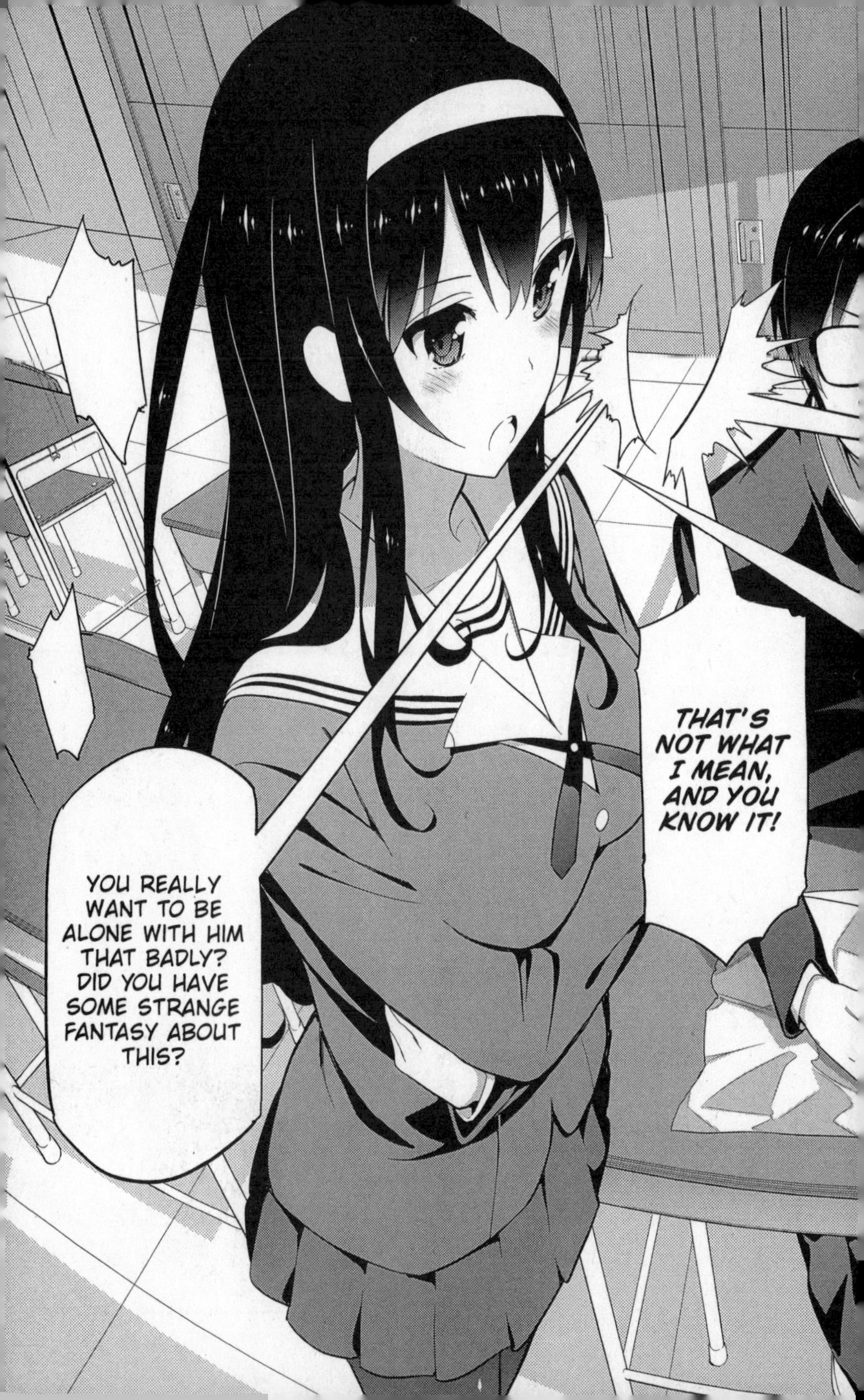
THAT'S NOT WHAT I MEAN, AND YOU KNOW IT!
YOU REALLY WANT TO BE ALONE WITH HIM THAT BADLY? DID YOU HAVE SOME STRANGE FANTASY ABOUT THIS?

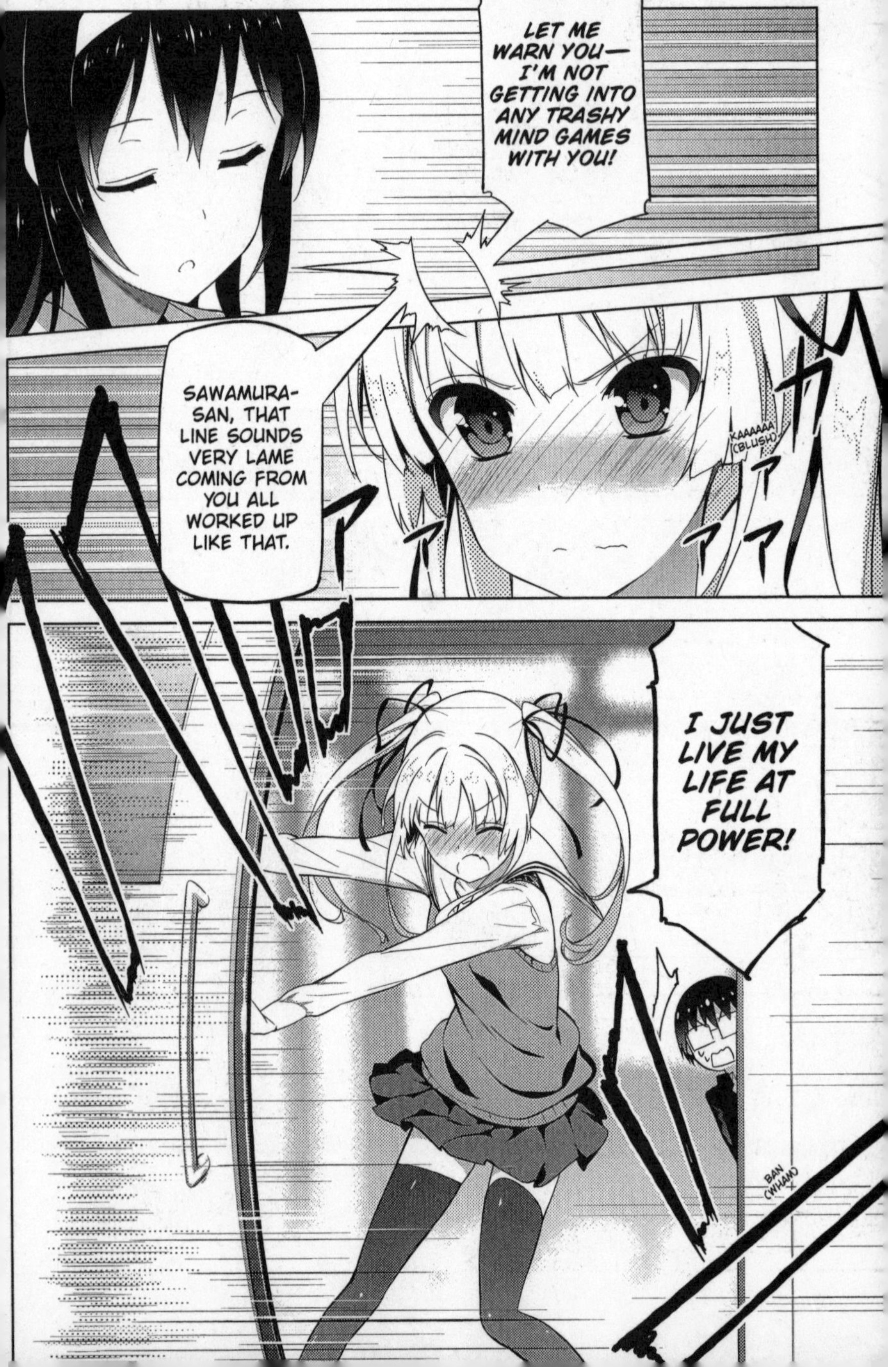
LET ME WARN YOU— I'M NOT GETTING INTO ANY TRASHY MIND GAMES WITH YOU!
KAAAAAA (BLUSH)
SAWAMURA-SAN, THAT LINE SOUNDS VERY LAME COMING FROM YOU ALL WORKED UP LIKE THAT.
I JUST LIVE MY LIFE AT FULL POWER!
BAN (WHAM)

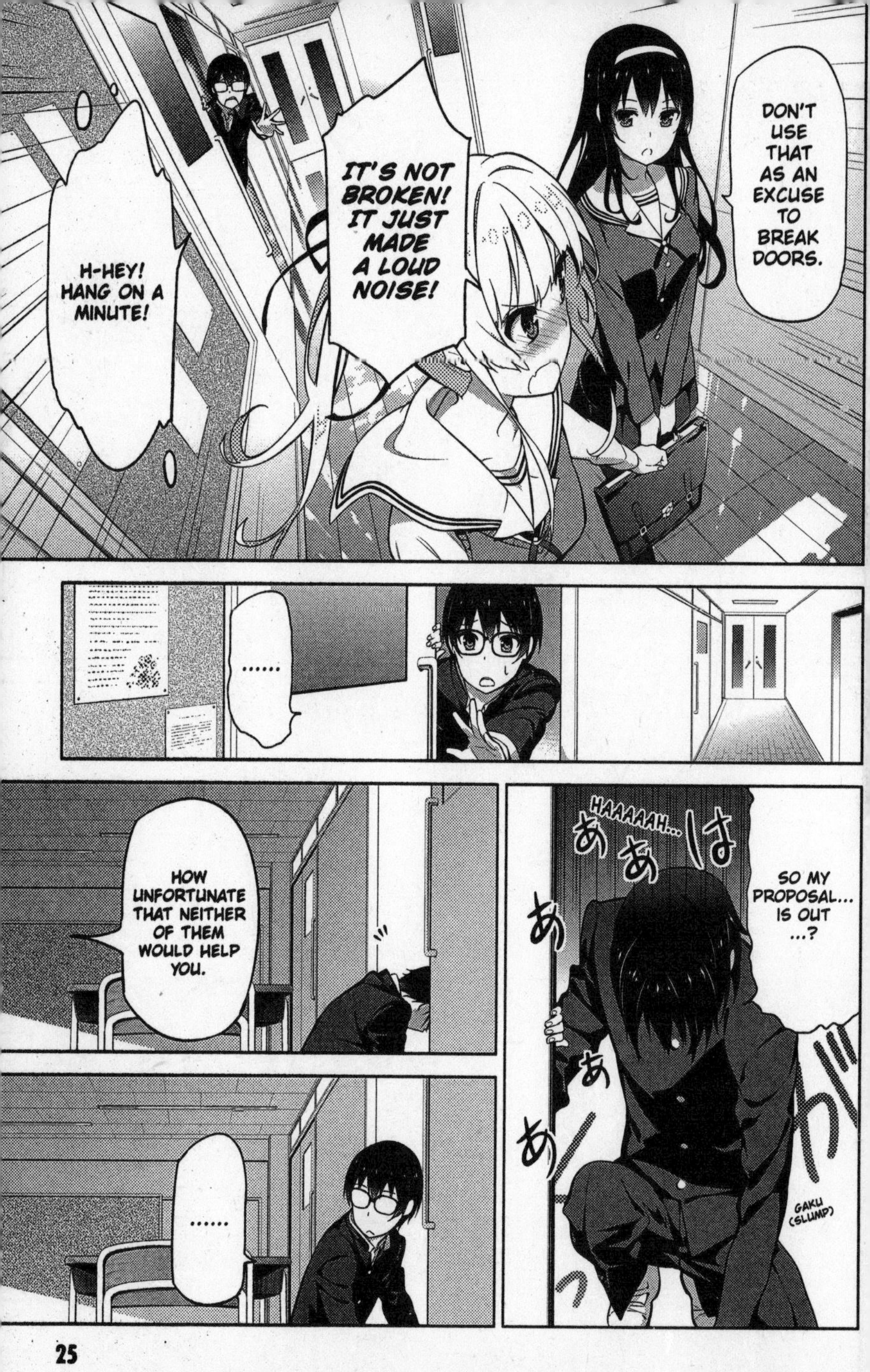

DON'T USE THAT AS AN EXCUSE TO BREAK DOORS.
IT'S NOT BROKEN! IT JUST MADE A LOUD NOISE!
H-HEY! HANG ON A MINUTE!
......
HAAAAAH...
はあああああっ
SO MY PROPOSAL... IS OUT ...?
GAKU (SLUMP)
HOW UNFORTUNATE THAT NEITHER OF THEM WOULD HELP YOU.
......

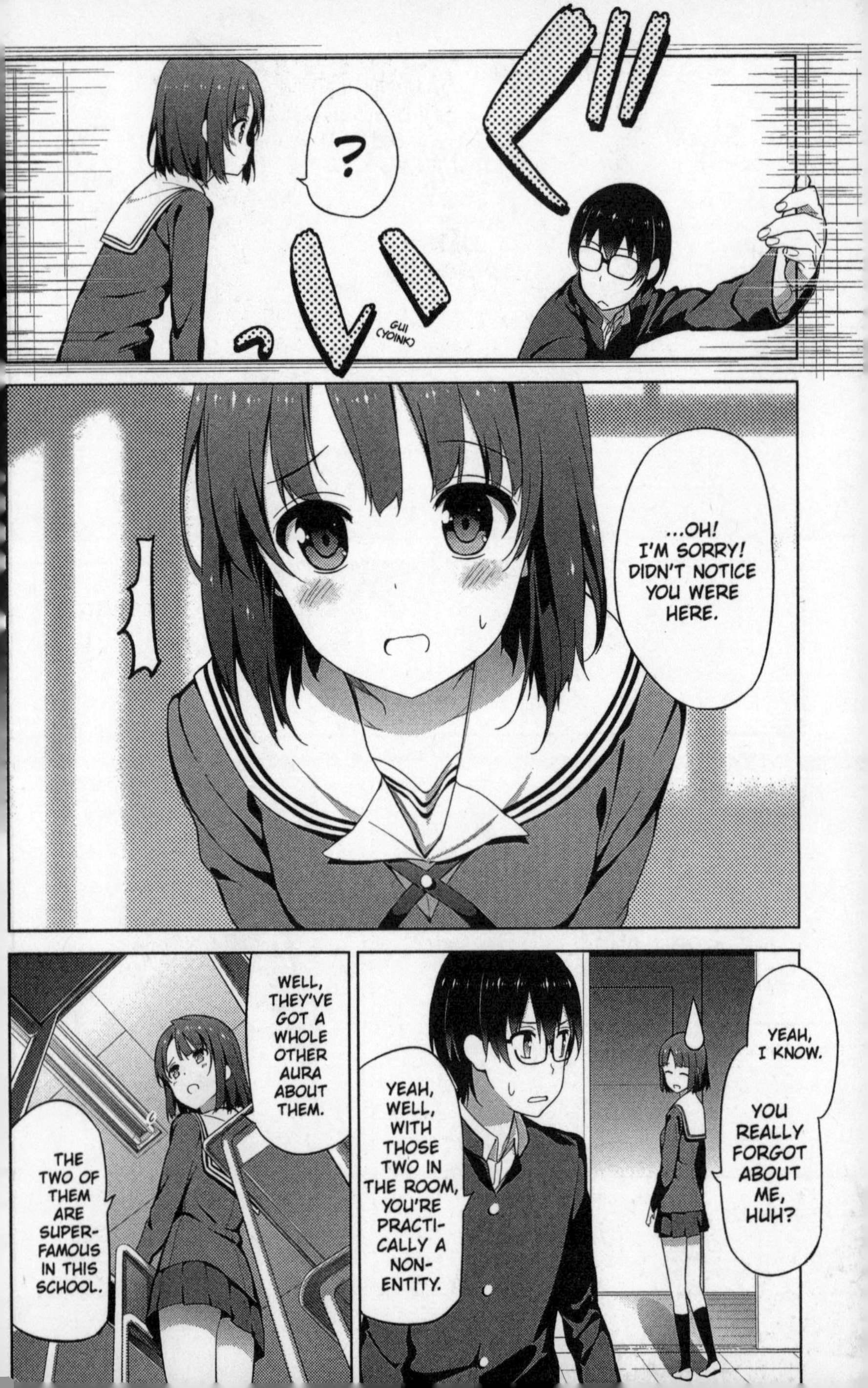
ぐいっ
GUI (YOINK)
?
...OH! I'M SORRY! DIDN'T NOTICE YOU WERE HERE.
YEAH, I KNOW.
YOU REALLY FORGOT ABOUT ME, HUH?
YEAH, WELL, WITH THOSE TWO IN THE ROOM, YOU'RE PRACTICALLY A NON-ENTITY.
WELL, THEY'VE GOT A WHOLE OTHER AURA ABOUT THEM.
THE TWO OF THEM ARE SUPER-FAMOUS IN THIS SCHOOL.

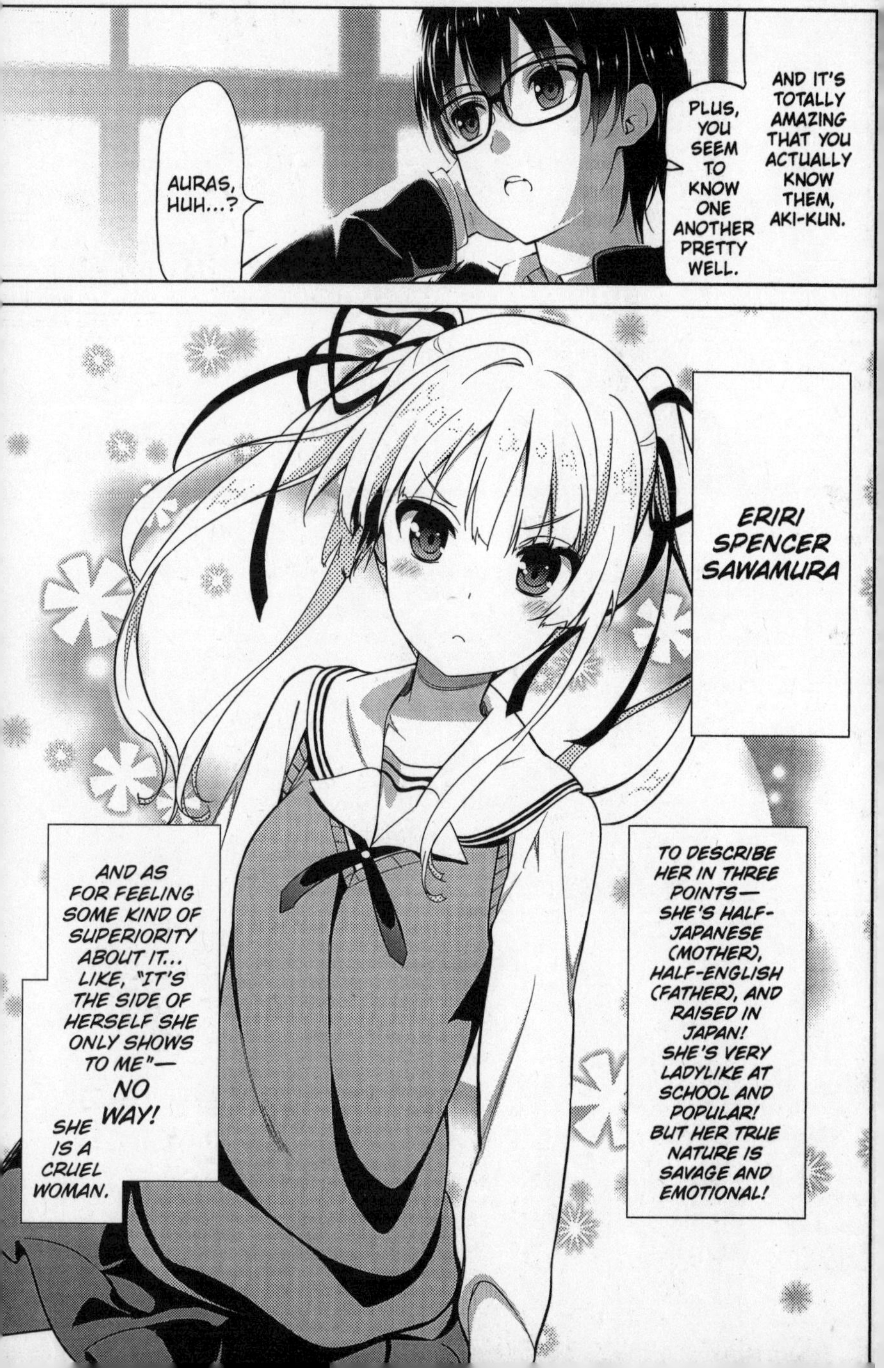
AND IT'S TOTALLY AMAZING THAT YOU ACTUALLY KNOW THEM, AKI-KUN.
PLUS, YOU SEEM TO KNOW ONE ANOTHER PRETTY WELL.
AURAS, HUH...?
ERIRI SPENCER SAWAMURA
TO DESCRIBE HER IN THREE POINTS—SHE'S HALF-JAPANESE (MOTHER), HALF-ENGLISH (FATHER), AND RAISED IN JAPAN! SHE'S VERY LADYLIKE AT SCHOOL AND POPULAR! BUT HER TRUE NATURE IS SAVAGE AND EMOTIONAL!
AND AS FOR FEELING SOME KIND OF SUPERIORITY ABOUT IT... LIKE, "IT'S THE SIDE OF HERSELF SHE ONLY SHOWS TO ME"—
NO WAY!
SHE IS A CRUEL WOMAN.

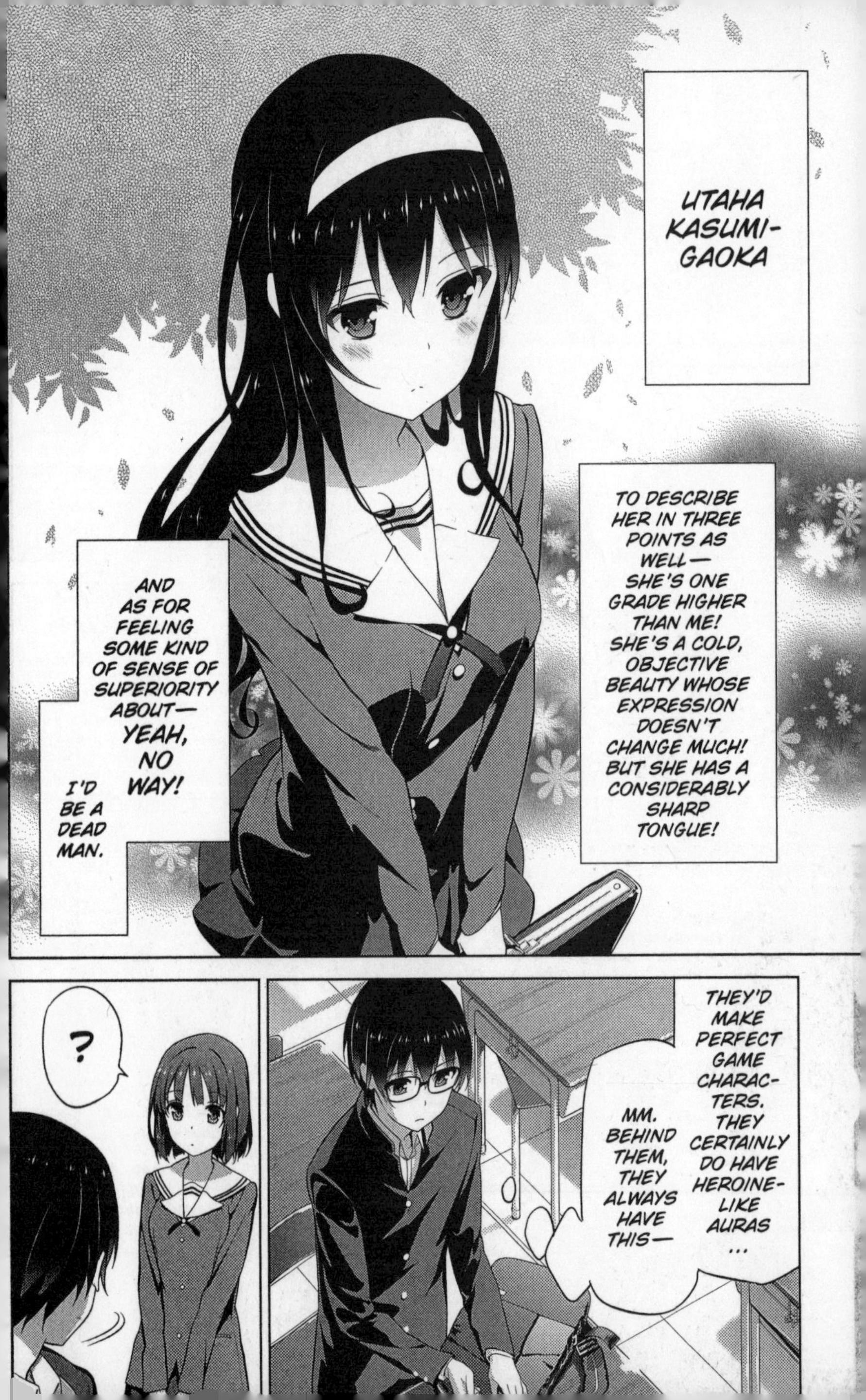
UTAHA KASUMI-GAOKA
TO DESCRIBE HER IN THREE POINTS AS WELL—SHE'S ONE GRADE HIGHER THAN ME! SHE'S A COLD, OBJECTIVE BEAUTY WHOSE EXPRESSION DOESN'T CHANGE MUCH! BUT SHE HAS A CONSIDERABLY SHARP TONGUE!
AND AS FOR FEELING SOME KIND OF SENSE OF SUPERIORITY ABOUT—YEAH, NO WAY!
I'D BE A DEAD MAN.
THEY'D MAKE PERFECT GAME CHARACTERS. THEY CERTAINLY DO HAVE HEROINE-LIKE AURAS ...
MM. BEHIND THEM, THEY ALWAYS HAVE THIS—
?

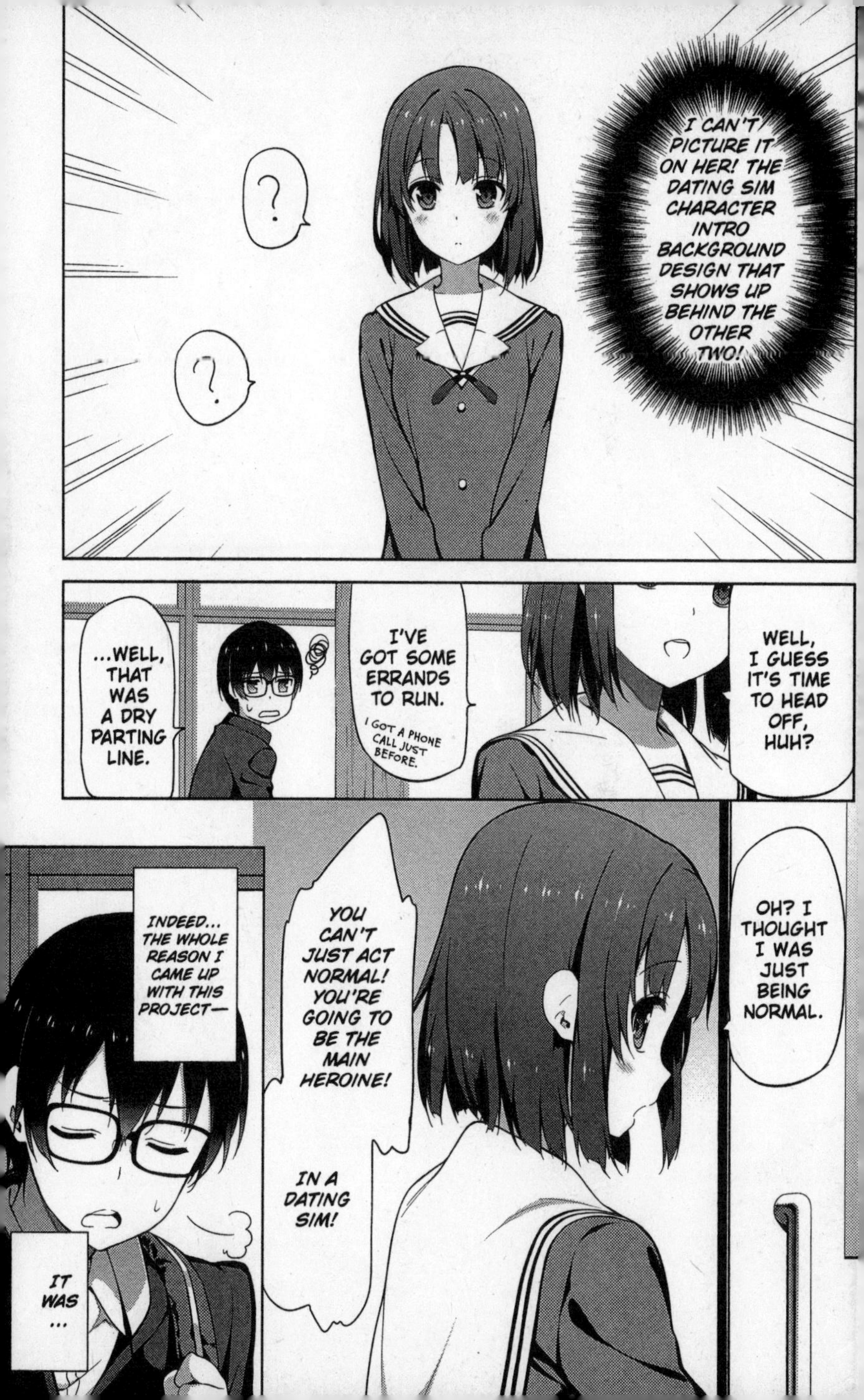
I CAN'T PICTURE IT ON HER! THE DATING SIM CHARACTER INTRO BACKGROUND DESIGN THAT SHOWS UP BEHIND THE OTHER TWO!
?
?
WELL, I GUESS IT'S TIME TO HEAD OFF, HUH?
I'VE GOT SOME ERRANDS TO RUN.
I GOT A PHONE CALL JUST BEFORE.
...WELL, THAT WAS A DRY PARTING LINE.
OH? I THOUGHT I WAS JUST BEING NORMAL.
YOU CAN'T JUST ACT NORMAL! YOU'RE GOING TO BE THE MAIN HEROINE!
IN A DATING SIM!
INDEED... THE WHOLE REASON I CAME UP WITH THIS PROJECT—
IT WAS...

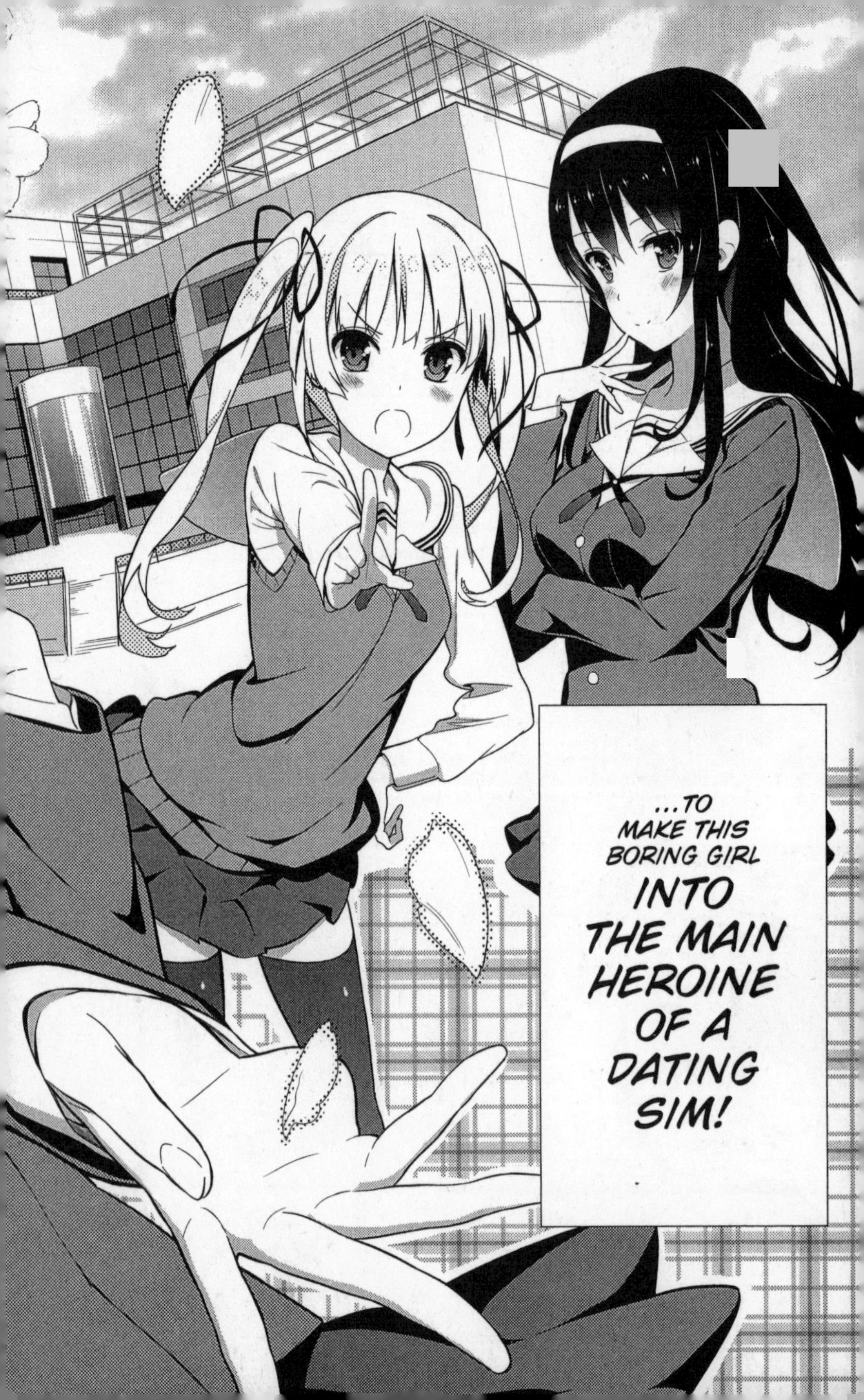
...TO MAKE THIS BORING GIRL INTO THE MAIN HEROINE OF A DATING SIM!

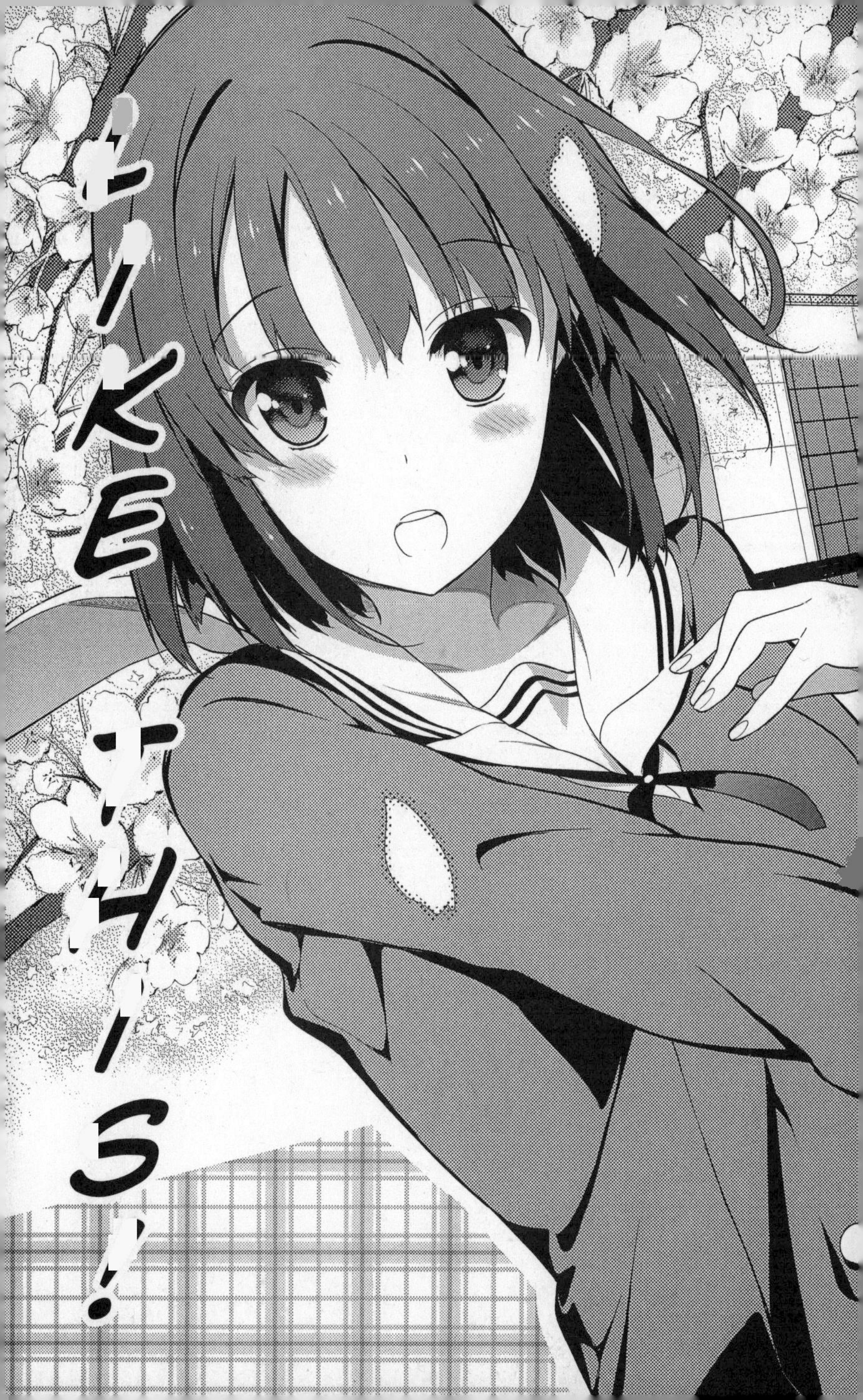
LIKE THIS!

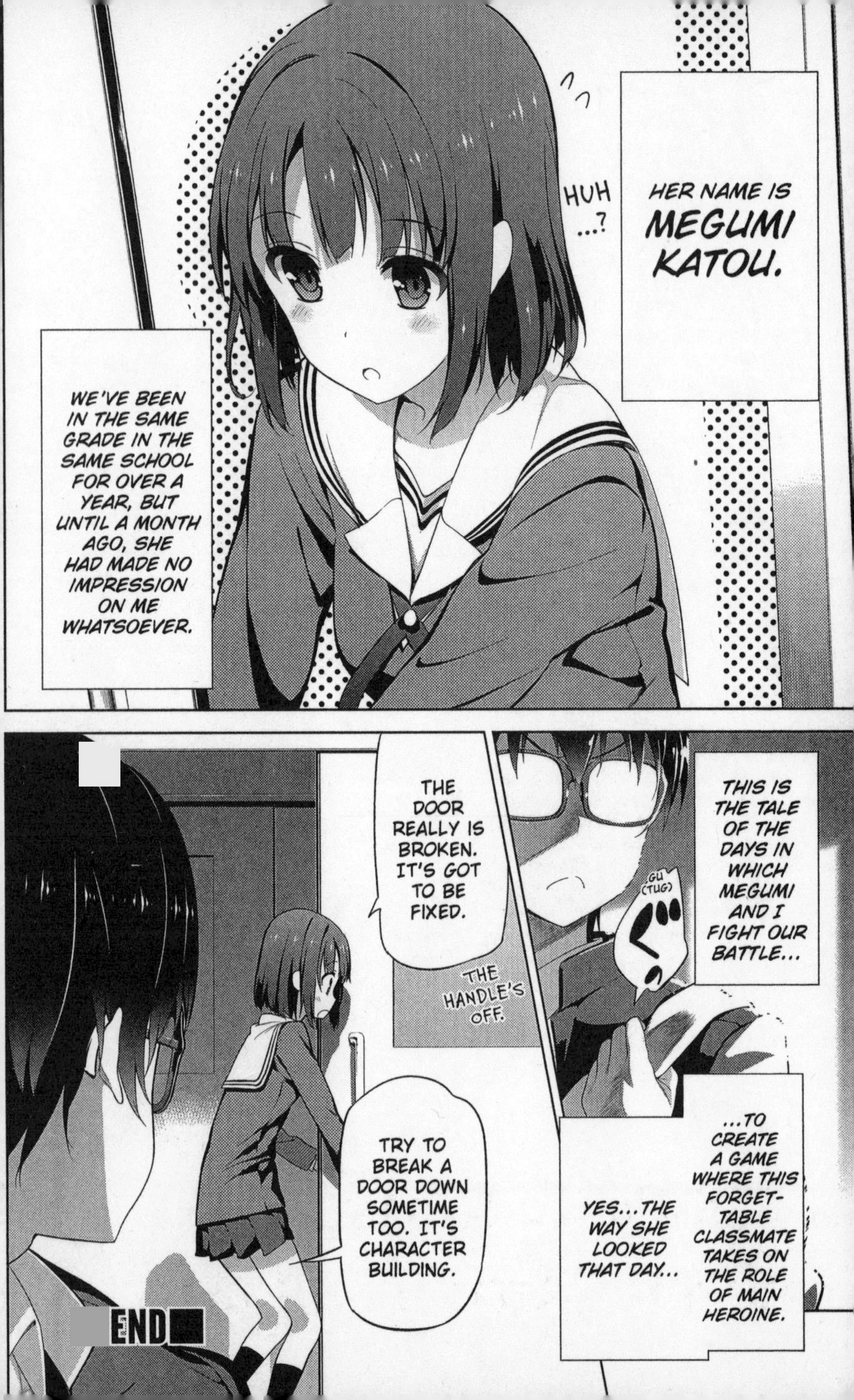
HER NAME IS MEGUMI KATOU.
HUH ...?
WE'VE BEEN IN THE SAME GRADE IN THE SAME SCHOOL FOR OVER A YEAR, BUT UNTIL A MONTH AGO, SHE HAD MADE NO IMPRESSION ON ME WHATSOEVER.
THIS IS THE TALE OF THE DAYS IN WHICH MEGUMI AND I FIGHT OUR BATTLE...
GU (TUG)
THE DOOR REALLY IS BROKEN. IT'S GOT TO BE FIXED.
THE HANDLE'S OFF.
...TO CREATE A GAME WHERE THIS FORGET-TABLE CLASSMATE TAKES ON THE ROLE OF MAIN HEROINE.
YES...THE WAY SHE LOOKED THAT DAY...
TRY TO BREAK A DOOR DOWN SOMETIME TOO. IT'S CHARACTER BUILDING.
END

How to Raise a Boring Girlfriend

How to Raise a Boring Girlfriend

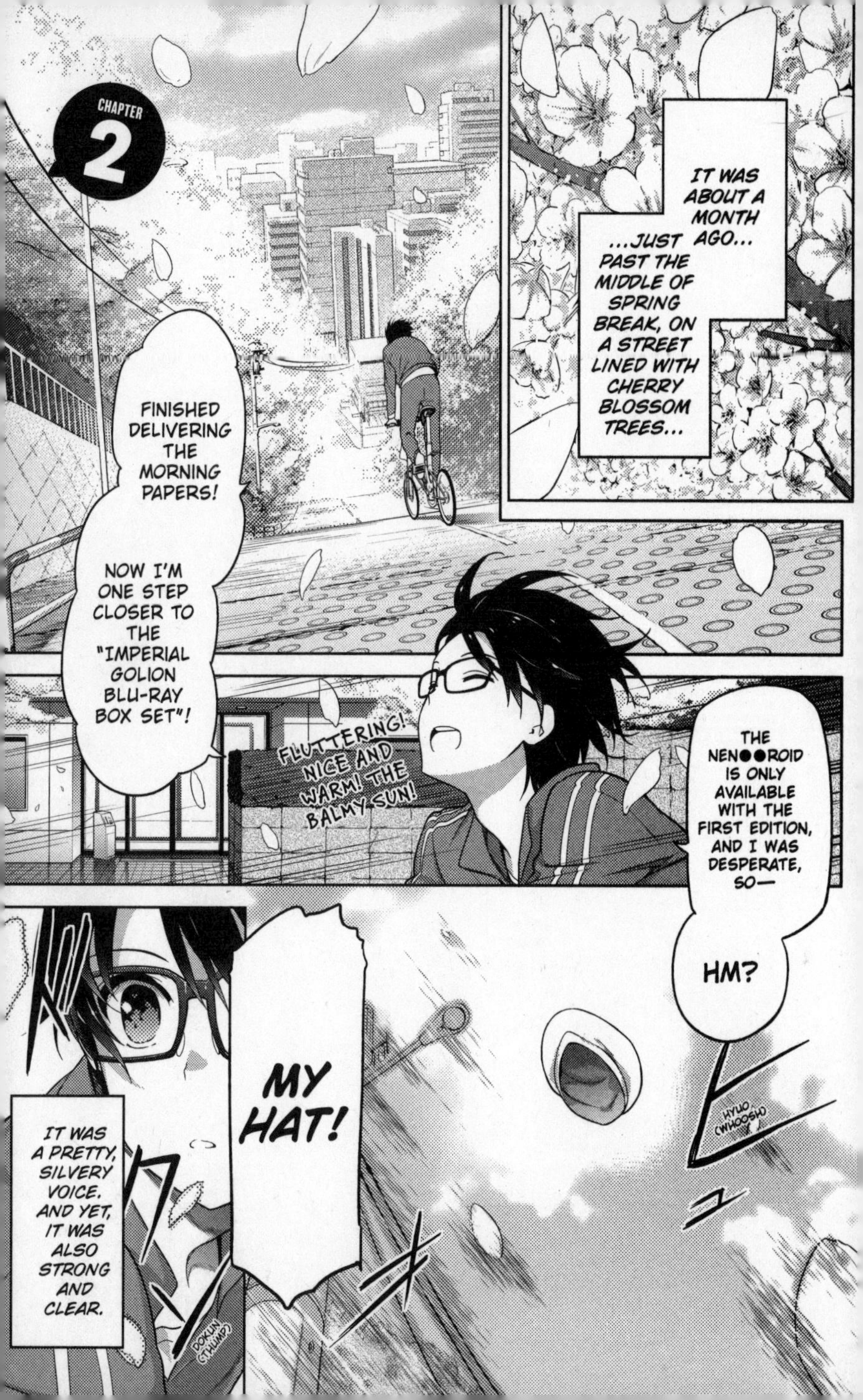
CHAPTER 2
IT WAS ABOUT A MONTH AGO...
...JUST PAST THE MIDDLE OF SPRING BREAK, ON A STREET LINED WITH CHERRY BLOSSOM TREES...
FINISHED DELIVERING THE MORNING PAPERS!
NOW I'M ONE STEP CLOSER TO THE "IMPERIAL GOLION BLU-RAY BOX SET"!
THE NEN●●ROID IS ONLY AVAILABLE WITH THE FIRST EDITION, AND I WAS DESPERATE, SO—
FLUTTERING!
NICE AND WARM! THE BALMY SUN!
HM?
HYUO (WHOOSH)
MY HAT!
IT WAS A PRETTY, SILVERY VOICE. AND YET, IT WAS ALSO STRONG AND CLEAR.
DOKUN (THUMP)

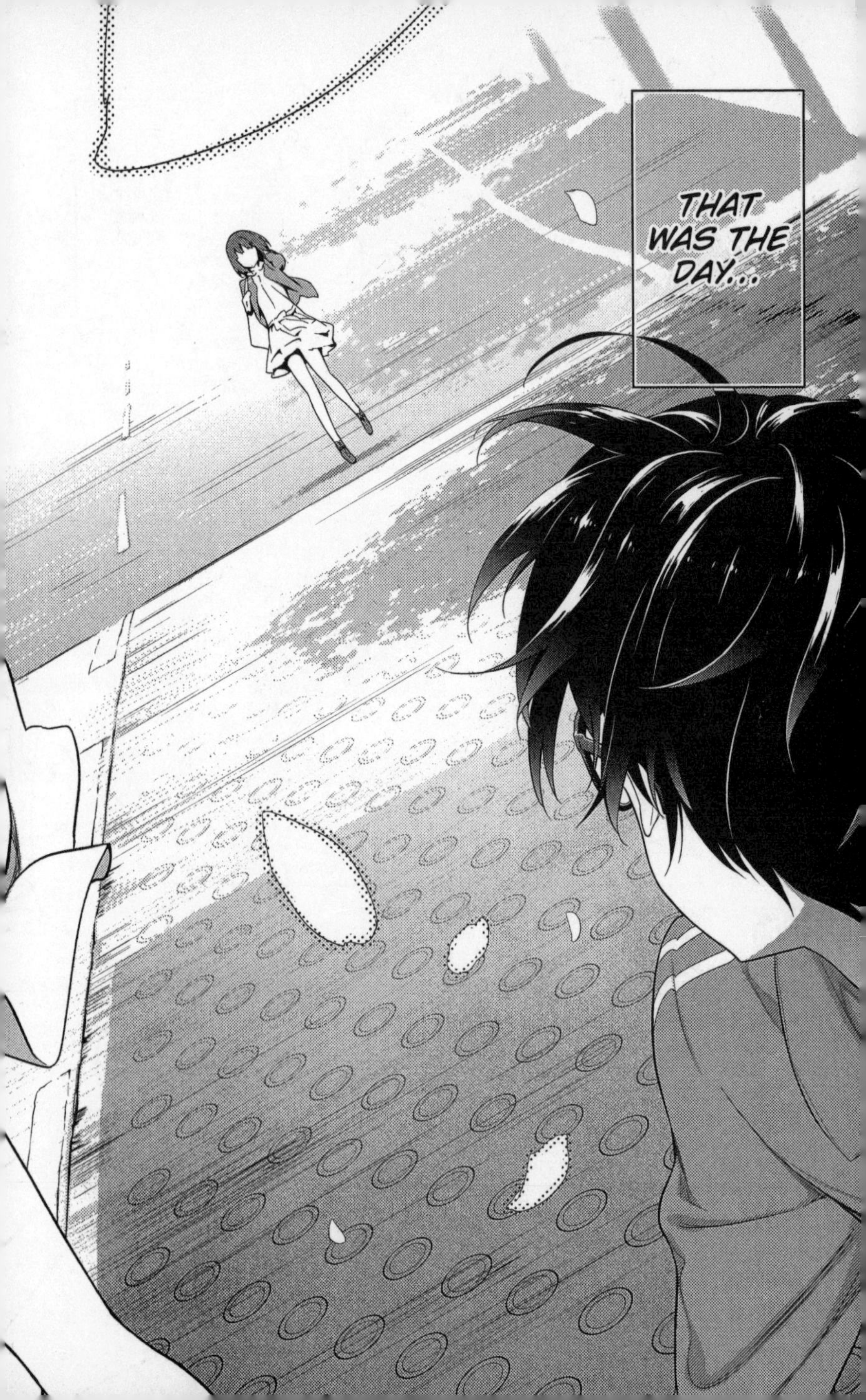
THAT WAS THE DAY...

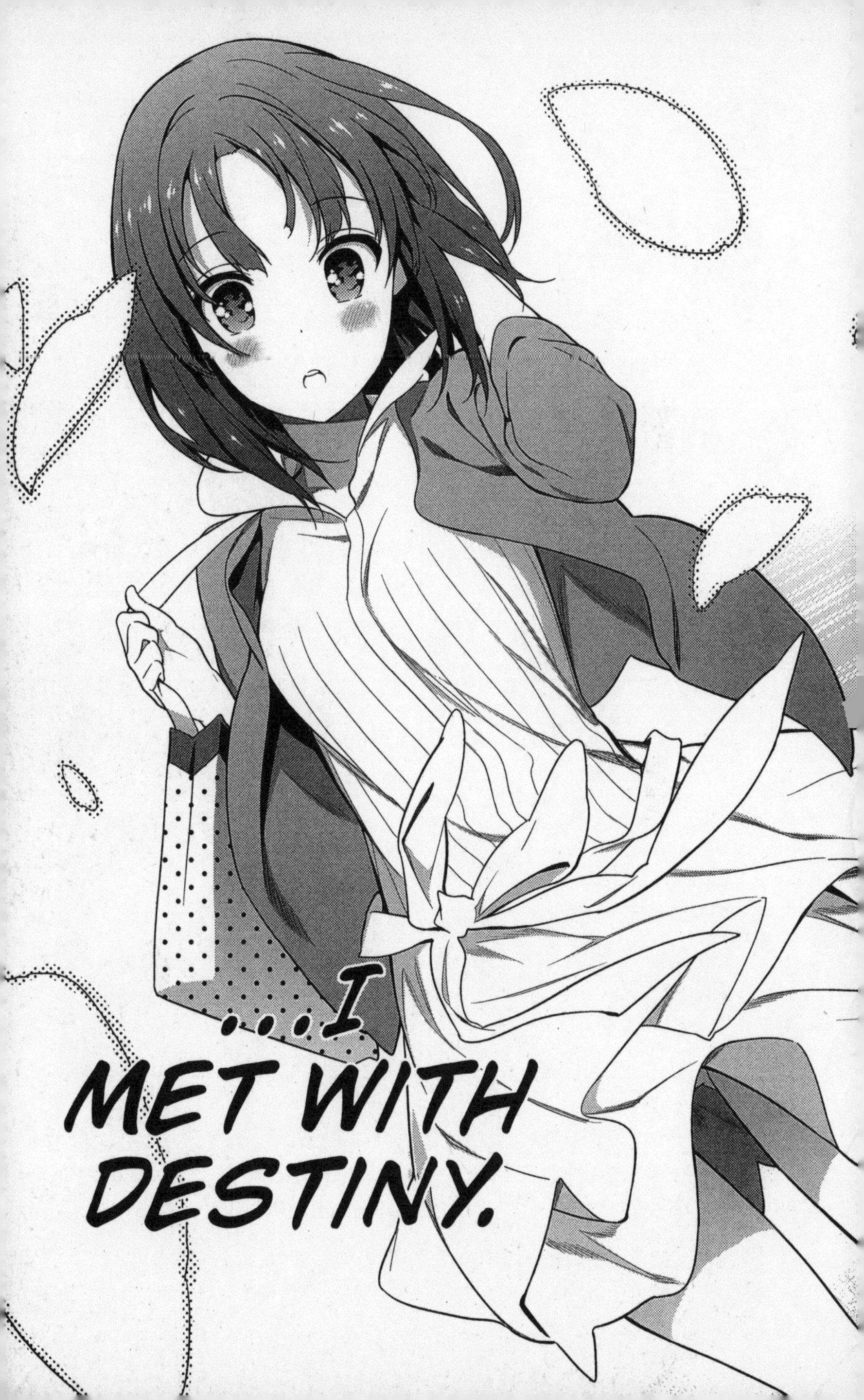
...I MET WITH DESTINY.

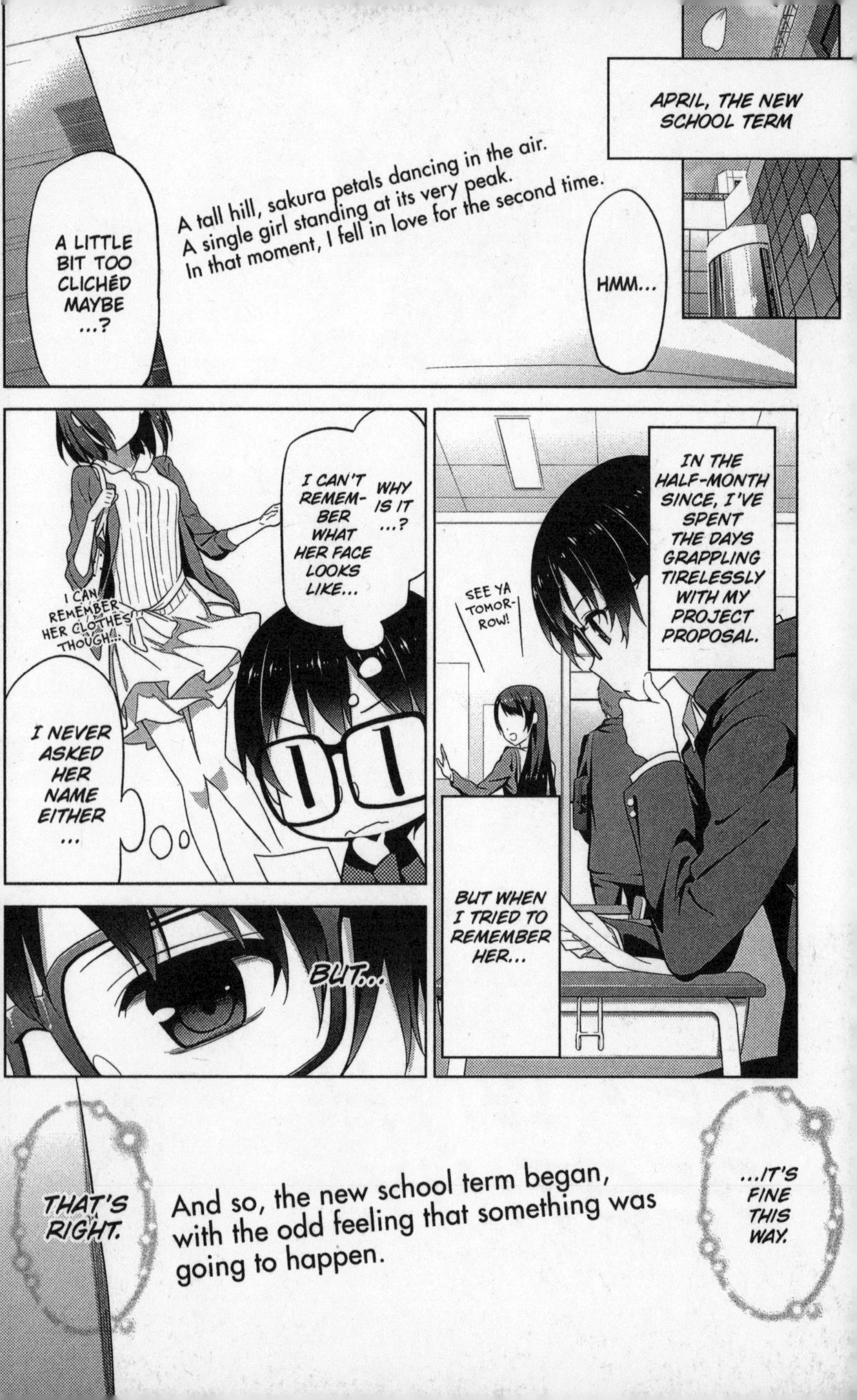
APRIL, THE NEW SCHOOL TERM
HMM...
A tall hill, sakura petals dancing in the air.
A single girl standing at its very peak.
In that moment, I fell in love for the second time.
A LITTLE BIT TOO CLICHÉD MAYBE ...?
IN THE HALF-MONTH SINCE, I'VE SPENT THE DAYS GRAPPLING TIRELESSLY WITH MY PROJECT PROPOSAL.
SEE YA TOMOR-ROW!
BUT WHEN I TRIED TO REMEMBER HER...
WHY IS IT ...?
I CAN'T REMEM-BER WHAT HER FACE LOOKS LIKE...
I CAN REMEMBER HER CLOTHES THOUGH...
I NEVER ASKED HER NAME EITHER ...
BUT...
...IT'S FINE THIS WAY.
And so, the new school term began,
with the odd feeling that something was
going to happen.
THAT'S RIGHT.

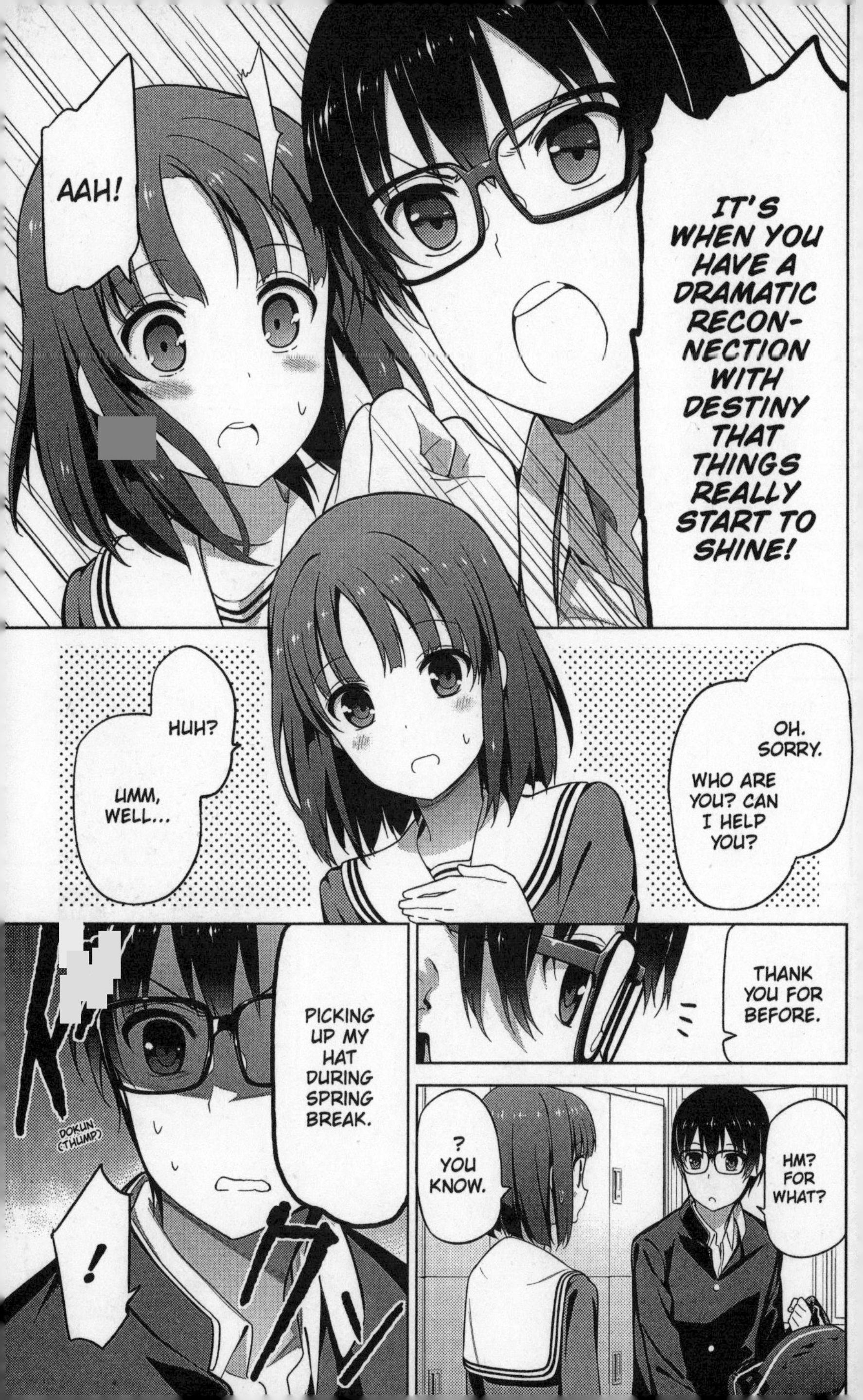
IT'S WHEN YOU HAVE A DRAMATIC RECON-NECTION WITH DESTINY THAT THINGS REALLY START TO SHINE!
AAH!
OH. SORRY.
WHO ARE YOU? CAN I HELP YOU?
HUH?
UMM, WELL...
THANK YOU FOR BEFORE.
HM? FOR WHAT?
? YOU KNOW.
PICKING UP MY HAT DURING SPRING BREAK.
DOKUN (THUMP)
!

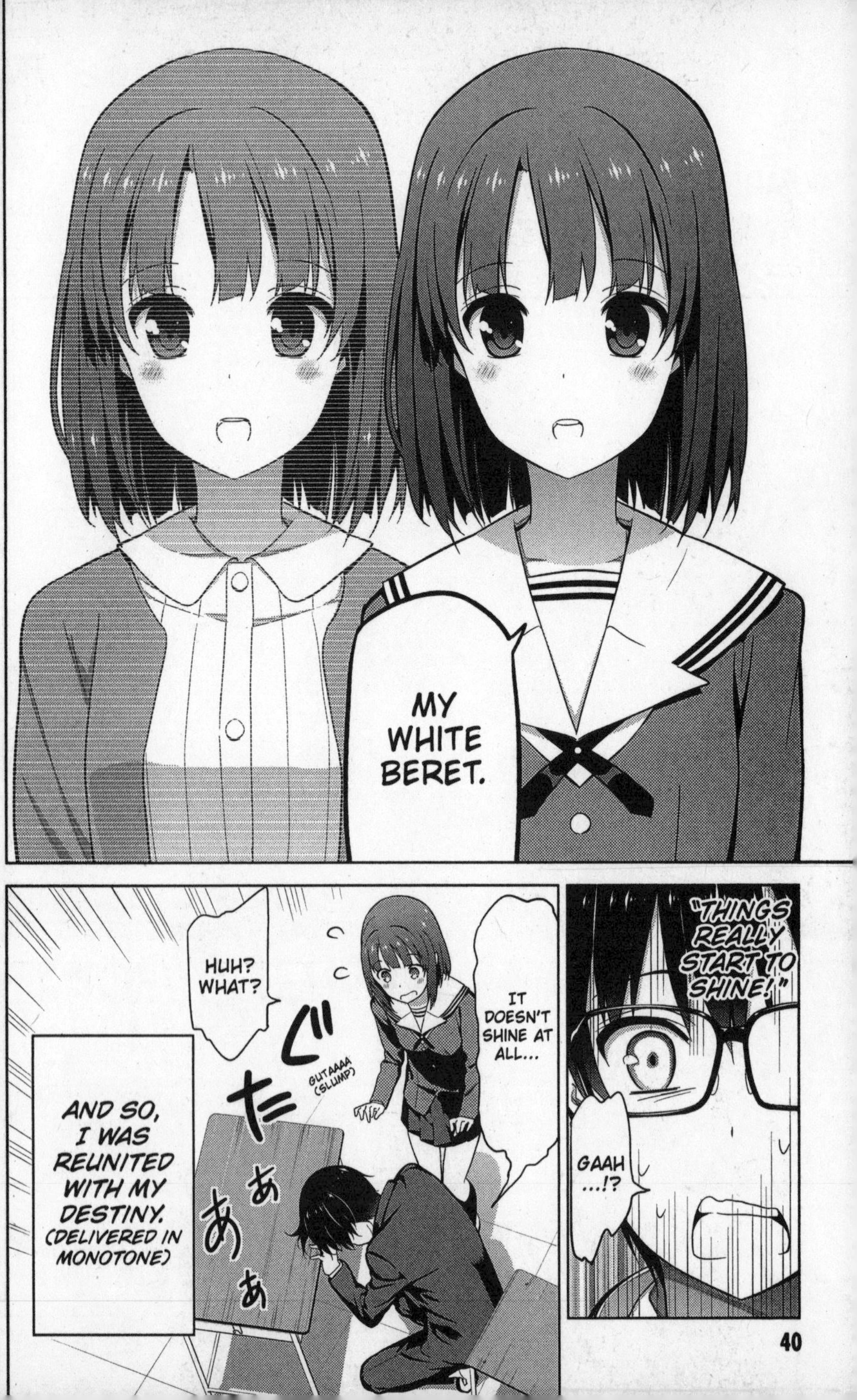
MY WHITE BERET.
"THINGS REALLY START TO SHINE!"
GAAH ...!?
IT DOESN'T SHINE AT ALL...
HUH? WHAT?
ぐたぁあぁ
GUTAAAA (SLUMP)
AND SO, I WAS REUNITED WITH MY DESTINY. (DELIVERED IN MONOTONE)

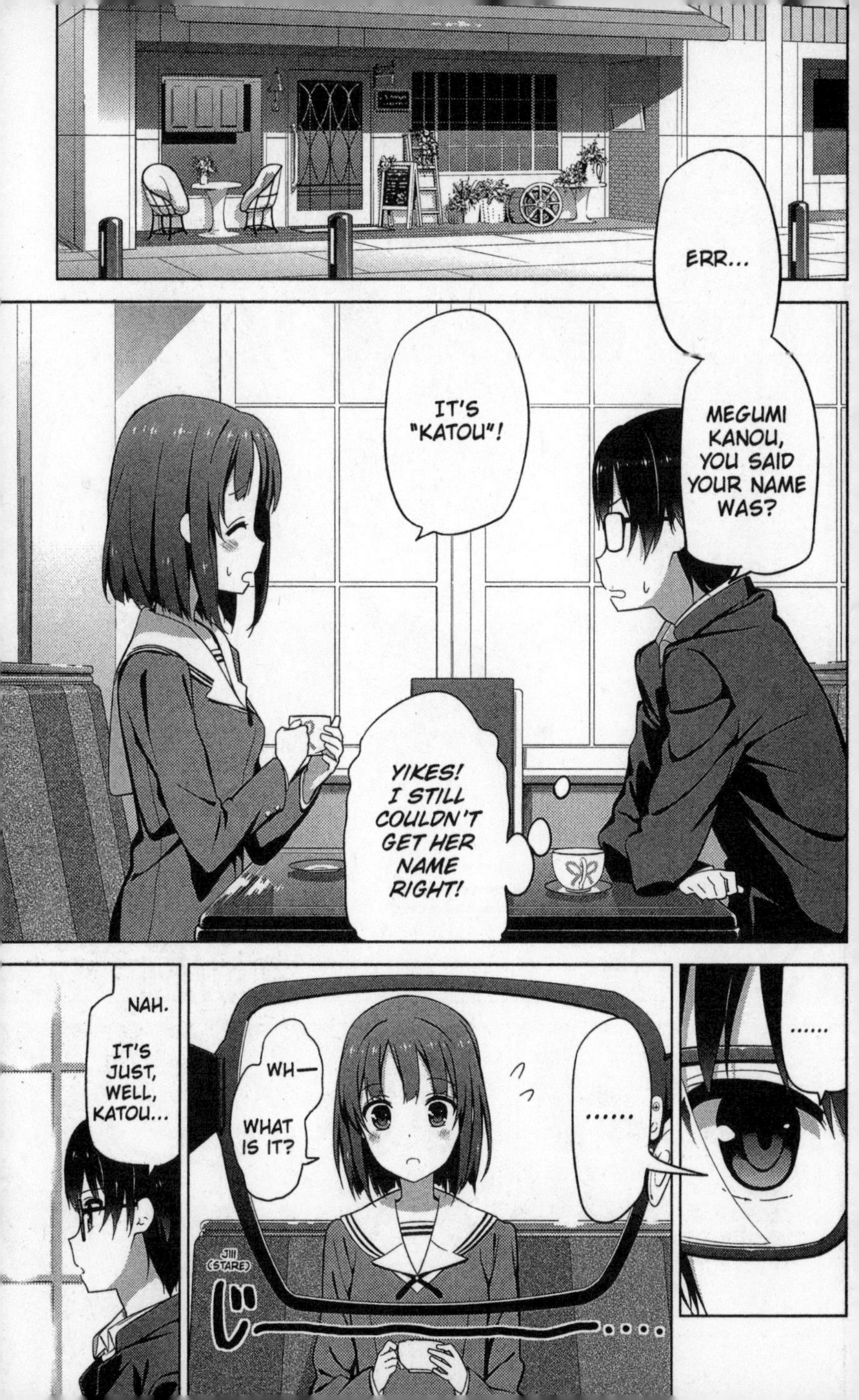
ERR...
MEGUMI KANOU, YOU SAID YOUR NAME WAS?
IT'S "KATOU"!
YIKES! I STILL COULDN'T GET HER NAME RIGHT!
......
......
WH—
WHAT IS IT?
JIII (STARE)
じ————....
NAH.
IT'S JUST, WELL, KATOU...

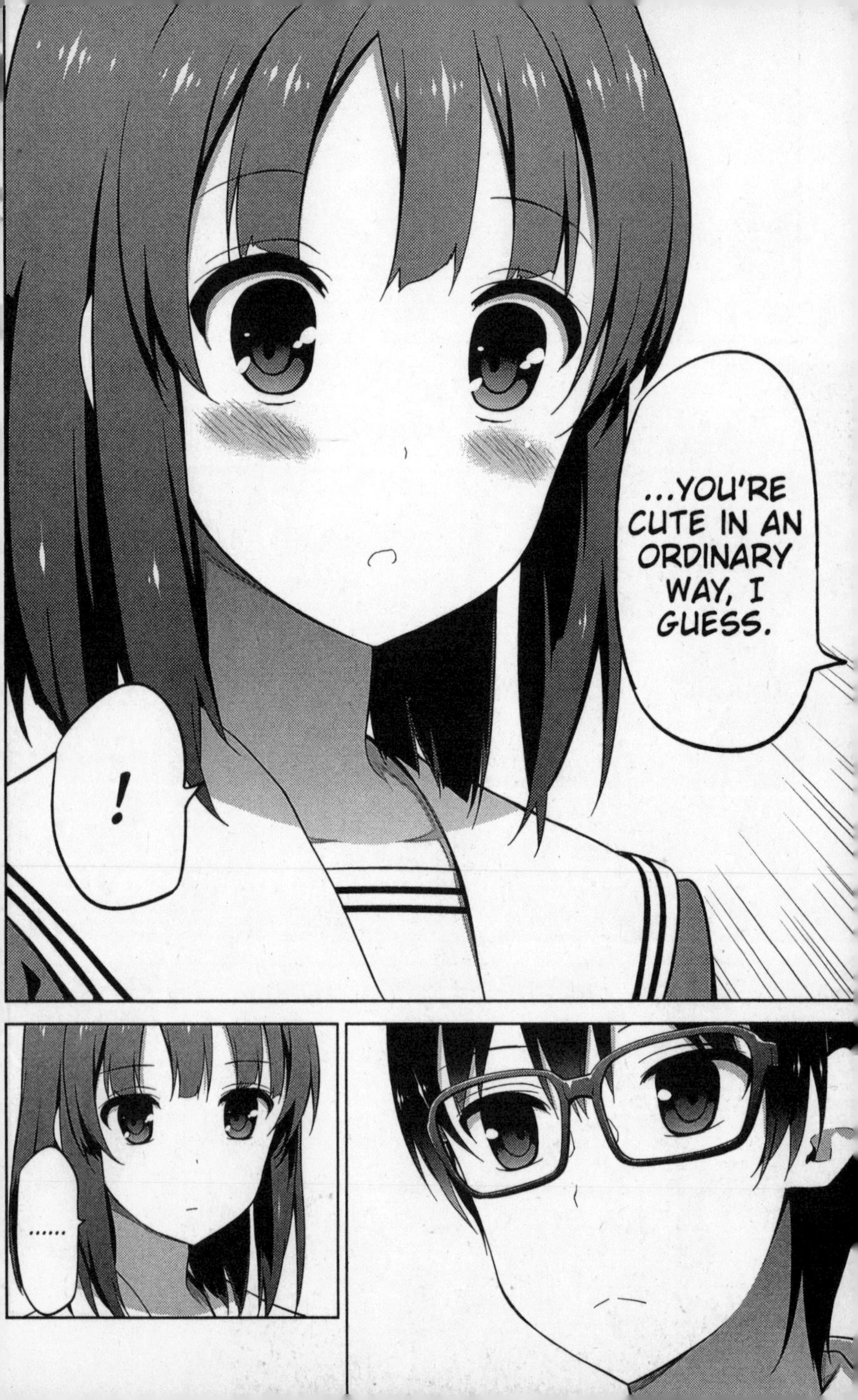
...YOU'RE CUTE IN AN ORDINARY WAY, I GUESS.
!
......

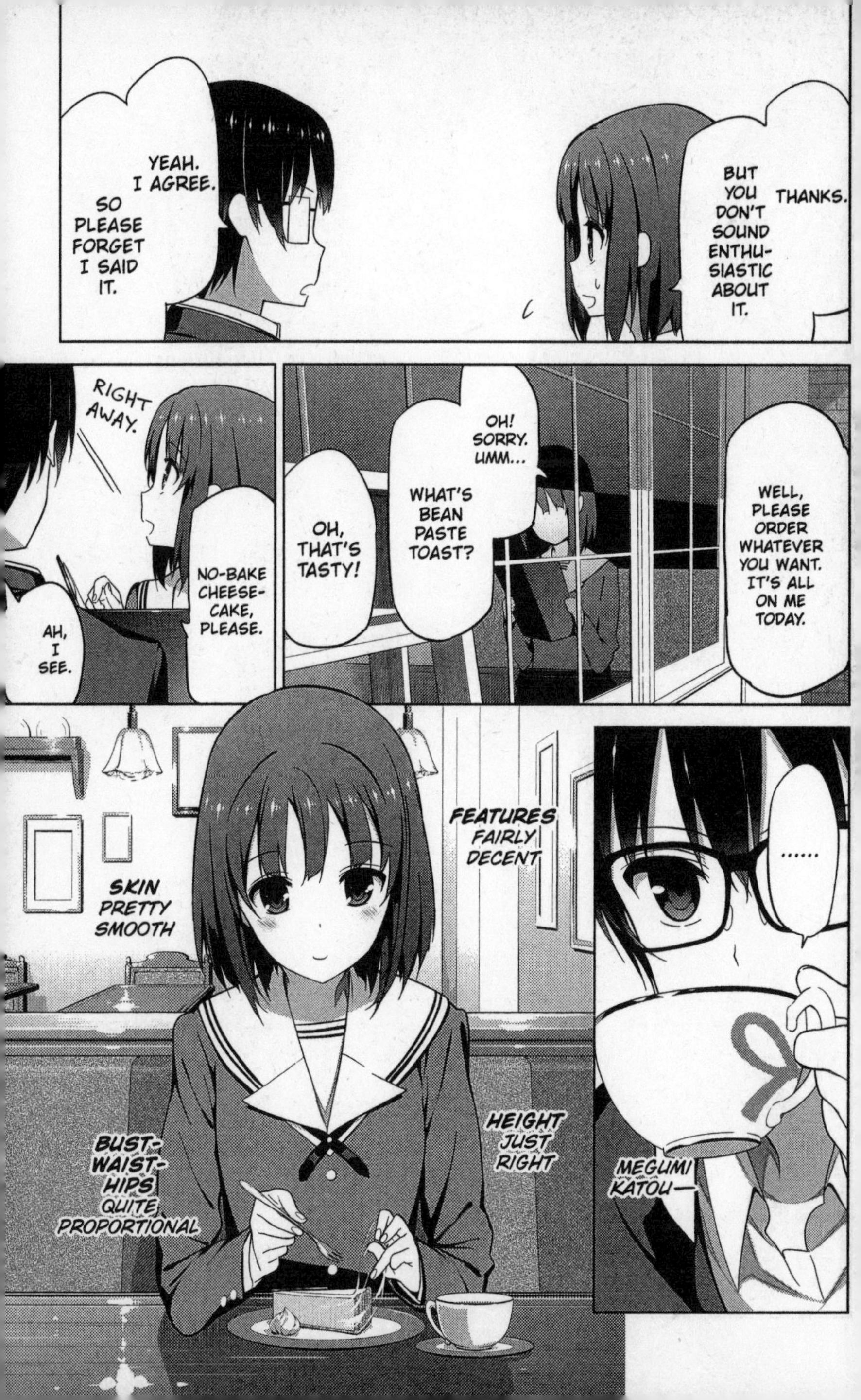
THANKS.
BUT YOU DON'T SOUND ENTHU-SIASTIC ABOUT IT.
YEAH. I AGREE.
SO PLEASE FORGET I SAID IT.
WELL, PLEASE ORDER WHATEVER YOU WANT. IT'S ALL ON ME TODAY.
OH! SORRY. UMM...
WHAT'S BEAN PASTE TOAST?
OH, THAT'S TASTY!
NO-BAKE CHEESE-CAKE, PLEASE.
RIGHT AWAY.
AH, I SEE.
......
MEGUMI KATOU—
FEATURES FAIRLY DECENT
SKIN PRETTY SMOOTH
HEIGHT JUST RIGHT
BUST-WAIST-HIPS QUITE PROPORTIONAL

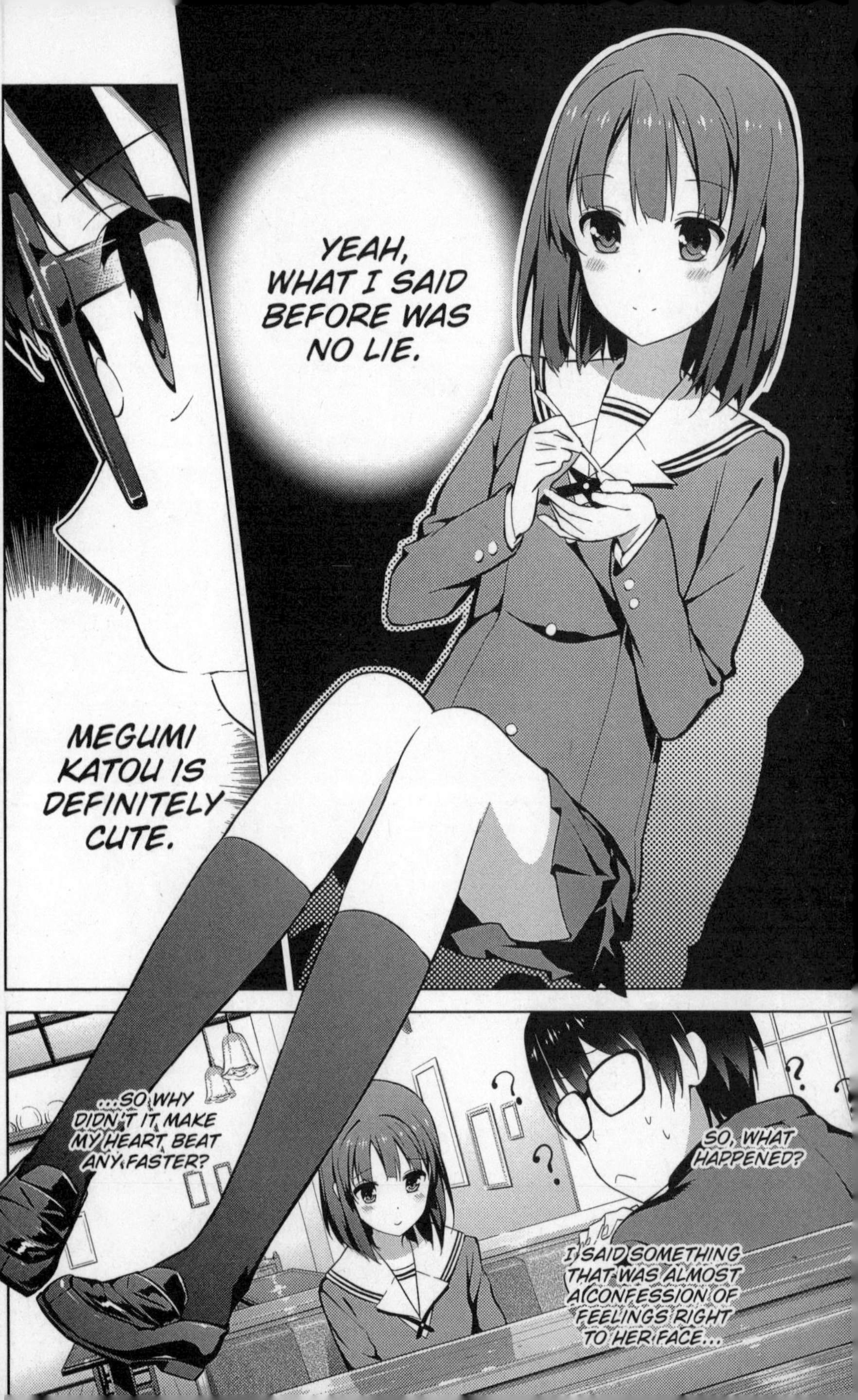
YEAH, WHAT I SAID BEFORE WAS NO LIE.
MEGUMI KATOU IS DEFINITELY CUTE.
SO, WHAT HAPPENED?
I SAID SOMETHING THAT WAS ALMOST A CONFESSION OF FEELINGS RIGHT TO HER FACE...
...SO WHY DIDN'T IT MAKE MY HEART BEAT ANY FASTER?

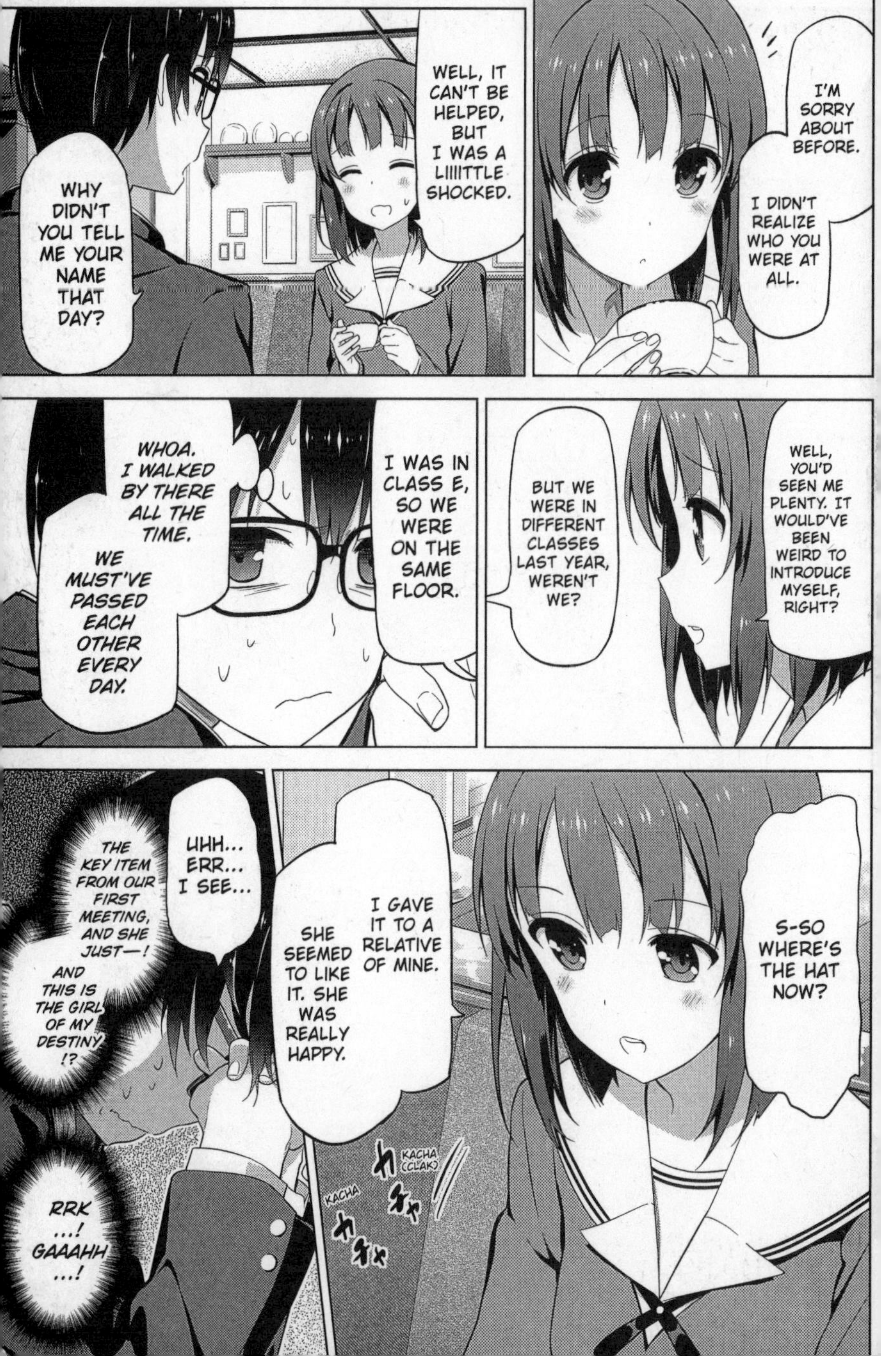
I'M SORRY ABOUT BEFORE.
I DIDN'T REALIZE WHO YOU WERE AT ALL.
WELL, IT CAN'T BE HELPED, BUT I WAS A LIIIITTLE SHOCKED.
WHY DIDN'T YOU TELL ME YOUR NAME THAT DAY?
WELL, YOU'D SEEN ME PLENTY. IT WOULD'VE BEEN WEIRD TO INTRODUCE MYSELF, RIGHT?
BUT WE WERE IN DIFFERENT CLASSES LAST YEAR, WEREN'T WE?
I WAS IN CLASS E, SO WE WERE ON THE SAME FLOOR.
WHOA. I WALKED BY THERE ALL THE TIME.
WE MUST'VE PASSED EACH OTHER EVERY DAY.
S-SO WHERE'S THE HAT NOW?
I GAVE IT TO A RELATIVE OF MINE.
SHE SEEMED TO LIKE IT. SHE WAS REALLY HAPPY.
KACHA (CLAK)
KACHA
UHH... ERR... I SEE...
THE KEY ITEM FROM OUR FIRST MEETING, AND SHE JUST—!
AND THIS IS THE GIRL OF MY DESTINY!?
RRK...! GAAAHH...!

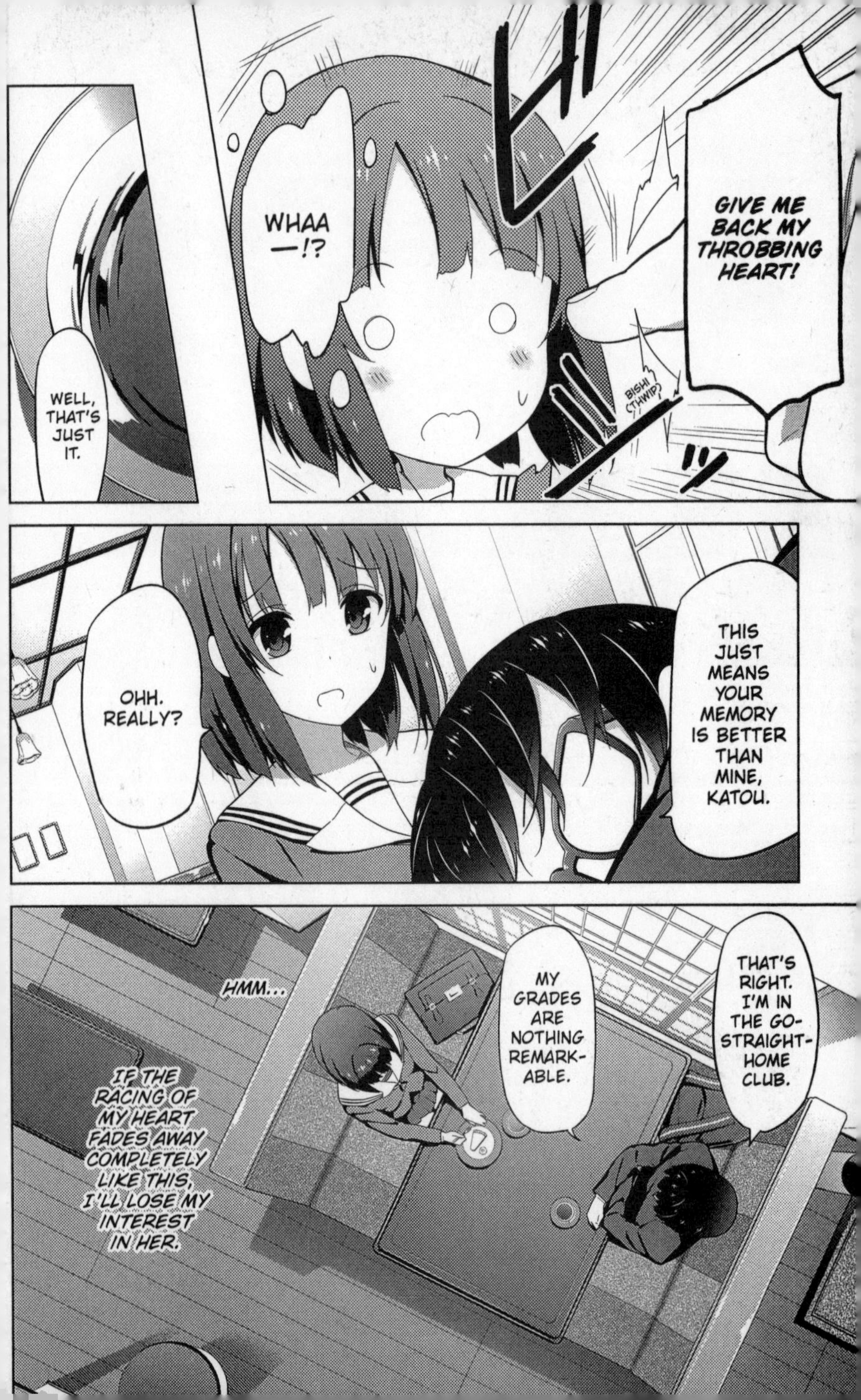
GIVE ME BACK MY THROBBING HEART!
WHAA—!?
BISHI (THWIP)
WELL, THAT'S JUST IT.
THIS JUST MEANS YOUR MEMORY IS BETTER THAN MINE, KATOU.
OHH. REALLY?
THAT'S RIGHT. I'M IN THE GO-STRAIGHT-HOME CLUB.
MY GRADES ARE NOTHING REMARKABLE.
HMM...
IF THE RACING OF MY HEART FADES AWAY COMPLETELY LIKE THIS, I'LL LOSE MY INTEREST IN HER.

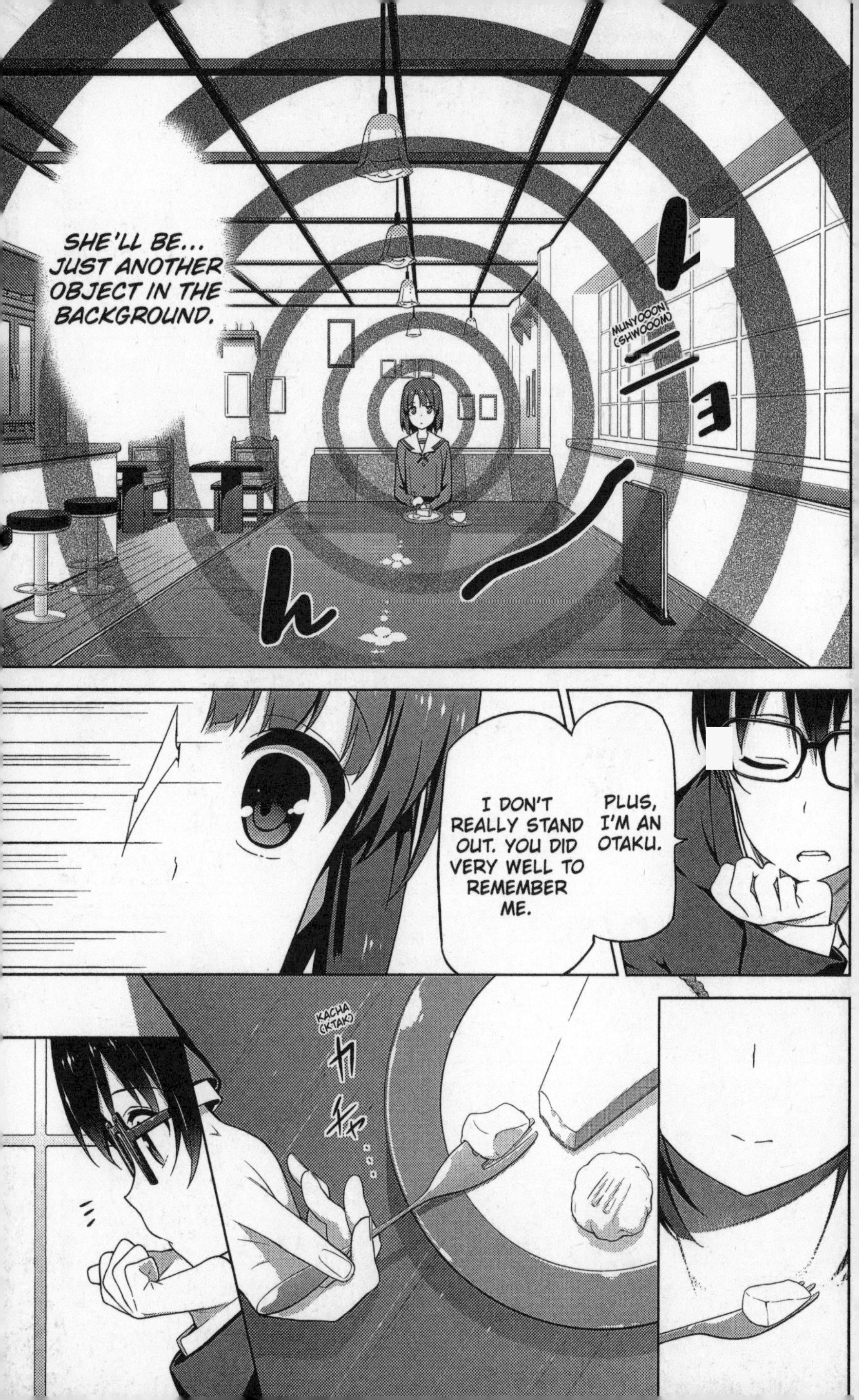
SHE'LL BE... JUST ANOTHER OBJECT IN THE BACKGROUND.
MUNYOOON (SHWOOOM)
I DON'T REALLY STAND OUT. YOU DID VERY WELL TO REMEMBER ME.
PLUS, I'M AN OTAKU.
KACHA (KTAK)

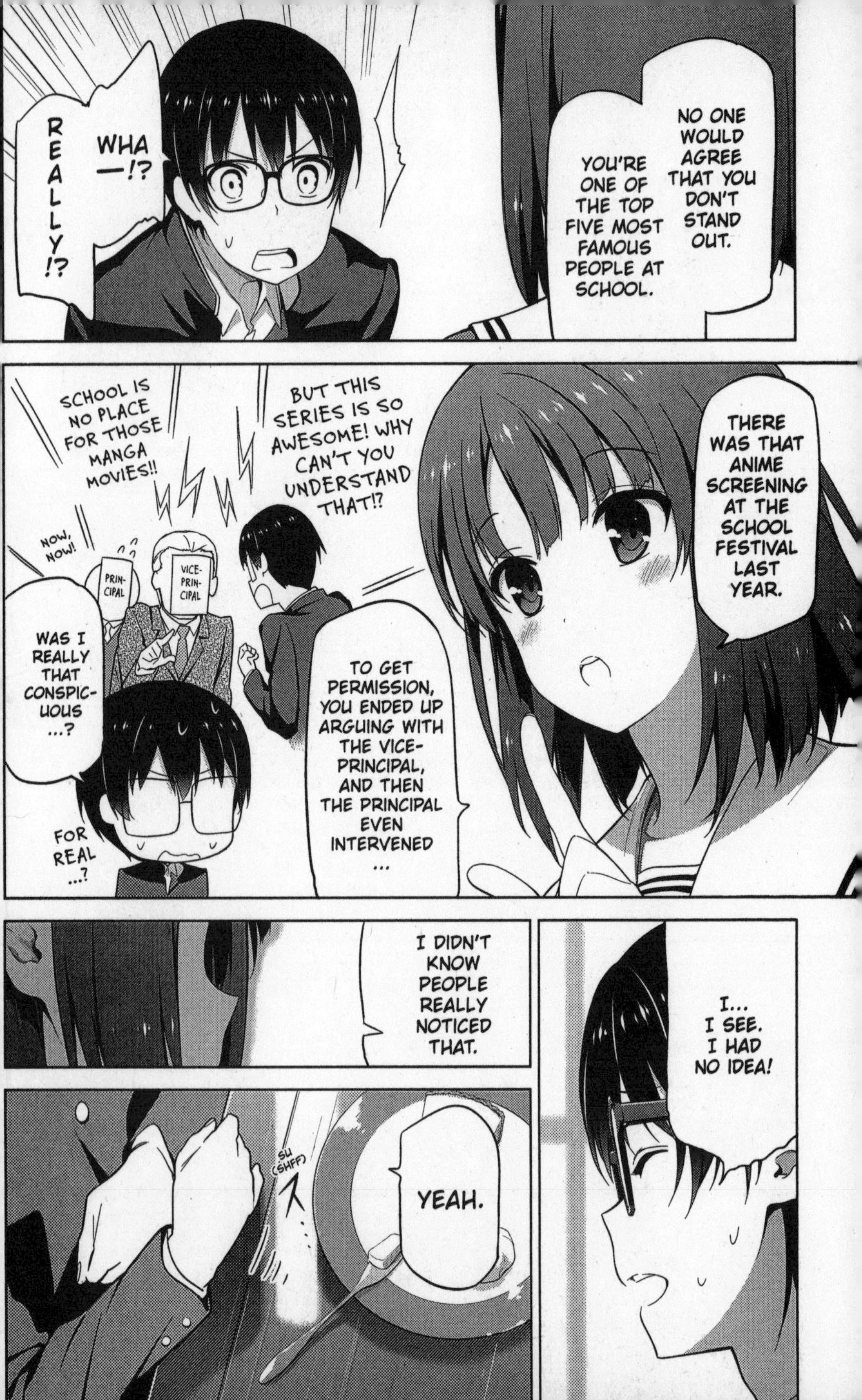
NO ONE WOULD AGREE THAT YOU DON'T STAND OUT.
YOU'RE ONE OF THE TOP FIVE MOST FAMOUS PEOPLE AT SCHOOL.
WHA—!?
REALLY!?
THERE WAS THAT ANIME SCREENING AT THE SCHOOL FESTIVAL LAST YEAR.
TO GET PERMISSION, YOU ENDED UP ARGUING WITH THE VICE-PRINCIPAL, AND THEN THE PRINCIPAL EVEN INTERVENED...
BUT THIS SERIES IS SO AWESOME! WHY CAN'T YOU UNDERSTAND THAT!?
SCHOOL IS NO PLACE FOR THOSE MANGA MOVIES!!
VICE-PRINCIPAL
NOW, NOW!
PRINCIPAL
WAS I REALLY THAT CONSPICUOUS...?
FOR REAL...?
I... I SEE. I HAD NO IDEA!
I DIDN'T KNOW PEOPLE REALLY NOTICED THAT.
YEAH.
SU (SHFF)

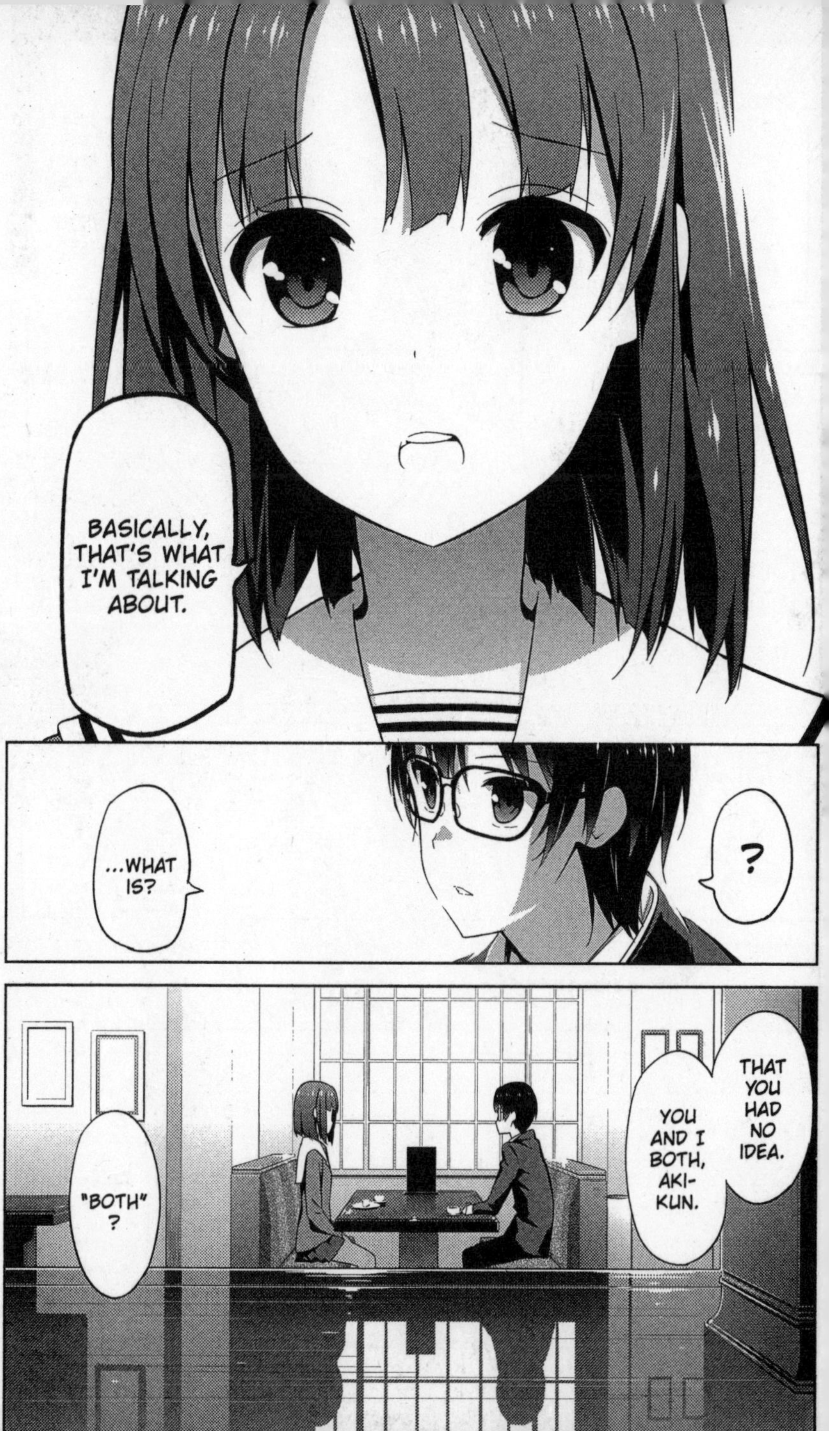
BASICALLY, THAT'S WHAT I'M TALKING ABOUT.
?
...WHAT IS?
THAT YOU HAD NO IDEA.
YOU AND I BOTH, AKI-KUN.
"BOTH"?

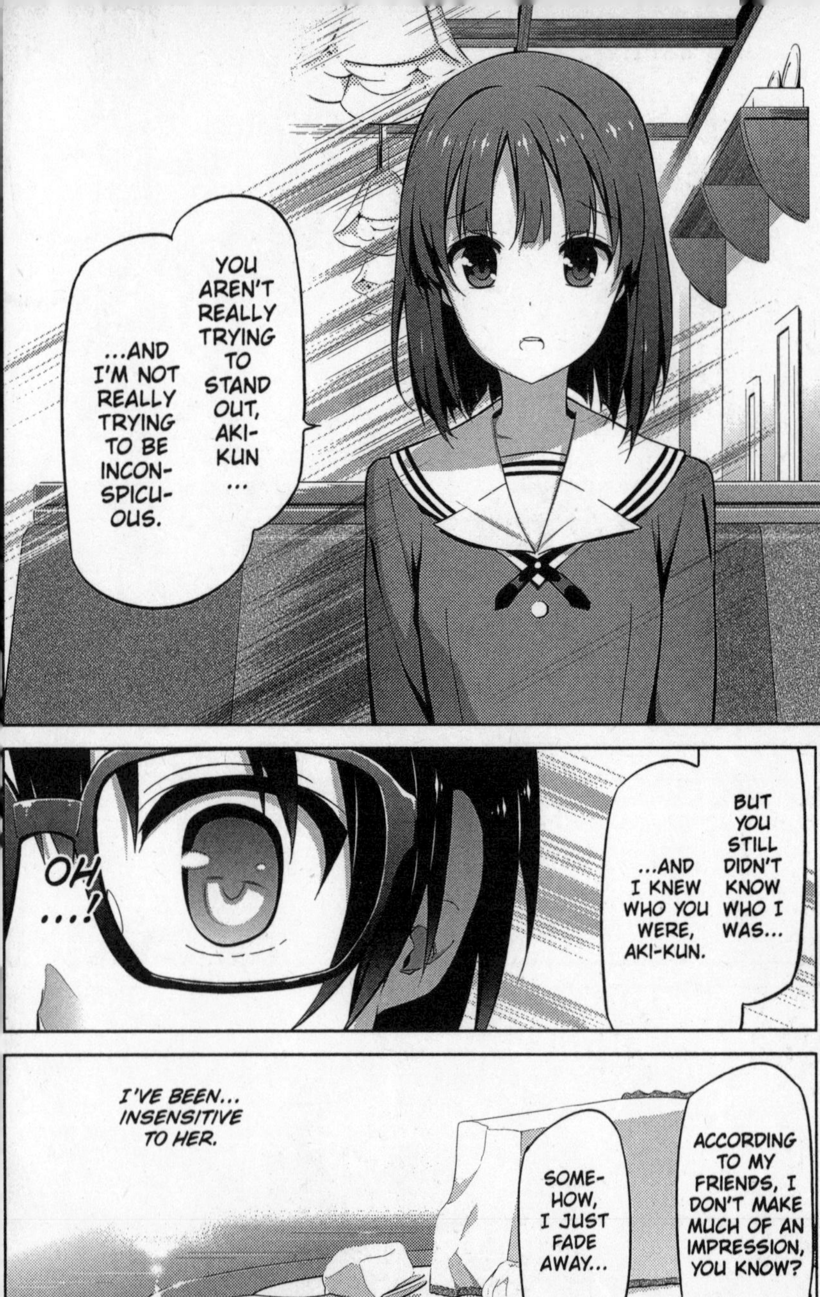
YOU AREN'T REALLY TRYING TO STAND OUT, AKI-KUN...
...AND I'M NOT REALLY TRYING TO BE INCONSPICUOUS.
BUT YOU STILL DIDN'T KNOW WHO I WAS...
...AND I KNEW WHO YOU WERE, AKI-KUN.
OH...!
ACCORDING TO MY FRIENDS, I DON'T MAKE MUCH OF AN IMPRESSION, YOU KNOW?
SOMEHOW, I JUST FADE AWAY...
I'VE BEEN... INSENSITIVE TO HER.

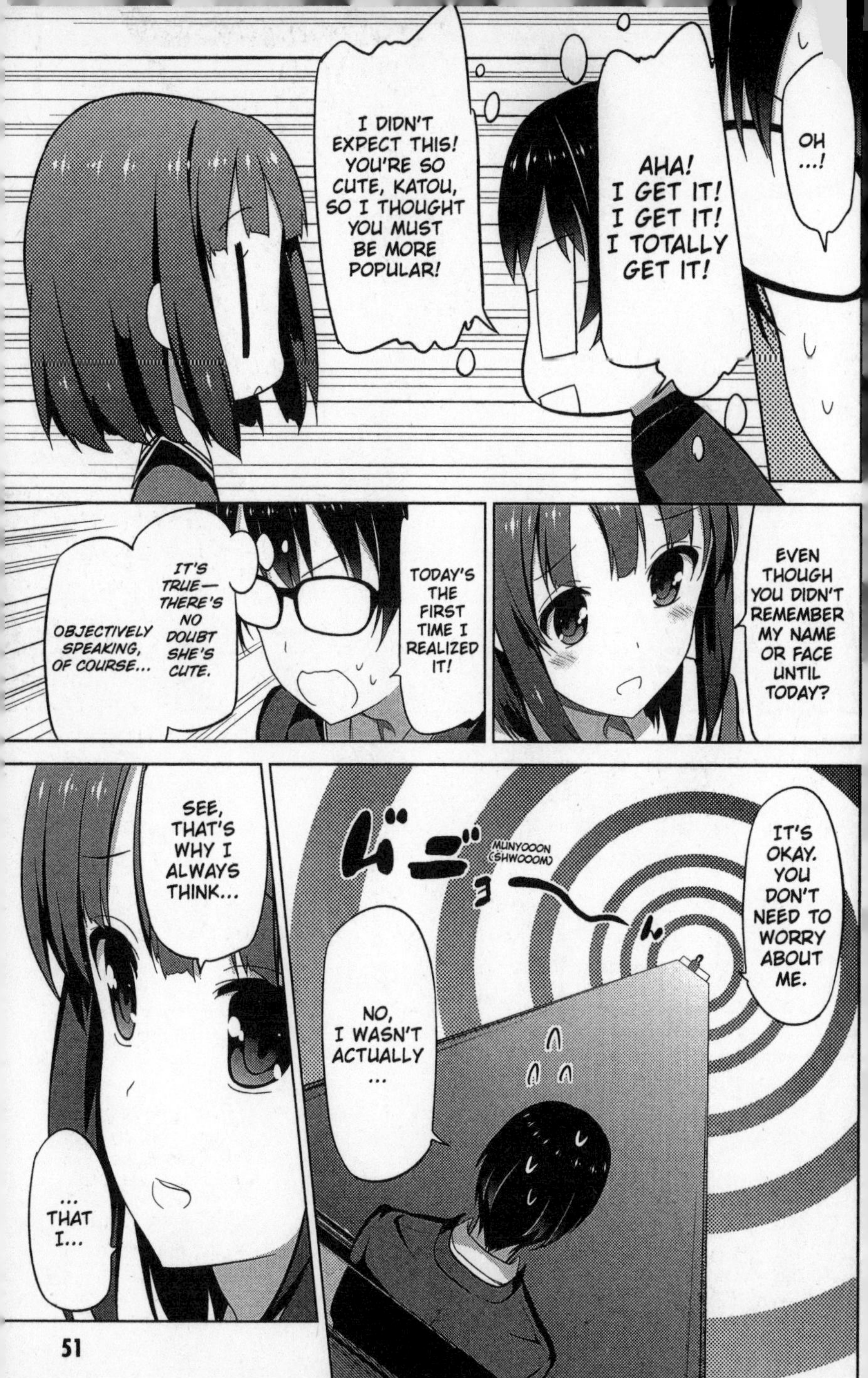
OH ...!
AHA! I GET IT! I GET IT! I TOTALLY GET IT!
I DIDN'T EXPECT THIS! YOU'RE SO CUTE, KATOU, SO I THOUGHT YOU MUST BE MORE POPULAR!
EVEN THOUGH YOU DIDN'T REMEMBER MY NAME OR FACE UNTIL TODAY?
TODAY'S THE FIRST TIME I REALIZED IT!
IT'S TRUE— THERE'S NO DOUBT SHE'S CUTE.
OBJECTIVELY SPEAKING, OF COURSE...
IT'S OKAY. YOU DON'T NEED TO WORRY ABOUT ME.
MUNYOOON (SHWOOOM)
NO, I WASN'T ACTUALLY ...
SEE, THAT'S WHY I ALWAYS THINK...
... THAT I...

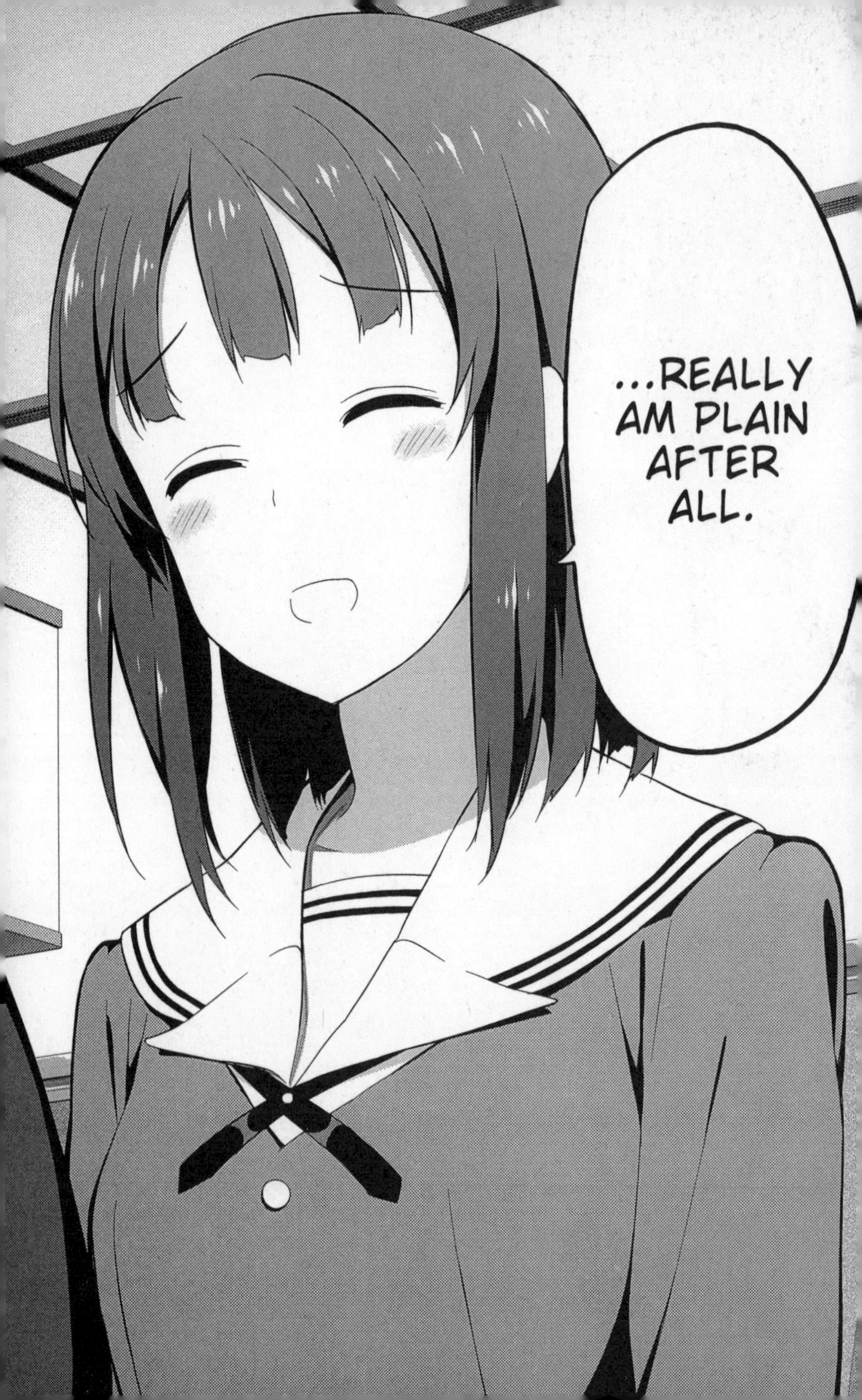
...REALLY AM PLAIN AFTER ALL.

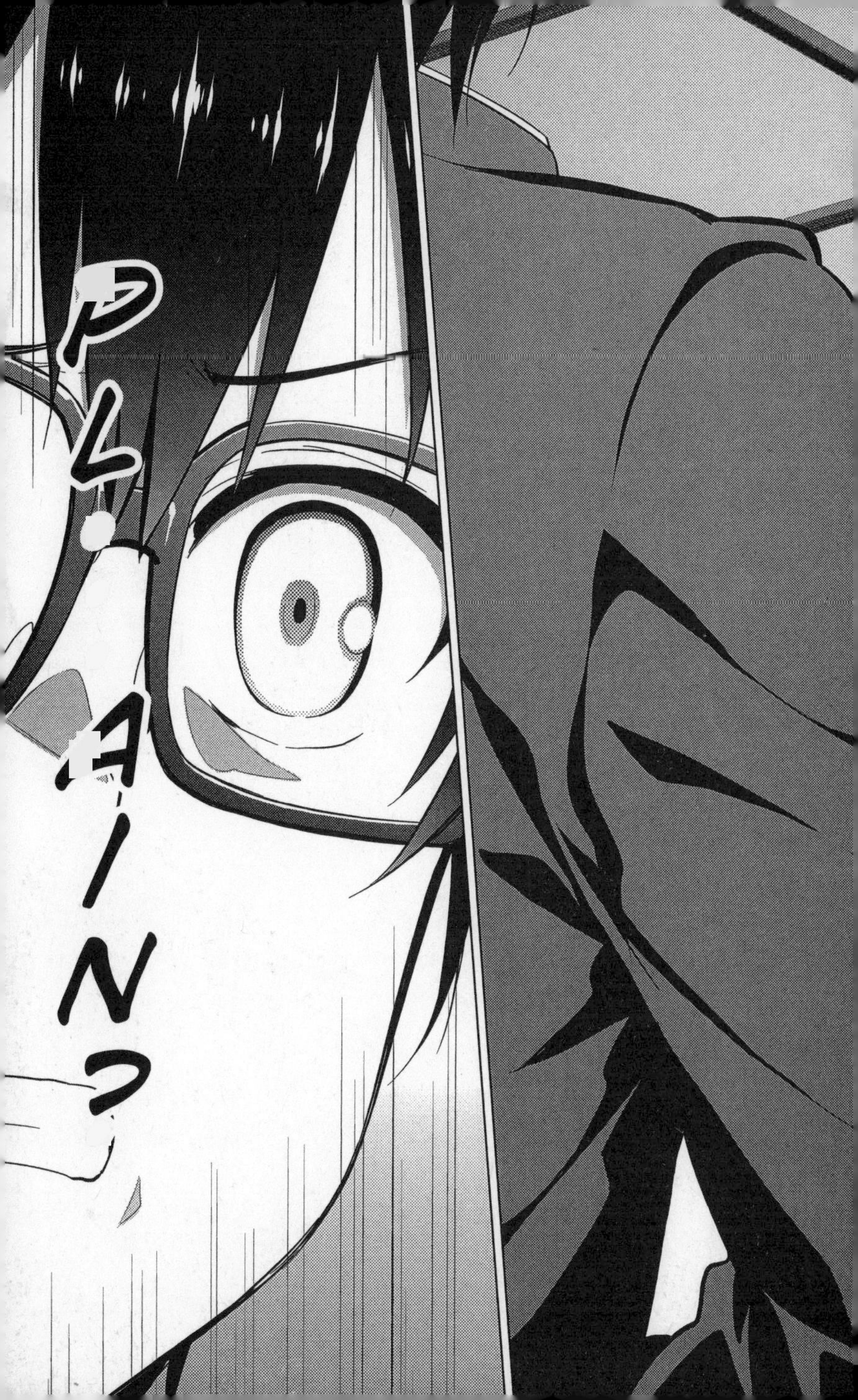
PL
A-N?

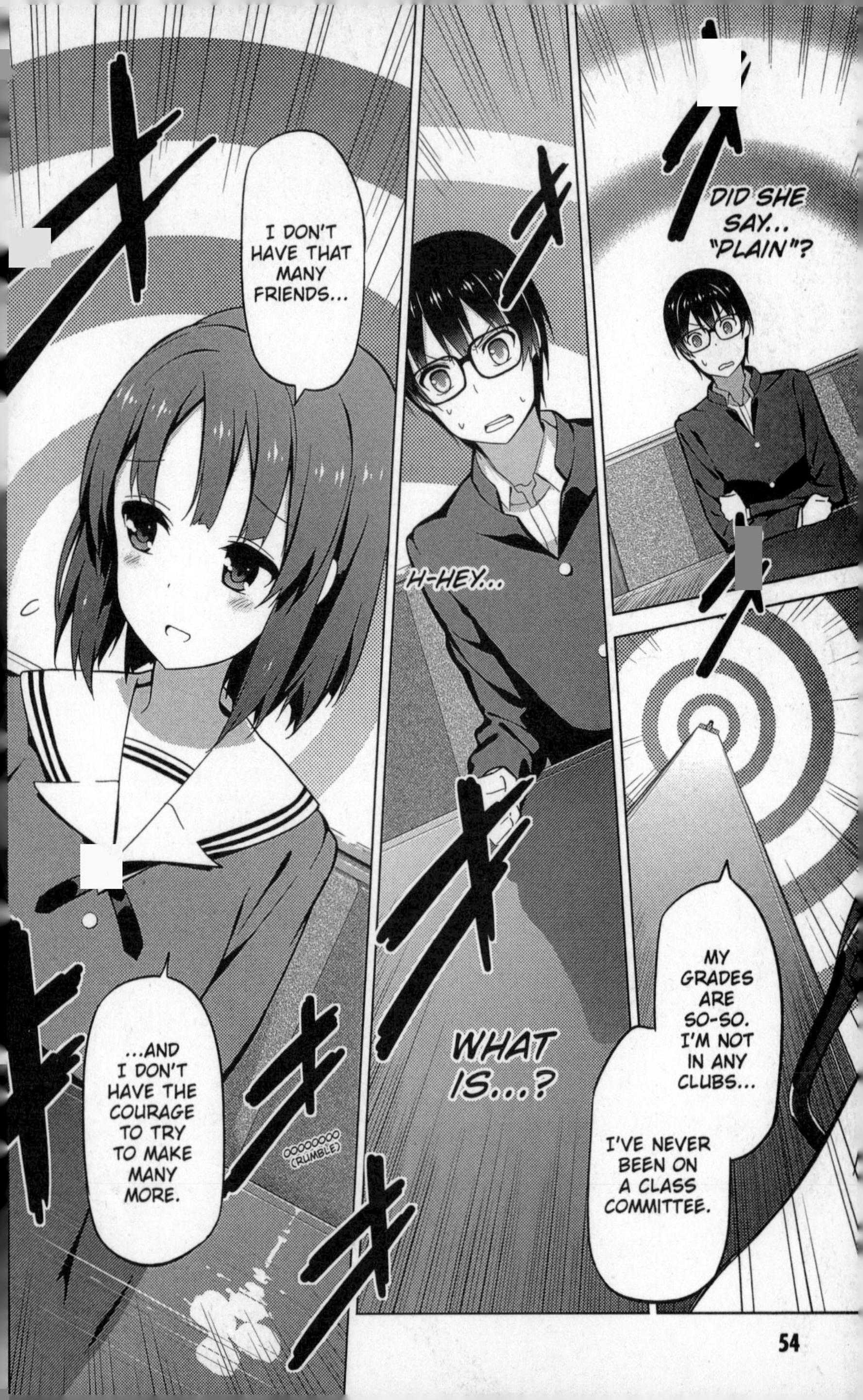
DID SHE SAY... "PLAIN"?
MY GRADES ARE SO-SO. I'M NOT IN ANY CLUBS...
I'VE NEVER BEEN ON A CLASS COMMITTEE.
H-HEY...
WHAT IS...?
I DON'T HAVE THAT MANY FRIENDS...
...AND I DON'T HAVE THE COURAGE TO TRY TO MAKE MANY MORE.
OOOOOOOO (RUMBLE)

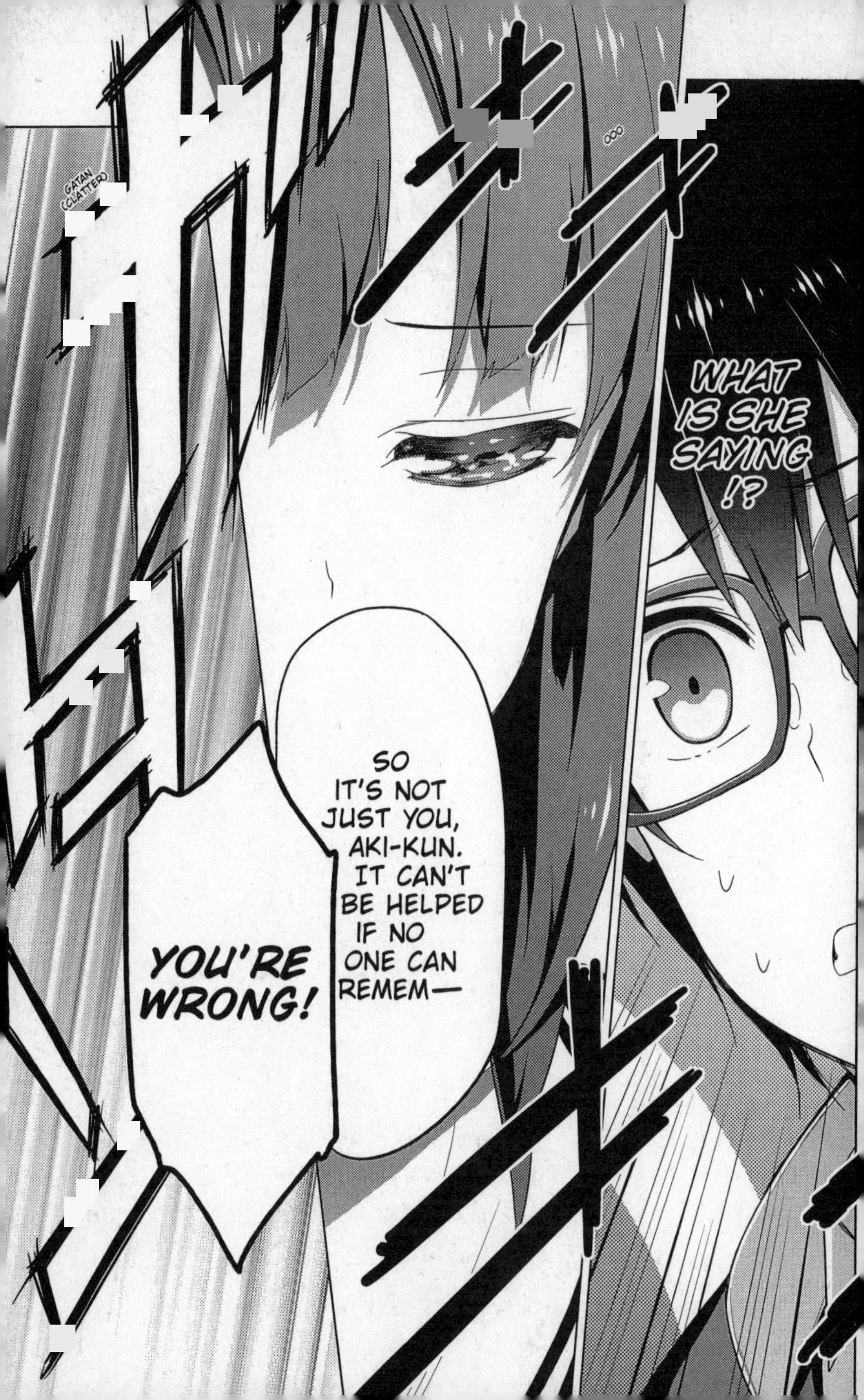
WHAT IS SHE SAYING !?
GATAN (CLATTER)
SO IT'S NOT JUST YOU, AKI-KUN. IT CAN'T BE HELPED IF NO ONE CAN REMEM—
YOU'RE WRONG!

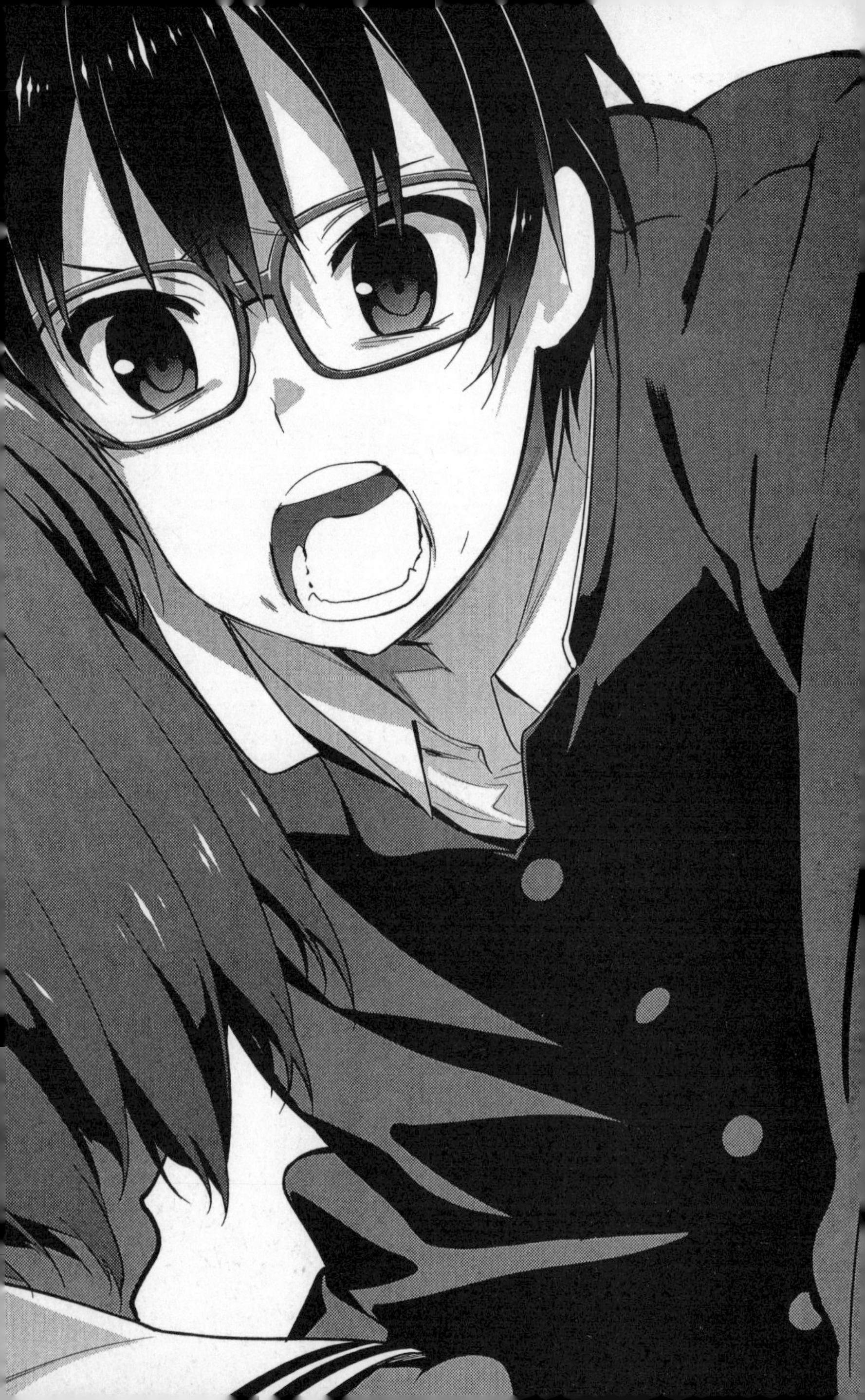

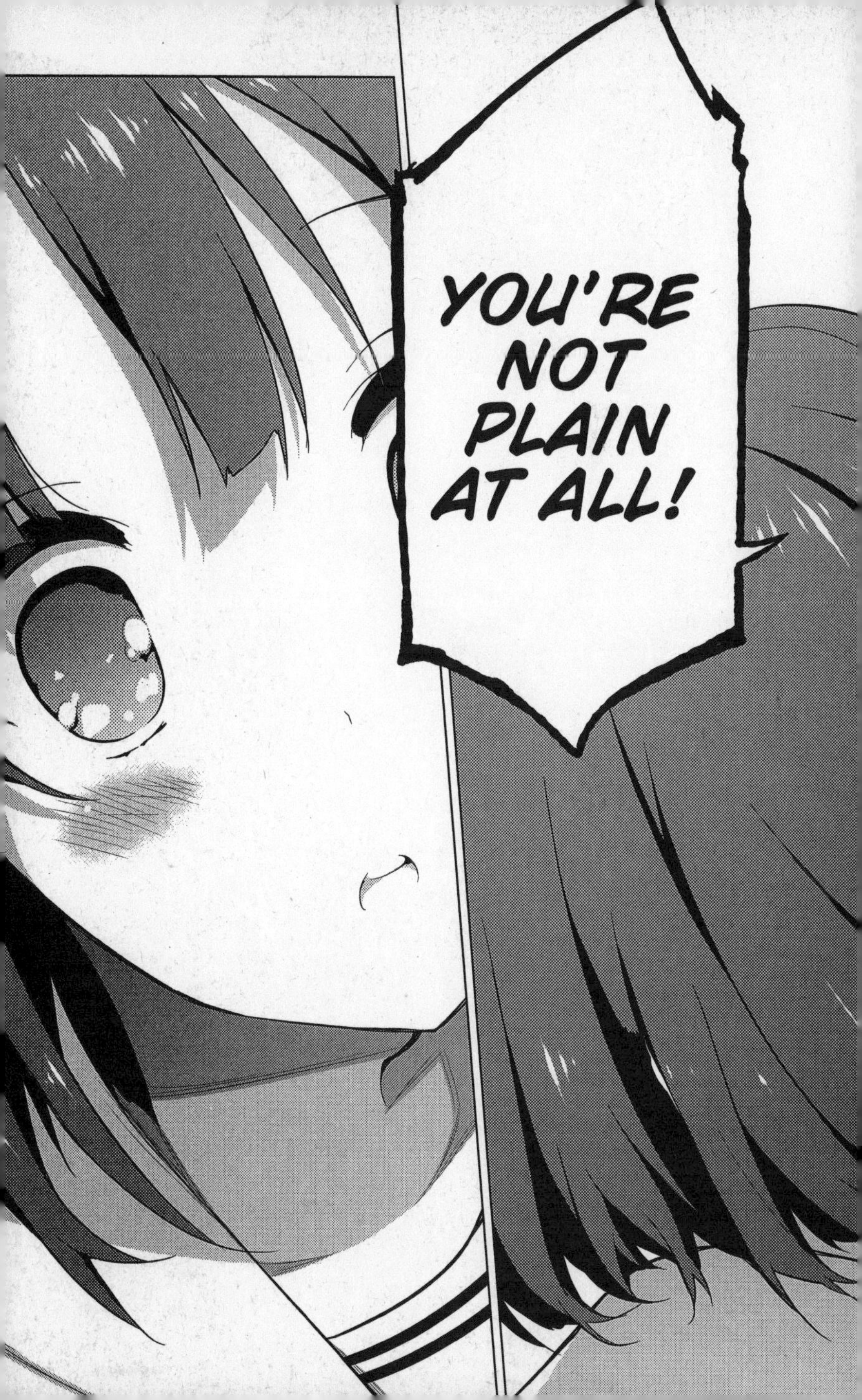
YOU'RE NOT PLAIN AT ALL!

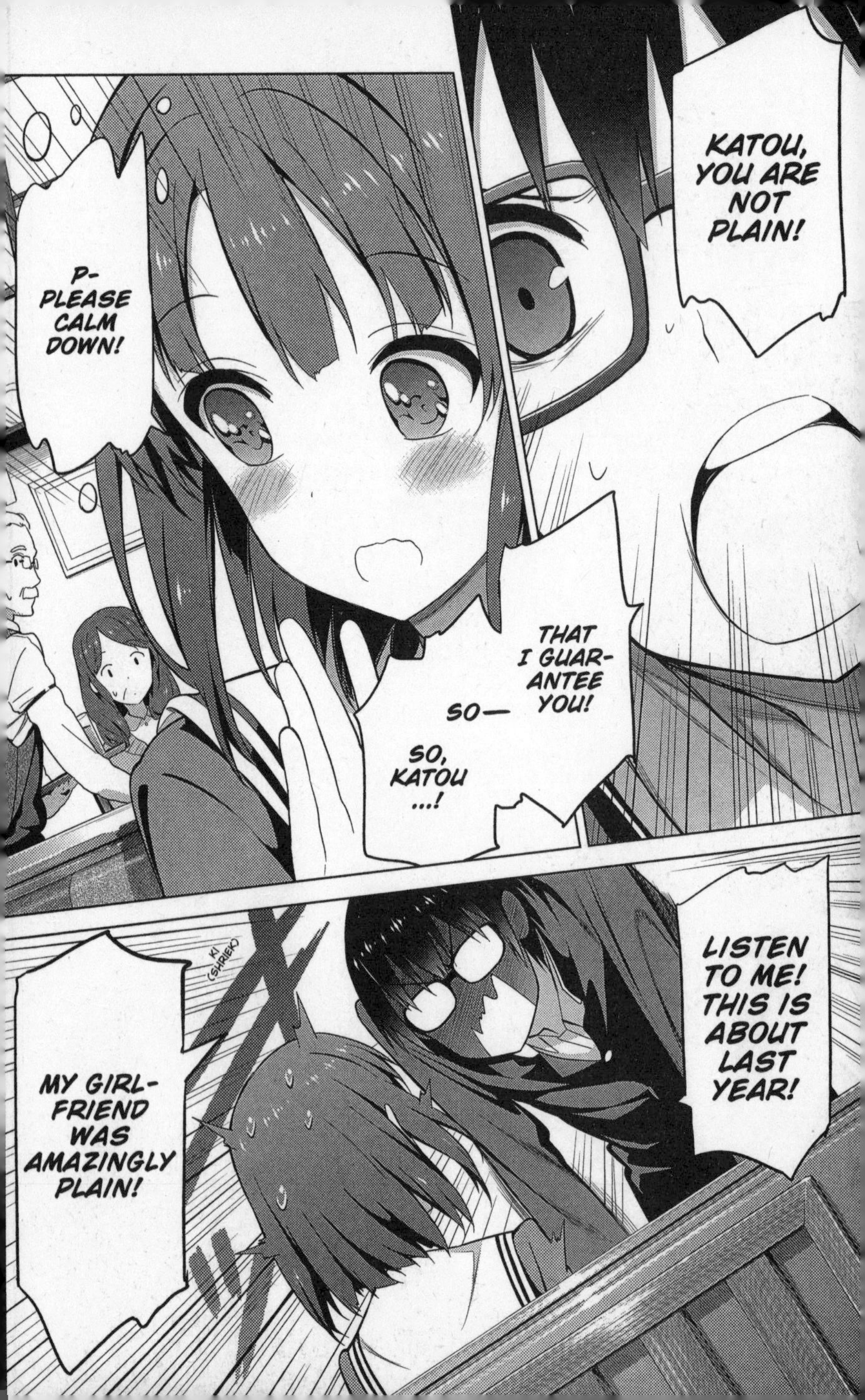
KATOU, YOU ARE NOT PLAIN!
THAT I GUARANTEE YOU!
SO—
SO, KATOU...!
P-PLEASE CALM DOWN!
LISTEN TO ME! THIS IS ABOUT LAST YEAR!
KI (SHRIEK)
MY GIRLFRIEND WAS AMAZINGLY PLAIN!

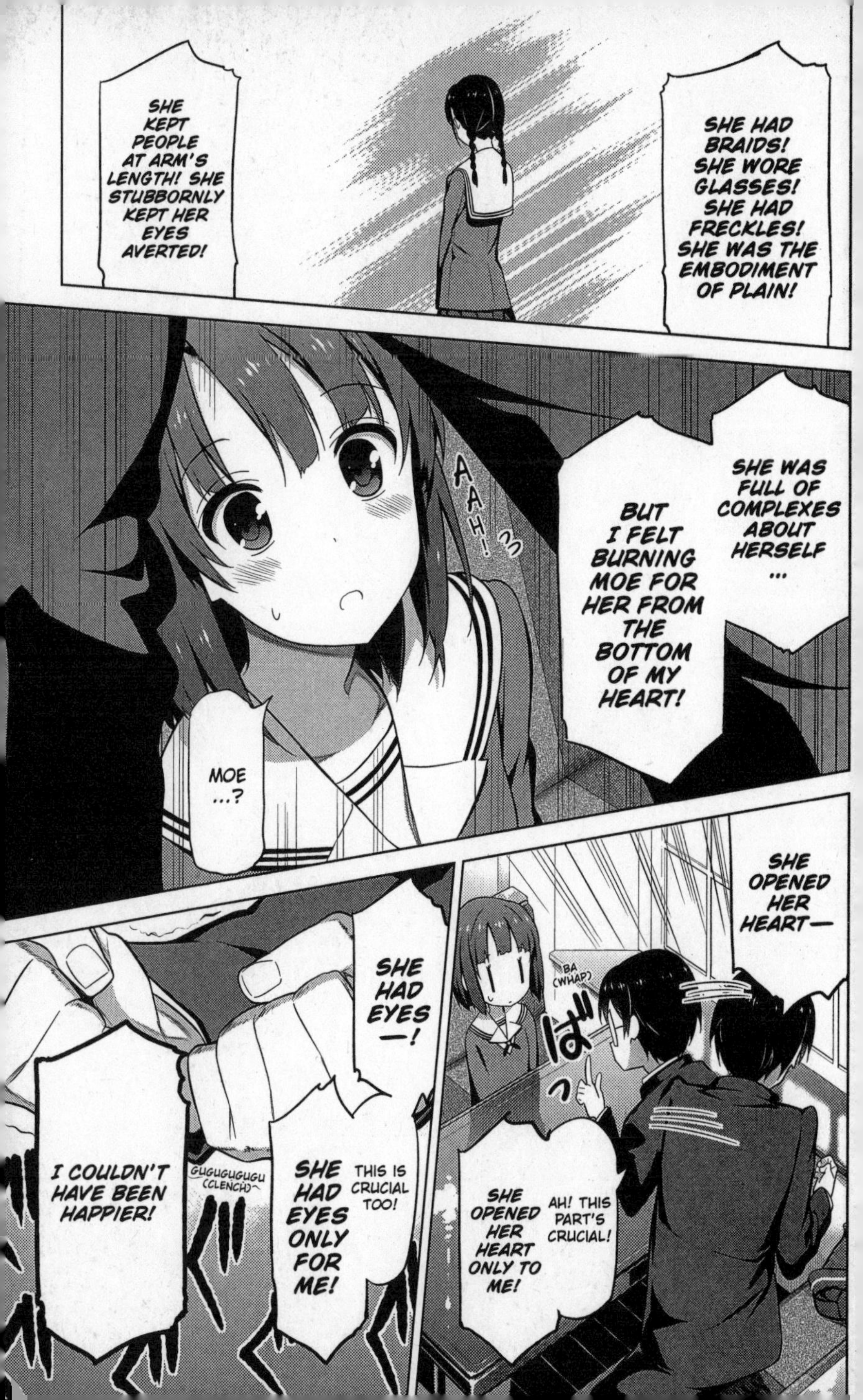
SHE HAD BRAIDS! SHE WORE GLASSES! SHE HAD FRECKLES! SHE WAS THE EMBODIMENT OF PLAIN!
SHE KEPT PEOPLE AT ARM'S LENGTH! SHE STUBBORNLY KEPT HER EYES AVERTED!
SHE WAS FULL OF COMPLEXES ABOUT HERSELF ...
BUT I FELT BURNING MOE FOR HER FROM THE BOTTOM OF MY HEART!
AAH!
MOE ...?
SHE OPENED HER HEART—
BA (WHAP)
AH! THIS PART'S CRUCIAL!
SHE OPENED HER HEART ONLY TO ME!
SHE HAD EYES—!
THIS IS CRUCIAL TOO!
SHE HAD EYES ONLY FOR ME!
GUGUGUGUGU (CLENCH)
I COULDN'T HAVE BEEN HAPPIER!

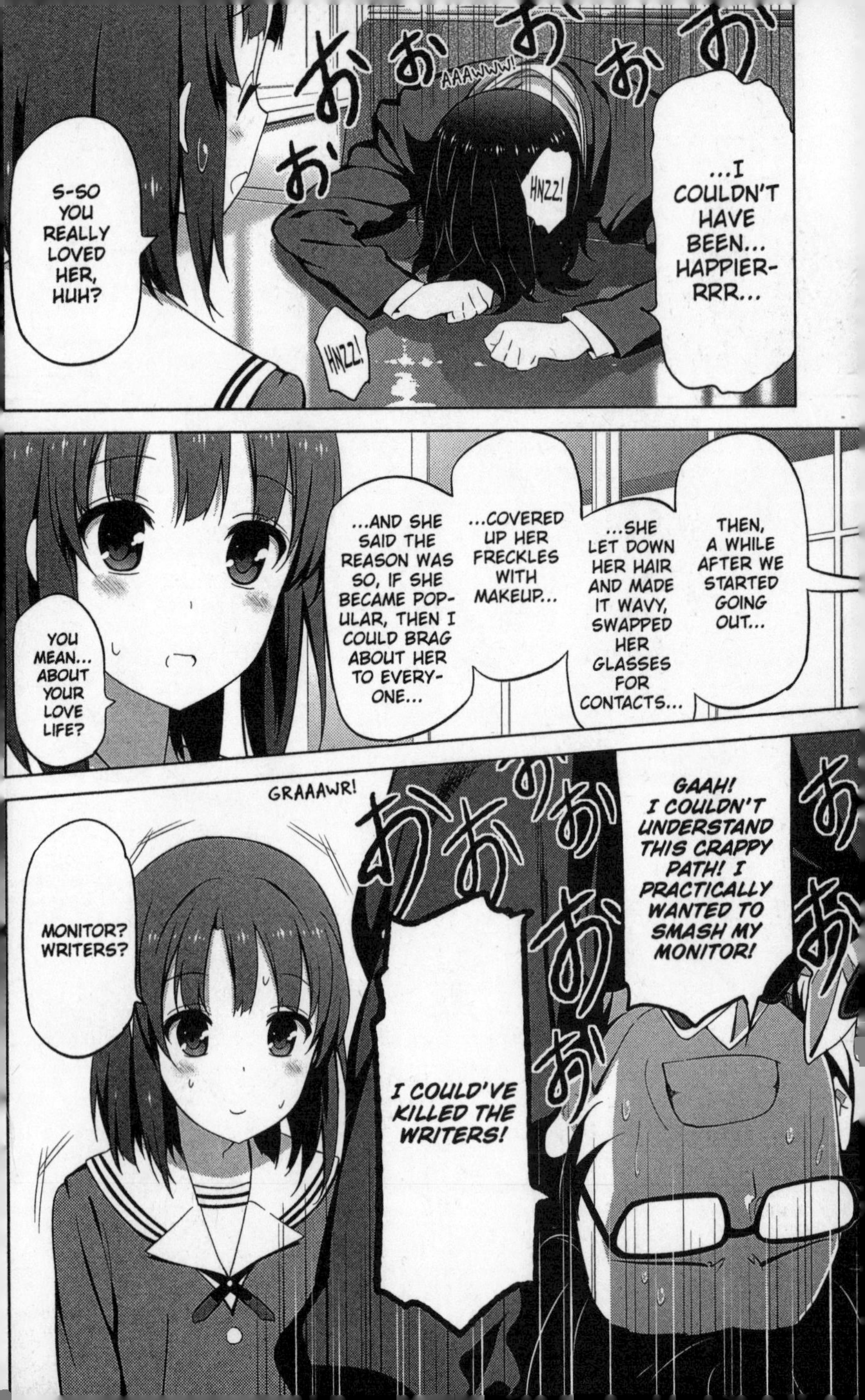
...I COULDN'T HAVE BEEN... HAPPIER-RRR...
AAAWWW!
HNZZ!
HNZZ!
S-SO YOU REALLY LOVED HER, HUH?
THEN, A WHILE AFTER WE STARTED GOING OUT...
...SHE LET DOWN HER HAIR AND MADE IT WAVY, SWAPPED HER GLASSES FOR CONTACTS...
...COVERED UP HER FRECKLES WITH MAKEUP...
...AND SHE SAID THE REASON WAS SO, IF SHE BECAME POP-ULAR, THEN I COULD BRAG ABOUT HER TO EVERY-ONE...
YOU MEAN... ABOUT YOUR LOVE LIFE?
GAAH! I COULDN'T UNDERSTAND THIS CRAPPY PATH! I PRACTICALLY WANTED TO SMASH MY MONITOR!
GRAAAWR!
I COULD'VE KILLED THE WRITERS!
MONITOR? WRITERS?

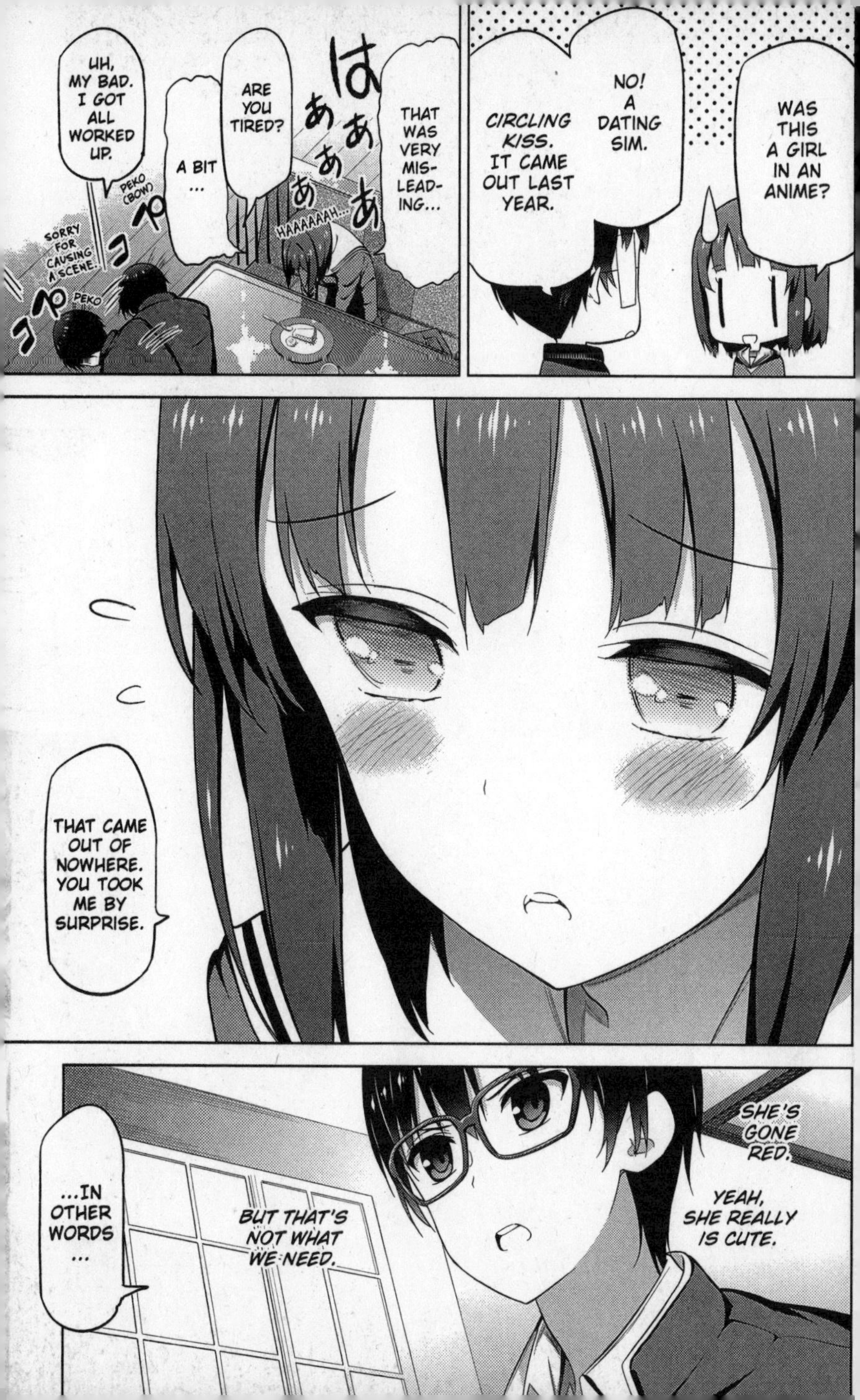
WAS THIS A GIRL IN AN ANIME?
NO! A DATING SIM.
CIRCLING KISS. IT CAME OUT LAST YEAR.
THAT WAS VERY MIS-LEADING...
HAAAAAAH...
ARE YOU TIRED?
A BIT...
UH, MY BAD. I GOT ALL WORKED UP.
PEKO (BOW)
SORRY FOR CAUSING A SCENE.
PEKO
THAT CAME OUT OF NOWHERE. YOU TOOK ME BY SURPRISE.
SHE'S GONE RED.
YEAH, SHE REALLY IS CUTE.
BUT THAT'S NOT WHAT WE NEED.
...IN OTHER WORDS...

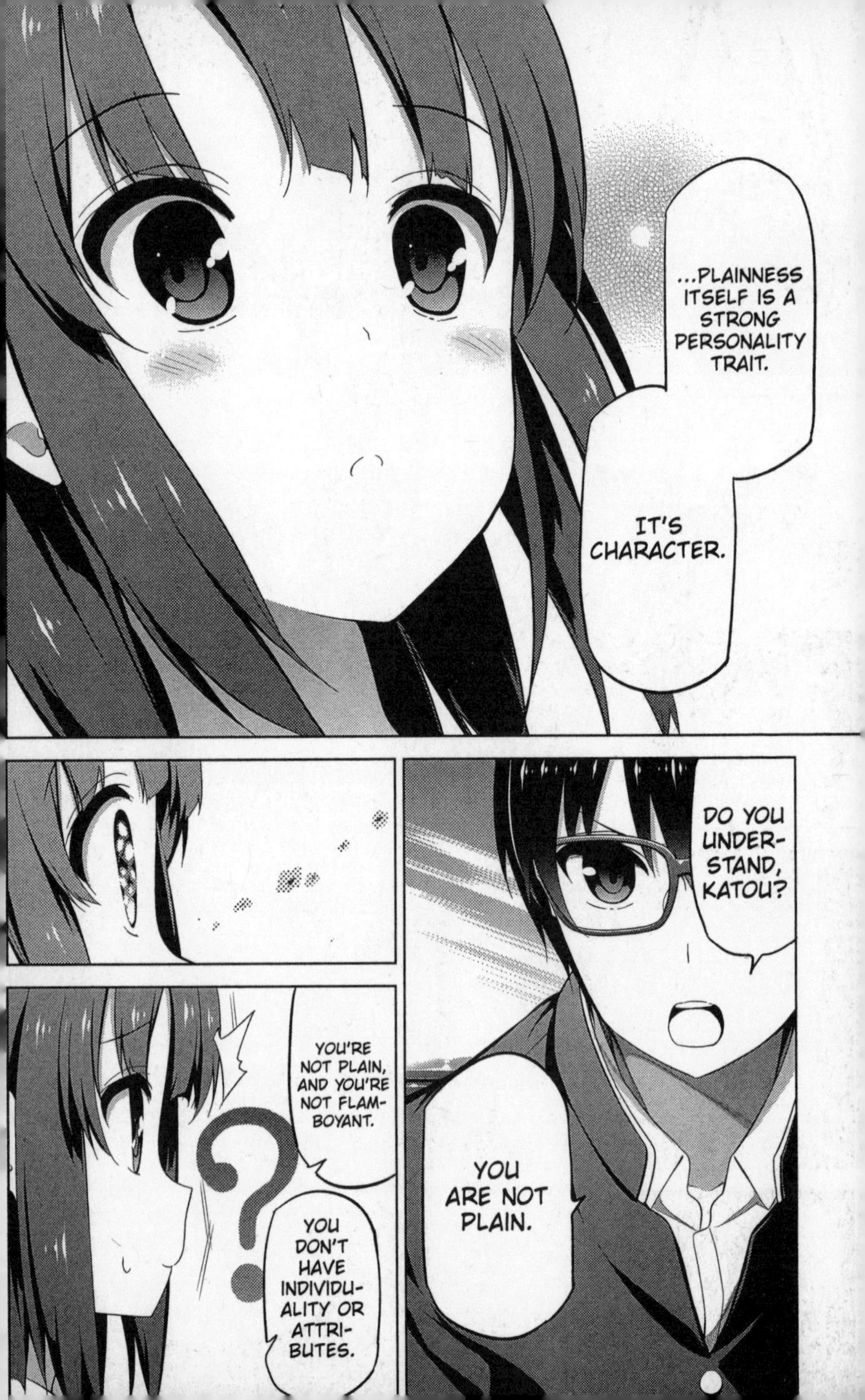
...PLAINNESS ITSELF IS A STRONG PERSONALITY TRAIT.
IT'S CHARACTER.
DO YOU UNDERSTAND, KATOU?
YOU ARE NOT PLAIN.
YOU'RE NOT PLAIN, AND YOU'RE NOT FLAMBOYANT.
YOU DON'T HAVE INDIVIDUALITY OR ATTRIBUTES.

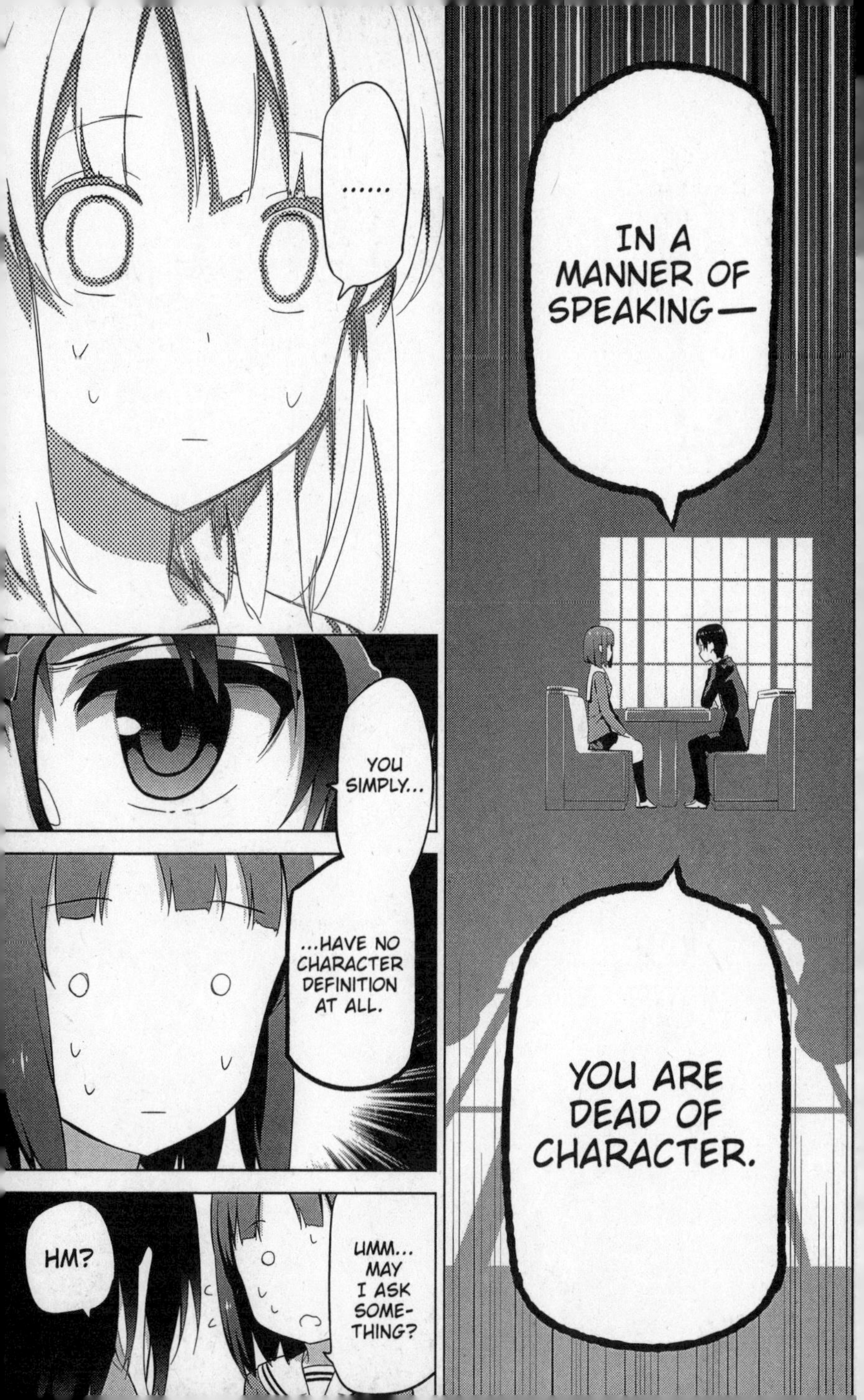
IN A MANNER OF SPEAKING—
YOU ARE DEAD OF CHARACTER.
......
YOU SIMPLY...
...HAVE NO CHARACTER DEFINITION AT ALL.
UMM... MAY I ASK SOME-THING?
HM?

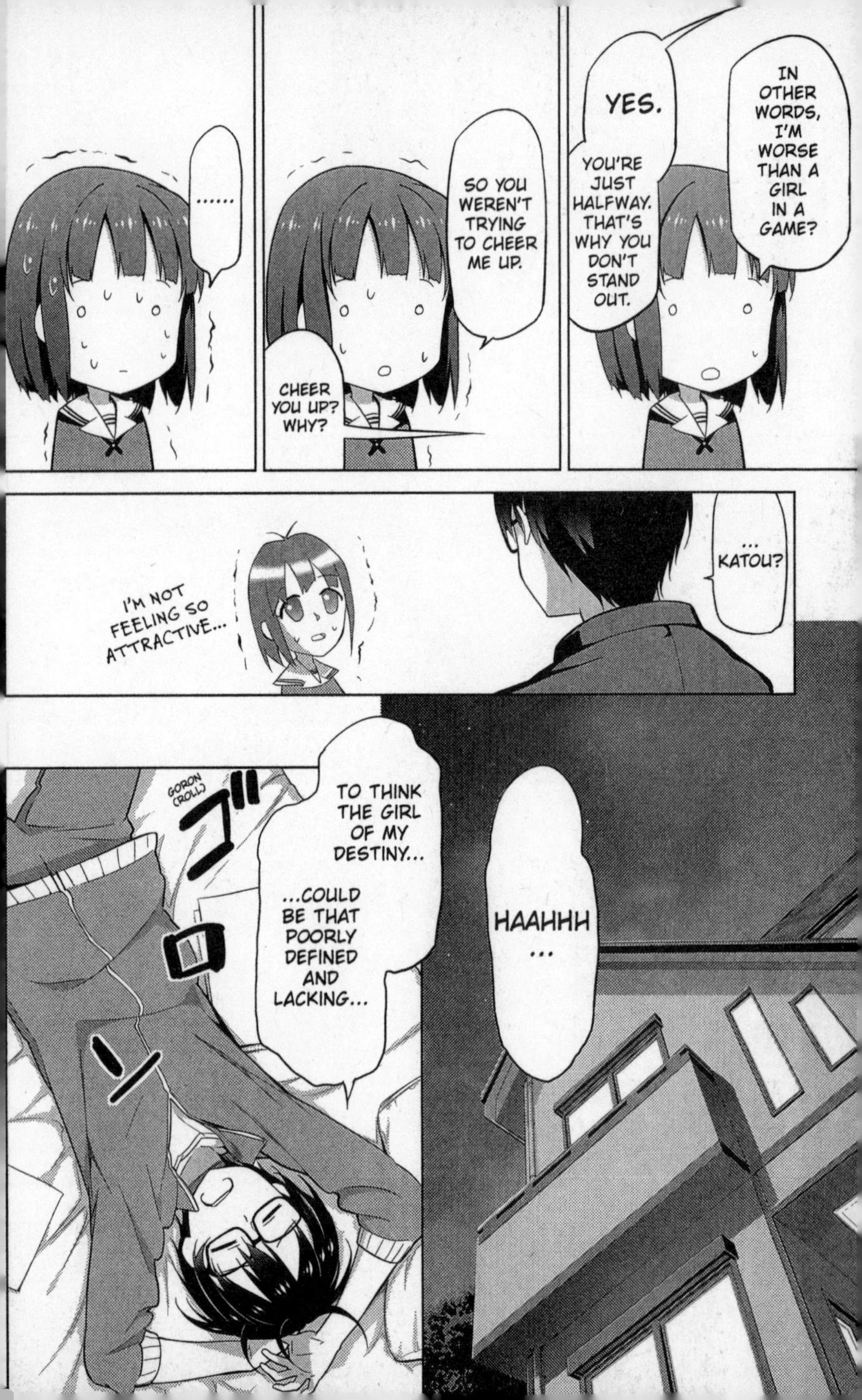
IN OTHER WORDS, I'M WORSE THAN A GIRL IN A GAME?
YES.
YOU'RE JUST HALFWAY. THAT'S WHY YOU DON'T STAND OUT.
SO YOU WEREN'T TRYING TO CHEER ME UP.
CHEER YOU UP? WHY?
......
...KATOU?
I'M NOT FEELING SO ATTRACTIVE...
HAAHHH...
TO THINK THE GIRL OF MY DESTINY...
...COULD BE THAT POORLY DEFINED AND LACKING...
GORON (ROLL)

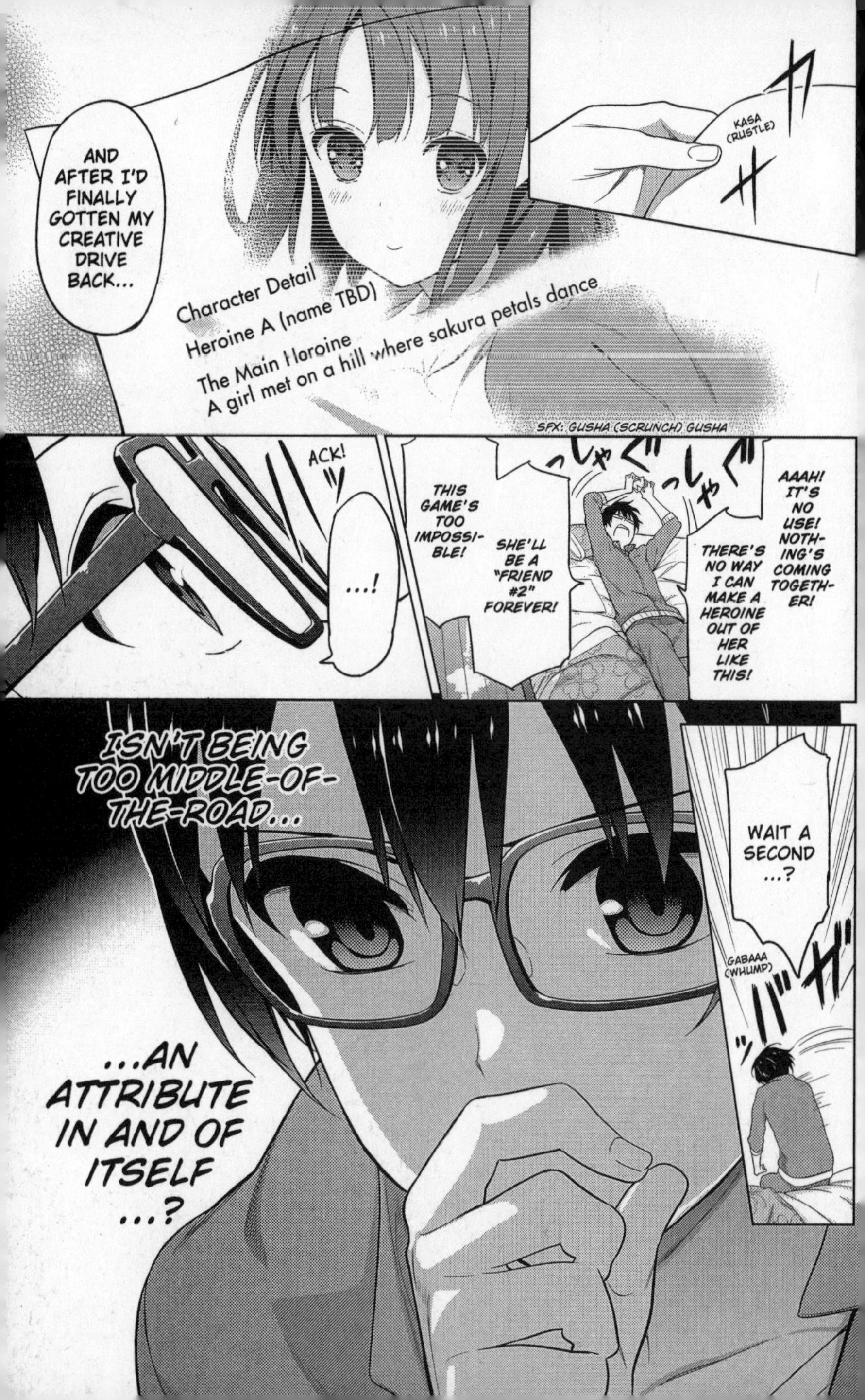
KASA (RUSTLE)
AND AFTER I'D FINALLY GOTTEN MY CREATIVE DRIVE BACK...
Character Detail
Heroine A (name TBD)
The Main Heroine
A girl met on a hill where sakura petals dance
SFX: GUSHA (SCRUNCH) GUSHA
AAAH! IT'S NO USE! NOTHING'S COMING TOGETHER!
THERE'S NO WAY I CAN MAKE A HEROINE OUT OF HER LIKE THIS!
THIS GAME'S TOO IMPOSSIBLE!
SHE'LL BE A "FRIEND #2" FOREVER!
ACK!
...!
WAIT A SECOND ...?
GABAAA (WHUMP)
ISN'T BEING TOO MIDDLE-OF-THE-ROAD...
...AN ATTRIBUTE IN AND OF ITSELF ...?

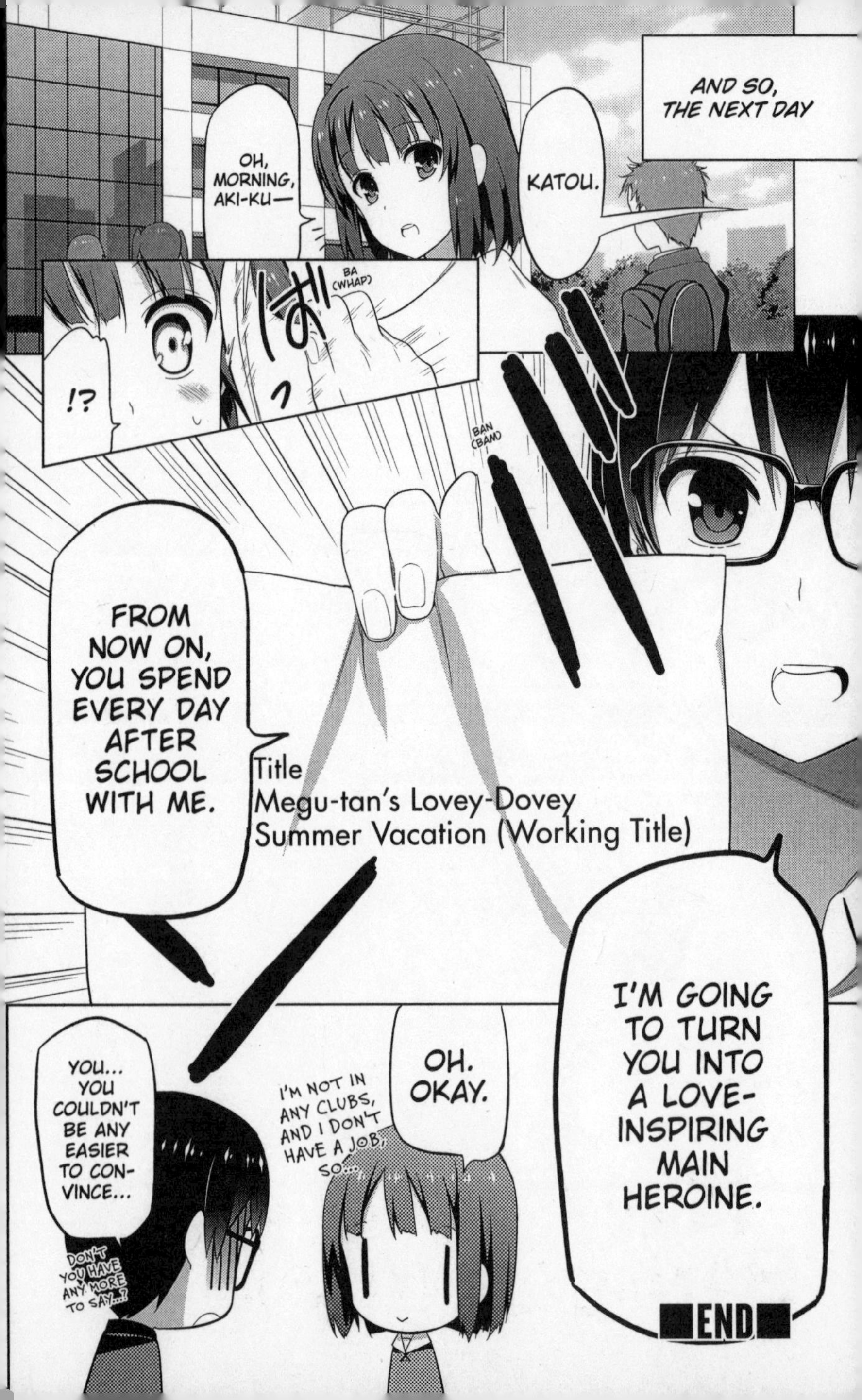
AND SO, THE NEXT DAY
KATOU.
OH, MORNING, AKI-KU—
BA (WHAP)
!?
BAN (BAM)
FROM NOW ON, YOU SPEND EVERY DAY AFTER SCHOOL WITH ME.
Title
Megu-tan's Lovey-Dovey Summer Vacation (Working Title)
I'M GOING TO TURN YOU INTO A LOVE-INSPIRING MAIN HEROINE.
OH. OKAY.
I'M NOT IN ANY CLUBS, AND I DON'T HAVE A JOB, SO...
YOU... YOU COULDN'T BE ANY EASIER TO CONVINCE...
DON'T YOU HAVE ANY MORE TO SAY...?
END

How to Raise a Boring Girlfriend

How to Raise a Boring Girlfriend

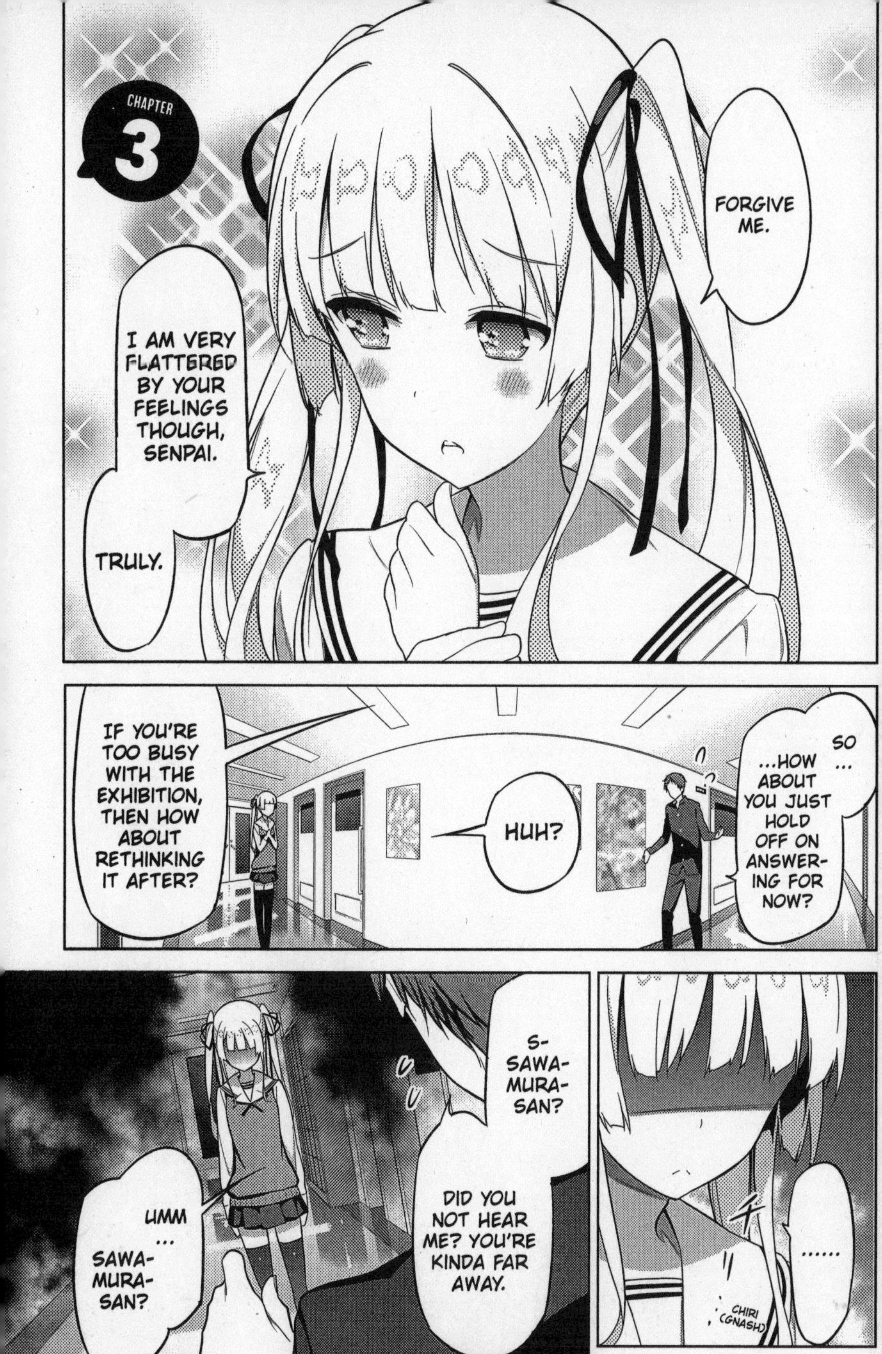
CHAPTER 3
FORGIVE ME.
I AM VERY FLATTERED BY YOUR FEELINGS THOUGH, SENPAI.
TRULY.
SO ...HOW ABOUT YOU JUST HOLD OFF ON ANSWERING FOR NOW?
HUH?
IF YOU'RE TOO BUSY WITH THE EXHIBITION, THEN HOW ABOUT RETHINKING IT AFTER?
......
CHIRI (GNASH)
S-SAWAMURA-SAN?
DID YOU NOT HEAR ME? YOU'RE KINDA FAR AWAY.
UMM ... SAWAMURA-SAN?

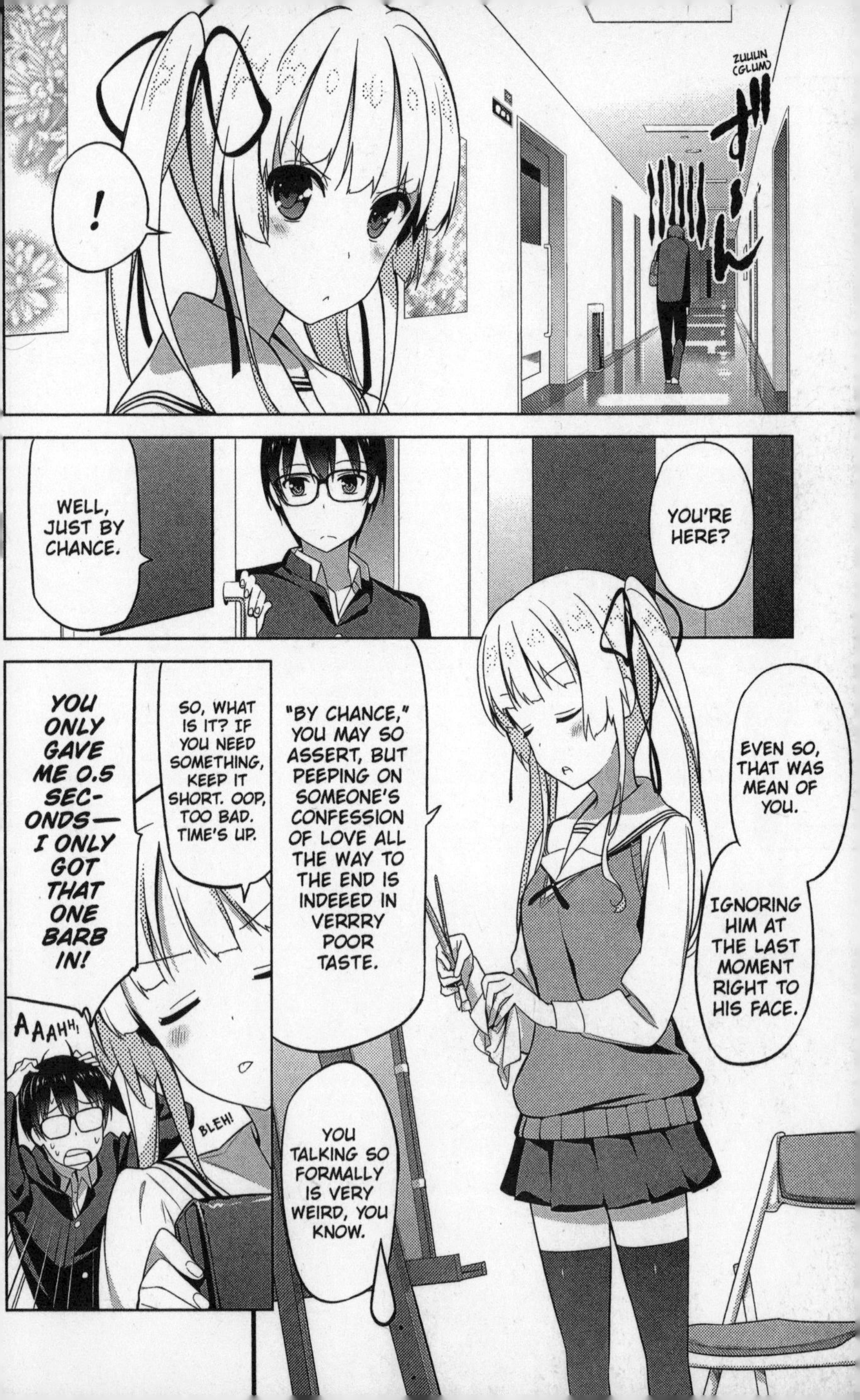
ZUUUN (GLUM)
!
YOU'RE HERE?
WELL, JUST BY CHANCE.
EVEN SO, THAT WAS MEAN OF YOU.
IGNORING HIM AT THE LAST MOMENT RIGHT TO HIS FACE.
"BY CHANCE," YOU MAY SO ASSERT, BUT PEEPING ON SOMEONE'S CONFESSION OF LOVE ALL THE WAY TO THE END IS INDEEED IN VERRRY POOR TASTE.
YOU TALKING SO FORMALLY IS VERY WEIRD, YOU KNOW.
SO, WHAT IS IT? IF YOU NEED SOMETHING, KEEP IT SHORT. OOP, TOO BAD. TIME'S UP.
YOU ONLY GAVE ME 0.5 SEC-ONDS— I ONLY GOT THAT ONE BARB IN!
AAAHH!
BLEH!

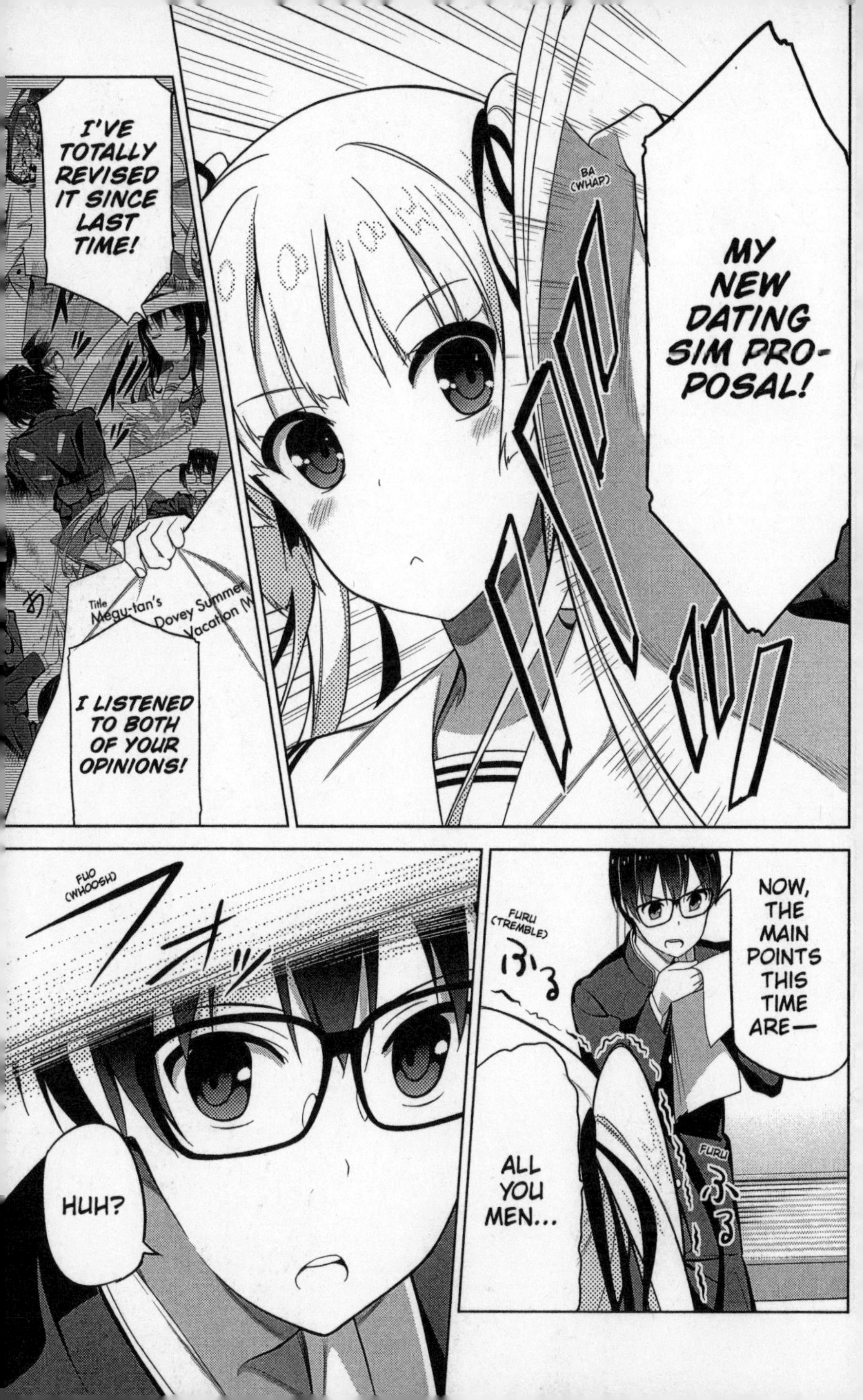

BA (WHAP)
MY NEW DATING SIM PROPOSAL!
I'VE TOTALLY REVISED IT SINCE LAST TIME!
Title Megu-tan's Dovey Summer Vacation (W
I LISTENED TO BOTH OF YOUR OPINIONS!
NOW, THE MAIN POINTS THIS TIME ARE—
FURU (TREMBLE)
ふる
FURU
ふる
ALL YOU MEN...
FUO (WHOOSH)
HUH?

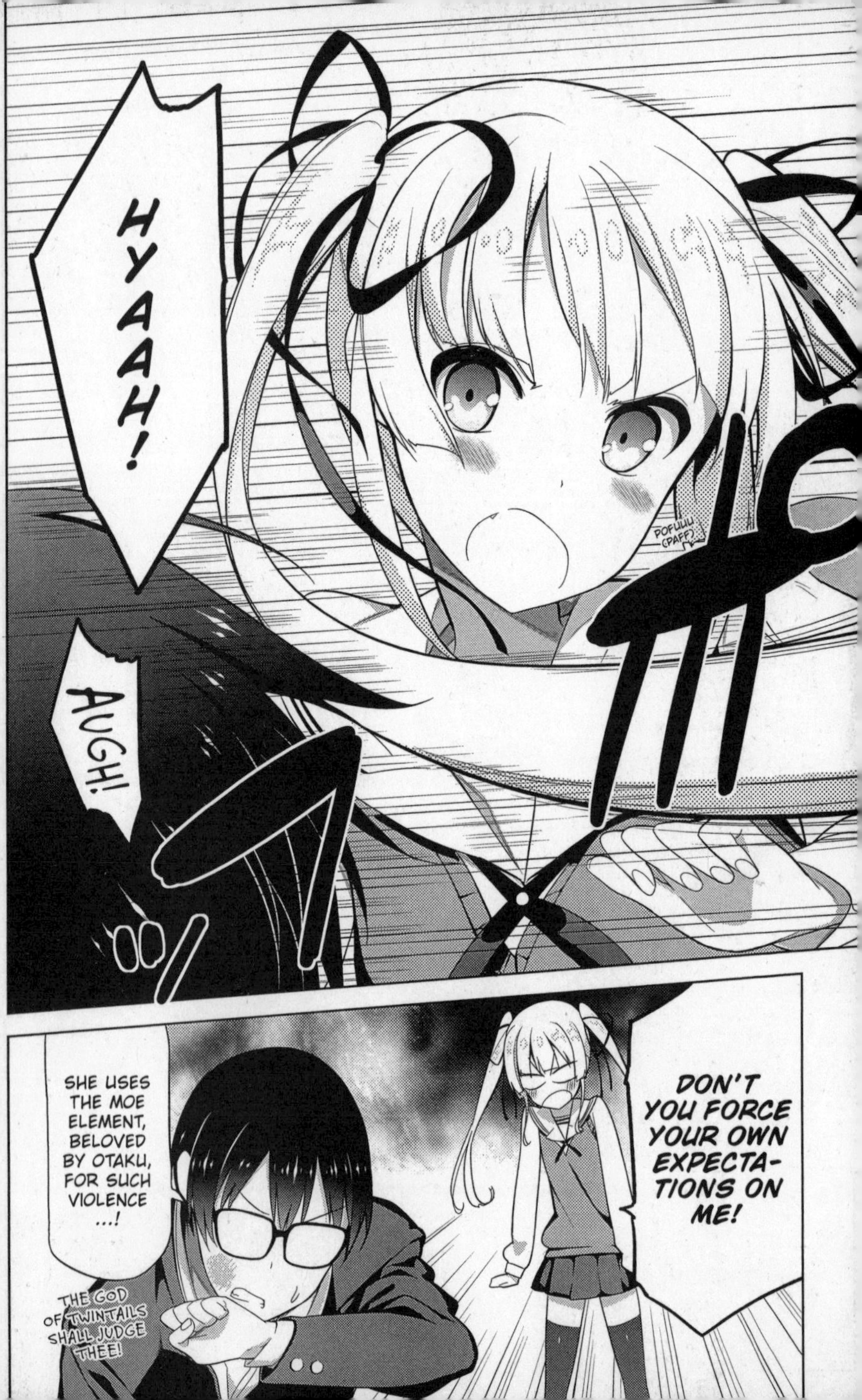
HYAAAH!
POFUUU (PAFF)
AUGH!
DON'T YOU FORCE YOUR OWN EXPECTATIONS ON ME!
SHE USES THE MOE ELEMENT, BELOVED BY OTAKU, FOR SUCH VIOLENCE ...!
THE GOD OF TWINTAILS SHALL JUDGE THEE!

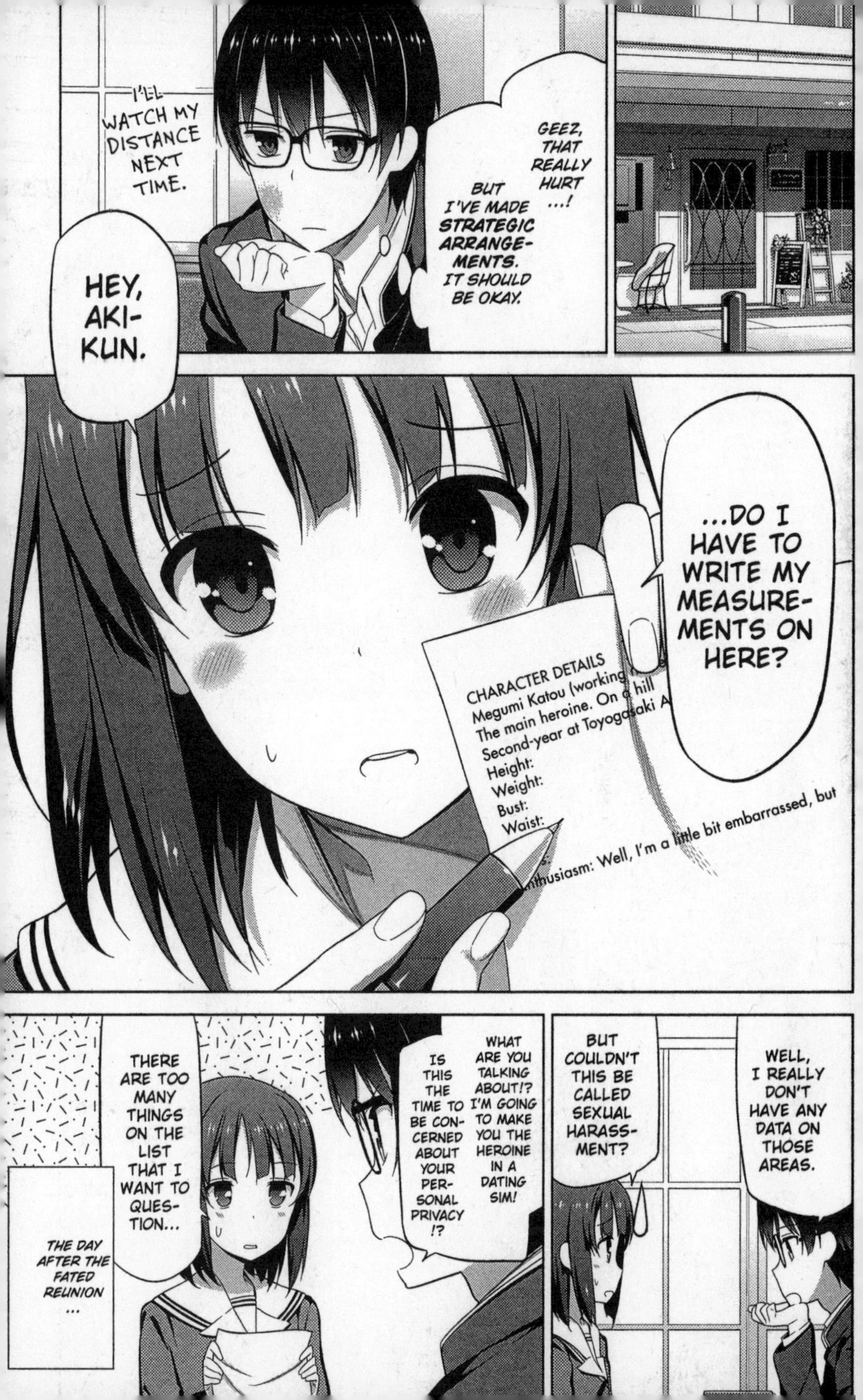
GEEZ, THAT REALLY HURT ...!
BUT I'VE MADE STRATEGIC ARRANGEMENTS. IT SHOULD BE OKAY.
I'LL WATCH MY DISTANCE NEXT TIME.
HEY, AKI-KUN.
...DO I HAVE TO WRITE MY MEASUREMENTS ON HERE?
CHARACTER DETAILS
Megumi Katou (working
The main heroine. On a hill
Second-year at Toyogasaki A
Height:
Weight:
Bust:
Waist:
nthusiasm: Well, I'm a little bit embarrassed, but
WELL, I REALLY DON'T HAVE ANY DATA ON THOSE AREAS.
BUT COULDN'T THIS BE CALLED SEXUAL HARASSMENT?
WHAT ARE YOU TALKING ABOUT!? I'M GOING TO MAKE YOU THE HEROINE IN A DATING SIM!
IS THIS THE TIME TO BE CONCERNED ABOUT YOUR PERSONAL PRIVACY!?
THERE ARE TOO MANY THINGS ON THE LIST THAT I WANT TO QUESTION...
THE DAY AFTER THE FATED REUNION ...

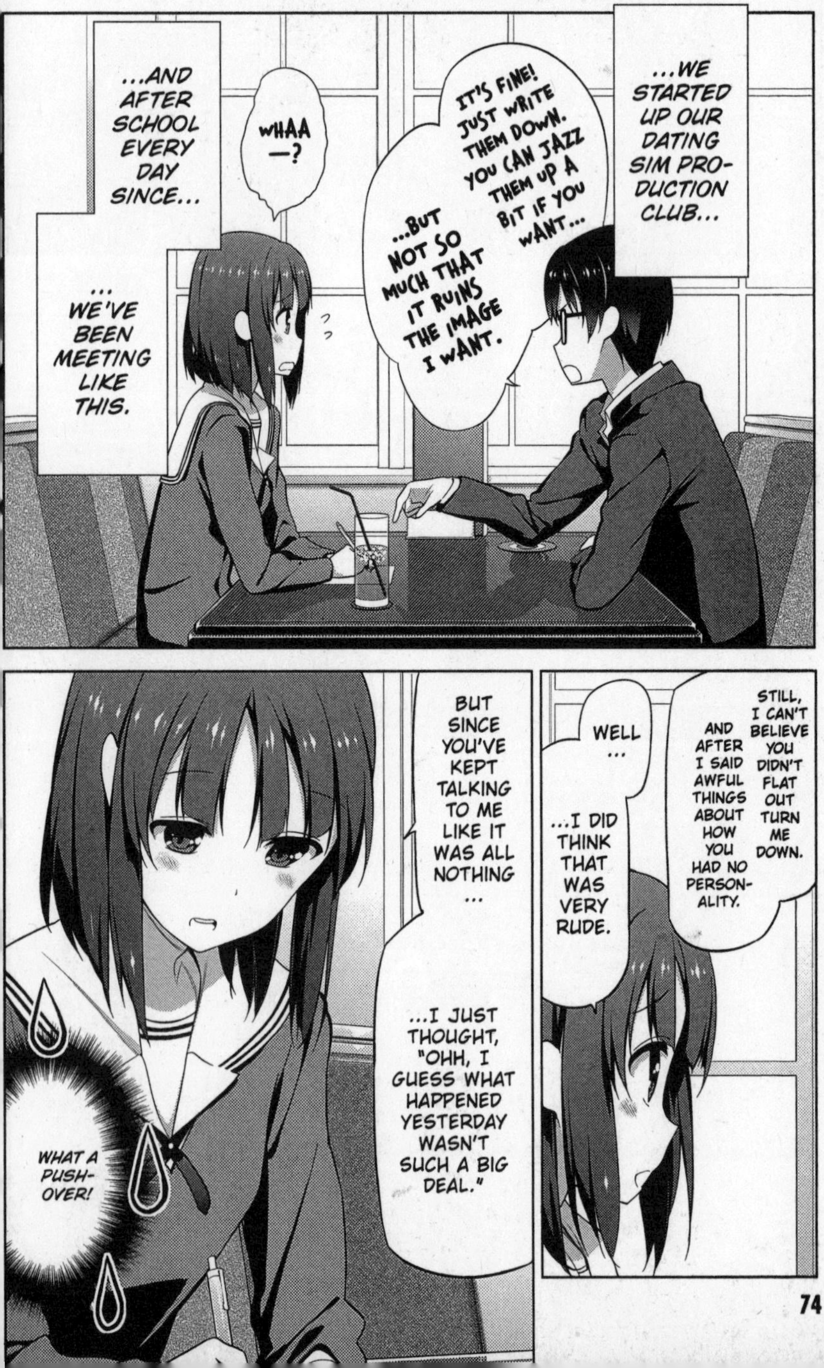
...WE STARTED UP OUR DATING SIM PRODUCTION CLUB...
IT'S FINE! JUST WRITE THEM DOWN. YOU CAN JAZZ THEM UP A BIT IF YOU WANT...
...BUT NOT SO MUCH THAT IT RUINS THE IMAGE I WANT.
WHAA—?
...AND AFTER SCHOOL EVERY DAY SINCE...
...WE'VE BEEN MEETING LIKE THIS.
STILL, I CAN'T BELIEVE YOU DIDN'T FLAT OUT TURN ME DOWN.
AND AFTER I SAID AWFUL THINGS ABOUT HOW YOU HAD NO PERSONALITY.
WELL...
...I DID THINK THAT WAS VERY RUDE.
BUT SINCE YOU'VE KEPT TALKING TO ME LIKE IT WAS ALL NOTHING...
...I JUST THOUGHT, "OHH, I GUESS WHAT HAPPENED YESTERDAY WASN'T SUCH A BIG DEAL."
WHAT A PUSH-OVER!

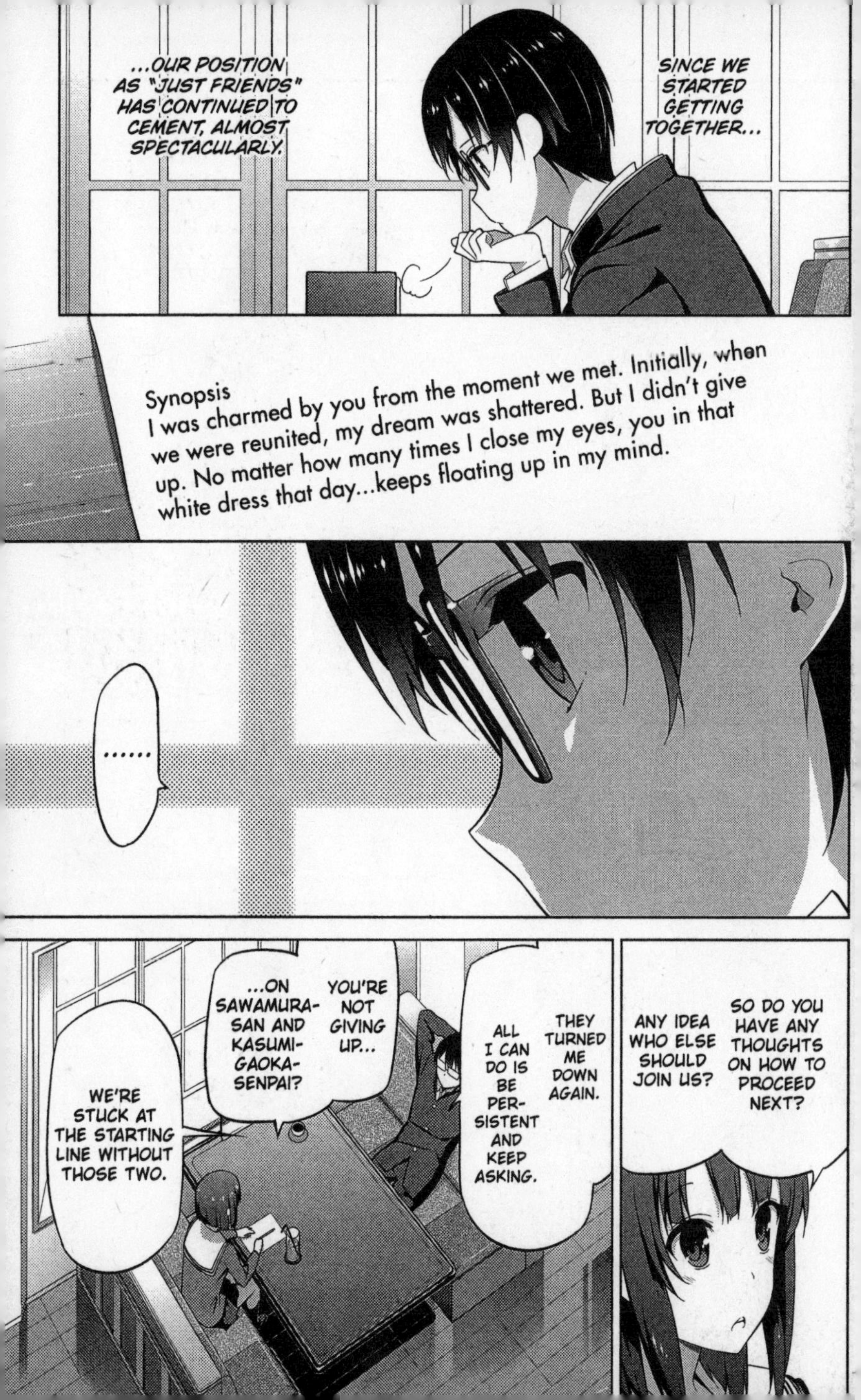
SINCE WE STARTED GETTING TOGETHER...
...OUR POSITION AS "JUST FRIENDS" HAS CONTINUED TO CEMENT, ALMOST SPECTACULARLY.
Synopsis
I was charmed by you from the moment we met. Initially, when we were reunited, my dream was shattered. But I didn't give up. No matter how many times I close my eyes, you in that white dress that day...keeps floating up in my mind.
......
SO DO YOU HAVE ANY THOUGHTS ON HOW TO PROCEED NEXT?
ANY IDEA WHO ELSE SHOULD JOIN US?
THEY TURNED ME DOWN AGAIN.
ALL I CAN DO IS BE PER-SISTENT AND KEEP ASKING.
YOU'RE NOT GIVING UP...
...ON SAWAMURA-SAN AND KASUMI-GAOKA-SENPAI?
WE'RE STUCK AT THE STARTING LINE WITHOUT THOSE TWO.

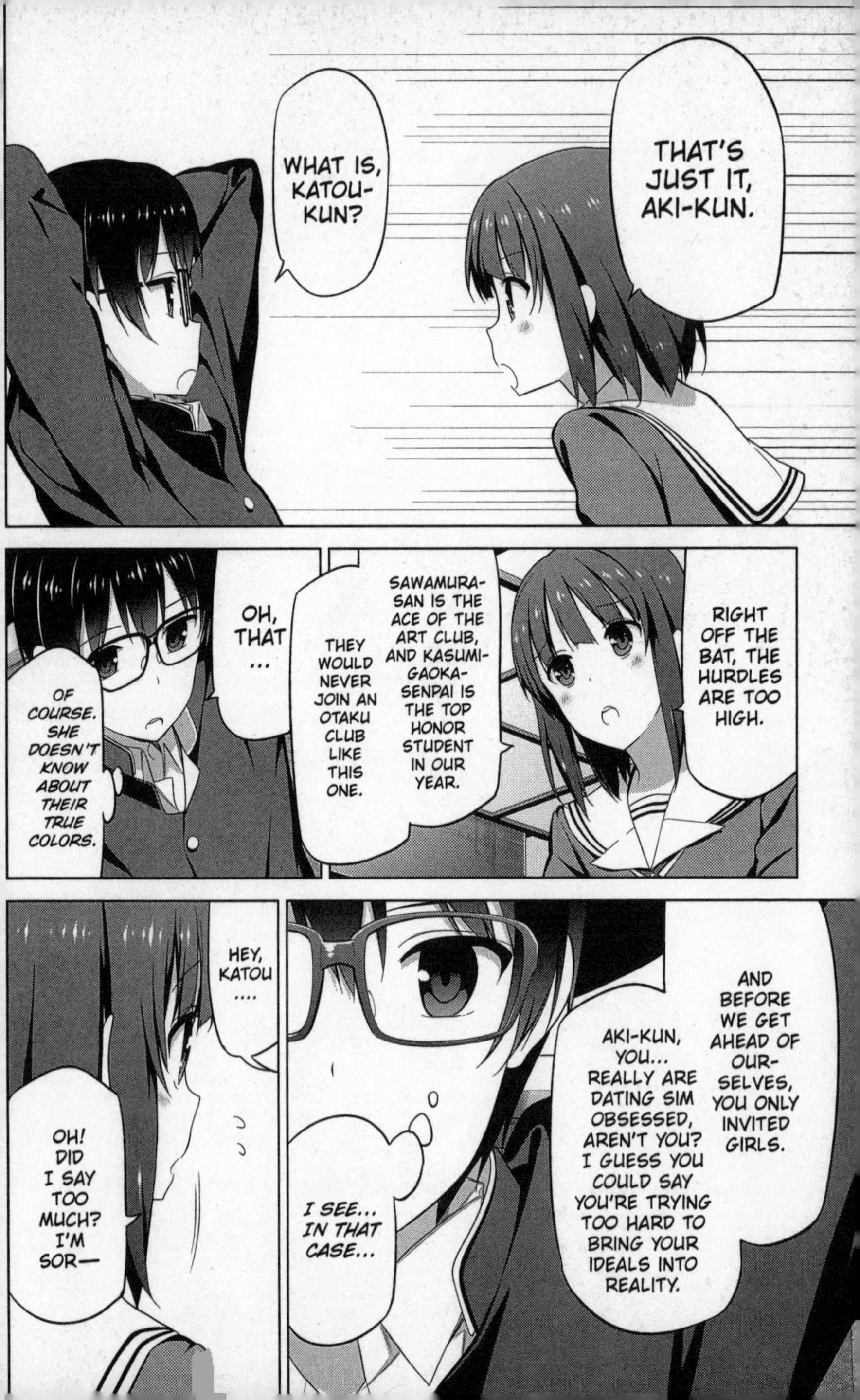
THAT'S JUST IT, AKI-KUN.
WHAT IS, KATOU-KUN?
RIGHT OFF THE BAT, THE HURDLES ARE TOO HIGH.
SAWAMURA-SAN IS THE ACE OF THE ART CLUB, AND KASUMIGAOKA-SENPAI IS THE TOP HONOR STUDENT IN OUR YEAR.
THEY WOULD NEVER JOIN AN OTAKU CLUB LIKE THIS ONE.
OH, THAT...
OF COURSE. SHE DOESN'T KNOW ABOUT THEIR TRUE COLORS.
AND BEFORE WE GET AHEAD OF OUR-SELVES, YOU ONLY INVITED GIRLS.
AKI-KUN, YOU... REALLY ARE DATING SIM OBSESSED, AREN'T YOU? I GUESS YOU COULD SAY YOU'RE TRYING TOO HARD TO BRING YOUR IDEALS INTO REALITY.
I SEE... IN THAT CASE...
HEY, KATOU....
OH! DID I SAY TOO MUCH? I'M SOR—

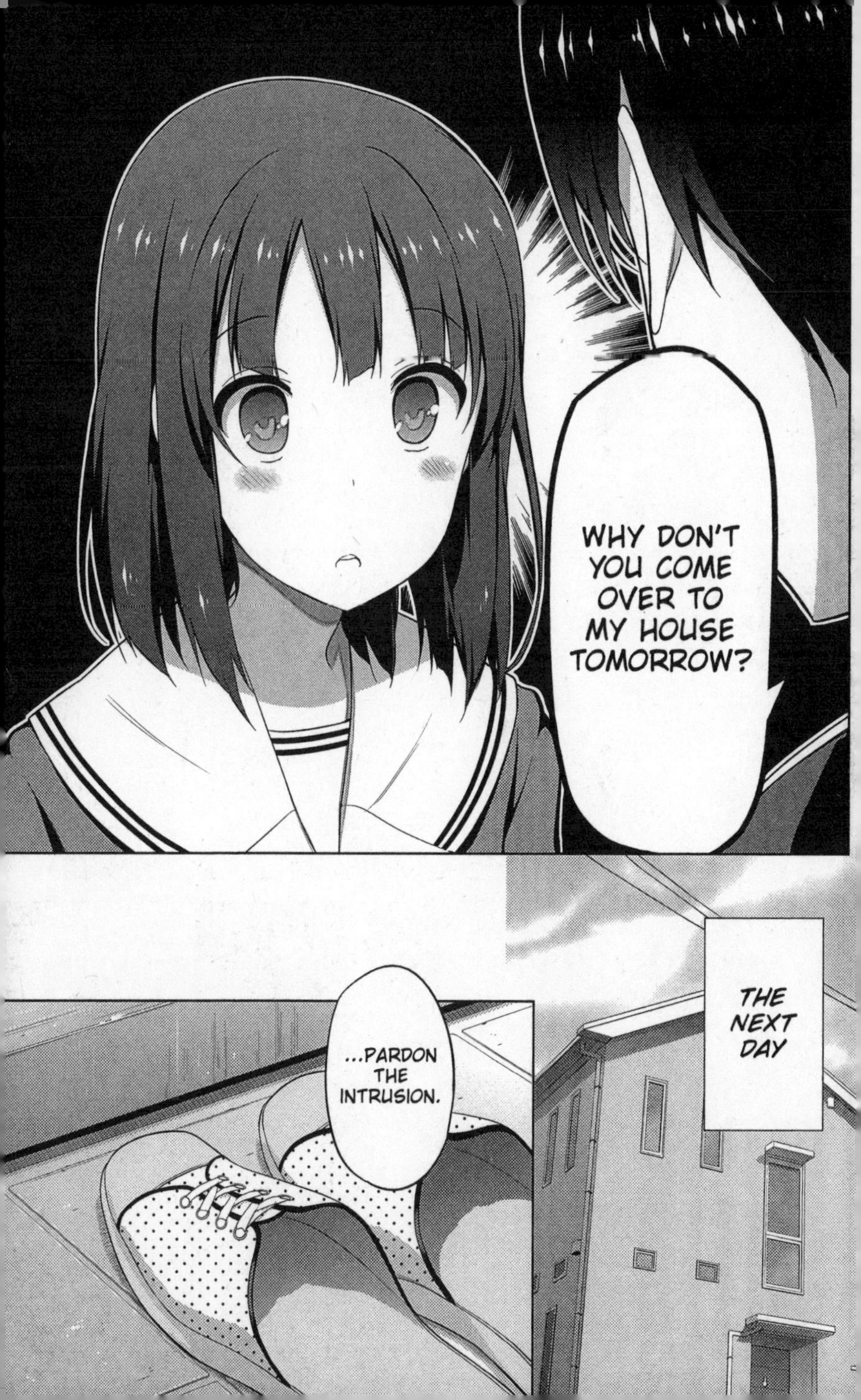
WHY DON'T YOU COME OVER TO MY HOUSE TOMORROW?
THE NEXT DAY
...PARDON THE INTRUSION.

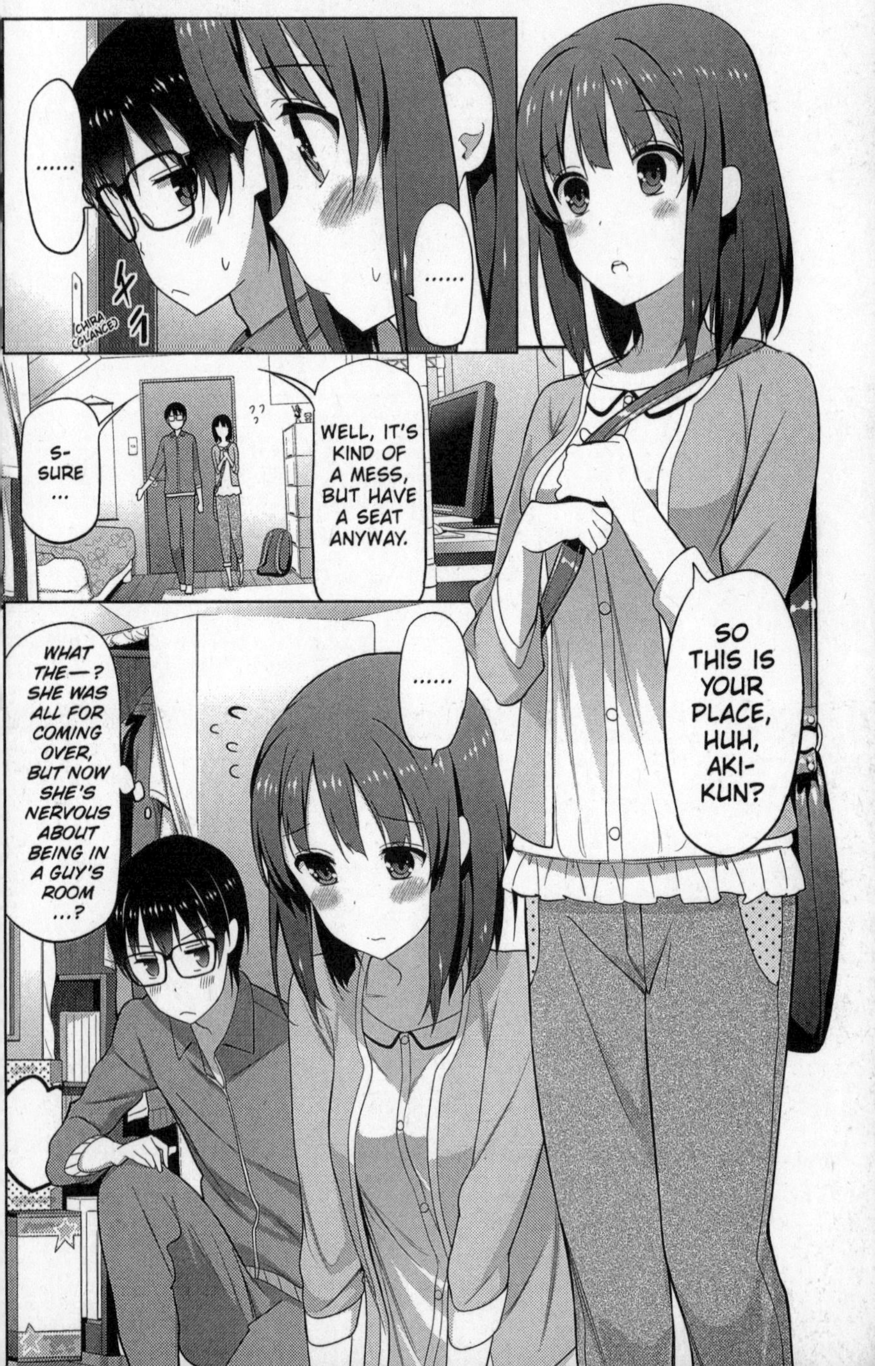

SO THIS IS YOUR PLACE, HUH, AKI-KUN?
......
......
CHIRA (GLANCE)
WELL, IT'S KIND OF A MESS, BUT HAVE A SEAT ANYWAY.
S-SURE...
......
WHAT THE—? SHE WAS ALL FOR COMING OVER, BUT NOW SHE'S NERVOUS ABOUT BEING IN A GUY'S ROOM...?

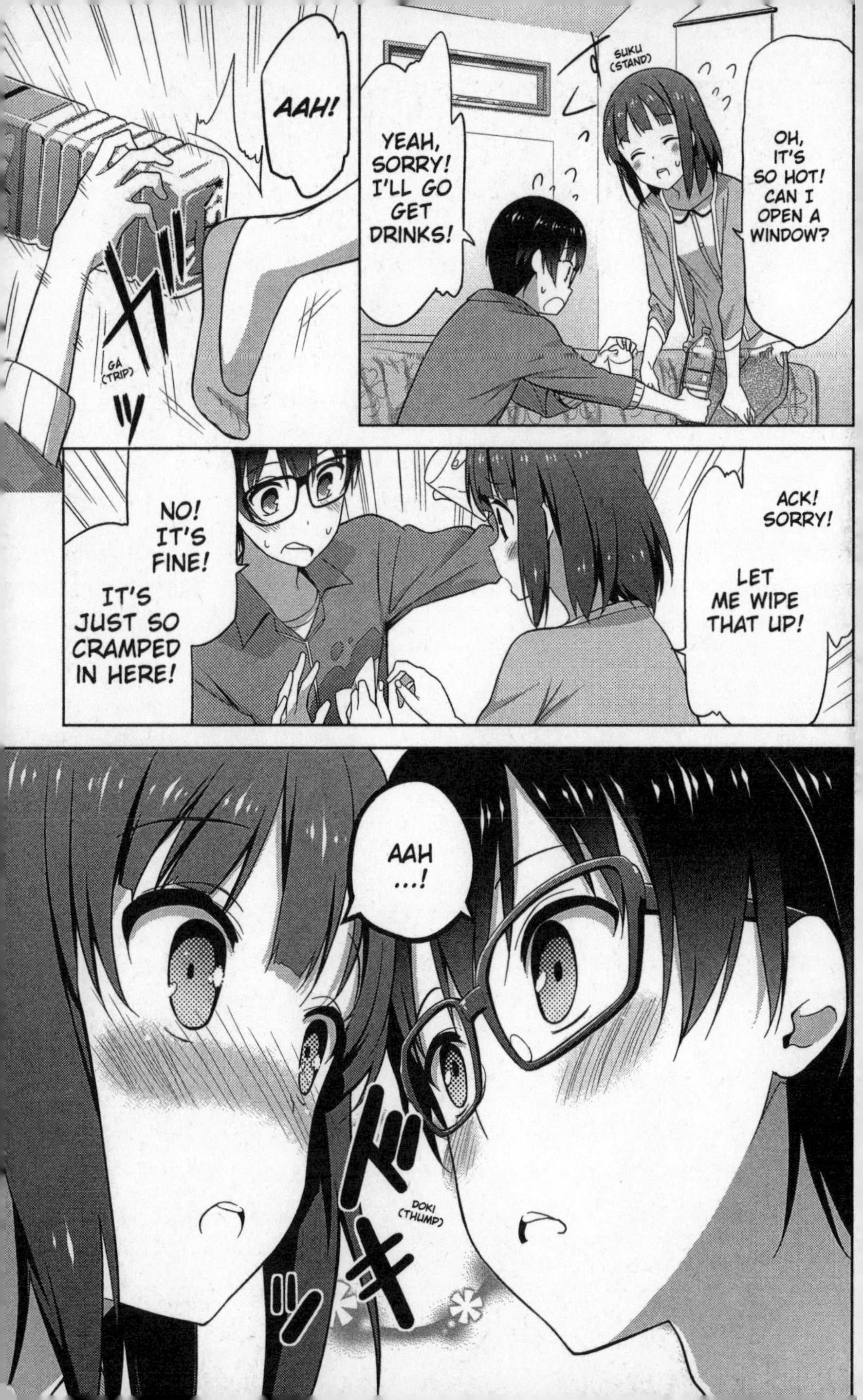
SUKU (STAND)
OH, IT'S SO HOT! CAN I OPEN A WINDOW?
YEAH, SORRY! I'LL GO GET DRINKS!
AAH!
GA (TRIP)
ACK! SORRY!
LET ME WIPE THAT UP!
NO! IT'S FINE!
IT'S JUST SO CRAMPED IN HERE!
AAH ...!
DOKI (THUMP)

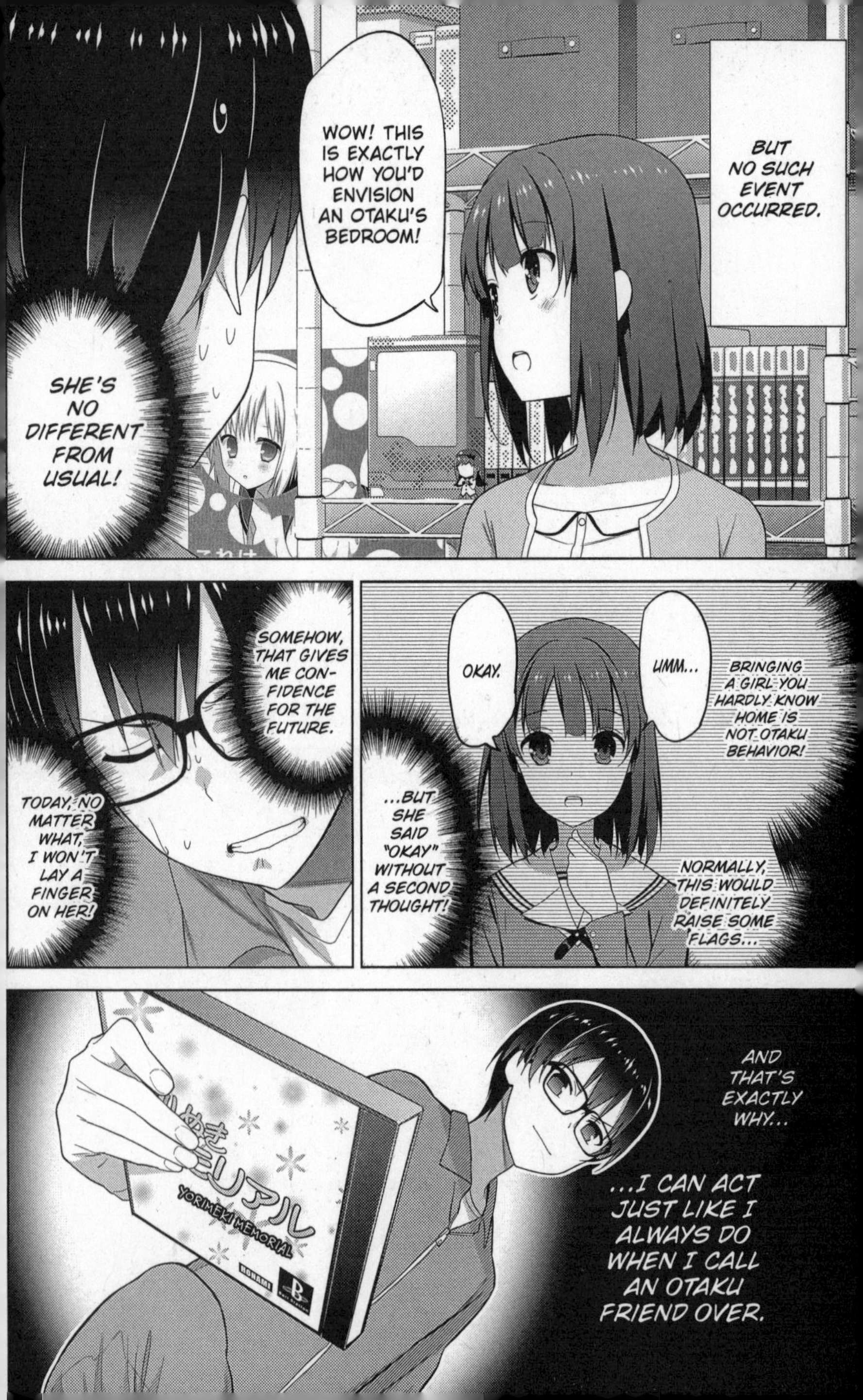
BUT NO SUCH EVENT OCCURRED.
WOW! THIS IS EXACTLY HOW YOU'D ENVISION AN OTAKU'S BEDROOM!
SHE'S NO DIFFERENT FROM USUAL!
UMM...
BRINGING A GIRL YOU HARDLY KNOW HOME IS NOT OTAKU BEHAVIOR!
OKAY.
NORMALLY, THIS WOULD DEFINITELY RAISE SOME FLAGS...
...BUT SHE SAID "OKAY" WITHOUT A SECOND THOUGHT!
SOMEHOW, THAT GIVES ME CON-FIDENCE FOR THE FUTURE.
TODAY, NO MATTER WHAT, I WON'T LAY A FINGER ON HER!
AND THAT'S EXACTLY WHY...
...I CAN ACT JUST LIKE I ALWAYS DO WHEN I CALL AN OTAKU FRIEND OVER.
YORIMEKI MEMORIAL

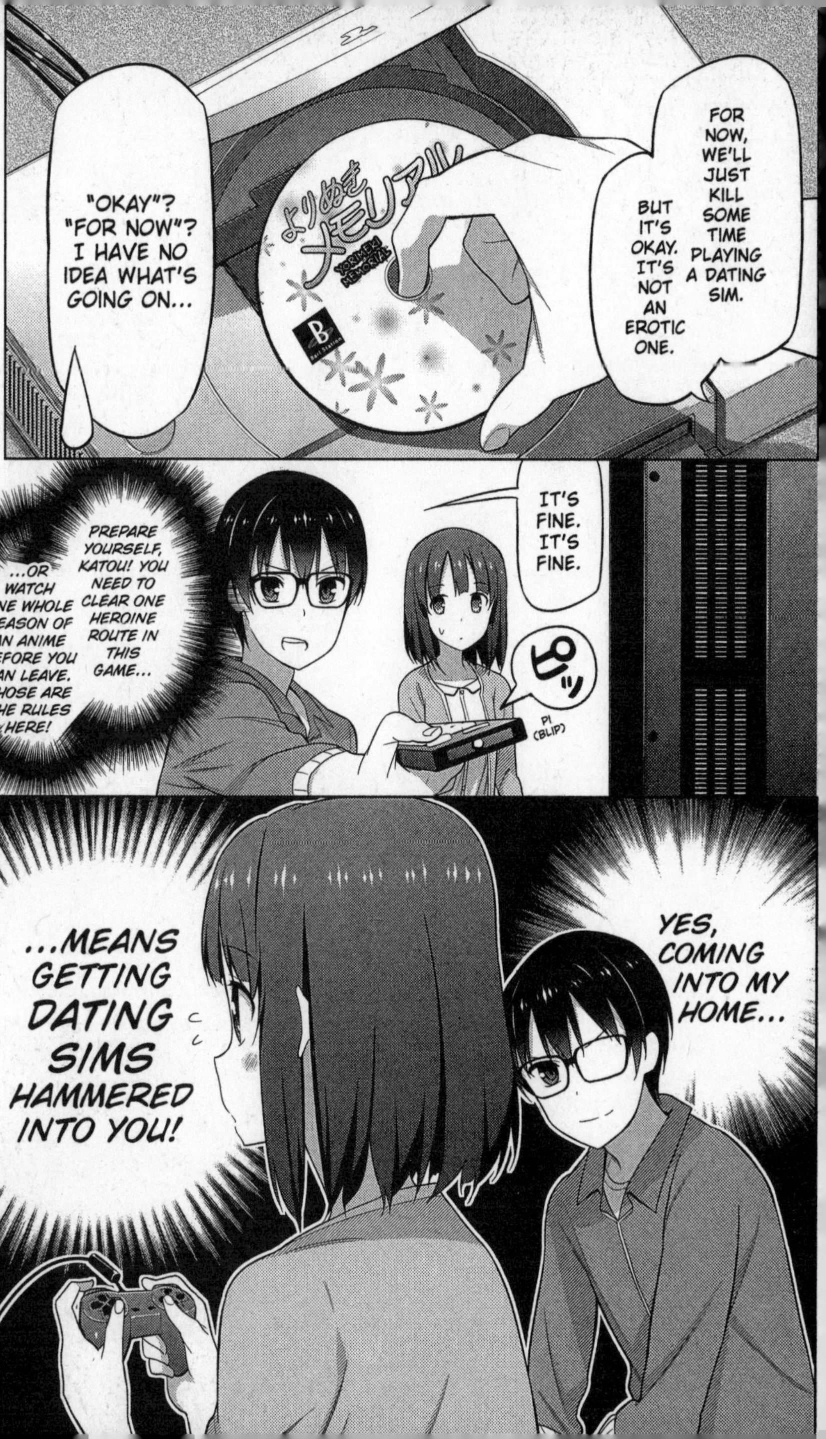

FOR NOW, WE'LL JUST KILL SOME TIME PLAYING A DATING SIM.
BUT IT'S OKAY. IT'S NOT AN EROTIC ONE.
よりめきメモリアル
YORIMEKI MEMORIAL
"OKAY"? "FOR NOW"? I HAVE NO IDEA WHAT'S GOING ON...
IT'S FINE. IT'S FINE.
ピッ
PI (BLIP)
PREPARE YOURSELF, KATOU! YOU NEED TO CLEAR ONE HEROINE ROUTE IN THIS GAME...
...OR WATCH ONE WHOLE SEASON OF AN ANIME BEFORE YOU CAN LEAVE. THOSE ARE THE RULES HERE!
YES, COMING INTO MY HOME...
...MEANS GETTING DATING SIMS HAMMERED INTO YOU!

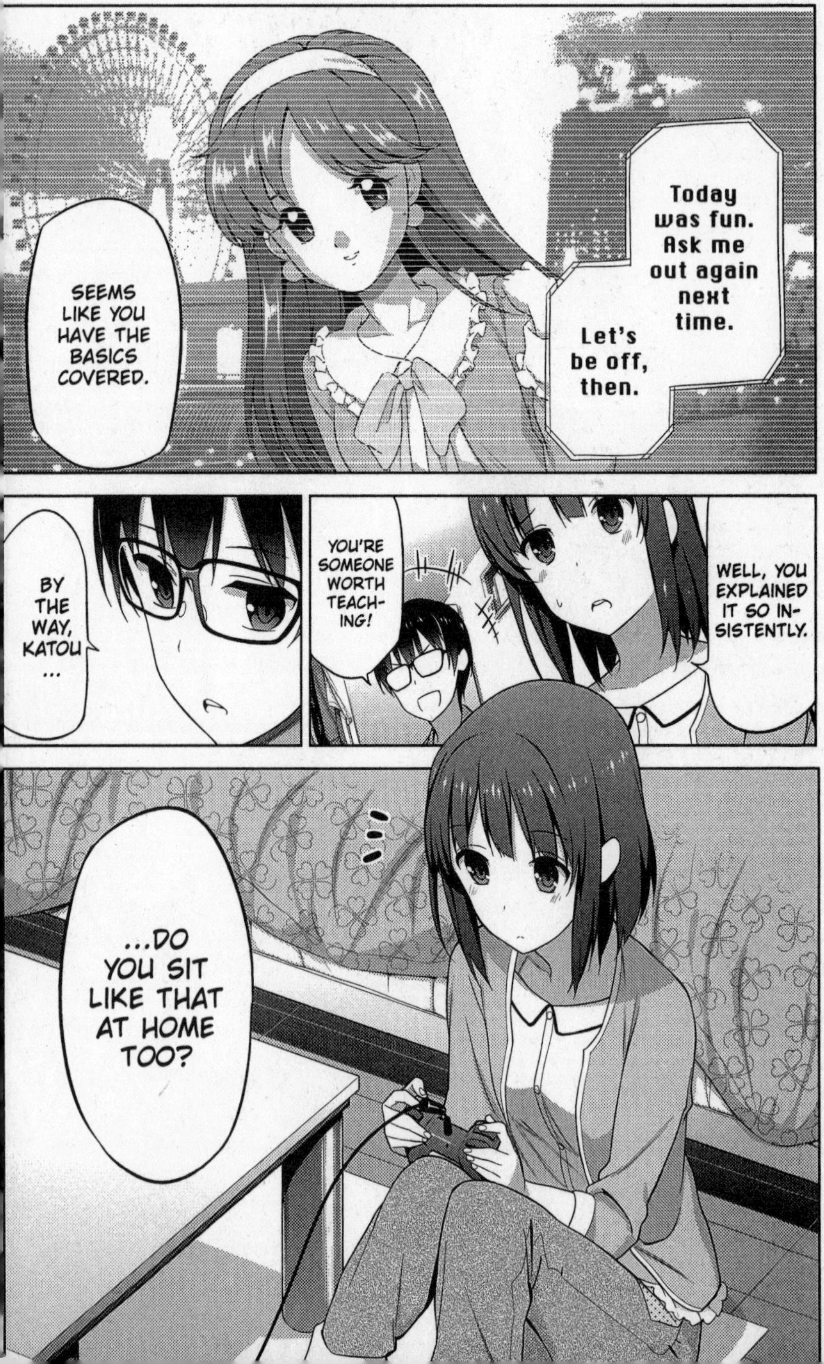
Today was fun. Ask me out again next time.
Let's be off, then.
SEEMS LIKE YOU HAVE THE BASICS COVERED.
WELL, YOU EXPLAINED IT SO IN-SISTENTLY.
YOU'RE SOMEONE WORTH TEACH-ING!
BY THE WAY, KATOU ...
...DO YOU SIT LIKE THAT AT HOME TOO?

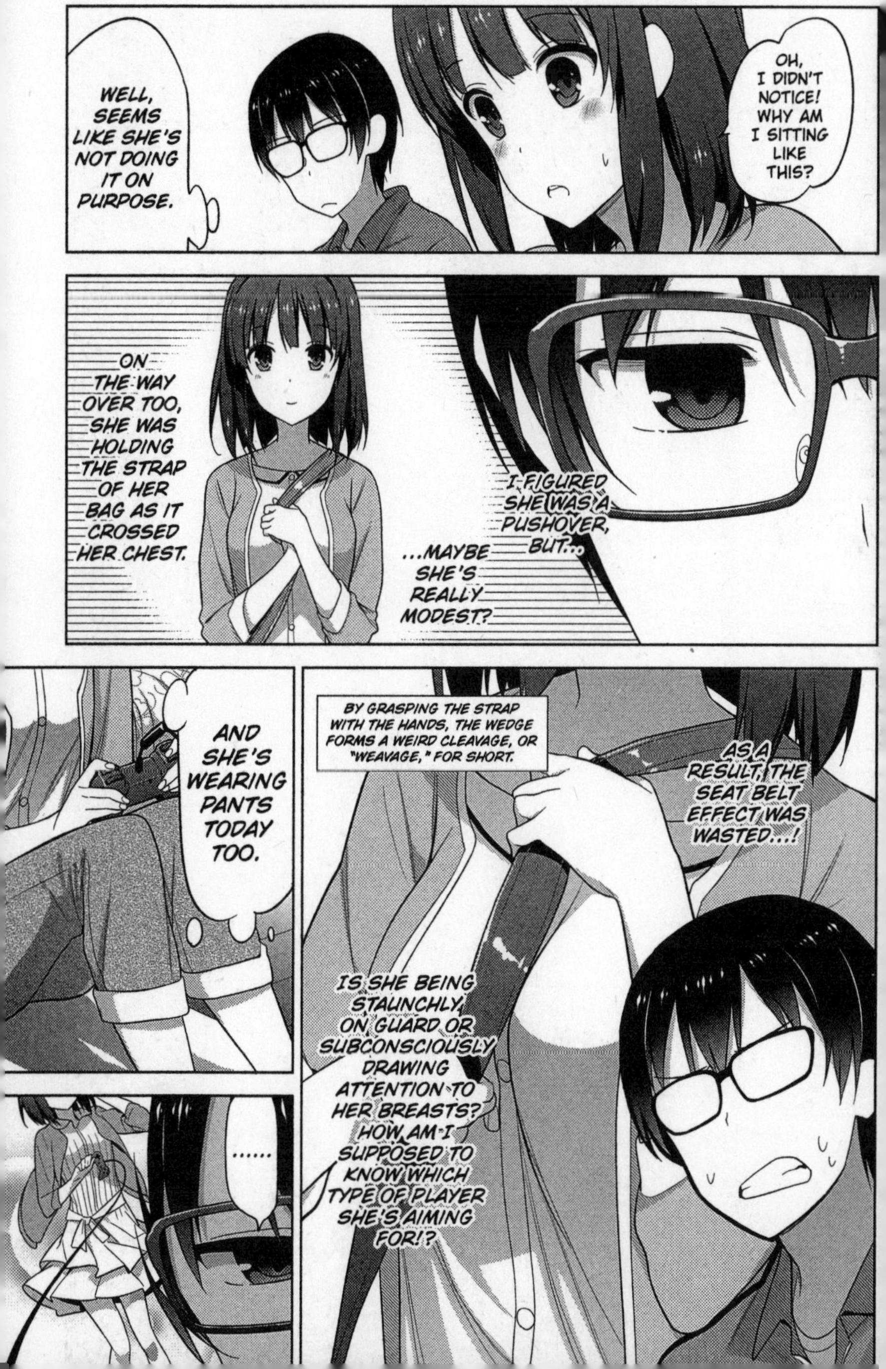

OH, I DIDN'T NOTICE! WHY AM I SITTING LIKE THIS?
WELL, SEEMS LIKE SHE'S NOT DOING IT ON PURPOSE.
ON THE WAY OVER TOO, SHE WAS HOLDING THE STRAP OF HER BAG AS IT CROSSED HER CHEST.
I FIGURED SHE WAS A PUSHOVER, BUT...
...MAYBE SHE'S REALLY MODEST?
BY GRASPING THE STRAP WITH THE HANDS, THE WEDGE FORMS A WEIRD CLEAVAGE, OR "WEAVAGE," FOR SHORT.
AS A RESULT, THE SEAT BELT EFFECT WAS WASTED...!
IS SHE BEING STAUNCHLY ON GUARD OR SUBCONSCIOUSLY DRAWING ATTENTION TO HER BREASTS? HOW AM I SUPPOSED TO KNOW WHICH TYPE OF PLAYER SHE'S AIMING FOR!?
AND SHE'S WEARING PANTS TODAY TOO.
......

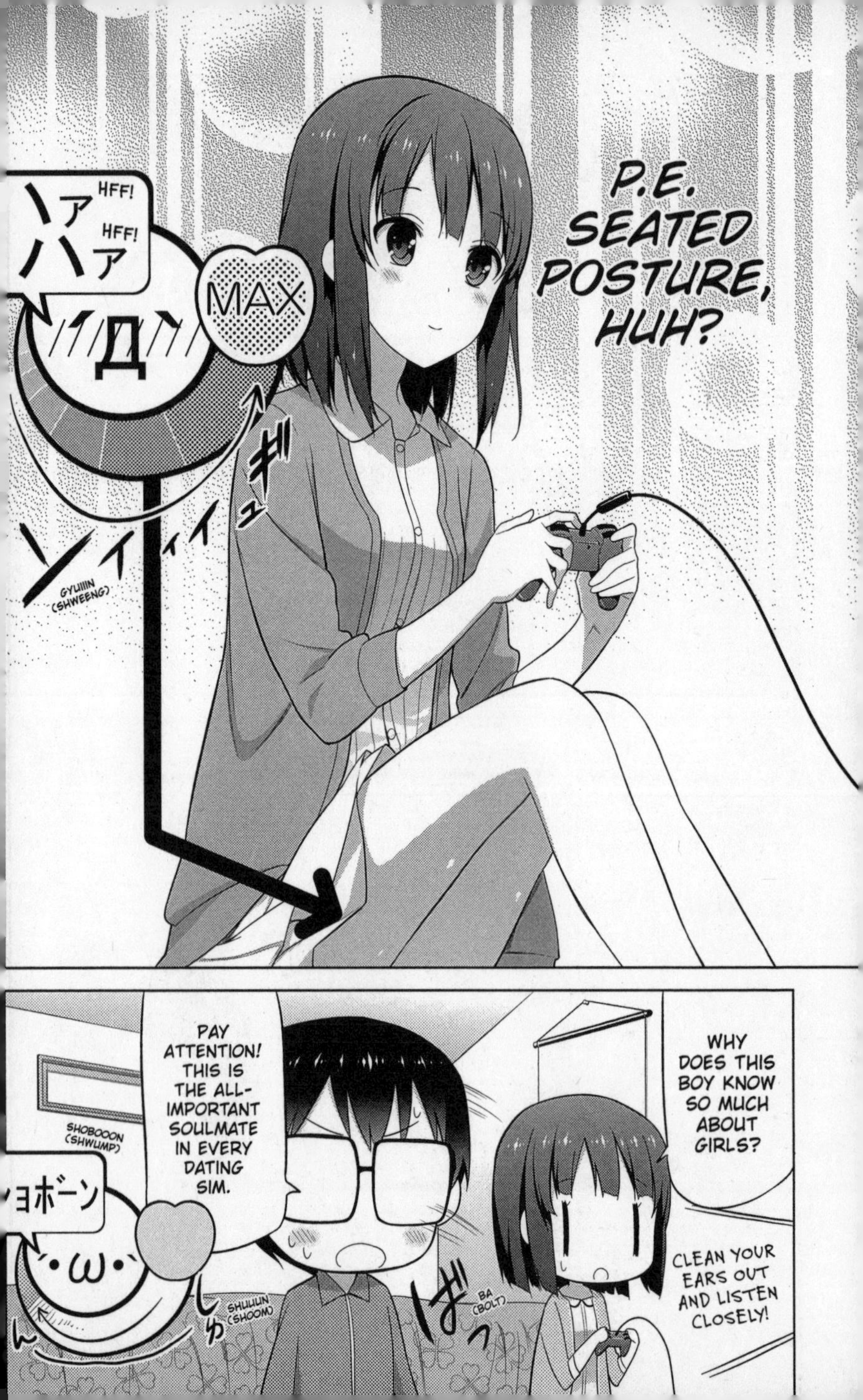
P.E. SEATED POSTURE, HUH?
ハァハァ
HFF! HFF!
MAX
ギュイイィン
GYUIIIN (SHWEENG)
WHY DOES THIS BOY KNOW SO MUCH ABOUT GIRLS?
CLEAN YOUR EARS OUT AND LISTEN CLOSELY!
ばっ
BA (BOLT)
PAY ATTENTION! THIS IS THE ALL-IMPORTANT SOULMATE IN EVERY DATING SIM.
しゅん
SHUUUN (SHOOM)
ショボーン
SHOBOOON (SHWUMP)

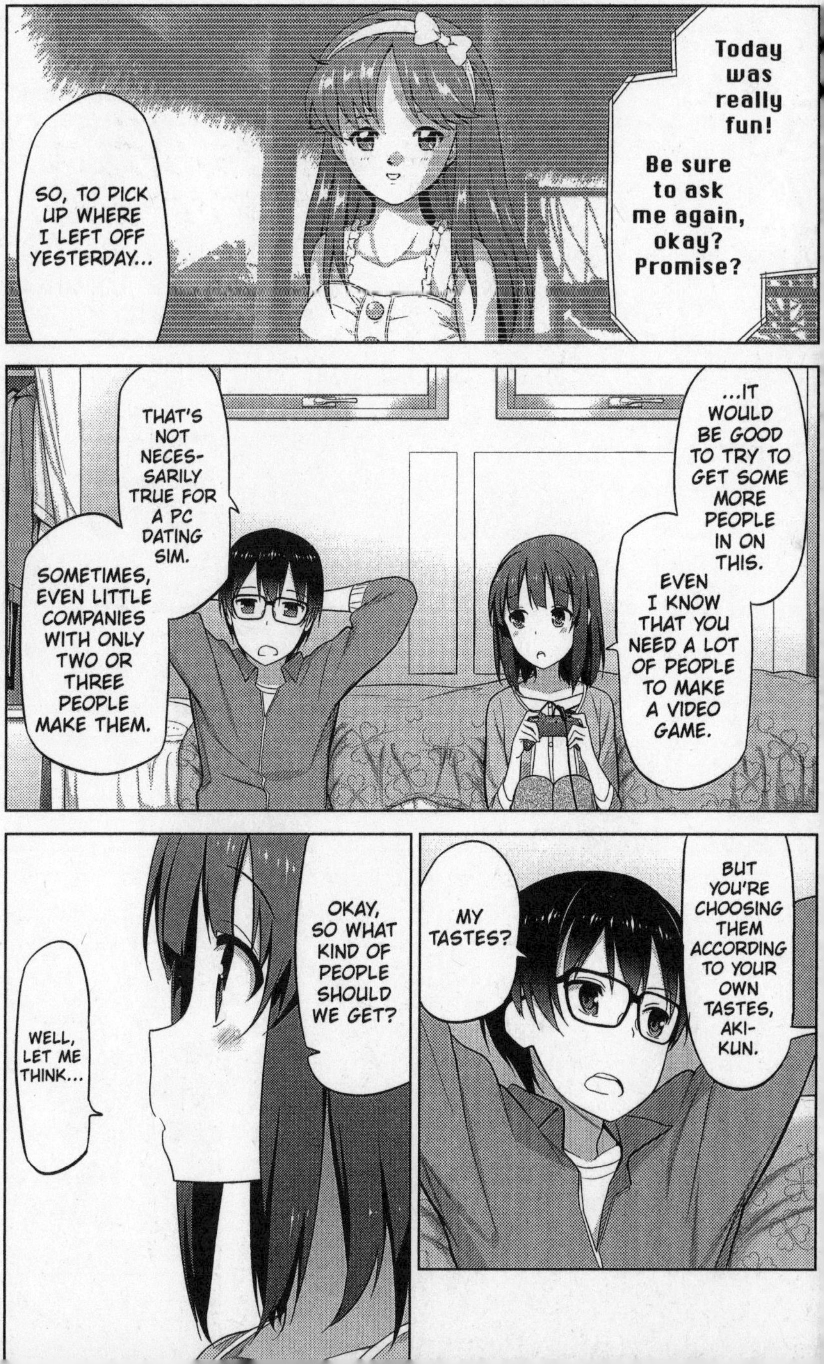
Today was really fun!
Be sure to ask me again, okay? Promise?
SO, TO PICK UP WHERE I LEFT OFF YESTERDAY...
...IT WOULD BE GOOD TO TRY TO GET SOME MORE PEOPLE IN ON THIS.
EVEN I KNOW THAT YOU NEED A LOT OF PEOPLE TO MAKE A VIDEO GAME.
THAT'S NOT NECES-SARILY TRUE FOR A PC DATING SIM.
SOMETIMES, EVEN LITTLE COMPANIES WITH ONLY TWO OR THREE PEOPLE MAKE THEM.
BUT YOU'RE CHOOSING THEM ACCORDING TO YOUR OWN TASTES, AKI-KUN.
MY TASTES?
OKAY, SO WHAT KIND OF PEOPLE SHOULD WE GET?
WELL, LET ME THINK...

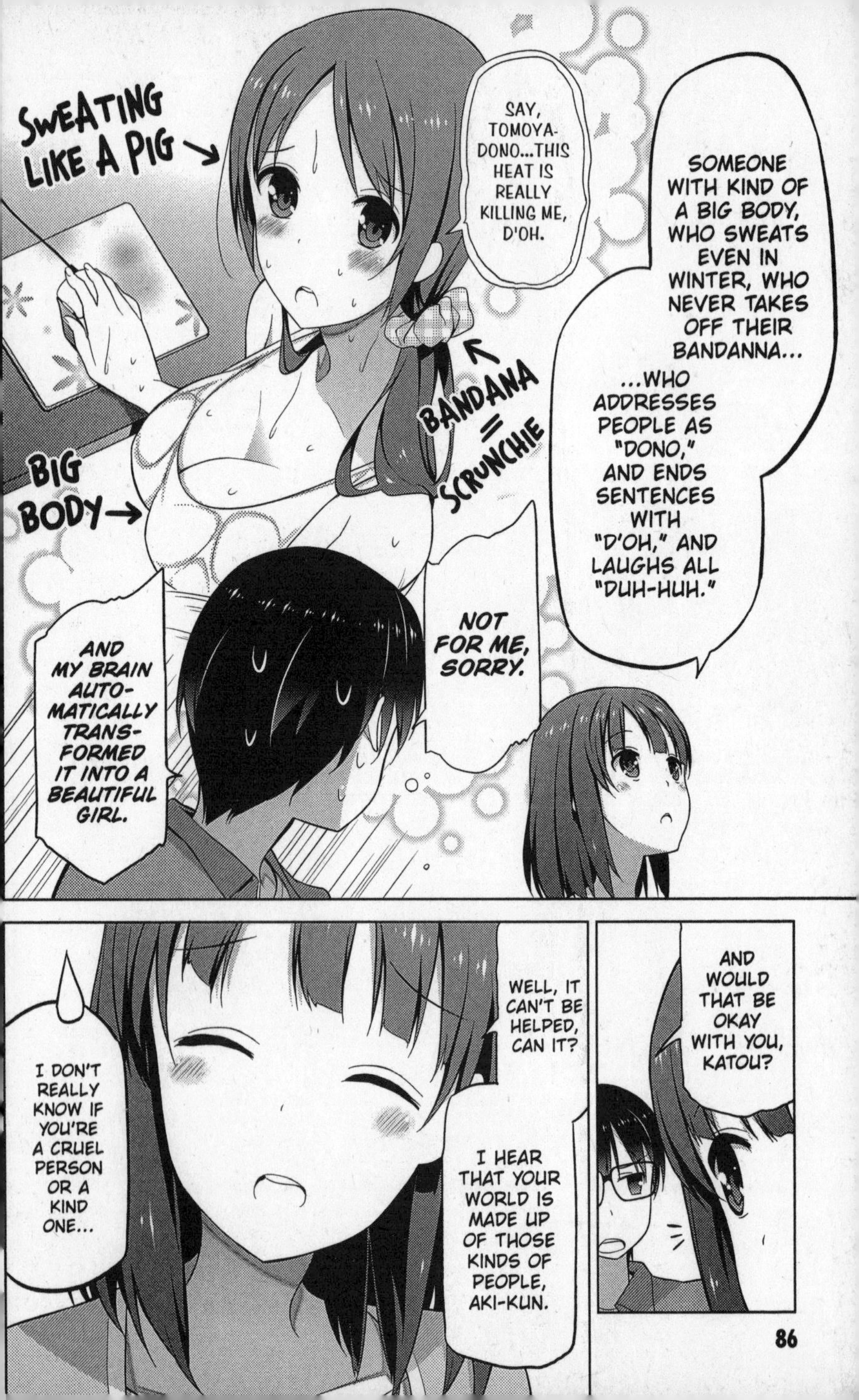
SOMEONE WITH KIND OF A BIG BODY, WHO SWEATS EVEN IN WINTER, WHO NEVER TAKES OFF THEIR BANDANNA...
...WHO ADDRESSES PEOPLE AS "DONO," AND ENDS SENTENCES WITH "D'OH," AND LAUGHS ALL "DUH-HUH."
SAY, TOMOYA-DONO...THIS HEAT IS REALLY KILLING ME, D'OH.
SWEATING LIKE A PIG
BANDANA = SCRUNCHIE
BIG BODY
NOT FOR ME, SORRY.
AND MY BRAIN AUTO-MATICALLY TRANS-FORMED IT INTO A BEAUTIFUL GIRL.
AND WOULD THAT BE OKAY WITH YOU, KATOU?
WELL, IT CAN'T BE HELPED, CAN IT?
I HEAR THAT YOUR WORLD IS MADE UP OF THOSE KINDS OF PEOPLE, AKI-KUN.
I DON'T REALLY KNOW IF YOU'RE A CRUEL PERSON OR A KIND ONE...

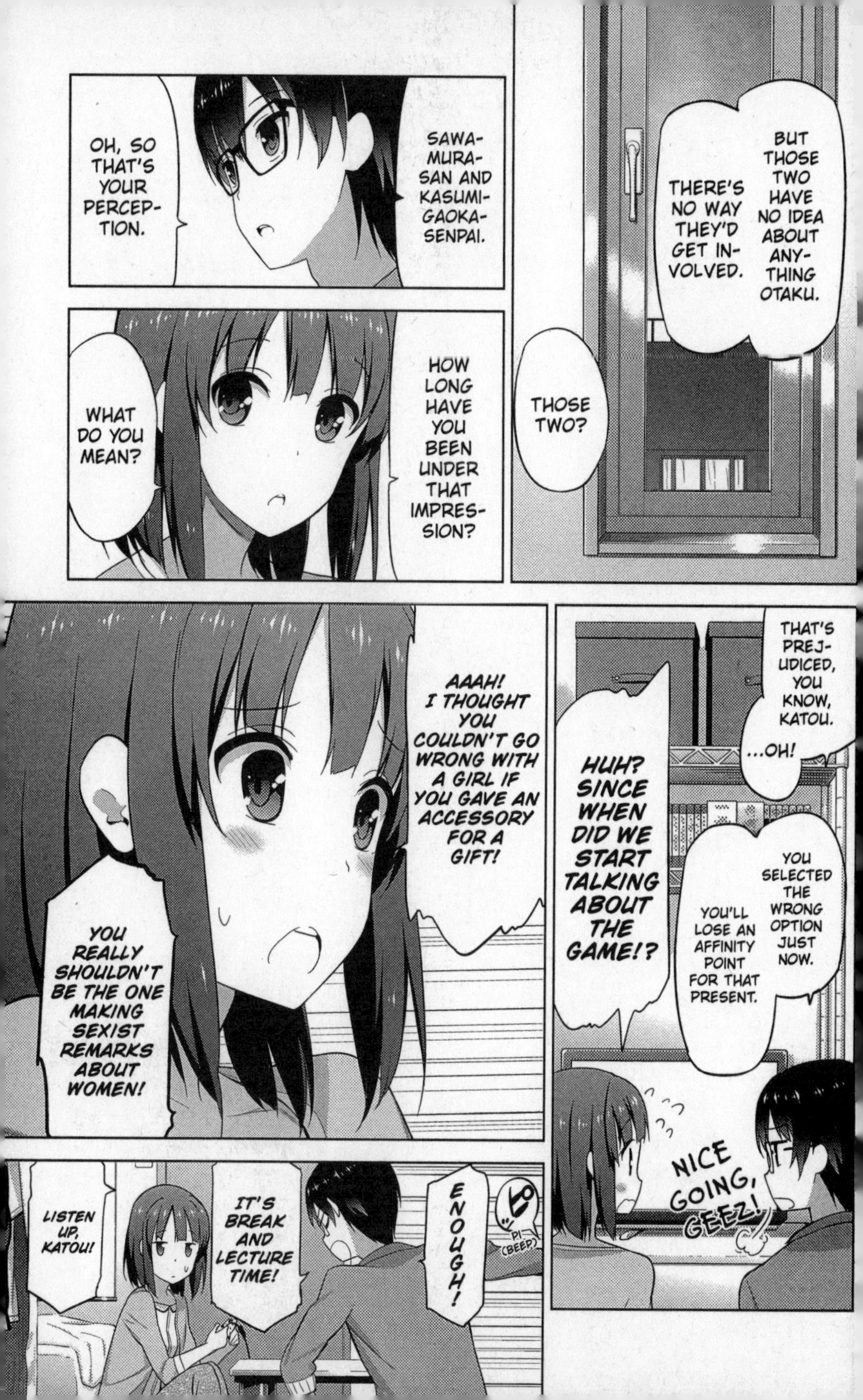
BUT THOSE TWO HAVE NO IDEA ABOUT ANYTHING OTAKU.
THERE'S NO WAY THEY'D GET INVOLVED.
THOSE TWO?
SAWAMURA-SAN AND KASUMIGAOKA-SENPAI.
OH, SO THAT'S YOUR PERCEPTION.
HOW LONG HAVE YOU BEEN UNDER THAT IMPRESSION?
WHAT DO YOU MEAN?
THAT'S PREJUDICED, YOU KNOW, KATOU.
...OH!
YOU SELECTED THE WRONG OPTION JUST NOW.
YOU'LL LOSE AN AFFINITY POINT FOR THAT PRESENT.
HUH? SINCE WHEN DID WE START TALKING ABOUT THE GAME!?
NICE GOING, GEEZ!
AAAH! I THOUGHT YOU COULDN'T GO WRONG WITH A GIRL IF YOU GAVE AN ACCESSORY FOR A GIFT!
YOU REALLY SHOULDN'T BE THE ONE MAKING SEXIST REMARKS ABOUT WOMEN!
PI (BEEP)
ENOUGH!
IT'S BREAK AND LECTURE TIME!
LISTEN UP, KATOU!

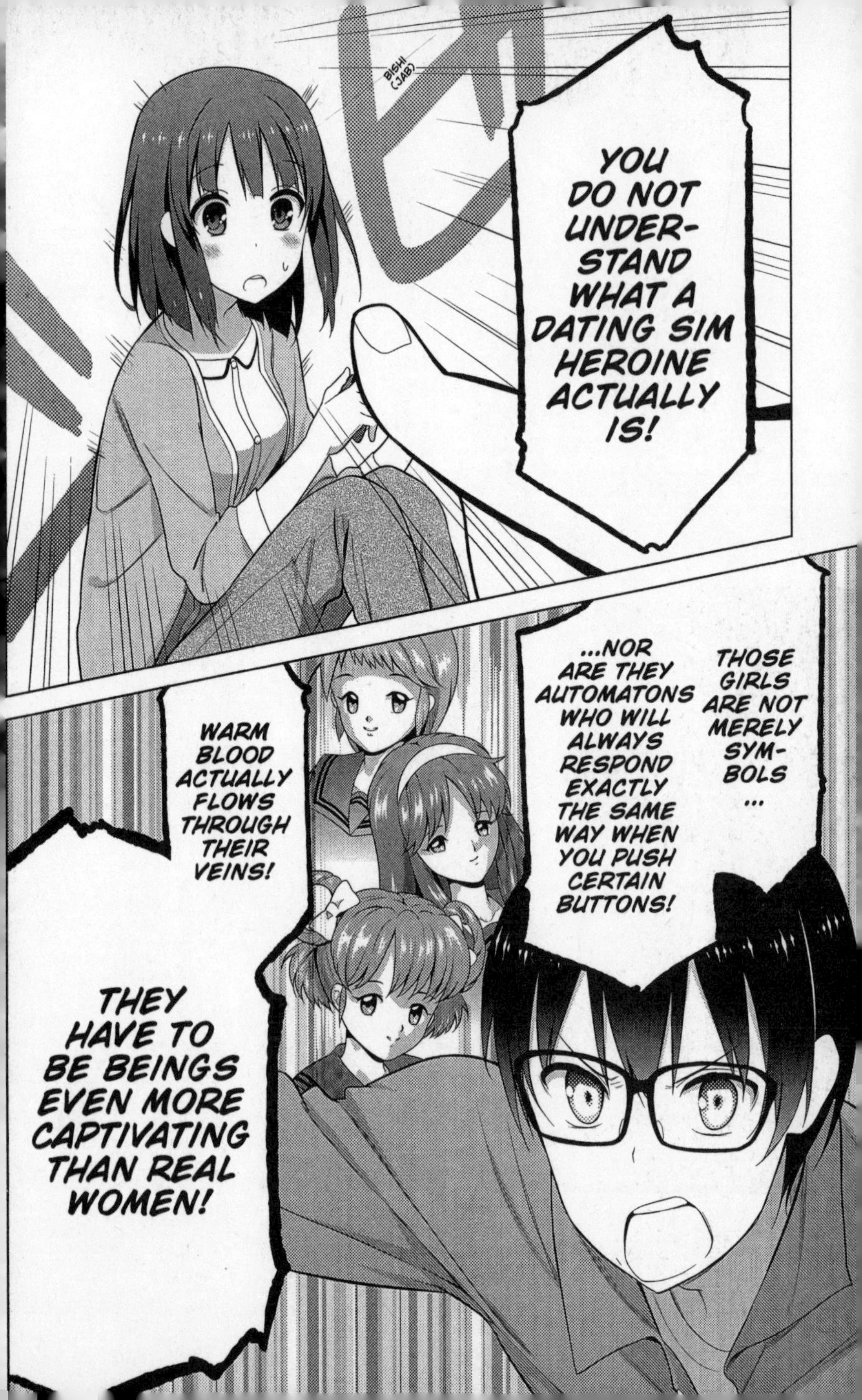
BISHI (JAB)
YOU DO NOT UNDER-STAND WHAT A DATING SIM HEROINE ACTUALLY IS!
THOSE GIRLS ARE NOT MERELY SYM-BOLS ...
...NOR ARE THEY AUTOMATONS WHO WILL ALWAYS RESPOND EXACTLY THE SAME WAY WHEN YOU PUSH CERTAIN BUTTONS!
WARM BLOOD ACTUALLY FLOWS THROUGH THEIR VEINS!
THEY HAVE TO BE BEINGS EVEN MORE CAPTIVATING THAN REAL WOMEN!

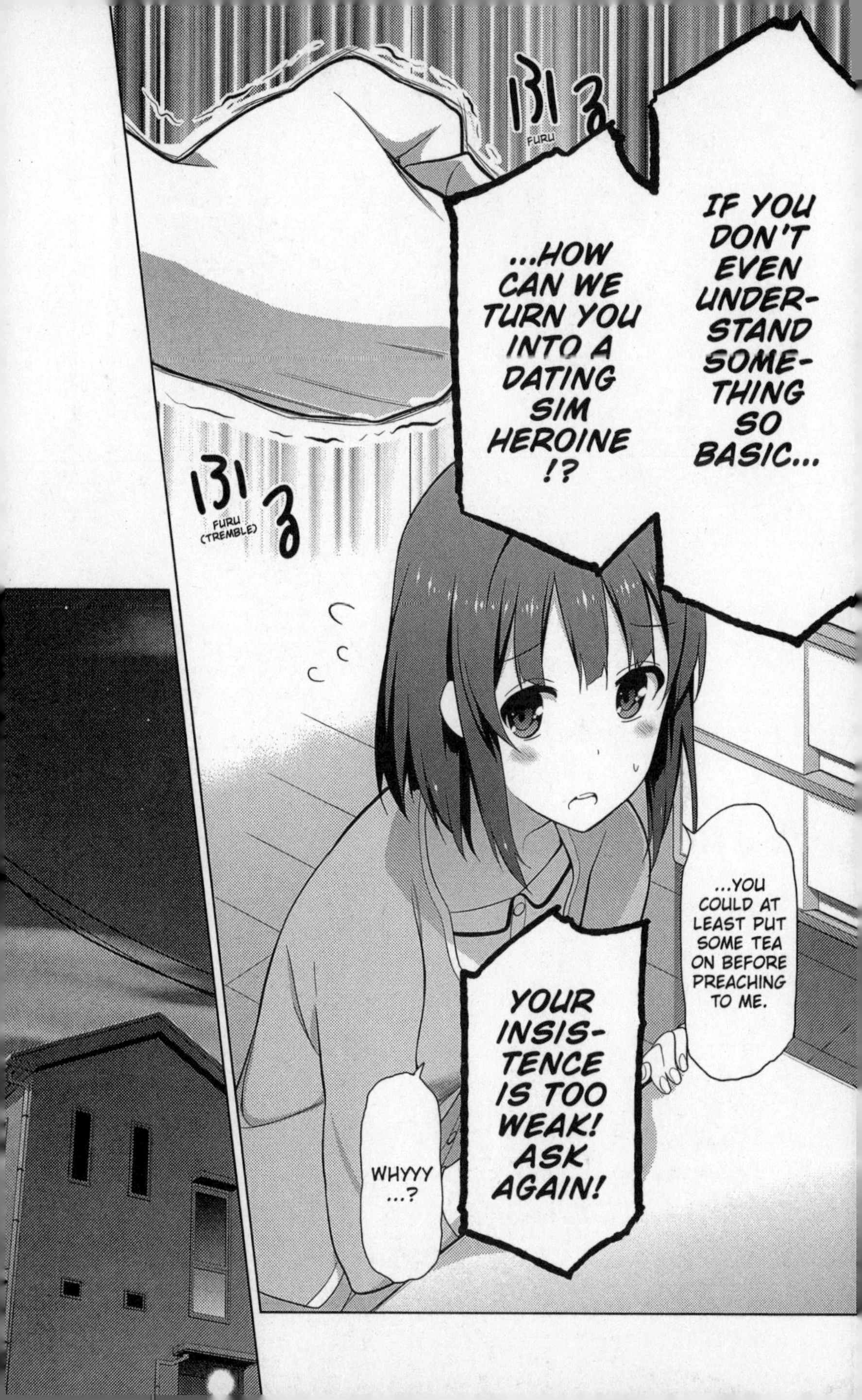
ふる
FURU
IF YOU DON'T EVEN UNDER-STAND SOME-THING SO BASIC...
...HOW CAN WE TURN YOU INTO A DATING SIM HEROINE !?
ふる
FURU (TREMBLE)
...YOU COULD AT LEAST PUT SOME TEA ON BEFORE PREACHING TO ME.
YOUR INSIS-TENCE IS TOO WEAK! ASK AGAIN!
WHYYY ...?

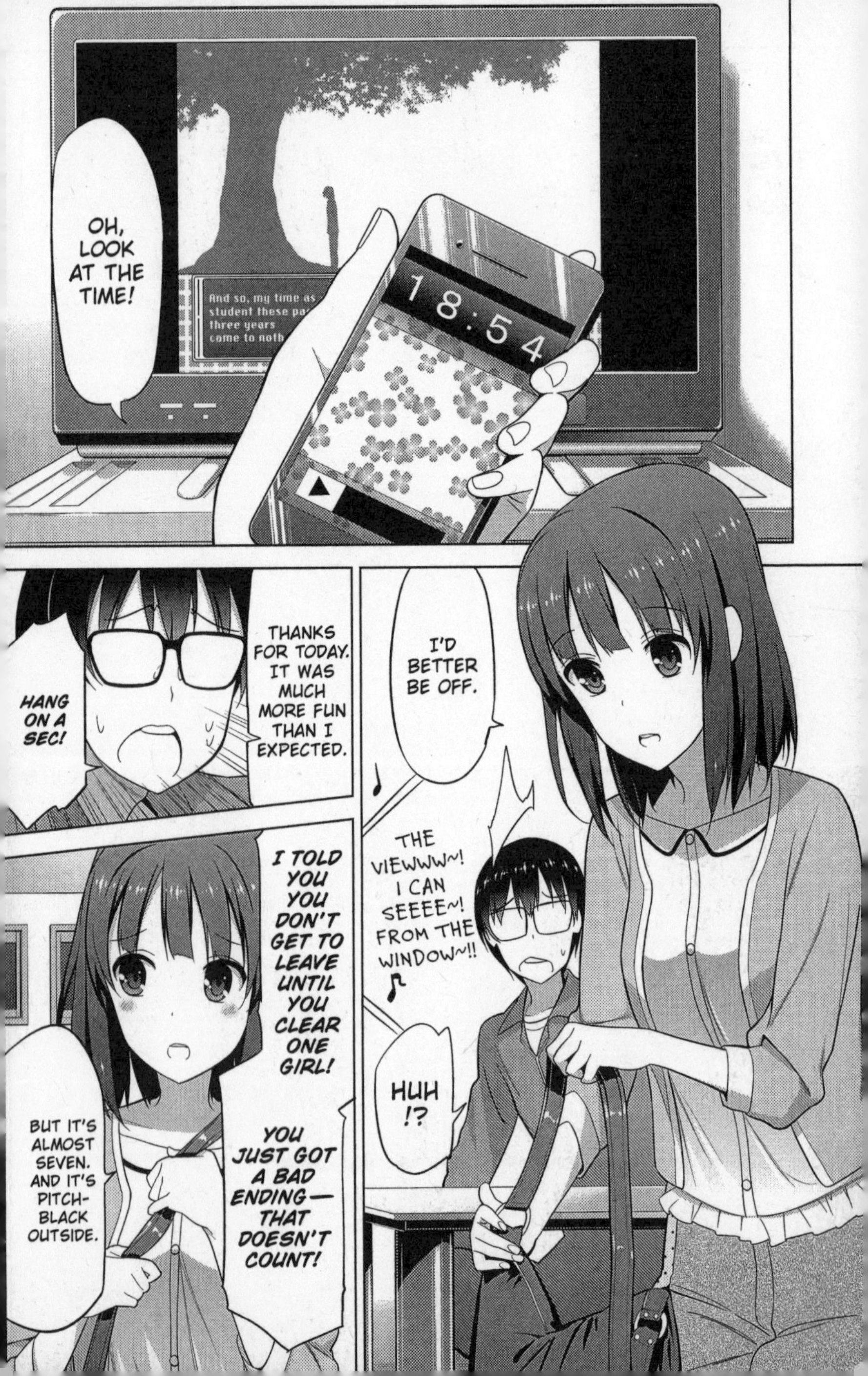
OH, LOOK AT THE TIME!
And so, my time as
student these pas
three years
come to noth
18:54
I'D BETTER BE OFF.
THE VIEWWW~! I CAN SEEEE~! FROM THE WINDOW~!!
HUH !?
THANKS FOR TODAY. IT WAS MUCH MORE FUN THAN I EXPECTED.
HANG ON A SEC!
I TOLD YOU YOU DON'T GET TO LEAVE UNTIL YOU CLEAR ONE GIRL!
YOU JUST GOT A BAD ENDING—THAT DOESN'T COUNT!
BUT IT'S ALMOST SEVEN. AND IT'S PITCH-BLACK OUTSIDE.

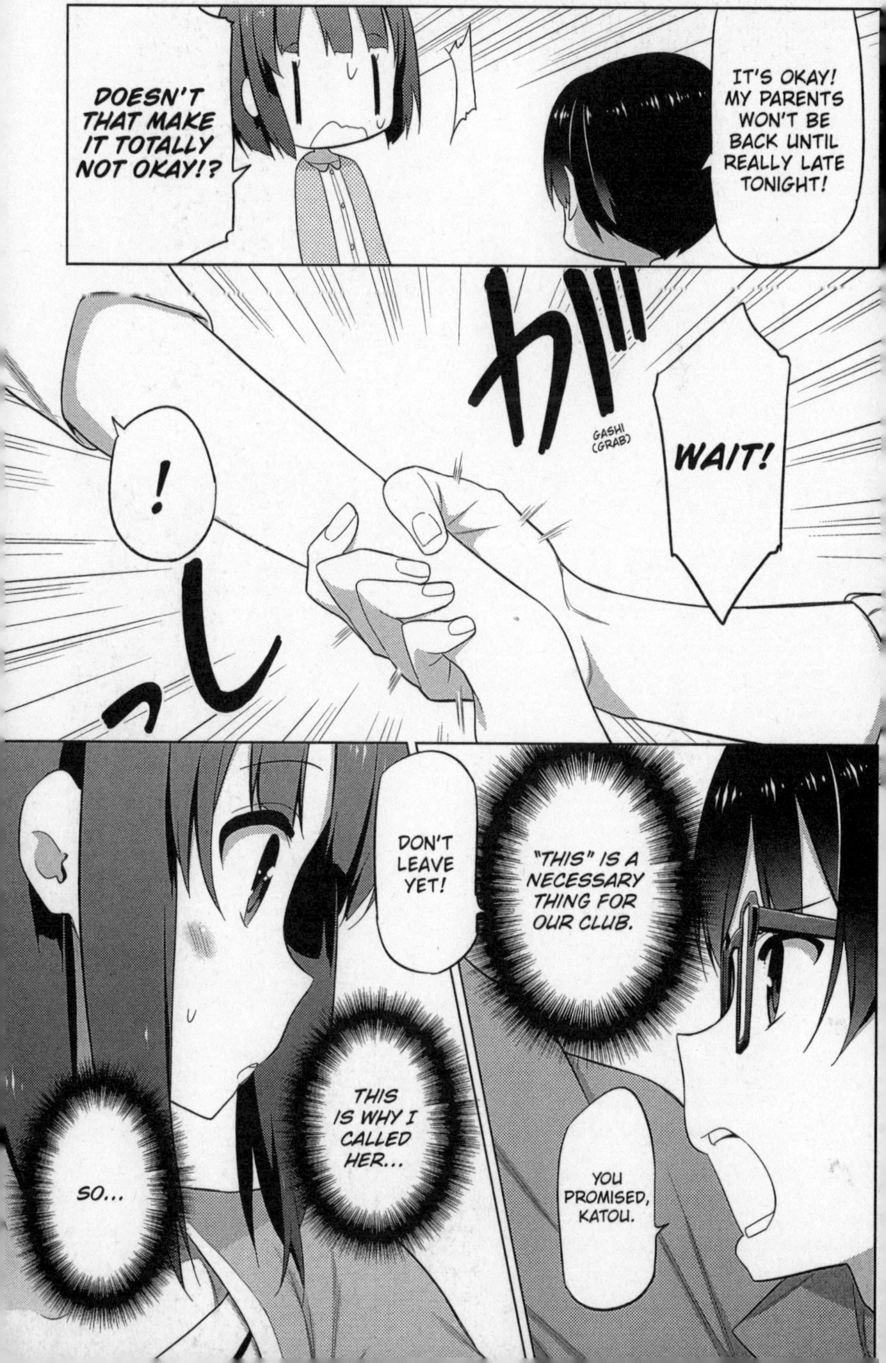
IT'S OKAY! MY PARENTS WON'T BE BACK UNTIL REALLY LATE TONIGHT!
DOESN'T THAT MAKE IT TOTALLY NOT OKAY!?
WAIT!
GASHI (GRAB)
!
"THIS" IS A NECESSARY THING FOR OUR CLUB.
DON'T LEAVE YET!
YOU PROMISED, KATOU.
THIS IS WHY I CALLED HER...
SO...

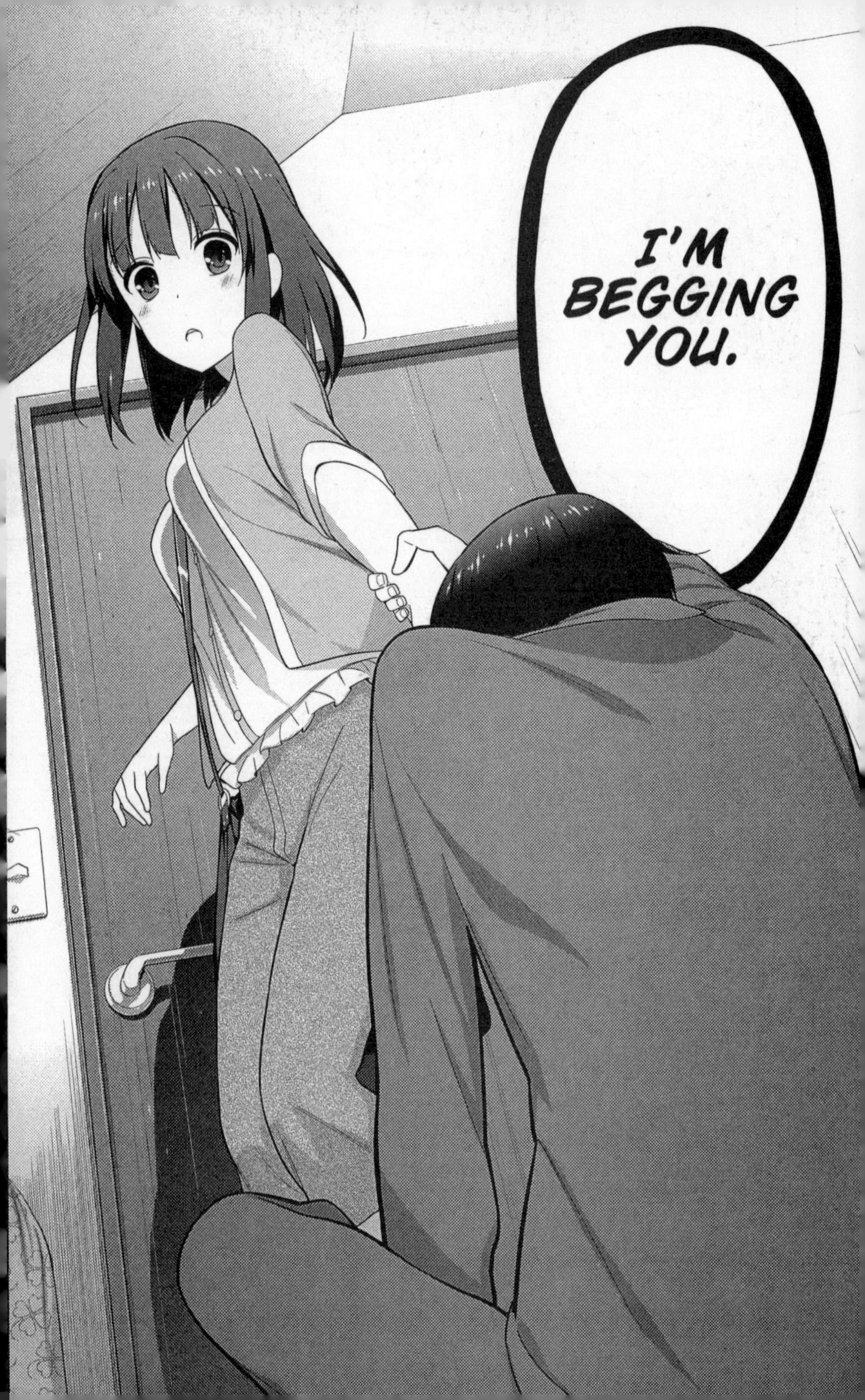
I'M BEGGING YOU.

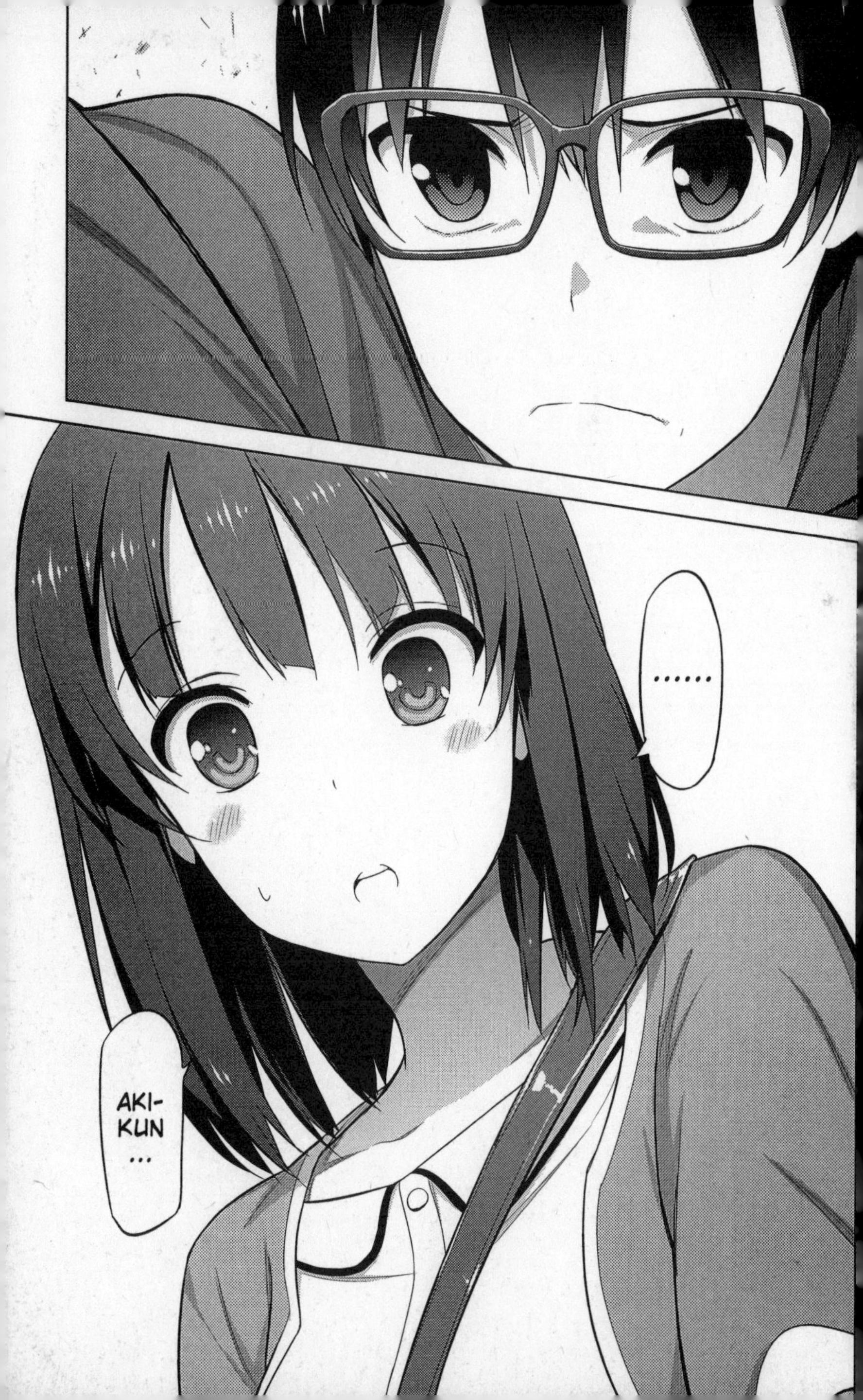
......
AKI-KUN...

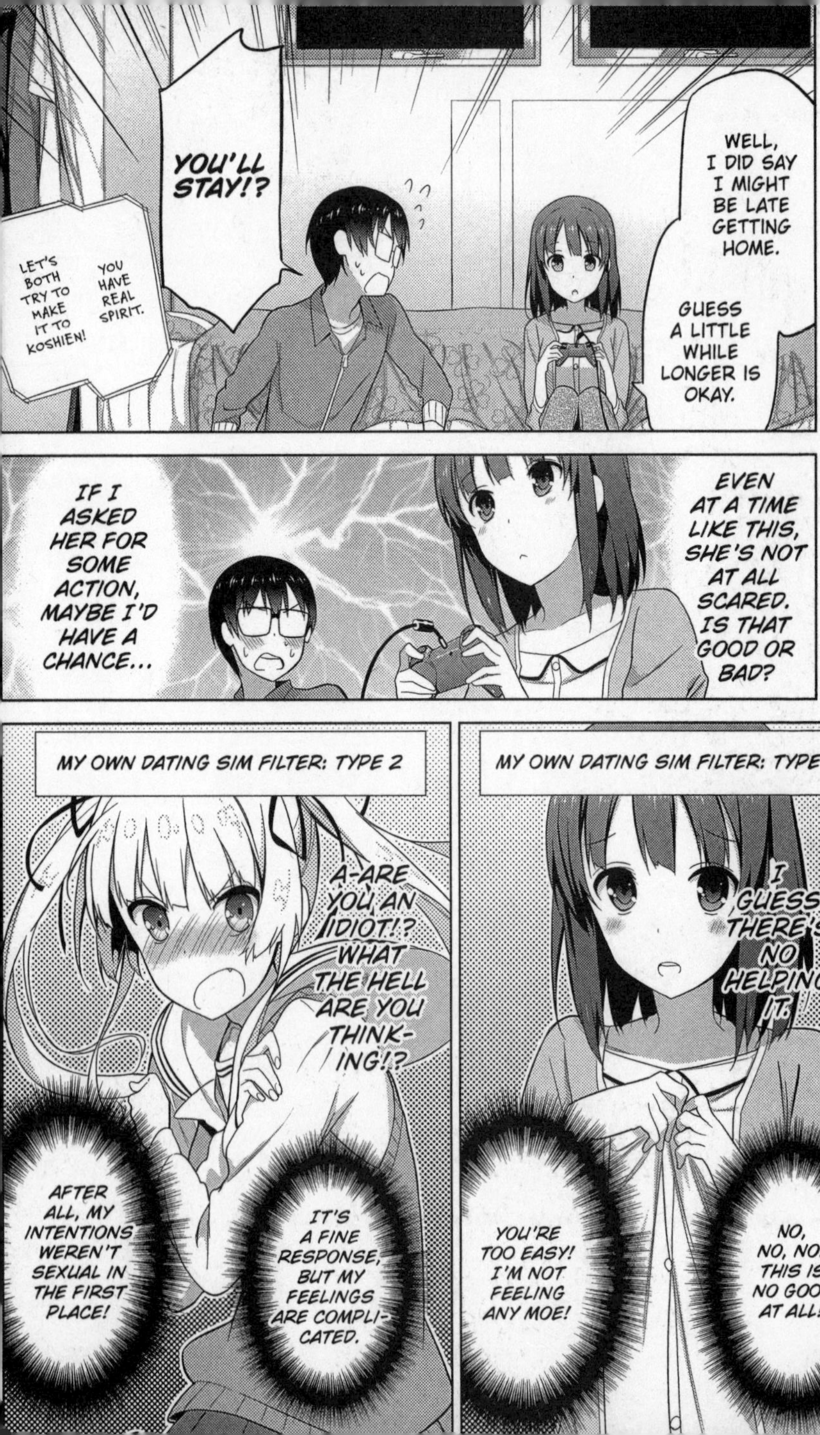
WELL, I DID SAY I MIGHT BE LATE GETTING HOME.
GUESS A LITTLE WHILE LONGER IS OKAY.
YOU'LL STAY!?
YOU HAVE REAL SPIRIT.
LET'S BOTH TRY TO MAKE IT TO KOSHIEN!
EVEN AT A TIME LIKE THIS, SHE'S NOT AT ALL SCARED. IS THAT GOOD OR BAD?
IF I ASKED HER FOR SOME ACTION, MAYBE I'D HAVE A CHANCE...
MY OWN DATING SIM FILTER: TYPE 1
I GUESS THERE'S NO HELPING IT.
NO, NO, NO! THIS IS NO GOOD AT ALL!
YOU'RE TOO EASY! I'M NOT FEELING ANY MOE!
MY OWN DATING SIM FILTER: TYPE 2
A-ARE YOU AN IDIOT!? WHAT THE HELL ARE YOU THINKING!?
IT'S A FINE RESPONSE, BUT MY FEELINGS ARE COMPLICATED.
AFTER ALL, MY INTENTIONS WEREN'T SEXUAL IN THE FIRST PLACE!

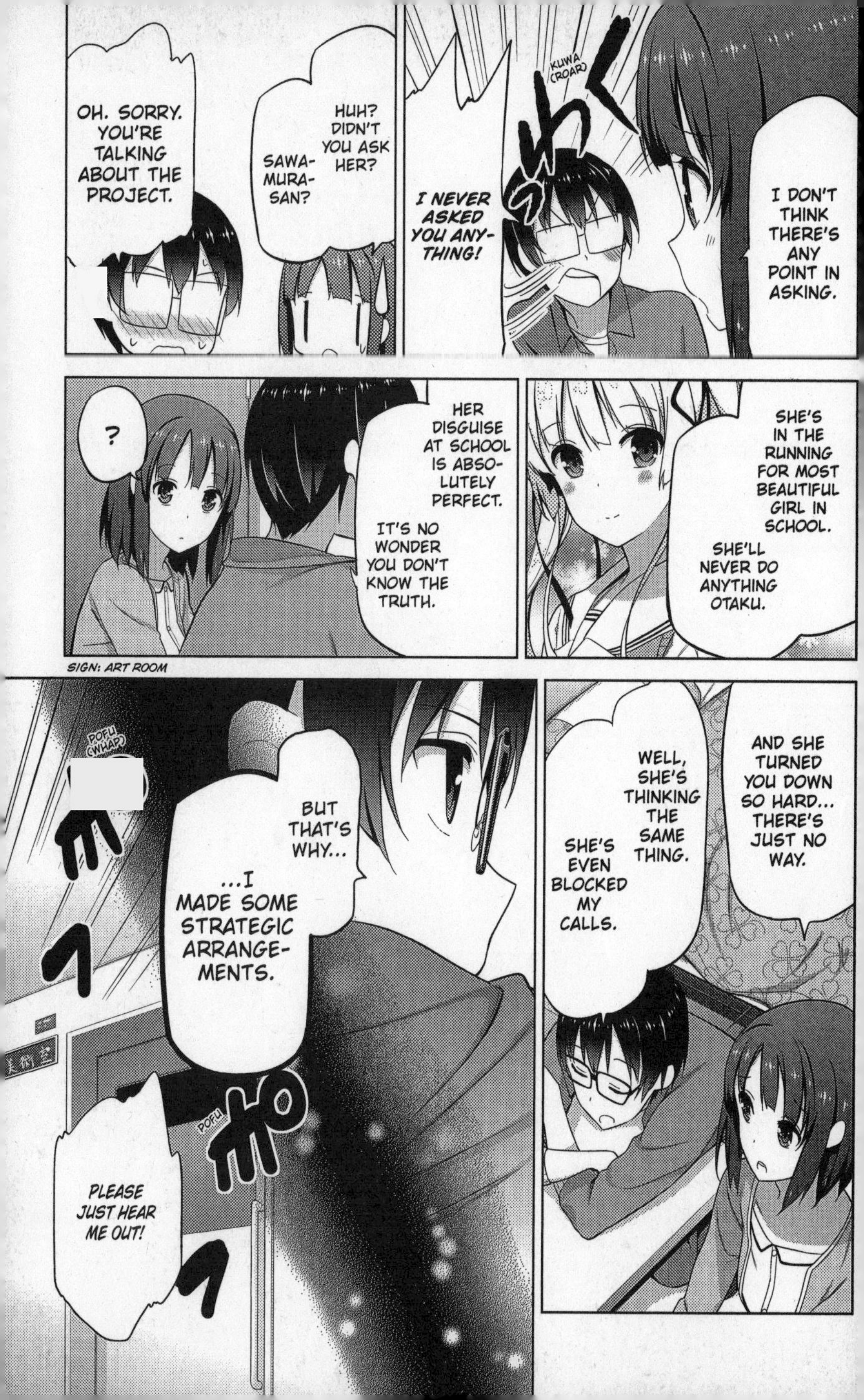
I DON'T THINK THERE'S ANY POINT IN ASKING.
KUWA (ROAR)
I NEVER ASKED YOU ANYTHING!
HUH? DIDN'T YOU ASK HER?
SAWAMURA-SAN?
OH. SORRY. YOU'RE TALKING ABOUT THE PROJECT.
SHE'S IN THE RUNNING FOR MOST BEAUTIFUL GIRL IN SCHOOL.
SHE'LL NEVER DO ANYTHING OTAKU.
HER DISGUISE AT SCHOOL IS ABSOLUTELY PERFECT.
IT'S NO WONDER YOU DON'T KNOW THE TRUTH.
?
SIGN: ART ROOM
AND SHE TURNED YOU DOWN SO HARD... THERE'S JUST NO WAY.
WELL, SHE'S THINKING THE SAME THING.
SHE'S EVEN BLOCKED MY CALLS.
BUT THAT'S WHY...
...I MADE SOME STRATEGIC ARRANGEMENTS.
POFU (WHAP)
POFU
PLEASE JUST HEAR ME OUT!

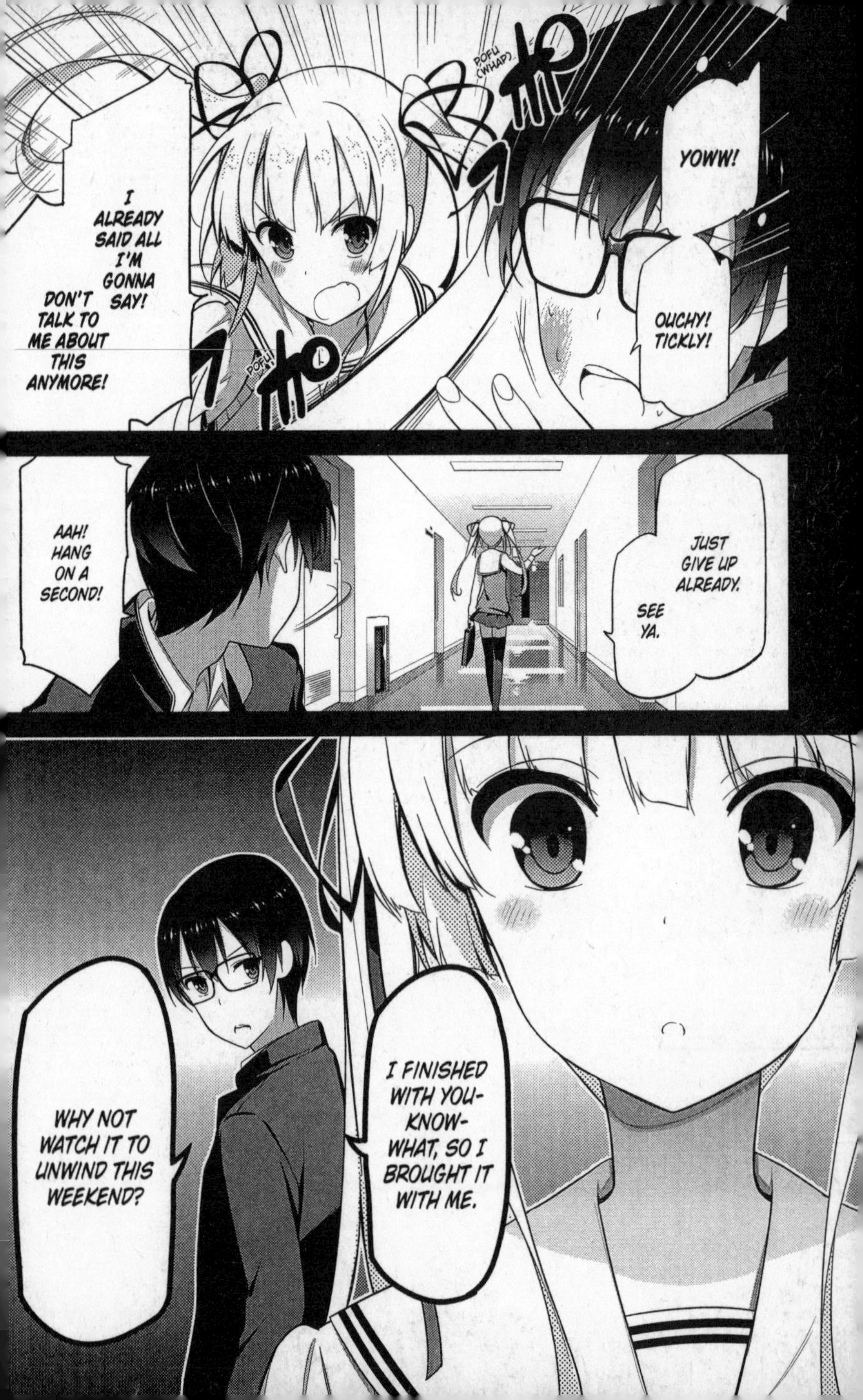
POFU (WHAP)
YOWW!
I ALREADY SAID ALL I'M GONNA SAY!
OUCHY! TICKLY!
POFU
DON'T TALK TO ME ABOUT THIS ANYMORE!
JUST GIVE UP ALREADY.
SEE YA.
AAH! HANG ON A SECOND!
I FINISHED WITH YOU-KNOW-WHAT, SO I BROUGHT IT WITH ME.
WHY NOT WATCH IT TO UNWIND THIS WEEKEND?

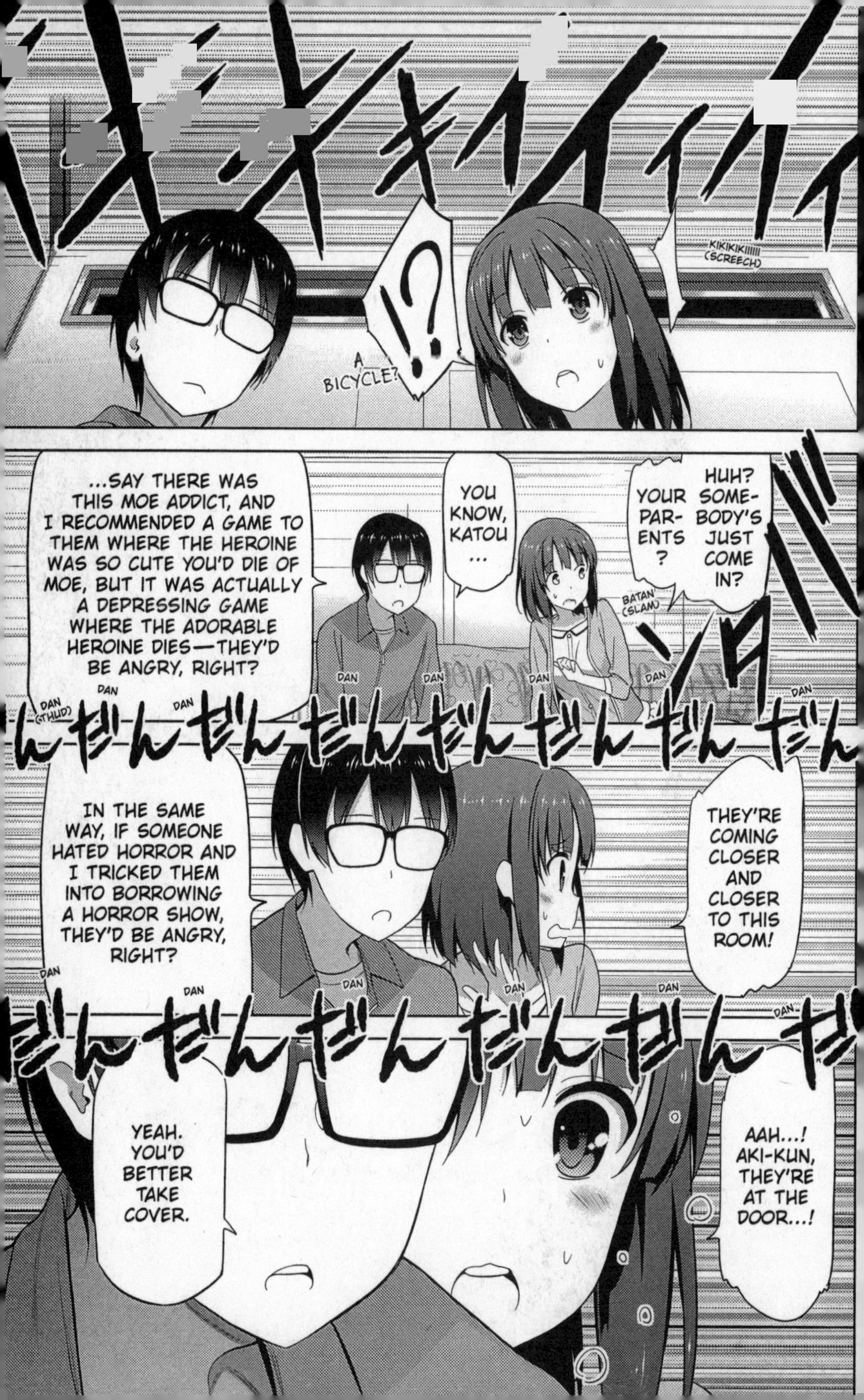
KIKIKIKIIIIII (SCREECH)
!?
A BICYCLE?
HUH? SOME-BODY'S JUST COME IN?
YOUR PAR-ENTS?
BATAN (SLAM)
YOU KNOW, KATOU...
...SAY THERE WAS THIS MOE ADDICT, AND I RECOMMENDED A GAME TO THEM WHERE THE HEROINE WAS SO CUTE YOU'D DIE OF MOE, BUT IT WAS ACTUALLY A DEPRESSING GAME WHERE THE ADORABLE HEROINE DIES—THEY'D BE ANGRY, RIGHT?
DAN DAN DAN DAN DAN DAN DAN DAN (THUD)
THEY'RE COMING CLOSER AND CLOSER TO THIS ROOM!
IN THE SAME WAY, IF SOMEONE HATED HORROR AND I TRICKED THEM INTO BORROWING A HORROR SHOW, THEY'D BE ANGRY, RIGHT?
DAN DAN DAN DAN DAN DAN
AAH...! AKI-KUN, THEY'RE AT THE DOOR...!
YEAH. YOU'D BETTER TAKE COVER.

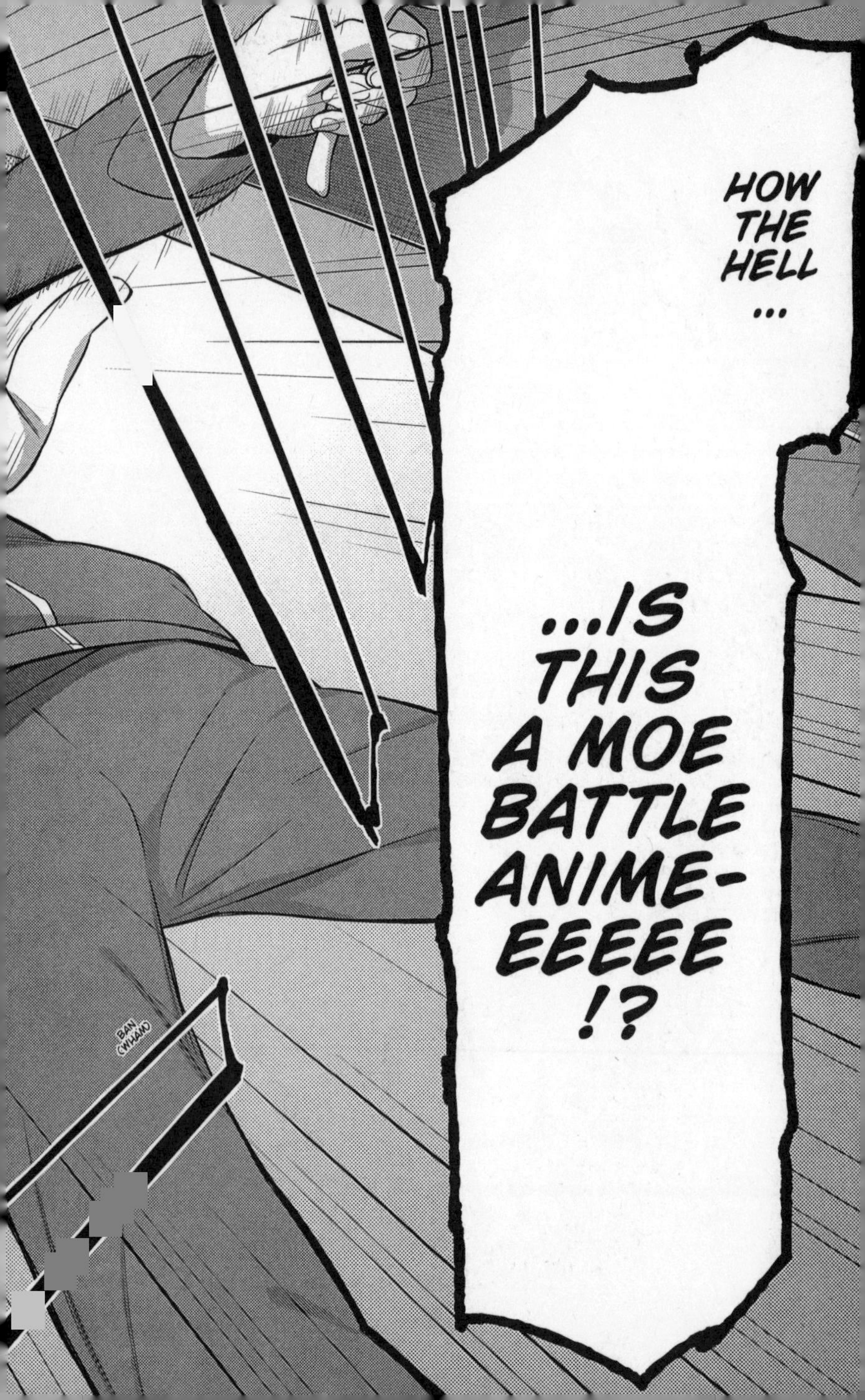
HOW THE HELL ...
...IS THIS A MOE BATTLE ANIME-EEEEE!?
BAN (WHAM)

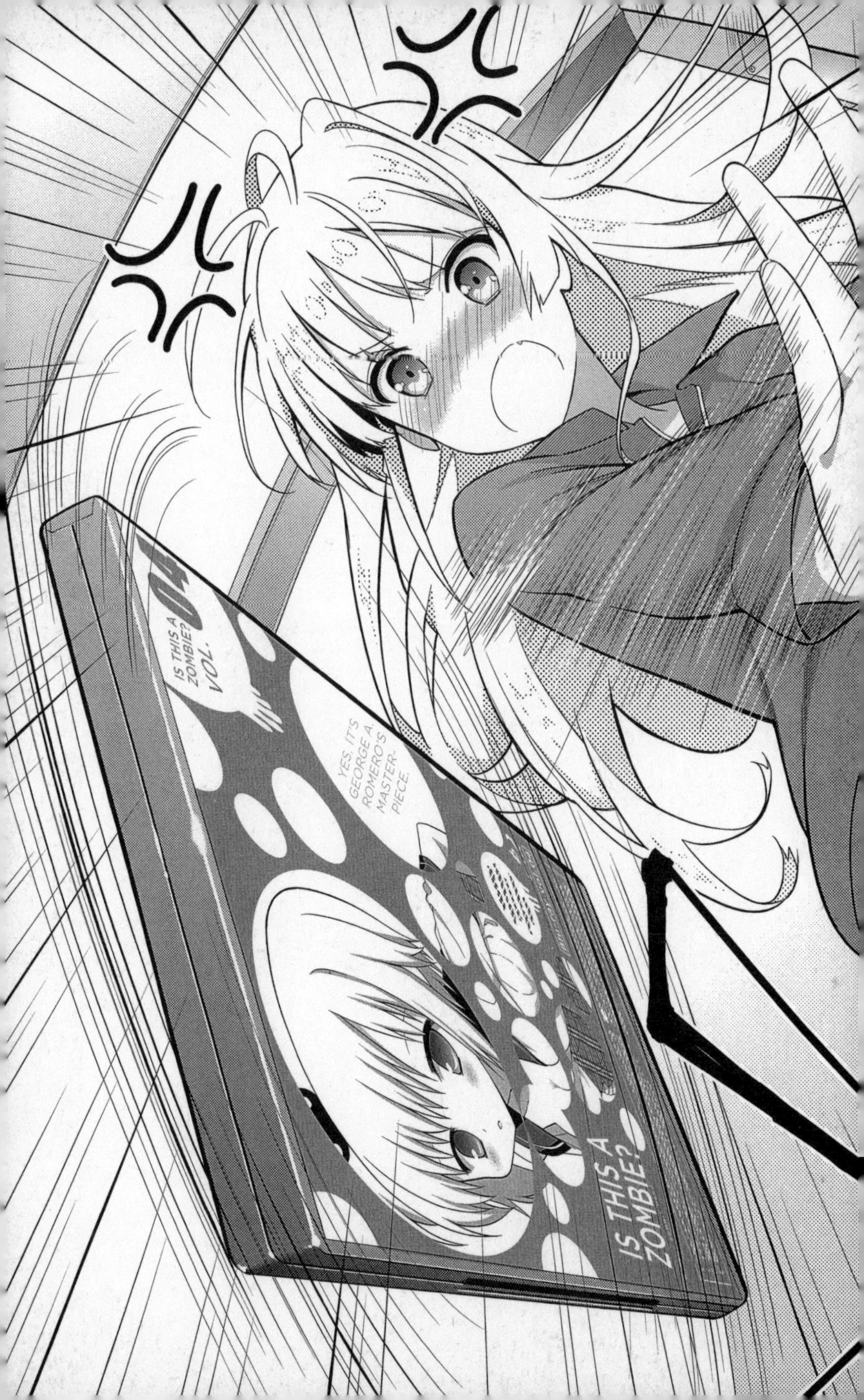
YES. IT'S GEORGE A. ROMERO'S MASTER-PIECE.
IS THIS A ZOMBIE? VOL. 04
IS THIS A ZOMBIE?

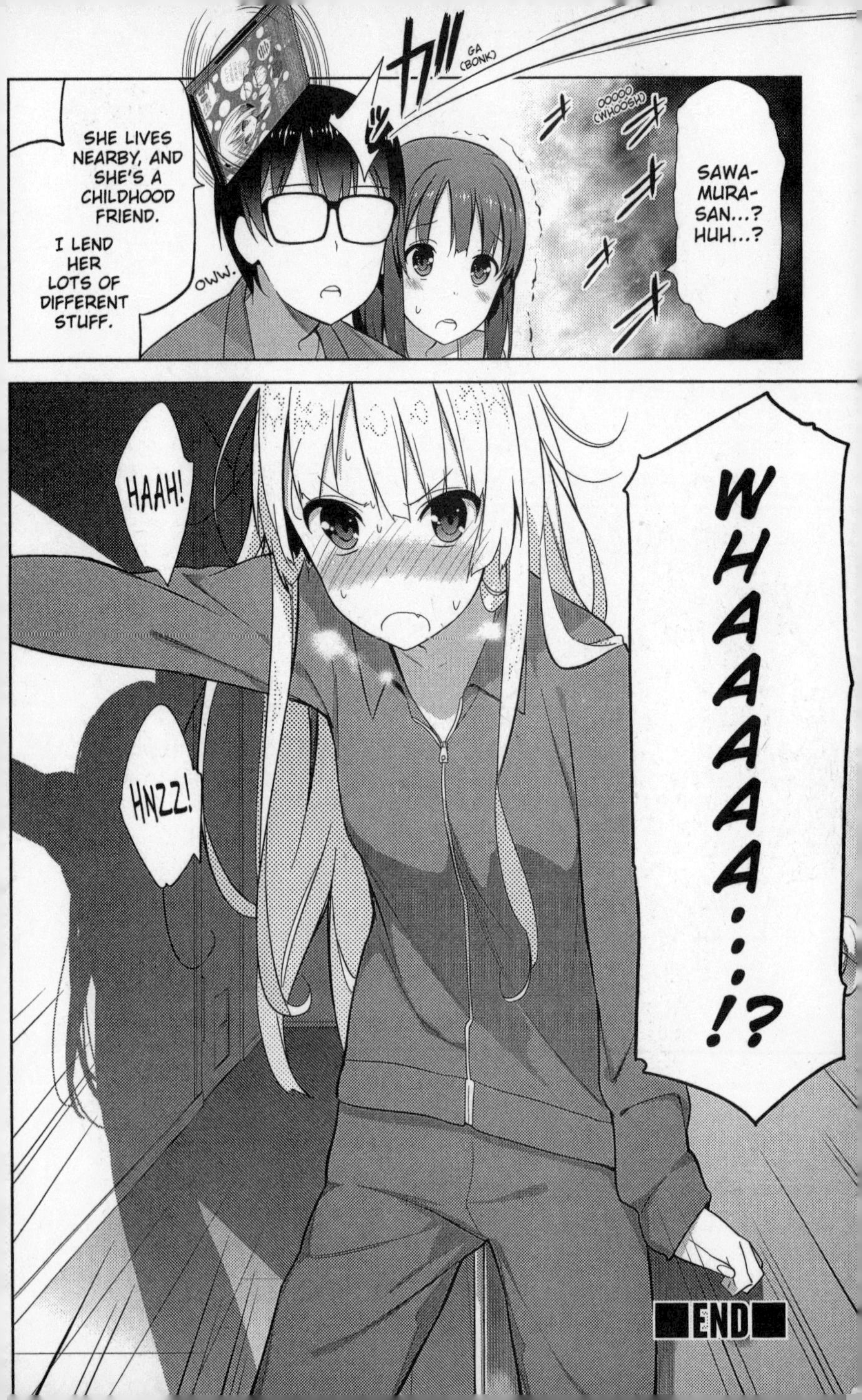
SAWA-MURA-SAN...? HUH...?
OOOOO (WHOOSH)
GA (BONK)
OWW.
SHE LIVES NEARBY, AND SHE'S A CHILDHOOD FRIEND.
I LEND HER LOTS OF DIFFERENT STUFF.
WHAAAAA...!?
HAAH!
HNZZ!
END

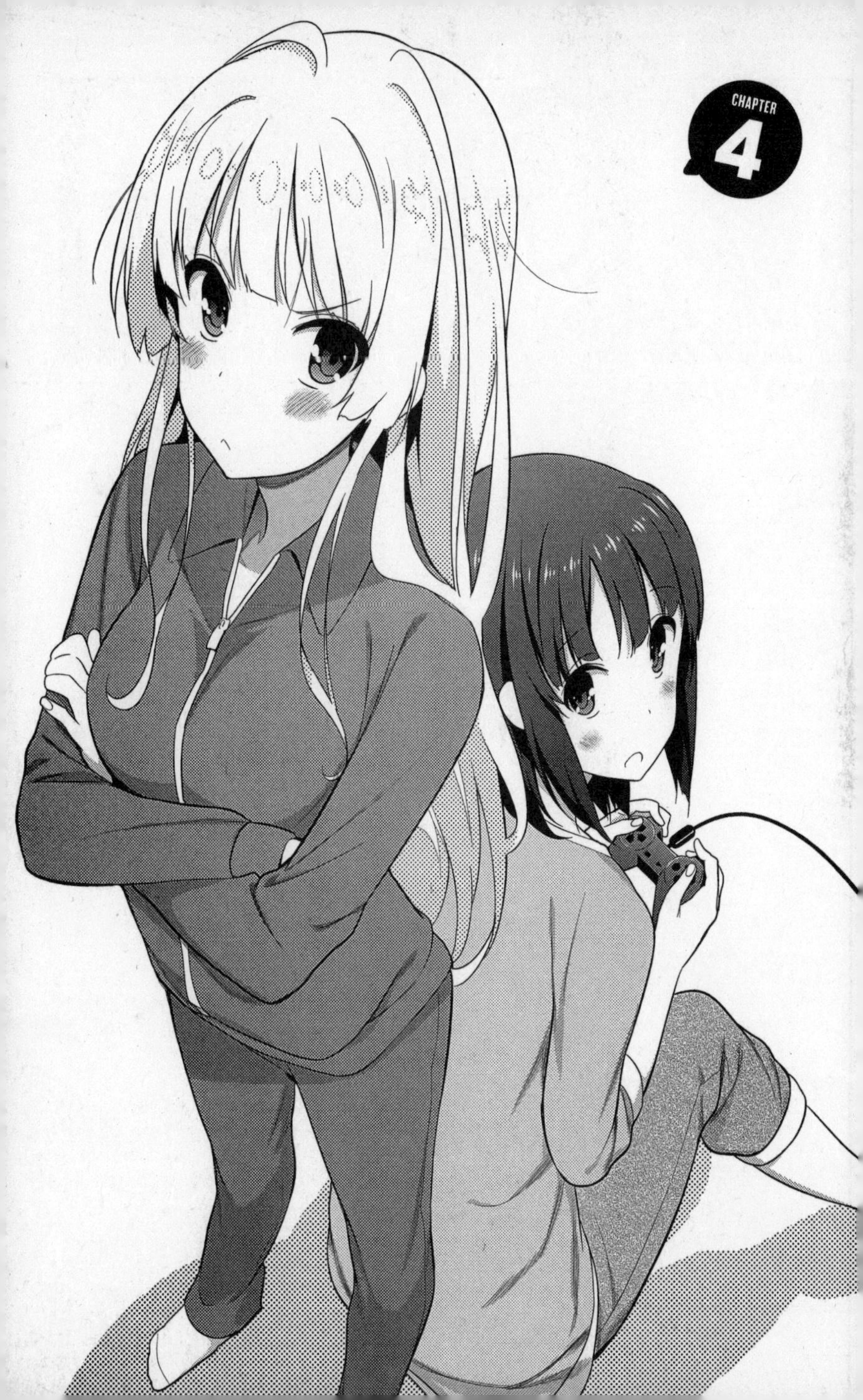
CHAPTER
4

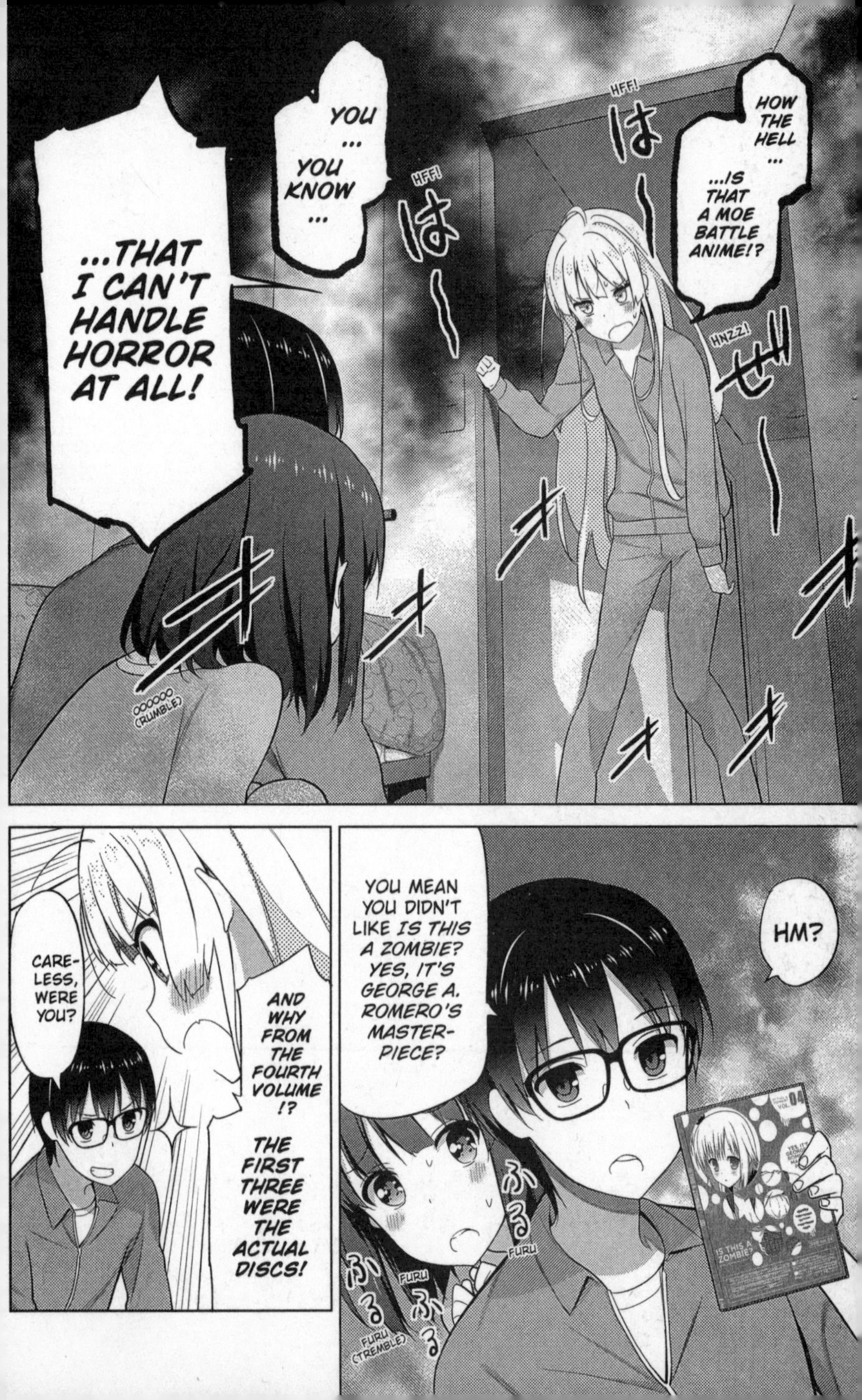
HFF! は～
HOW THE HELL... ...IS THAT A MOE BATTLE ANIME!?
HNZZ! ぜ～
HFF! は～
YOU... YOU KNOW...
...THAT I CAN'T HANDLE HORROR AT ALL!
オオオオ
OOOOOO (RUMBLE)
HM?
YOU MEAN YOU DIDN'T LIKE IS THIS A ZOMBIE? YES, IT'S GEORGE A. ROMERO'S MASTERPIECE?
ふる FURU
ふる FURU
ふる FURU (TREMBLE)
IS THIS A ZOMBIE?
AND WHY FROM THE FOURTH VOLUME!? THE FIRST THREE WERE THE ACTUAL DISCS!
CARE-LESS, WERE YOU?

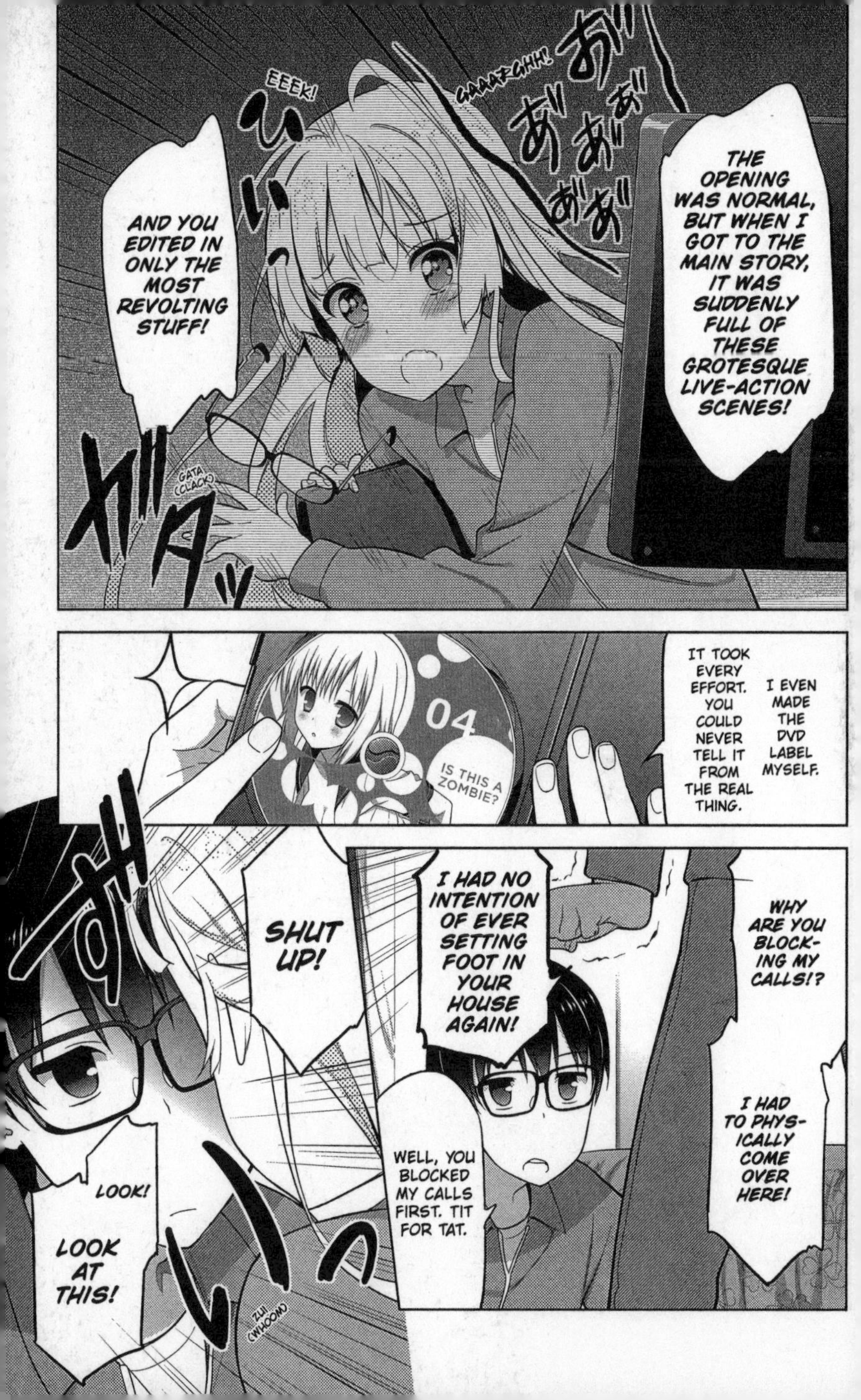
GAAARGHH!
THE OPENING WAS NORMAL, BUT WHEN I GOT TO THE MAIN STORY, IT WAS SUDDENLY FULL OF THESE GROTESQUE LIVE-ACTION SCENES!
EEEK!
AND YOU EDITED IN ONLY THE MOST REVOLTING STUFF!
GATA (CLACK)
IT TOOK EVERY EFFORT. YOU COULD NEVER TELL IT FROM THE REAL THING.
I EVEN MADE THE DVD LABEL MYSELF.
04
IS THIS A ZOMBIE?
WHY ARE YOU BLOCKING MY CALLS!?
I HAD TO PHYSICALLY COME OVER HERE!
I HAD NO INTENTION OF EVER SETTING FOOT IN YOUR HOUSE AGAIN!
WELL, YOU BLOCKED MY CALLS FIRST. TIT FOR TAT.
SHUT UP!
LOOK!
LOOK AT THIS!
ZUI (WHOOM)

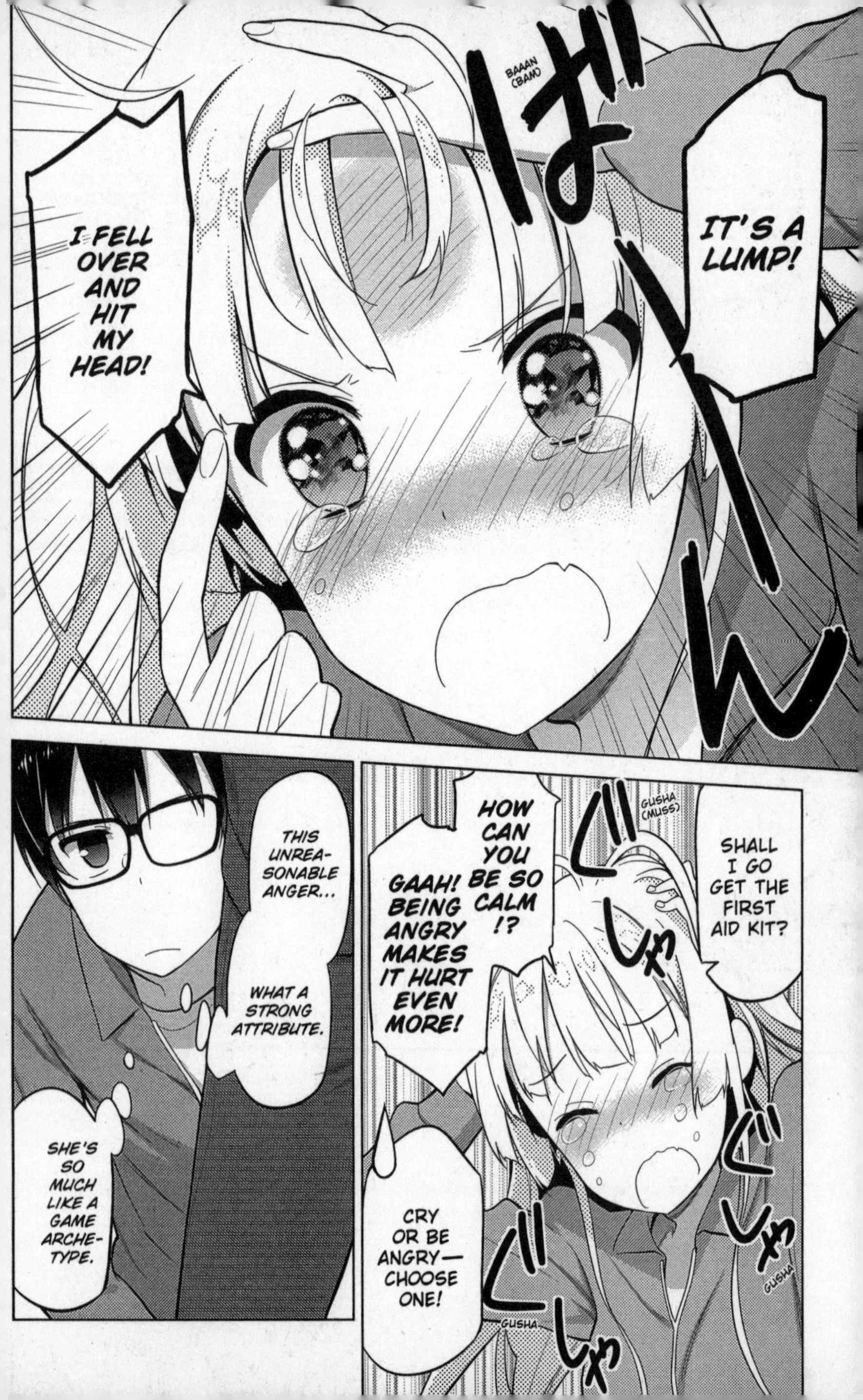
ばーん
BAAAN (BAM)
IT'S A LUMP!
I FELL OVER AND HIT MY HEAD!
SHALL I GO GET THE FIRST AID KIT?
ぐしゃ
GUSHA (MUSS)
HOW CAN YOU BE SO CALM!?
GAAH! BEING ANGRY MAKES IT HURT EVEN MORE!
ぐしゃ
GUSHA
ぐしゃ
GUSHA
CRY OR BE ANGRY—CHOOSE ONE!
THIS UNREA-SONABLE ANGER...
WHAT A STRONG ATTRIBUTE.
SHE'S SO MUCH LIKE A GAME ARCHE-TYPE.

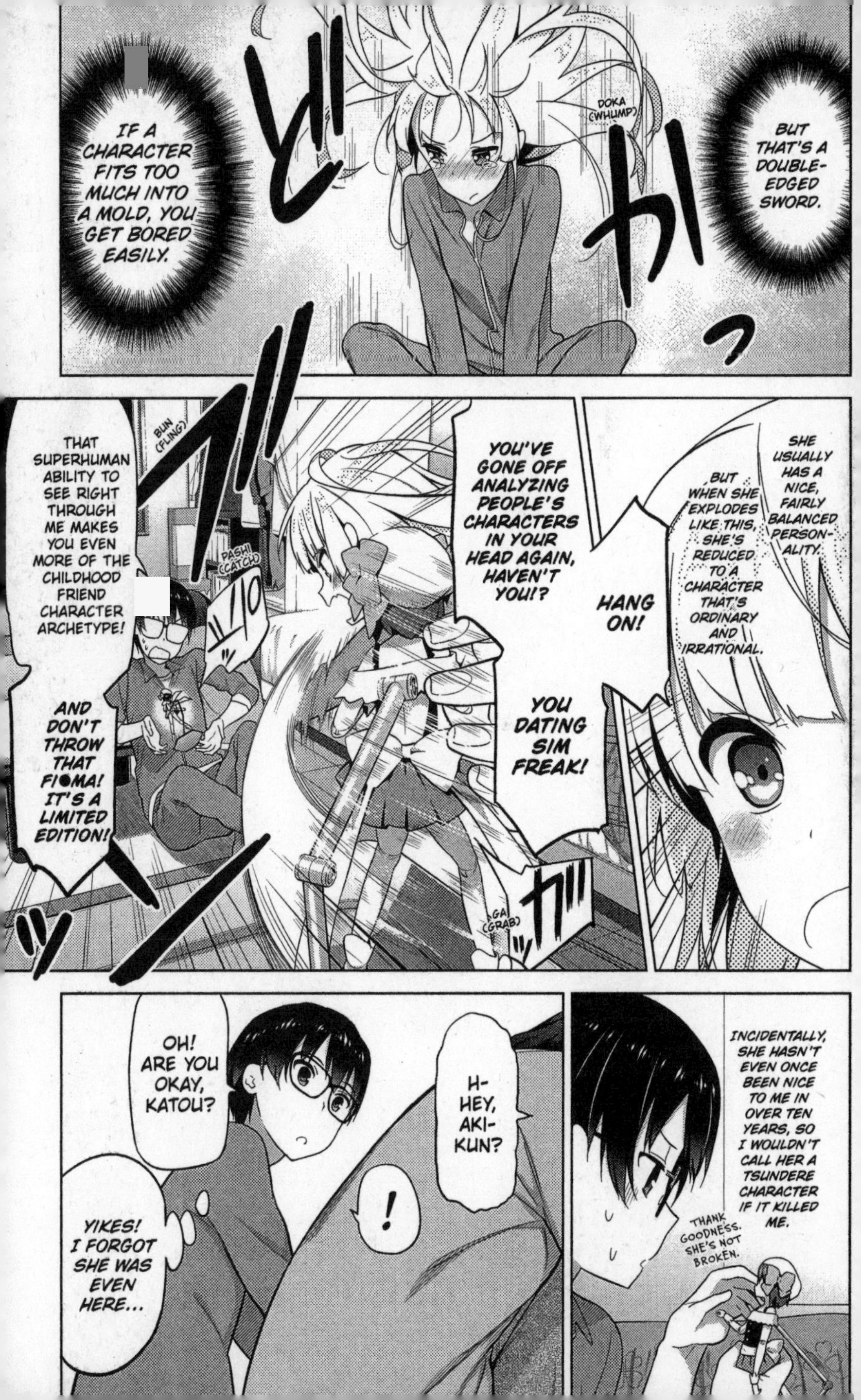

BUT THAT'S A DOUBLE-EDGED SWORD.
DOKA (WHUMP)
IF A CHARACTER FITS TOO MUCH INTO A MOLD, YOU GET BORED EASILY.
SHE USUALLY HAS A NICE, FAIRLY BALANCED PERSONALITY.
BUT WHEN SHE EXPLODES LIKE THIS, SHE'S REDUCED TO A CHARACTER THAT'S ORDINARY AND IRRATIONAL.
HANG ON!
YOU'VE GONE OFF ANALYZING PEOPLE'S CHARACTERS IN YOUR HEAD AGAIN, HAVEN'T YOU!?
YOU DATING SIM FREAK!
BUN (FLING)
PASHI (CATCH)
THAT SUPERHUMAN ABILITY TO SEE RIGHT THROUGH ME MAKES YOU EVEN MORE OF THE CHILDHOOD FRIEND CHARACTER ARCHETYPE!
AND DON'T THROW THAT FI●MA! IT'S A LIMITED EDITION!
GA (GRAB)
INCIDENTALLY, SHE HASN'T EVEN ONCE BEEN NICE TO ME IN OVER TEN YEARS, SO I WOULDN'T CALL HER A TSUNDERE CHARACTER IF IT KILLED ME.
THANK GOODNESS. SHE'S NOT BROKEN.
H-HEY, AKI-KUN?
OH! ARE YOU OKAY, KATOU?
!
YIKES! I FORGOT SHE WAS EVEN HERE...

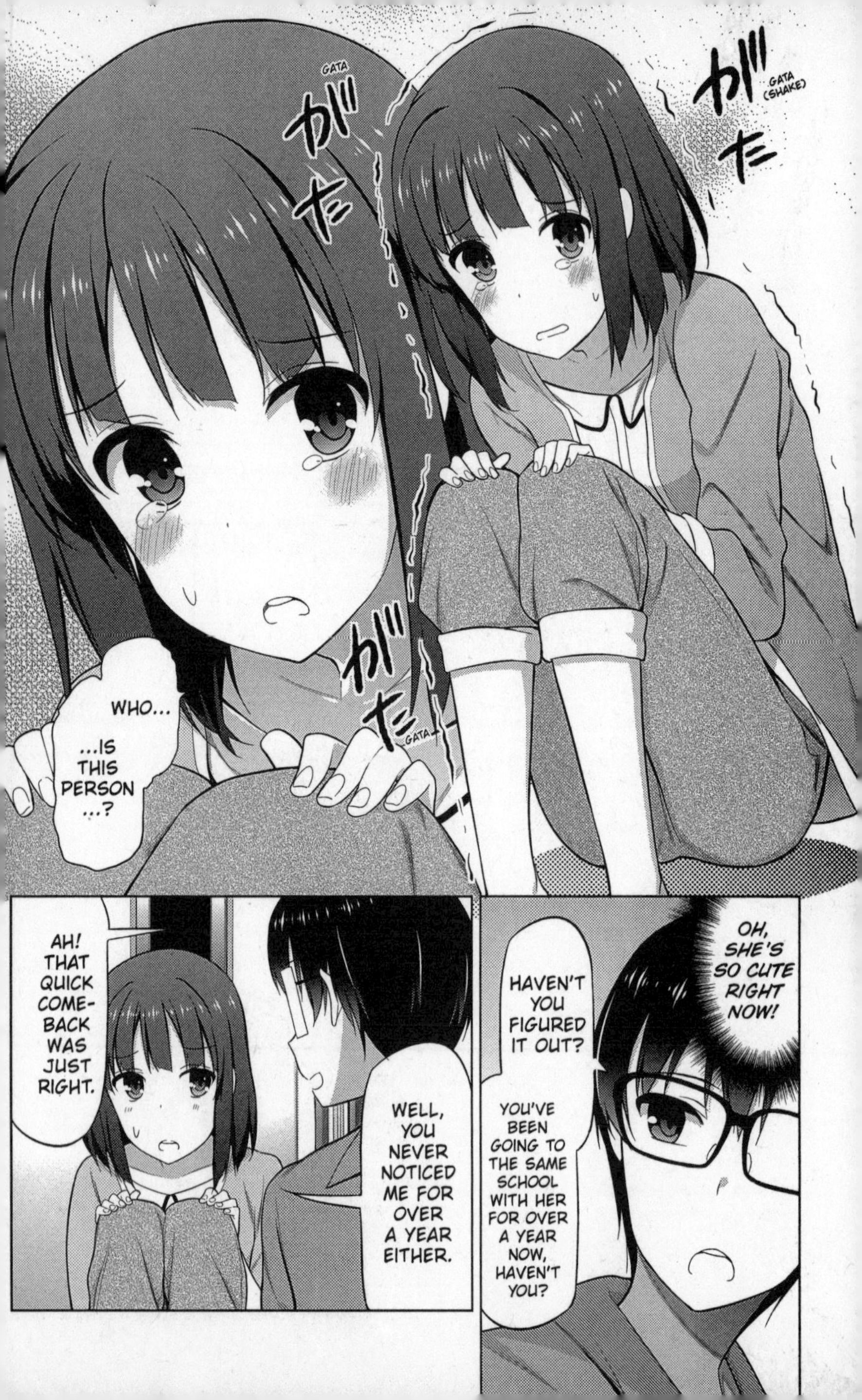

ガ GATA (SHAKE) た
ガ GATA た
ガ た GATA
WHO...
...IS THIS PERSON ...?
OH, SHE'S SO CUTE RIGHT NOW!
HAVEN'T YOU FIGURED IT OUT?
YOU'VE BEEN GOING TO THE SAME SCHOOL WITH HER FOR OVER A YEAR NOW, HAVEN'T YOU?
AH! THAT QUICK COME-BACK WAS JUST RIGHT.
WELL, YOU NEVER NOTICED ME FOR OVER A YEAR EITHER.

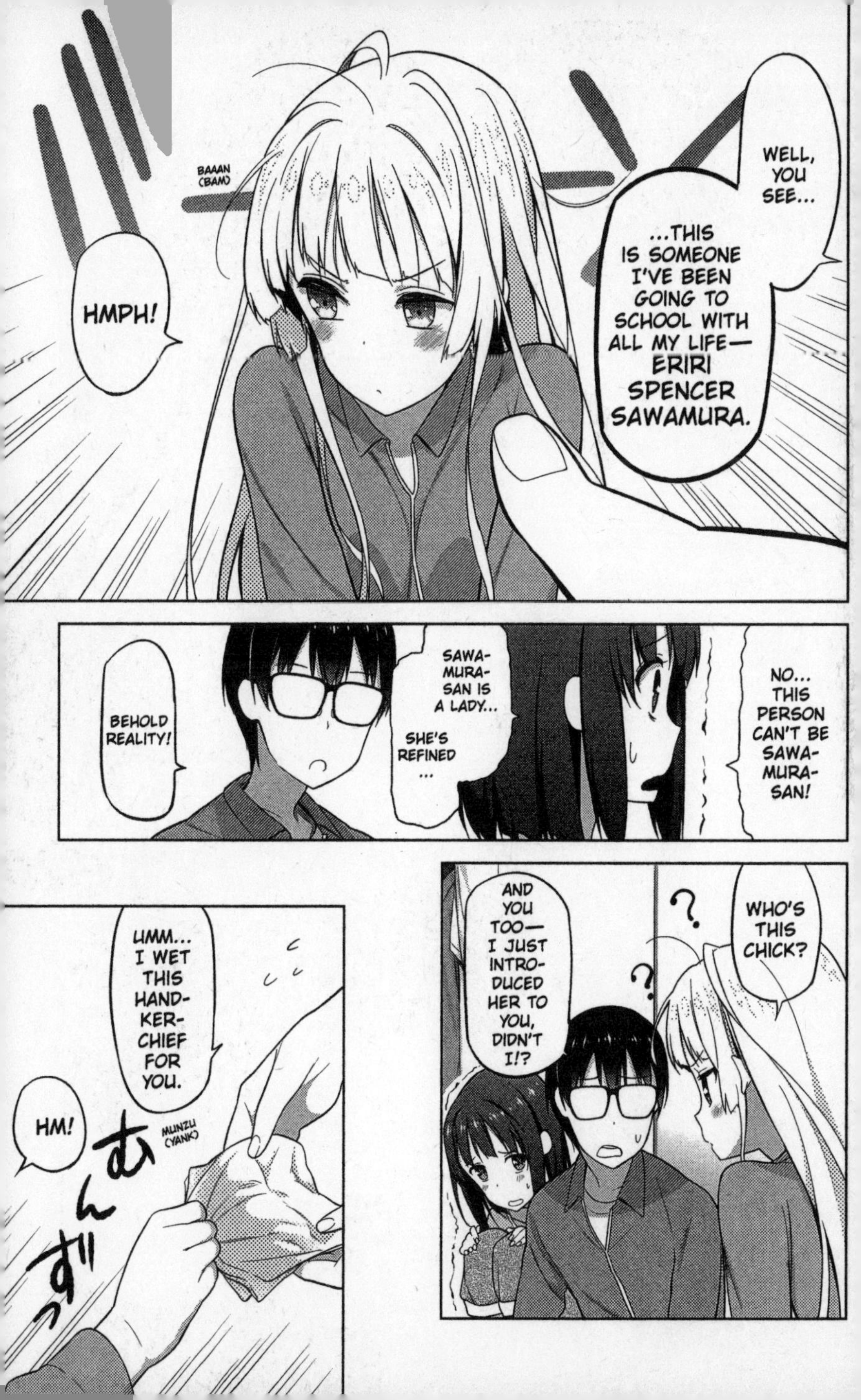
WELL, YOU SEE...
...THIS IS SOMEONE I'VE BEEN GOING TO SCHOOL WITH ALL MY LIFE—ERIRI SPENCER SAWAMURA.
BAAAN (BAM)
HMPH!
NO... THIS PERSON CAN'T BE SAWAMURA-SAN!
SAWAMURA-SAN IS A LADY...
SHE'S REFINED ...
BEHOLD REALITY!
WHO'S THIS CHICK?
AND YOU TOO—I JUST INTRODUCED HER TO YOU, DIDN'T I!?
UMM... I WET THIS HANDKERCHIEF FOR YOU.
MUNZU (YANK)
むんずっ
HM!

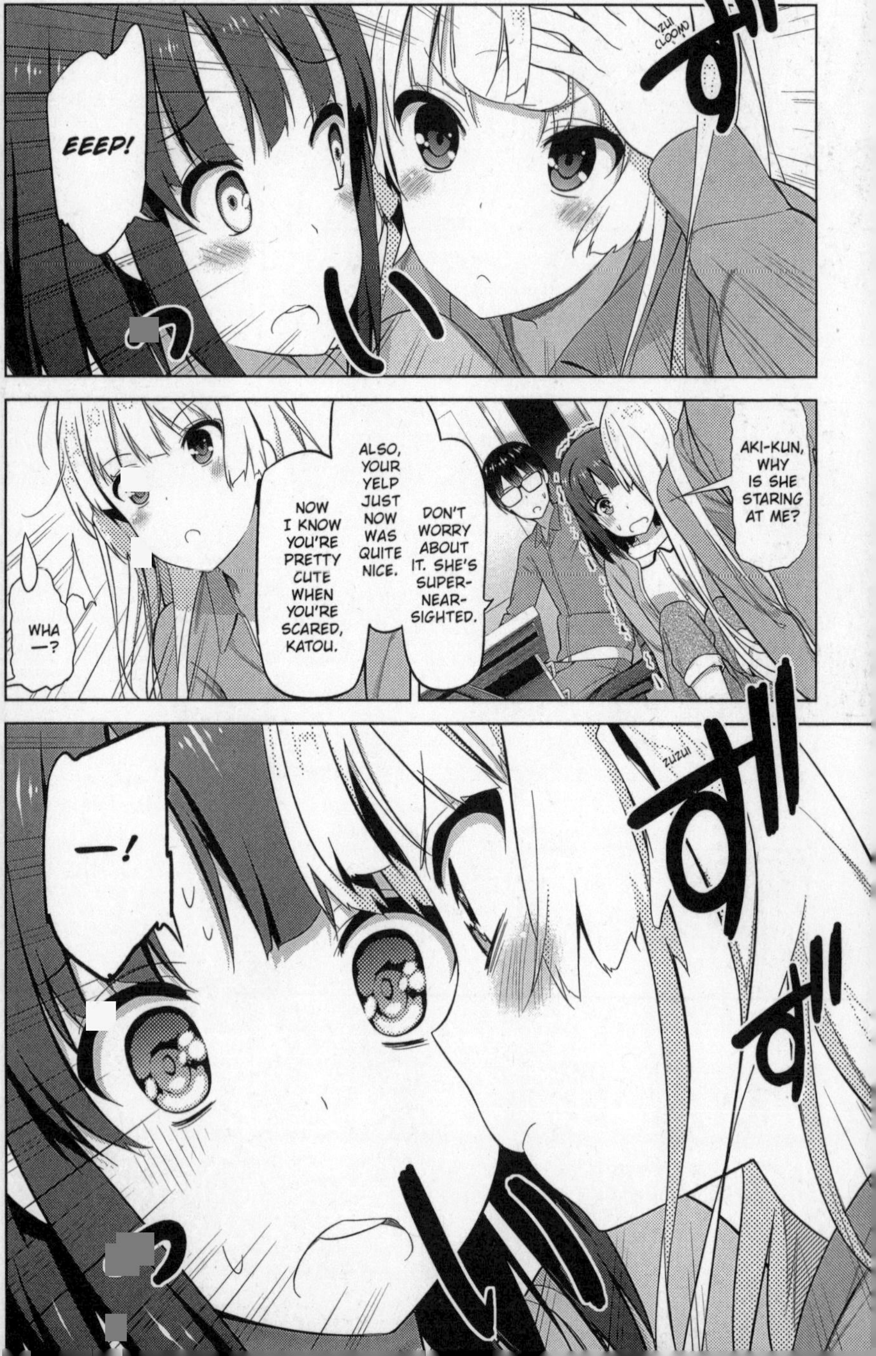
ZUI (LOOM)
EEEP!
AKI-KUN, WHY IS SHE STARING AT ME?
DON'T WORRY ABOUT IT. SHE'S SUPER-NEARSIGHTED.
ALSO, YOUR YELP JUST NOW WAS QUITE NICE.
NOW I KNOW YOU'RE PRETTY CUTE WHEN YOU'RE SCARED, KATOU.
WHA—?
ZUZUI
—!

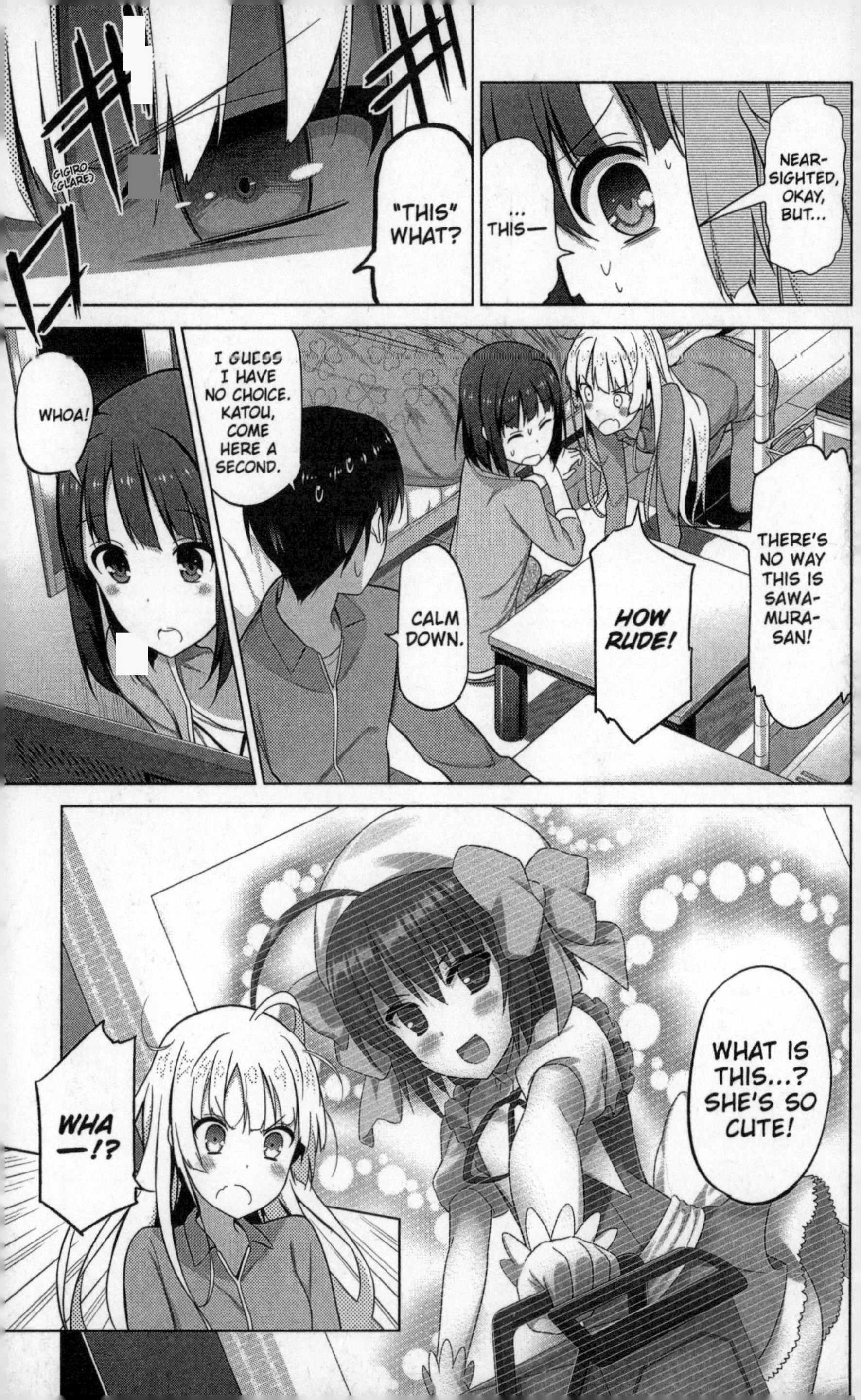
NEAR-SIGHTED, OKAY, BUT...
... THIS—
"THIS" WHAT?
GIGIRO (GLARE)
THERE'S NO WAY THIS IS SAWAMURA-SAN!
HOW RUDE!
CALM DOWN.
I GUESS I HAVE NO CHOICE. KATOU, COME HERE A SECOND.
WHOA!
WHAT IS THIS...? SHE'S SO CUTE!
WHA—!?

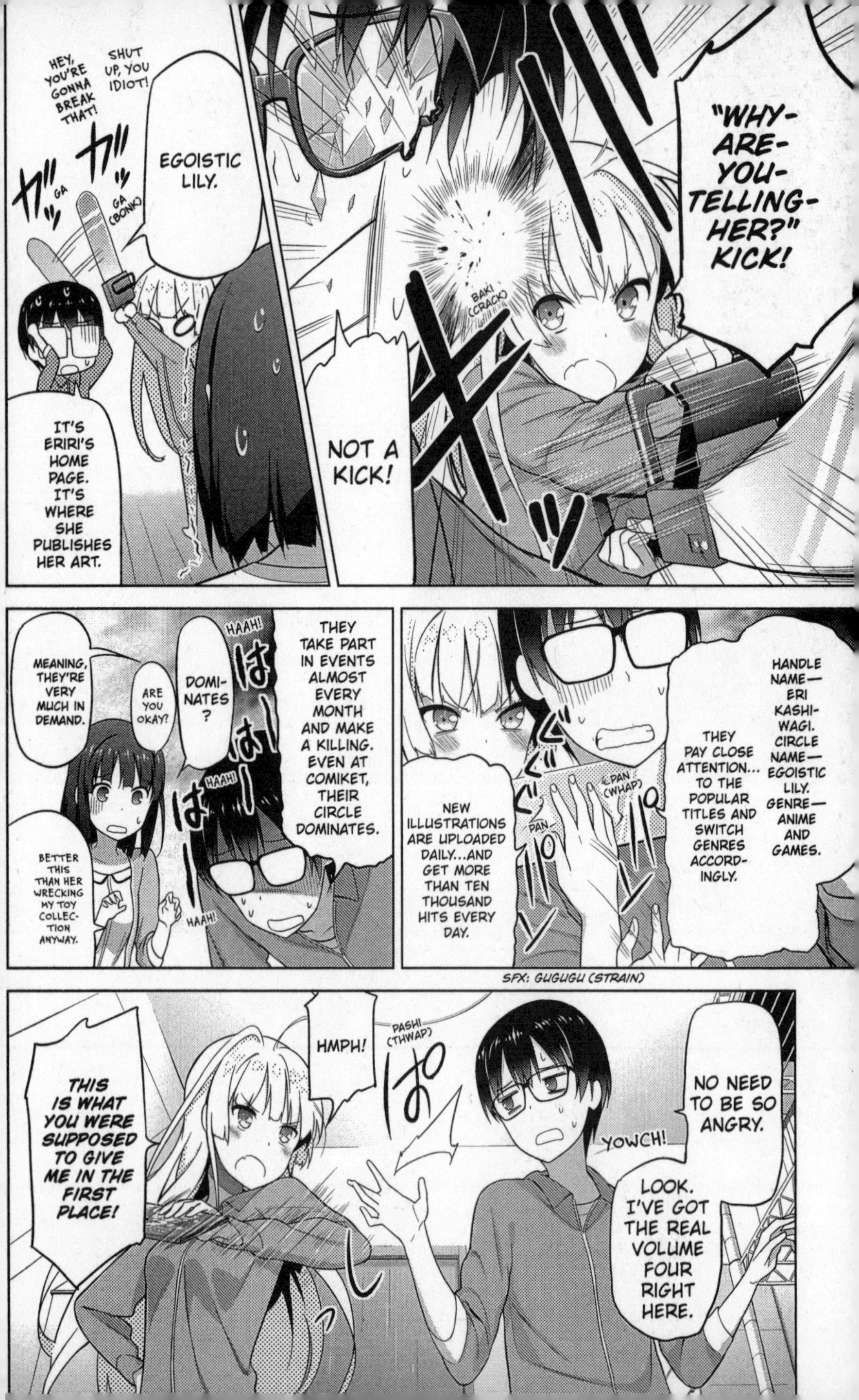
"WHY-ARE-YOU-TELLING-HER?" KICK!
BAKI (CRACK)
SHUT UP, YOU IDIOT!
HEY, YOU'RE GONNA BREAK THAT!
EGOISTIC LILY.
GA (BONK)
GA
NOT A KICK!
IT'S ERIRI'S HOME PAGE. IT'S WHERE SHE PUBLISHES HER ART.
HANDLE NAME—ERI KASHIWAGI. CIRCLE NAME—EGOISTIC LILY. GENRE—ANIME AND GAMES.
THEY PAY CLOSE ATTENTION... TO THE POPULAR TITLES AND SWITCH GENRES ACCORDINGLY.
PAN (WHAP)
PAN
NEW ILLUSTRATIONS ARE UPLOADED DAILY...AND GET MORE THAN TEN THOUSAND HITS EVERY DAY.
SFX: GUGUGU (STRAIN)
THEY TAKE PART IN EVENTS ALMOST EVERY MONTH AND MAKE A KILLING. EVEN AT COMIKET, THEIR CIRCLE DOMINATES.
HAAH!
DOMINATES?
ARE YOU OKAY?
MEANING, THEY'RE VERY MUCH IN DEMAND.
HAAH!
HAAH!
BETTER THIS THAN HER WRECKING MY TOY COLLECTION ANYWAY.
NO NEED TO BE SO ANGRY.
PASHI (THWAP)
HMPH!
YOWCH!
LOOK. I'VE GOT THE REAL VOLUME FOUR RIGHT HERE.
THIS IS WHAT YOU WERE SUPPOSED TO GIVE ME IN THE FIRST PLACE!

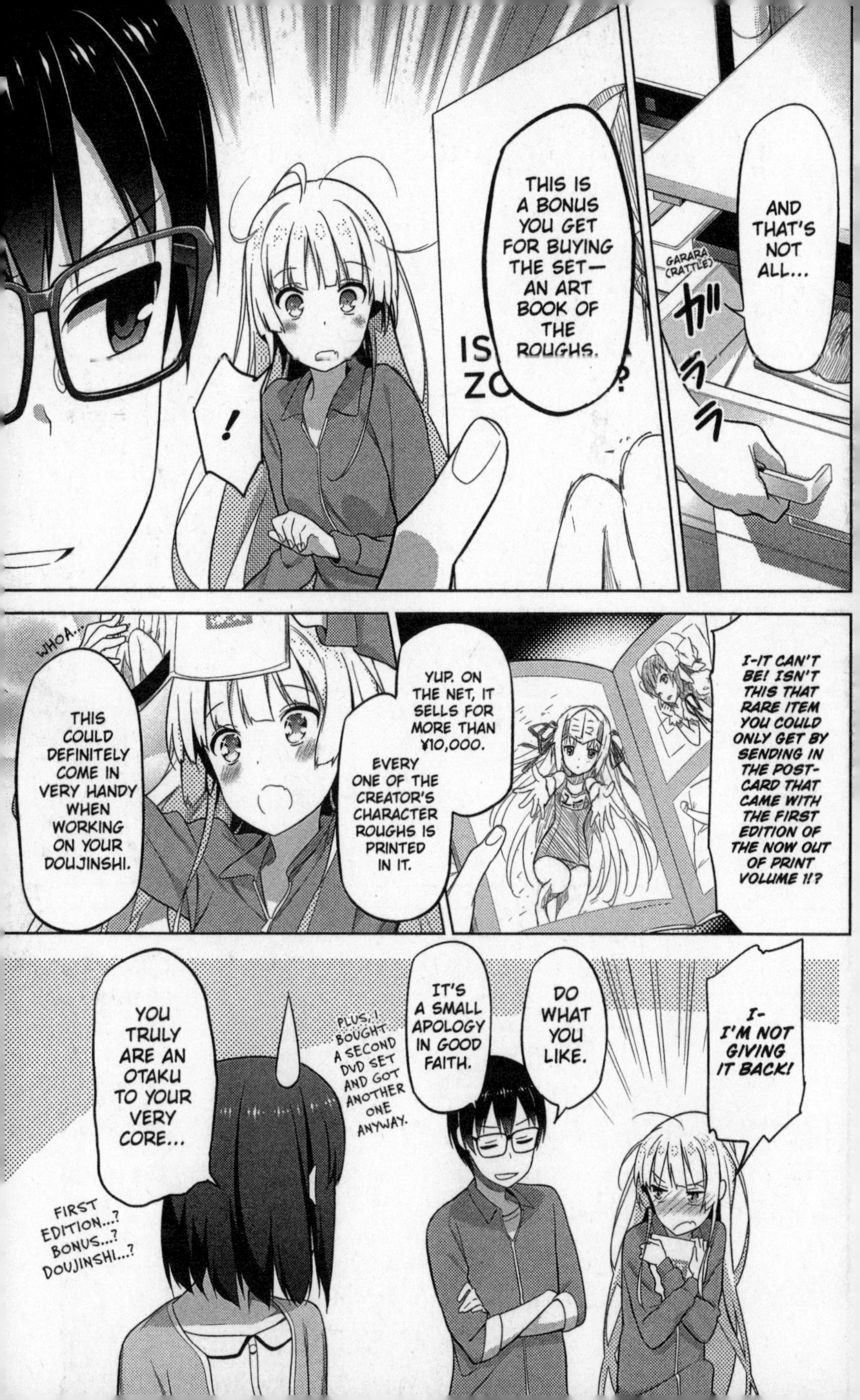
AND THAT'S NOT ALL...
GARARA (RATTLE)
THIS IS A BONUS YOU GET FOR BUYING THE SET—AN ART BOOK OF THE ROUGHS.
!
I-IT CAN'T BE! ISN'T THIS THAT RARE ITEM YOU COULD ONLY GET BY SENDING IN THE POST-CARD THAT CAME WITH THE FIRST EDITION OF THE NOW OUT OF PRINT VOLUME 1!?
YUP. ON THE NET, IT SELLS FOR MORE THAN ¥10,000.
EVERY ONE OF THE CREATOR'S CHARACTER ROUGHS IS PRINTED IN IT.
WHOA...
THIS COULD DEFINITELY COME IN VERY HANDY WHEN WORKING ON YOUR DOUJINSHI.
I- I'M NOT GIVING IT BACK!
DO WHAT YOU LIKE.
IT'S A SMALL APOLOGY IN GOOD FAITH.
PLUS, I BOUGHT A SECOND DVD SET AND GOT ANOTHER ONE ANYWAY.
YOU TRULY ARE AN OTAKU TO YOUR VERY CORE...
FIRST EDITION...? BONUS...? DOUJINSHI...?

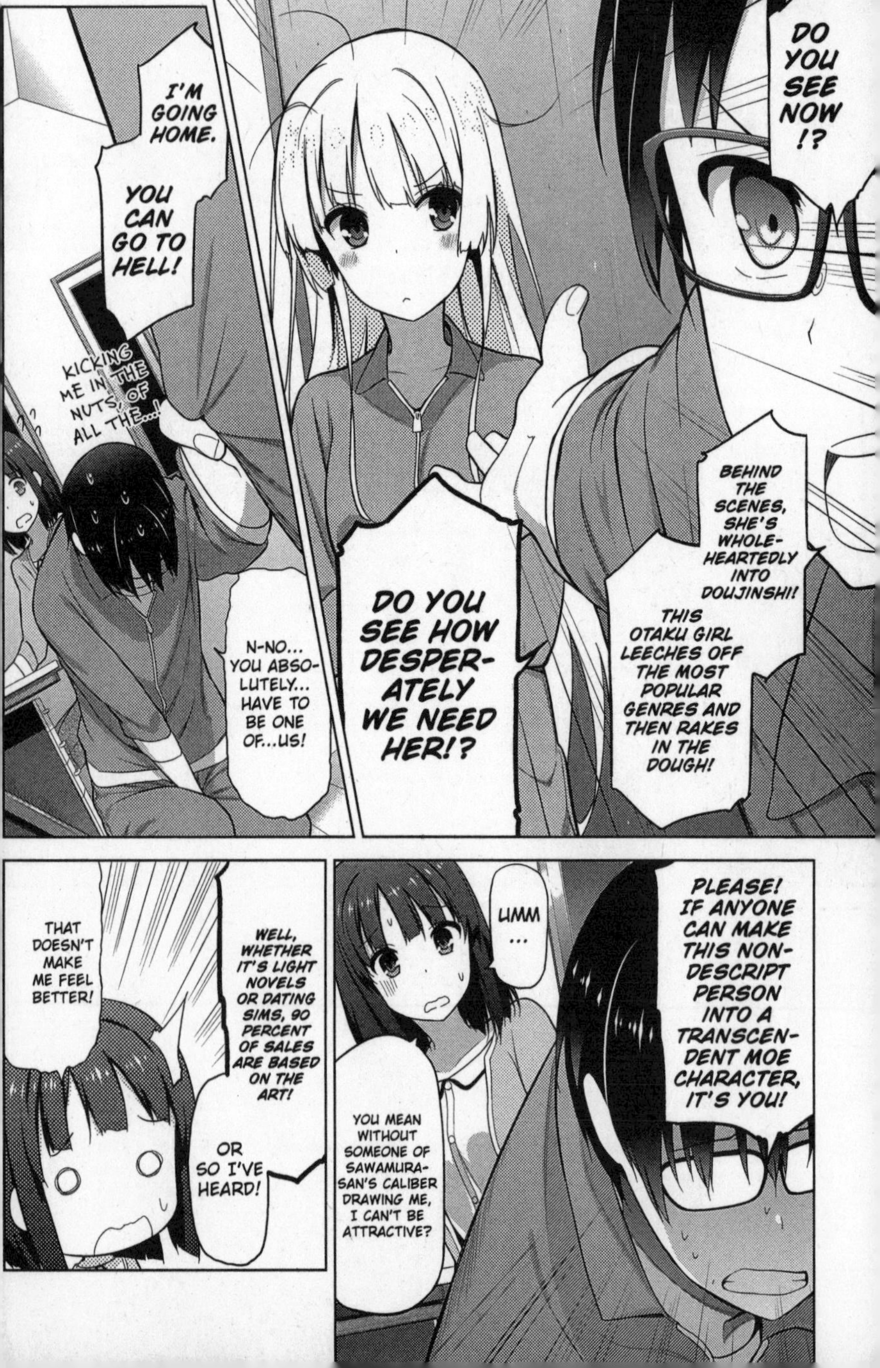
DO YOU SEE NOW!?
BEHIND THE SCENES, SHE'S WHOLE-HEARTEDLY INTO DOUJINSHI!
THIS OTAKU GIRL LEECHES OFF THE MOST POPULAR GENRES AND THEN RAKES IN THE DOUGH!
DO YOU SEE HOW DESPER-ATELY WE NEED HER!?
N-NO... YOU ABSO-LUTELY... HAVE TO BE ONE OF...US!
I'M GOING HOME.
YOU CAN GO TO HELL!
KICKING ME IN THE NUTS, OF ALL THE...!
PLEASE! IF ANYONE CAN MAKE THIS NON-DESCRIPT PERSON INTO A TRANSCEN-DENT MOE CHARACTER, IT'S YOU!
UMM...
YOU MEAN WITHOUT SOMEONE OF SAWAMURA-SAN'S CALIBER DRAWING ME, I CAN'T BE ATTRACTIVE?
WELL, WHETHER IT'S LIGHT NOVELS OR DATING SIMS, 90 PERCENT OF SALES ARE BASED ON THE ART!
OR SO I'VE HEARD!
THAT DOESN'T MAKE ME FEEL BETTER!

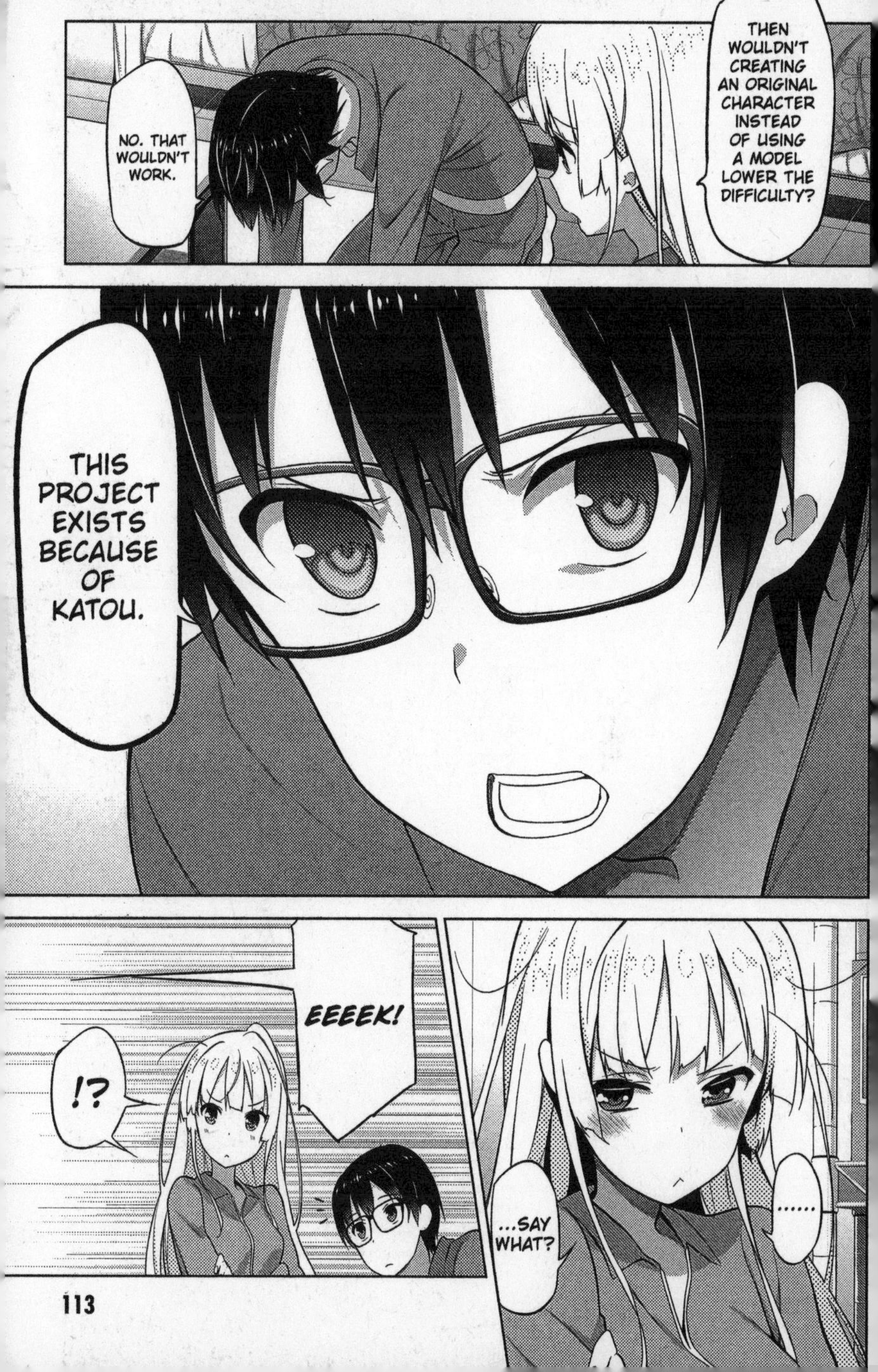
THEN WOULDN'T CREATING AN ORIGINAL CHARACTER INSTEAD OF USING A MODEL LOWER THE DIFFICULTY?
NO. THAT WOULDN'T WORK.
THIS PROJECT EXISTS BECAUSE OF KATOU.
......
...SAY WHAT?
EEEEK!
!?

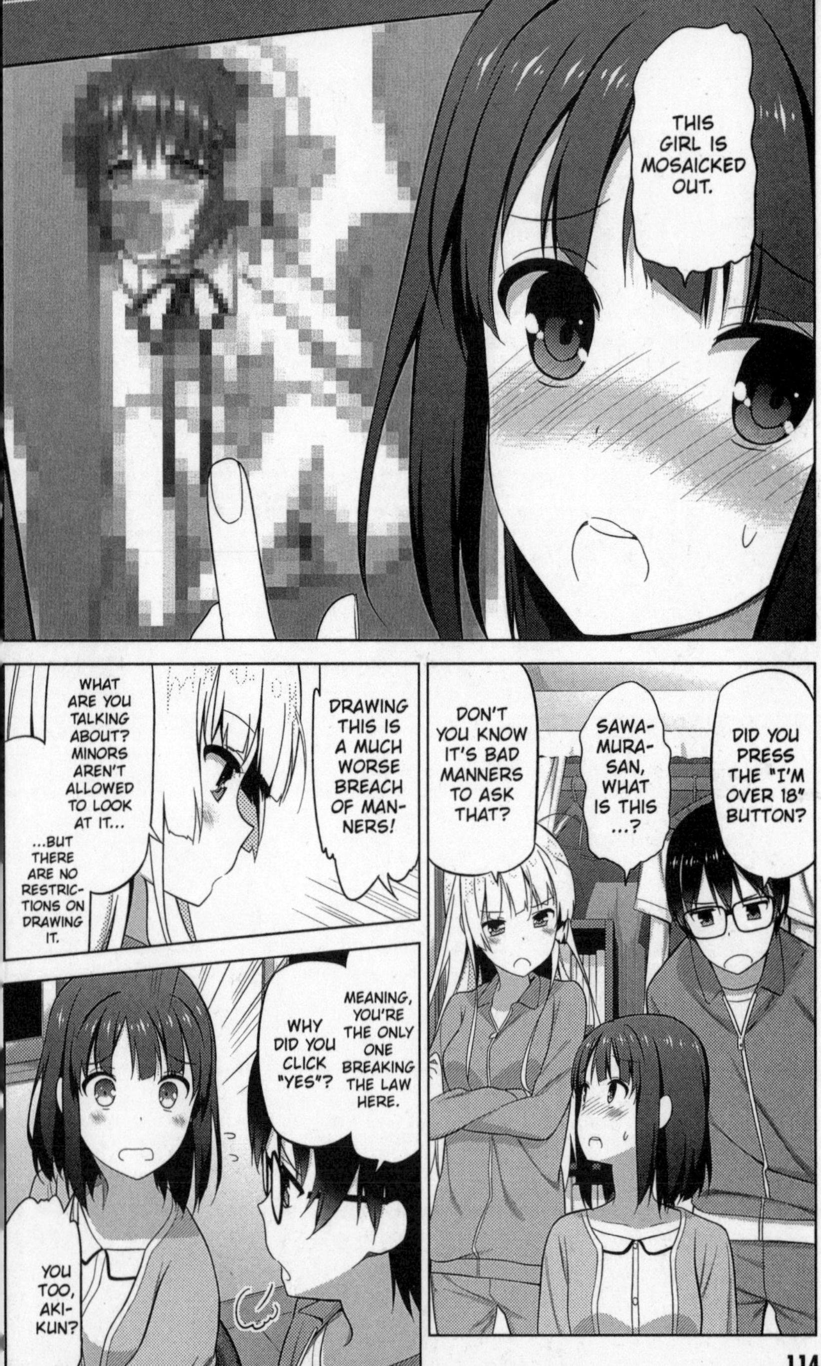
THIS GIRL IS MOSAICKED OUT.
DID YOU PRESS THE "I'M OVER 18" BUTTON?
SAWAMURA-SAN, WHAT IS THIS ...?
DON'T YOU KNOW IT'S BAD MANNERS TO ASK THAT?
DRAWING THIS IS A MUCH WORSE BREACH OF MAN-NERS!
WHAT ARE YOU TALKING ABOUT? MINORS AREN'T ALLOWED TO LOOK AT IT...
...BUT THERE ARE NO RESTRIC-TIONS ON DRAWING IT.
MEANING, YOU'RE THE ONLY ONE BREAKING THE LAW HERE.
WHY DID YOU CLICK "YES"?
YOU TOO, AKI-KUN?

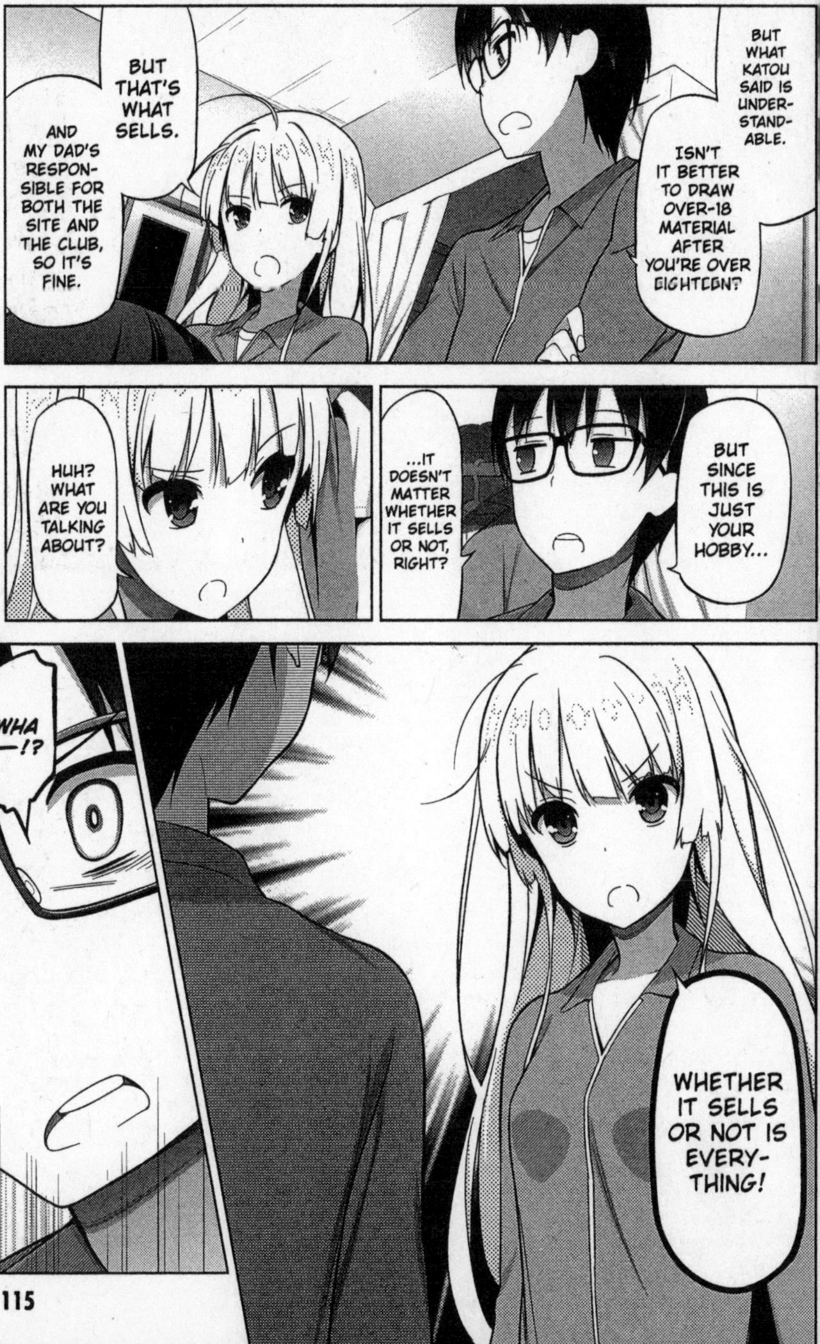
BUT WHAT KATOU SAID IS UNDER-STAND-ABLE.
ISN'T IT BETTER TO DRAW OVER-18 MATERIAL AFTER YOU'RE OVER EIGHTEEN?
BUT THAT'S WHAT SELLS.
AND MY DAD'S RESPON-SIBLE FOR BOTH THE SITE AND THE CLUB, SO IT'S FINE.
BUT SINCE THIS IS JUST YOUR HOBBY...
...IT DOESN'T MATTER WHETHER IT SELLS OR NOT, RIGHT?
HUH? WHAT ARE YOU TALKING ABOUT?
WHETHER IT SELLS OR NOT IS EVERY-THING!
WHA—!?

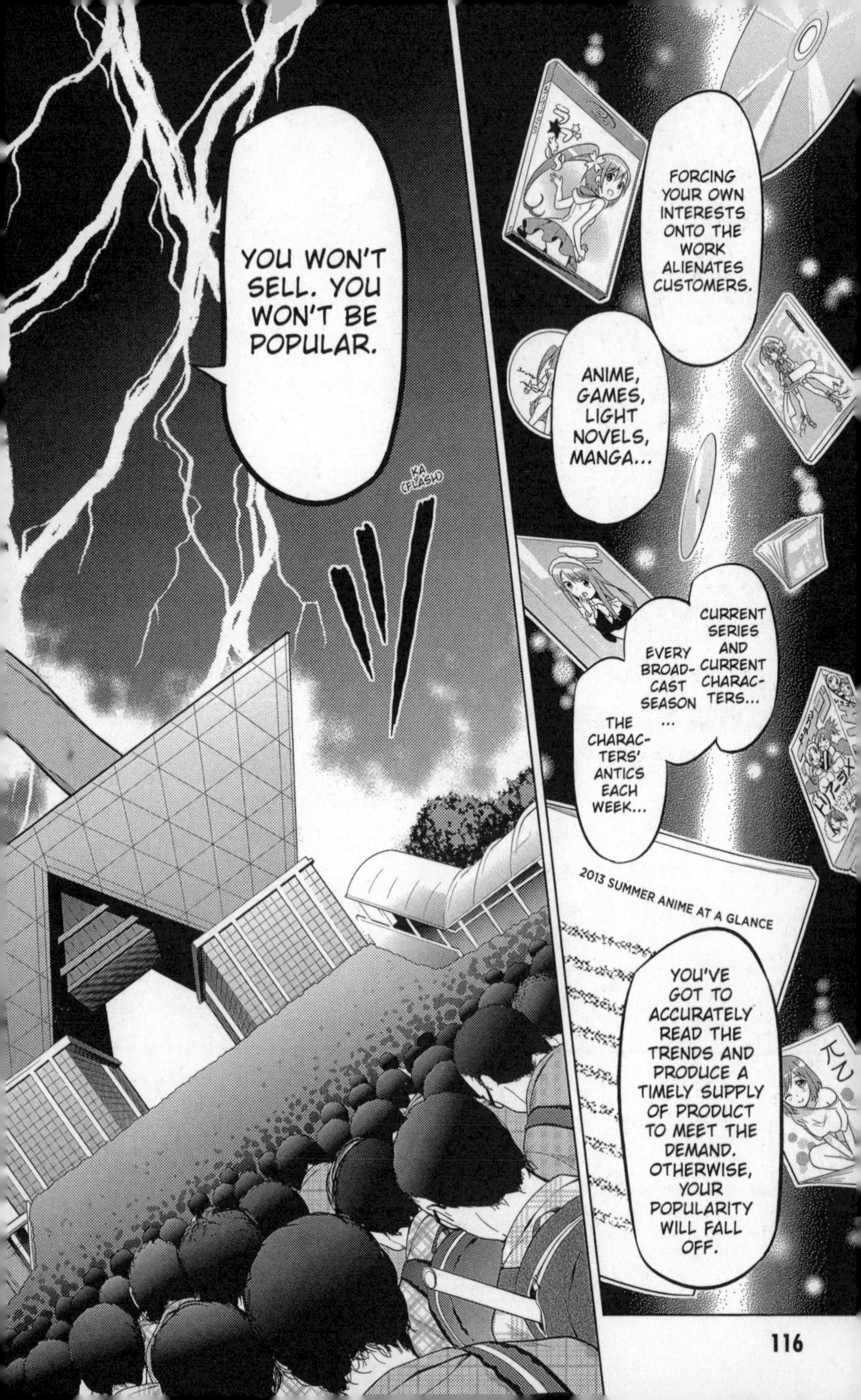
FORCING YOUR OWN INTERESTS ONTO THE WORK ALIENATES CUSTOMERS.
ANIME, GAMES, LIGHT NOVELS, MANGA...
CURRENT SERIES AND CURRENT CHARACTERS...
EVERY BROADCAST SEASON...
THE CHARACTERS' ANTICS EACH WEEK...
2013 SUMMER ANIME AT A GLANCE
YOU'VE GOT TO ACCURATELY READ THE TRENDS AND PRODUCE A TIMELY SUPPLY OF PRODUCT TO MEET THE DEMAND. OTHERWISE, YOUR POPULARITY WILL FALL OFF.
YOU WON'T SELL. YOU WON'T BE POPULAR.
KA (FLASH)

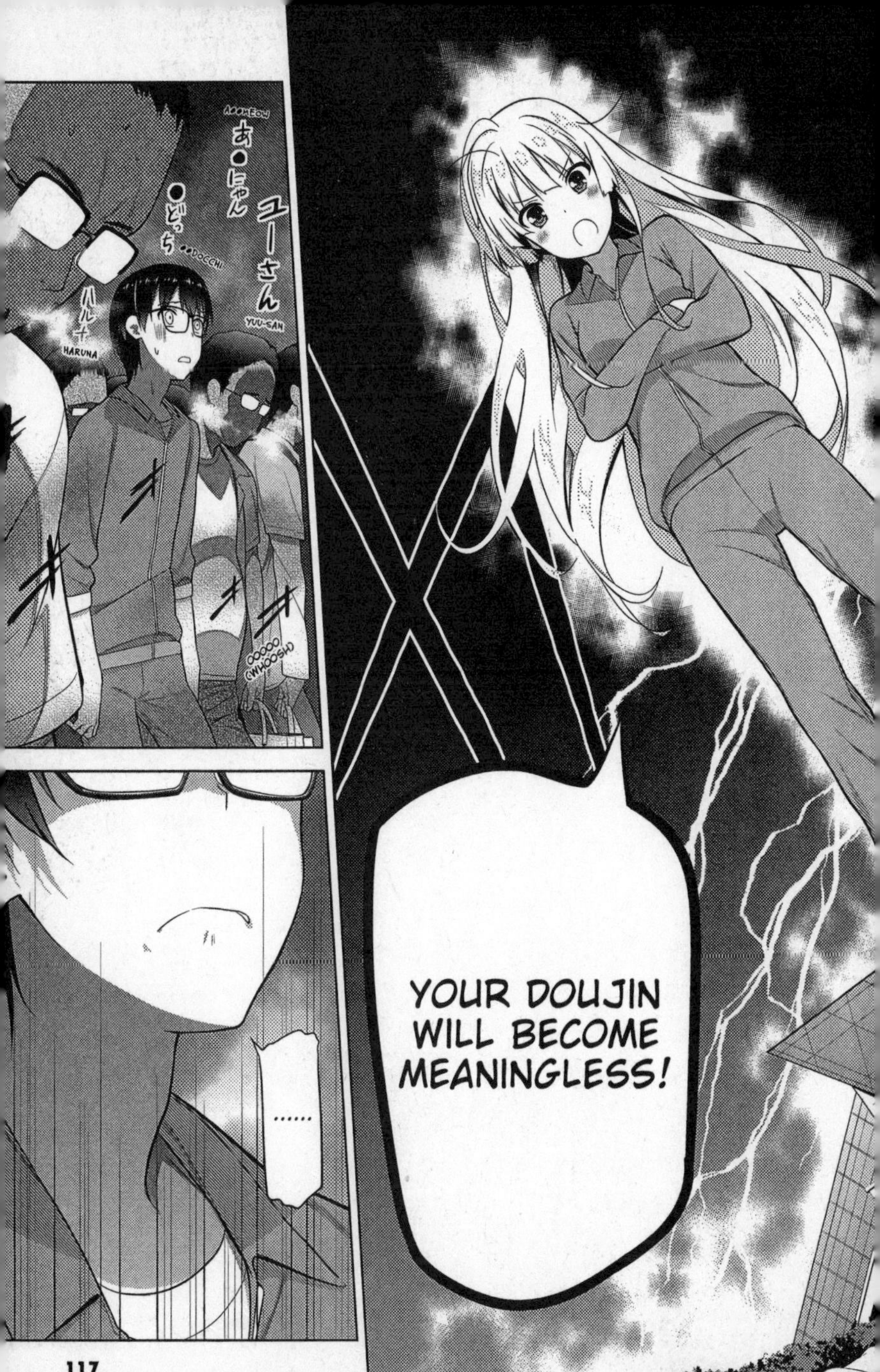
YOUR DOUJIN WILL BECOME MEANINGLESS!
ユーさん
YUU-SAN
あ●にゃん
A●●MEOW
●どっち
●●DOCCHI
ハルナ
HARUNA
OOOOO (WHOOSH)
......

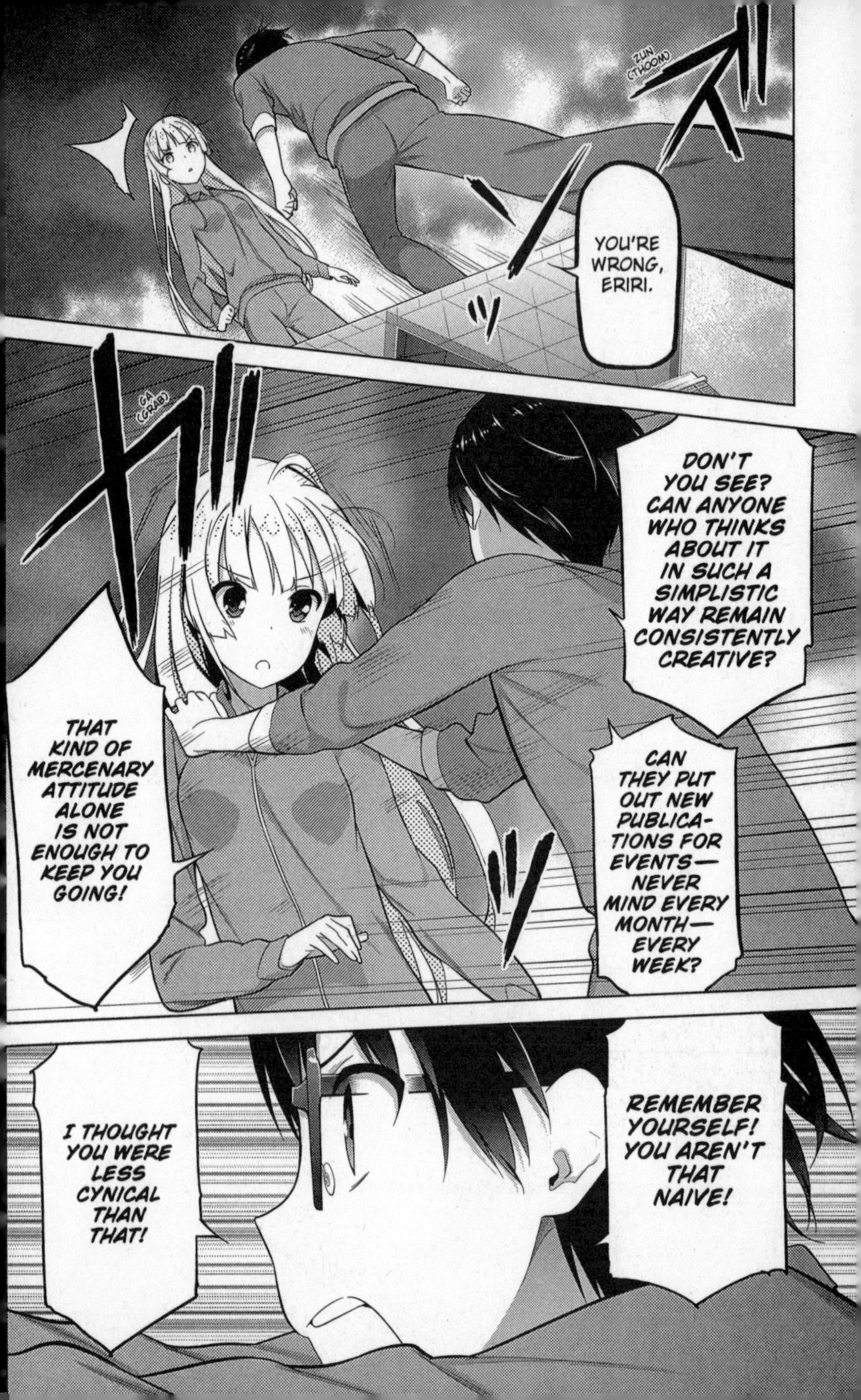
ZUN (THOOM)
YOU'RE WRONG, ERIRI.
GA (GRAB)
DON'T YOU SEE? CAN ANYONE WHO THINKS ABOUT IT IN SUCH A SIMPLISTIC WAY REMAIN CONSISTENTLY CREATIVE?
CAN THEY PUT OUT NEW PUBLICATIONS FOR EVENTS—NEVER MIND EVERY MONTH—EVERY WEEK?
THAT KIND OF MERCENARY ATTITUDE ALONE IS NOT ENOUGH TO KEEP YOU GOING!
REMEMBER YOURSELF! YOU AREN'T THAT NAIVE!
I THOUGHT YOU WERE LESS CYNICAL THAN THAT!

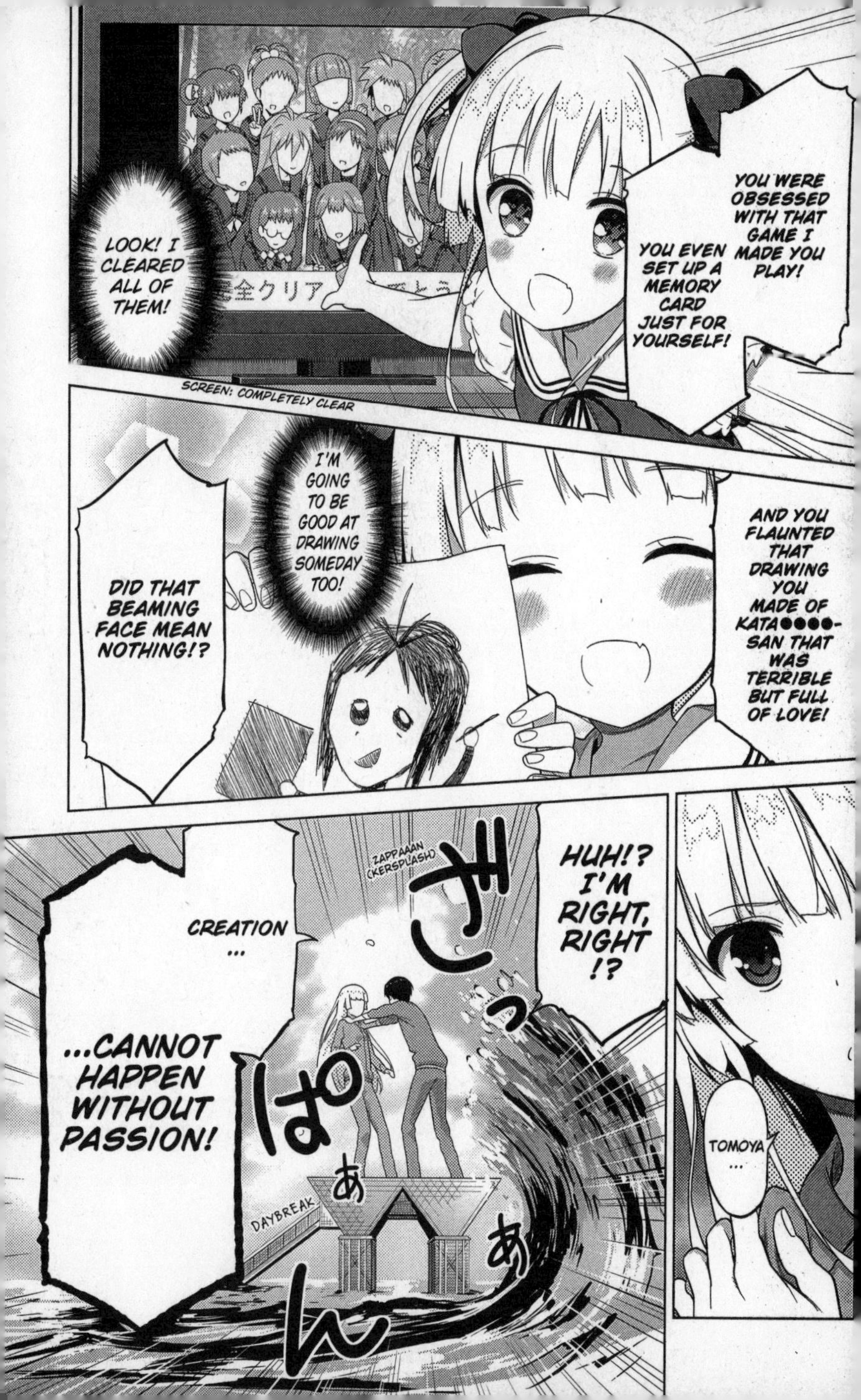
YOU WERE OBSESSED WITH THAT GAME I MADE YOU PLAY!
YOU EVEN SET UP A MEMORY CARD JUST FOR YOURSELF!
LOOK! I CLEARED ALL OF THEM!
完全クリア
SCREEN: COMPLETELY CLEAR
AND YOU FLAUNTED THAT DRAWING YOU MADE OF KATA●●●●-SAN THAT WAS TERRIBLE BUT FULL OF LOVE!
I'M GOING TO BE GOOD AT DRAWING SOMEDAY TOO!
DID THAT BEAMING FACE MEAN NOTHING!?
TOMOYA...
HUH!? I'M RIGHT, RIGHT!?
ZAPPAAAN (KERSPLASH)
ざっぱああん
CREATION...
...CANNOT HAPPEN WITHOUT PASSION!
DAYBREAK

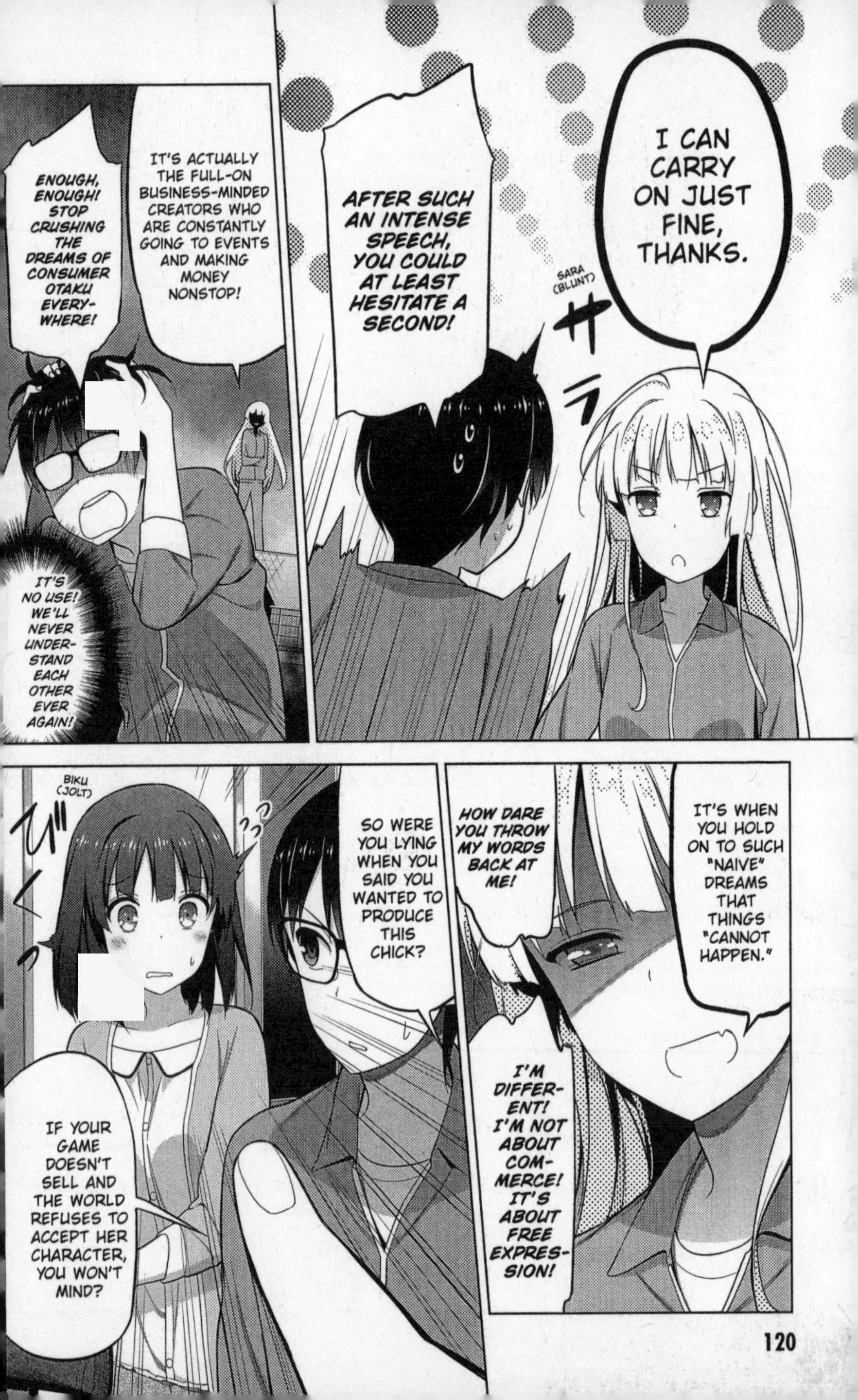
I CAN CARRY ON JUST FINE, THANKS.
SARA (BLUNT)
AFTER SUCH AN INTENSE SPEECH, YOU COULD AT LEAST HESITATE A SECOND!
IT'S ACTUALLY THE FULL-ON BUSINESS-MINDED CREATORS WHO ARE CONSTANTLY GOING TO EVENTS AND MAKING MONEY NONSTOP!
ENOUGH, ENOUGH! STOP CRUSHING THE DREAMS OF CONSUMER OTAKU EVERY-WHERE!
IT'S NO USE! WE'LL NEVER UNDER-STAND EACH OTHER EVER AGAIN!
IT'S WHEN YOU HOLD ON TO SUCH "NAIVE" DREAMS THAT THINGS "CANNOT HAPPEN."
HOW DARE YOU THROW MY WORDS BACK AT ME!
I'M DIFFER-ENT! I'M NOT ABOUT COM-MERCE! IT'S ABOUT FREE EXPRES-SION!
SO WERE YOU LYING WHEN YOU SAID YOU WANTED TO PRODUCE THIS CHICK?
BIKU (JOLT)
IF YOUR GAME DOESN'T SELL AND THE WORLD REFUSES TO ACCEPT HER CHARACTER, YOU WON'T MIND?

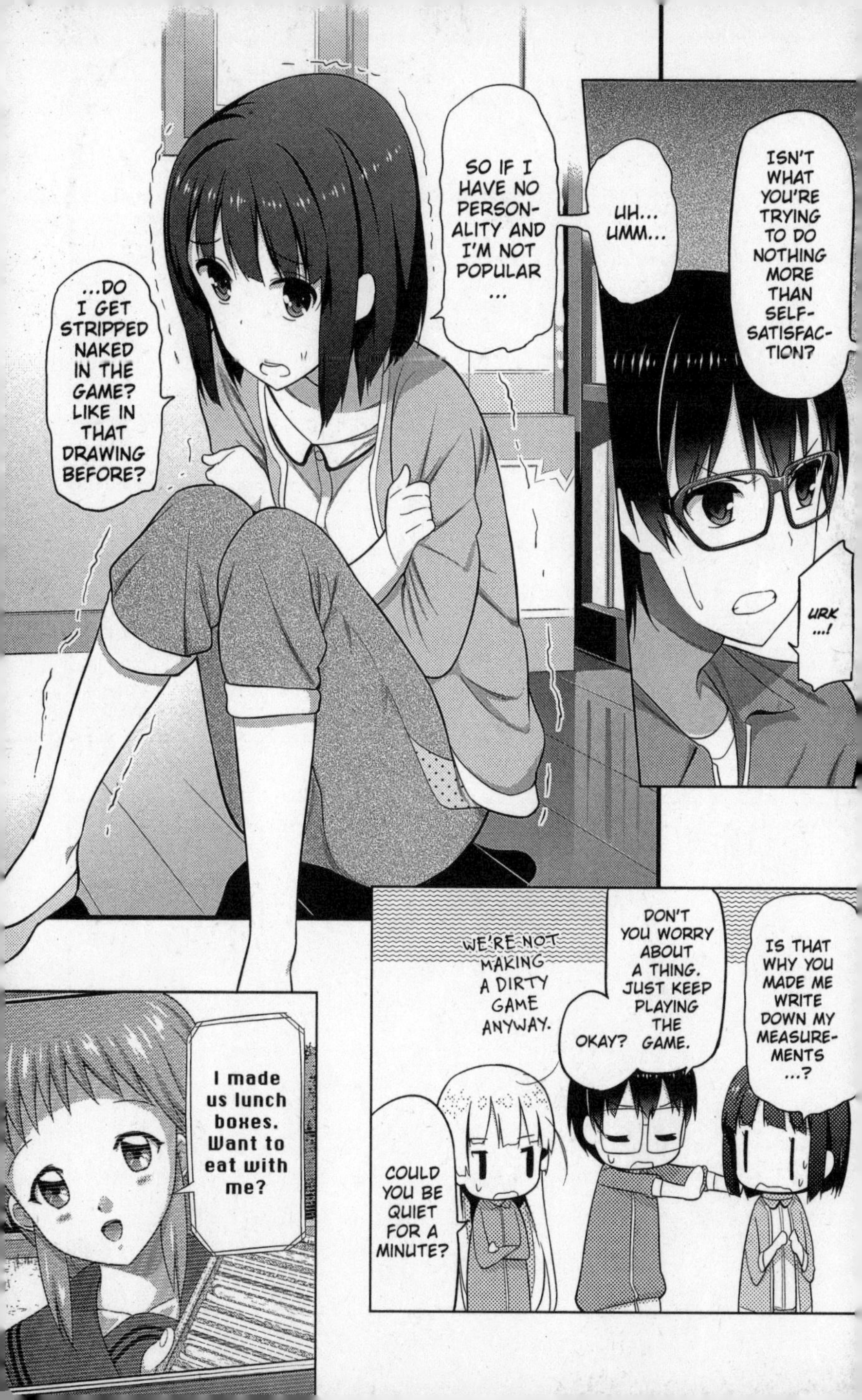
ISN'T WHAT YOU'RE TRYING TO DO NOTHING MORE THAN SELF-SATISFACTION?
URK ...!
UH... UMM...
SO IF I HAVE NO PERSON-ALITY AND I'M NOT POPULAR ...
...DO I GET STRIPPED NAKED IN THE GAME? LIKE IN THAT DRAWING BEFORE?
IS THAT WHY YOU MADE ME WRITE DOWN MY MEASURE-MENTS ...?
DON'T YOU WORRY ABOUT A THING. JUST KEEP PLAYING THE GAME.
OKAY?
WE'RE NOT MAKING A DIRTY GAME ANYWAY.
COULD YOU BE QUIET FOR A MINUTE?
I made us lunch boxes. Want to eat with me?

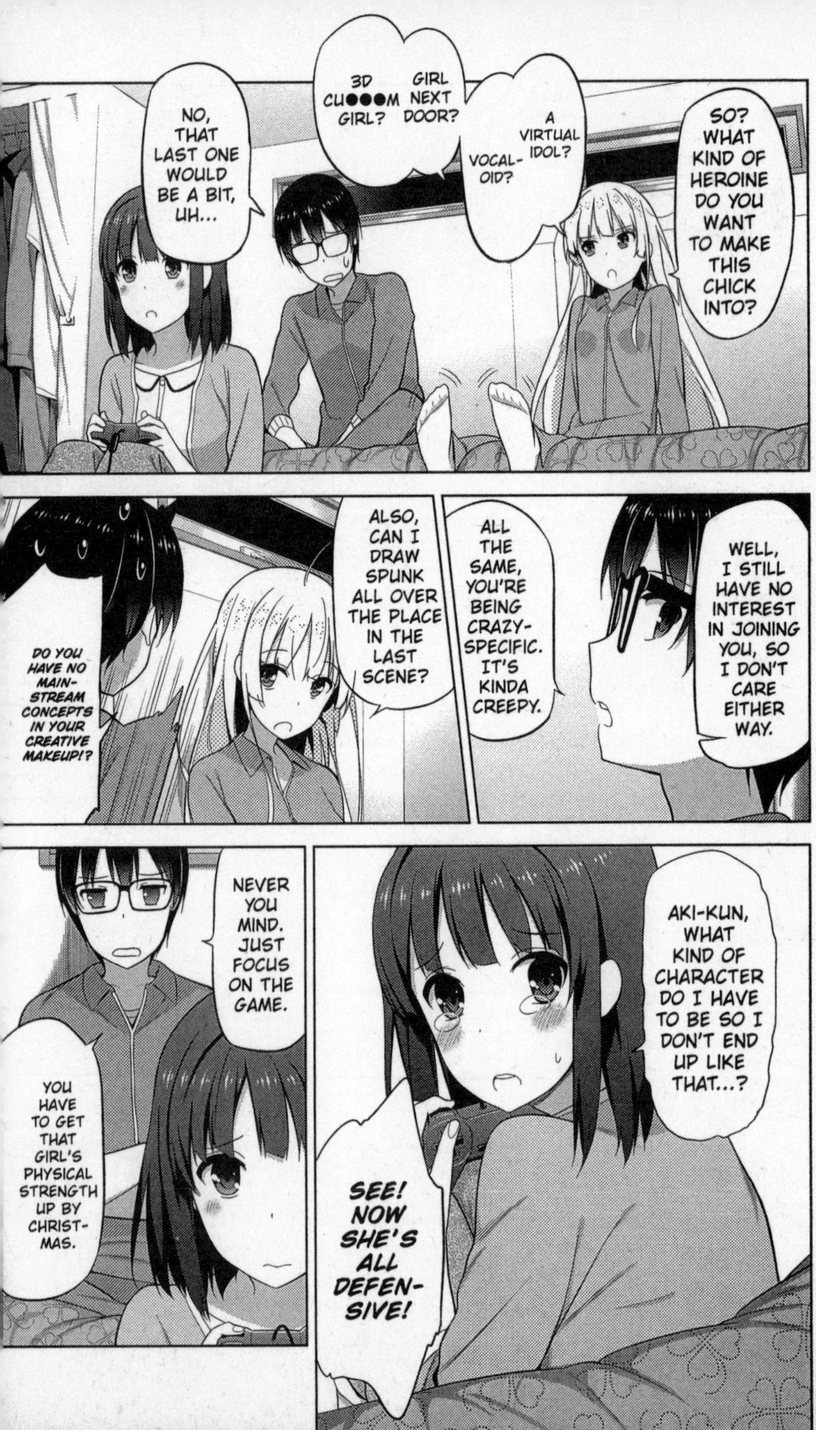
SO? WHAT KIND OF HEROINE DO YOU WANT TO MAKE THIS CHICK INTO?
A VIRTUAL IDOL?
VOCAL-OID?
GIRL NEXT DOOR?
3D CU●●●M GIRL?
NO, THAT LAST ONE WOULD BE A BIT, UH...
WELL, I STILL HAVE NO INTEREST IN JOINING YOU, SO I DON'T CARE EITHER WAY.
ALL THE SAME, YOU'RE BEING CRAZY-SPECIFIC. IT'S KINDA CREEPY.
ALSO, CAN I DRAW SPUNK ALL OVER THE PLACE IN THE LAST SCENE?
DO YOU HAVE NO MAIN-STREAM CONCEPTS IN YOUR CREATIVE MAKEUP!?
AKI-KUN, WHAT KIND OF CHARACTER DO I HAVE TO BE SO I DON'T END UP LIKE THAT...?
SEE! NOW SHE'S ALL DEFEN-SIVE!
NEVER YOU MIND. JUST FOCUS ON THE GAME.
YOU HAVE TO GET THAT GIRL'S PHYSICAL STRENGTH UP BY CHRIST-MAS.

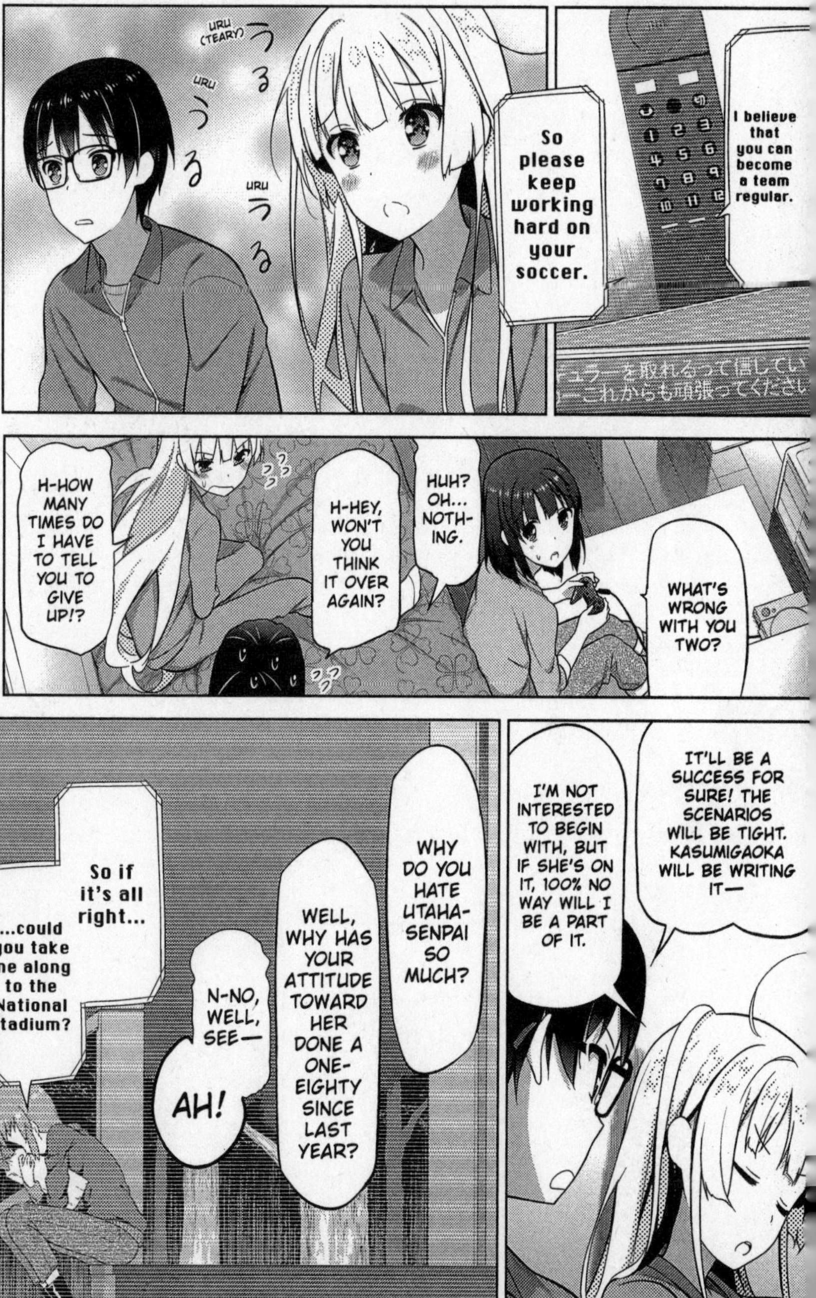
I believe that you can become a team regular.
So please keep working hard on your soccer.
URU (TEARY) うる
URU うる
URU うる
WHAT'S WRONG WITH YOU TWO?
HUH? OH... NOTHING.
H-HEY, WON'T YOU THINK IT OVER AGAIN?
H-HOW MANY TIMES DO I HAVE TO TELL YOU TO GIVE UP!?
IT'LL BE A SUCCESS FOR SURE! THE SCENARIOS WILL BE TIGHT. KASUMIGAOKA WILL BE WRITING IT—
I'M NOT INTERESTED TO BEGIN WITH, BUT IF SHE'S ON IT, 100% NO WAY WILL I BE A PART OF IT.
WHY DO YOU HATE UTAHA-SENPAI SO MUCH?
WELL, WHY HAS YOUR ATTITUDE TOWARD HER DONE A ONE-EIGHTY SINCE LAST YEAR?
N-NO, WELL, SEE—
AH!
So if it's all right...
...could you take me along to the National Stadium?

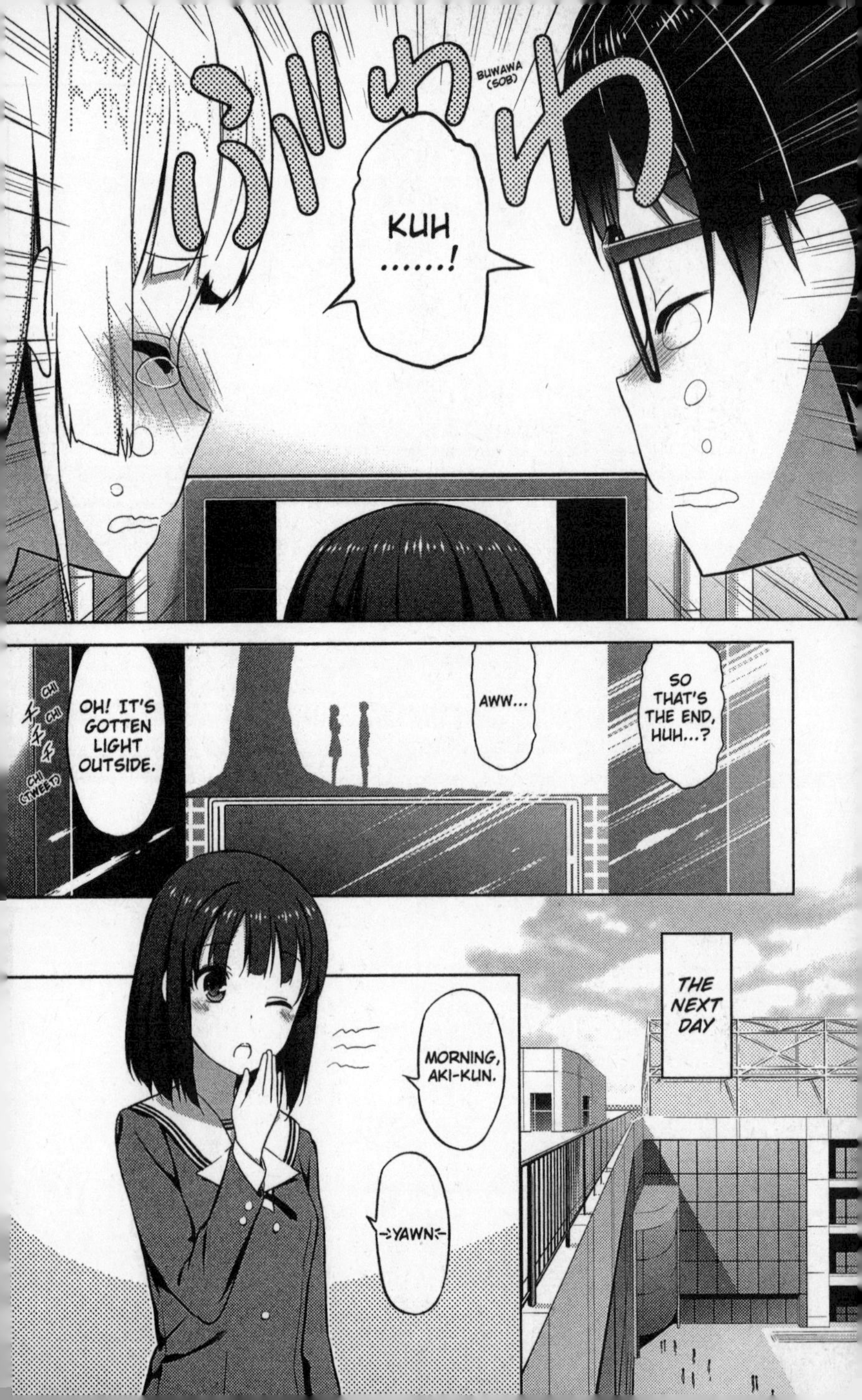
ぶわわ
BUWAWA (SOB)
KUH ......!
SO THAT'S THE END, HUH...?
AWW...
CHI CHI CHI (TWEET)
OH! IT'S GOTTEN LIGHT OUTSIDE.
THE NEXT DAY
MORNING, AKI-KUN.
~YAWN~

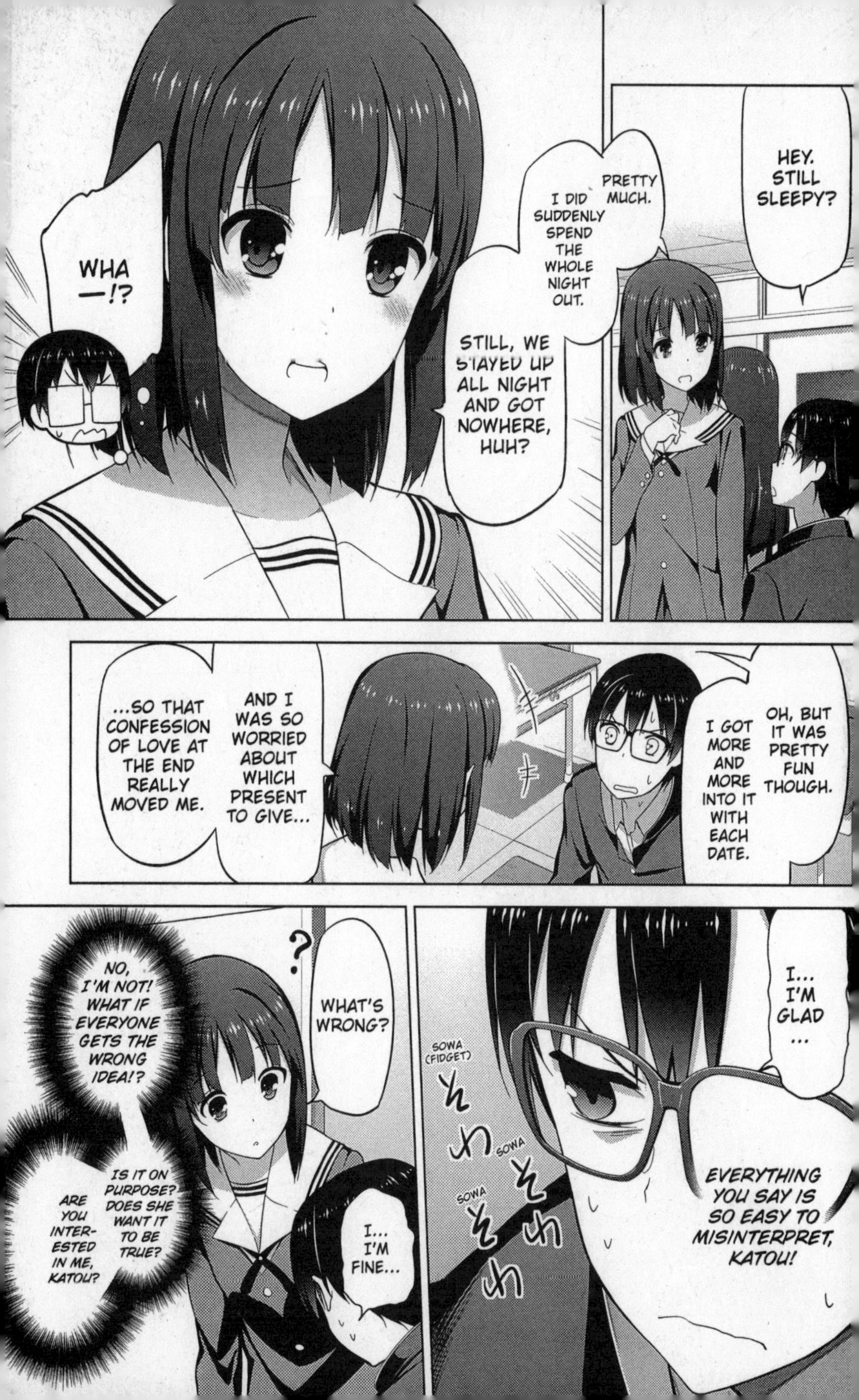
HEY. STILL SLEEPY?
PRETTY MUCH. I DID SUDDENLY SPEND THE WHOLE NIGHT OUT.
STILL, WE STAYED UP ALL NIGHT AND GOT NOWHERE, HUH?
WHA—!?
OH, BUT IT WAS PRETTY FUN THOUGH. I GOT MORE AND MORE INTO IT WITH EACH DATE.
AND I WAS SO WORRIED ABOUT WHICH PRESENT TO GIVE...
...SO THAT CONFESSION OF LOVE AT THE END REALLY MOVED ME.
I... I'M GLAD...
SOWA (FIDGET)
SOWA
SOWA
EVERYTHING YOU SAY IS SO EASY TO MISINTERPRET, KATOU!
?
WHAT'S WRONG?
NO, I'M NOT! WHAT IF EVERYONE GETS THE WRONG IDEA!?
IS IT ON PURPOSE? DOES SHE WANT IT TO BE TRUE?
ARE YOU INTER-ESTED IN ME, KATOU?
I... I'M FINE...

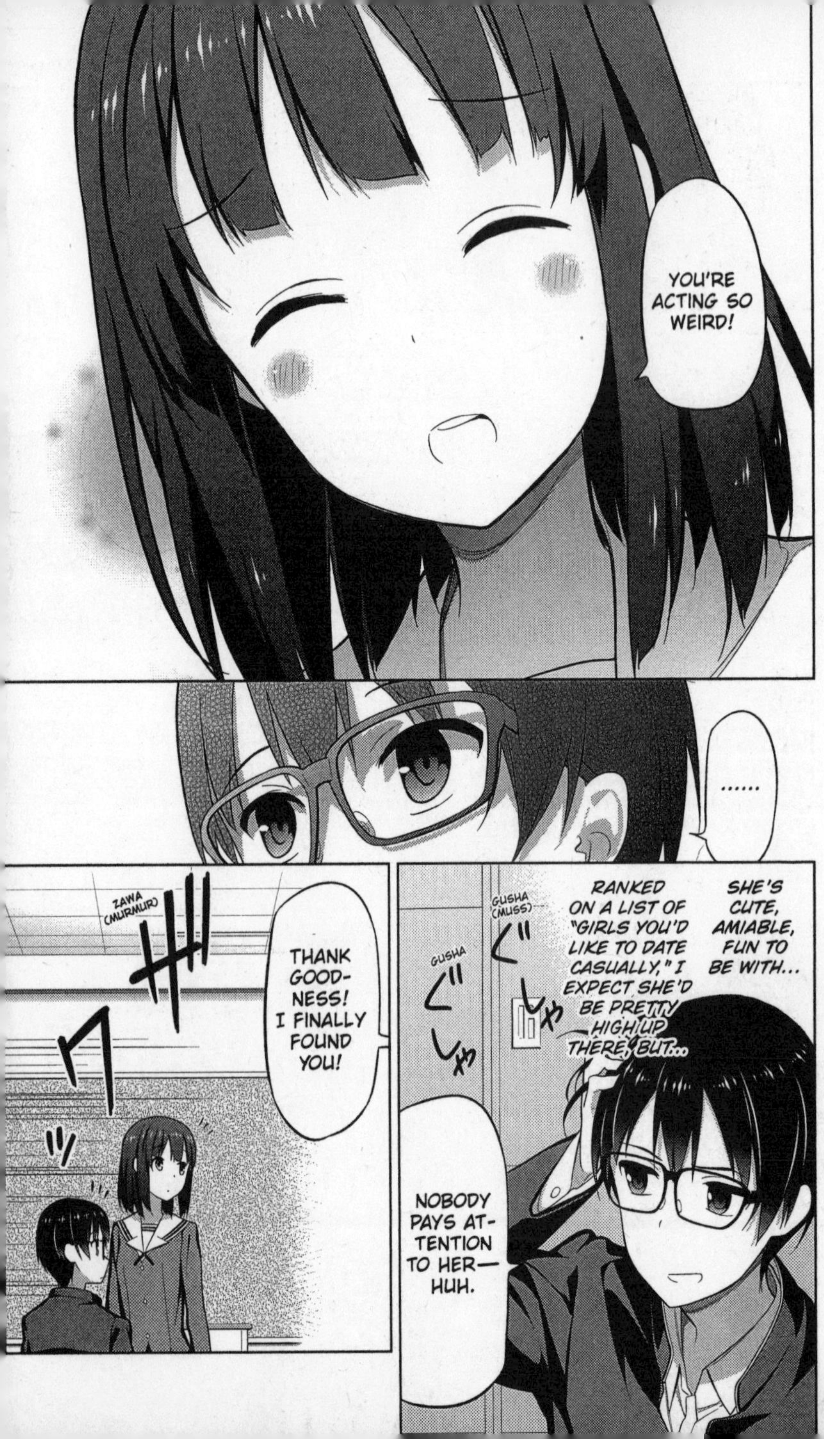
YOU'RE ACTING SO WEIRD!
......
SHE'S CUTE, AMIABLE, FUN TO BE WITH...
RANKED ON A LIST OF "GIRLS YOU'D LIKE TO DATE CASUALLY," I EXPECT SHE'D BE PRETTY HIGH UP THERE, BUT...
GUSHA (MUSS)
ぐしゃ
GUSHA
ぐしゃ
NOBODY PAYS AT-TENTION TO HER—HUH.
ZAWA (MURMUR)
THANK GOOD-NESS! I FINALLY FOUND YOU!

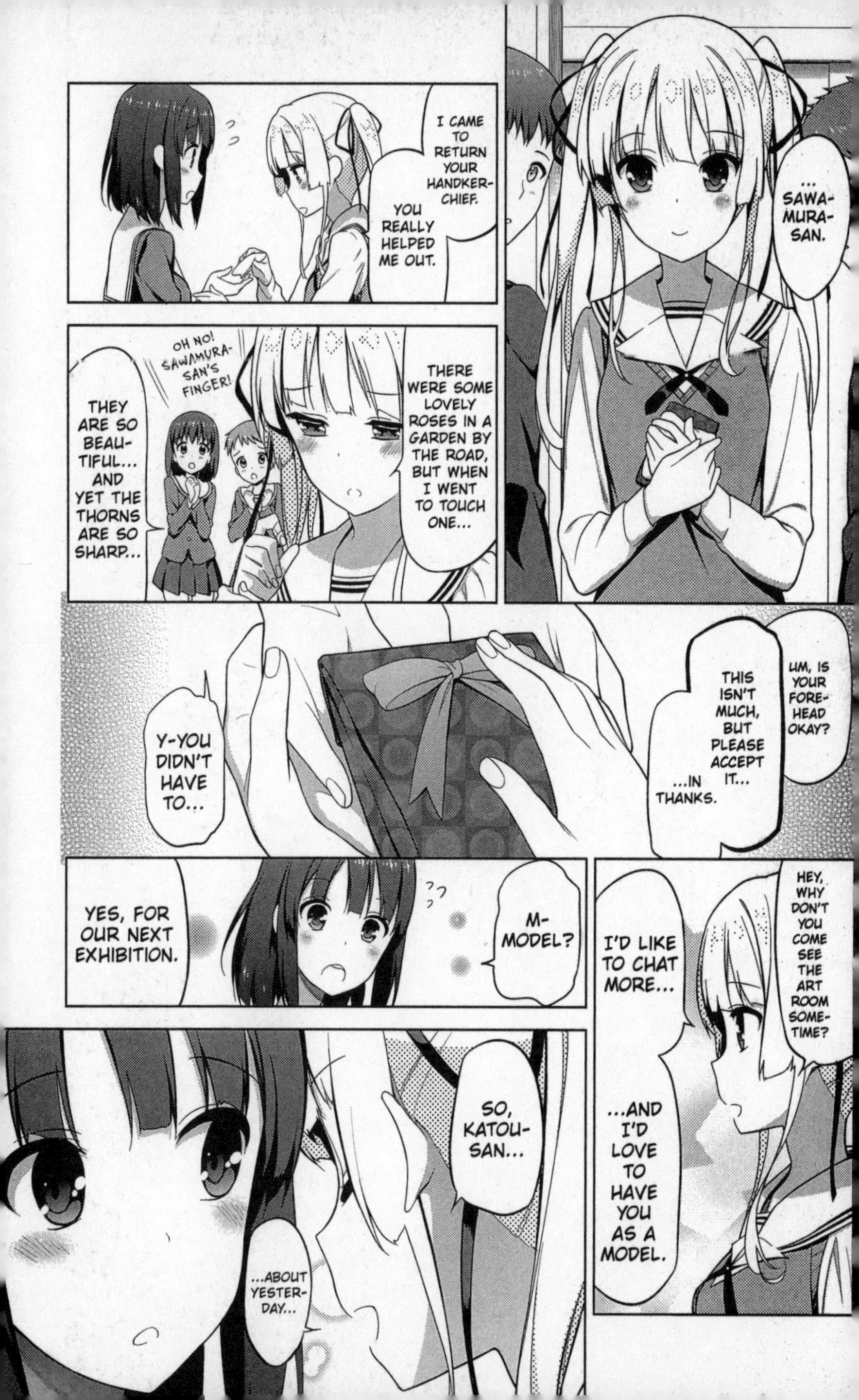
...SAWAMURA-SAN.
I CAME TO RETURN YOUR HANDKERCHIEF.
YOU REALLY HELPED ME OUT.
THERE WERE SOME LOVELY ROSES IN A GARDEN BY THE ROAD, BUT WHEN I WENT TO TOUCH ONE...
OH NO! SAWAMURA-SAN'S FINGER!
THEY ARE SO BEAUTIFUL... AND YET THE THORNS ARE SO SHARP...
UM, IS YOUR FOREHEAD OKAY?
THIS ISN'T MUCH, BUT PLEASE ACCEPT IT...
...IN THANKS.
Y-YOU DIDN'T HAVE TO...
HEY, WHY DON'T YOU COME SEE THE ART ROOM SOMETIME?
I'D LIKE TO CHAT MORE...
...AND I'D LOVE TO HAVE YOU AS A MODEL.
M-MODEL?
YES, FOR OUR NEXT EXHIBITION.
SO, KATOU-SAN...
...ABOUT YESTERDAY...

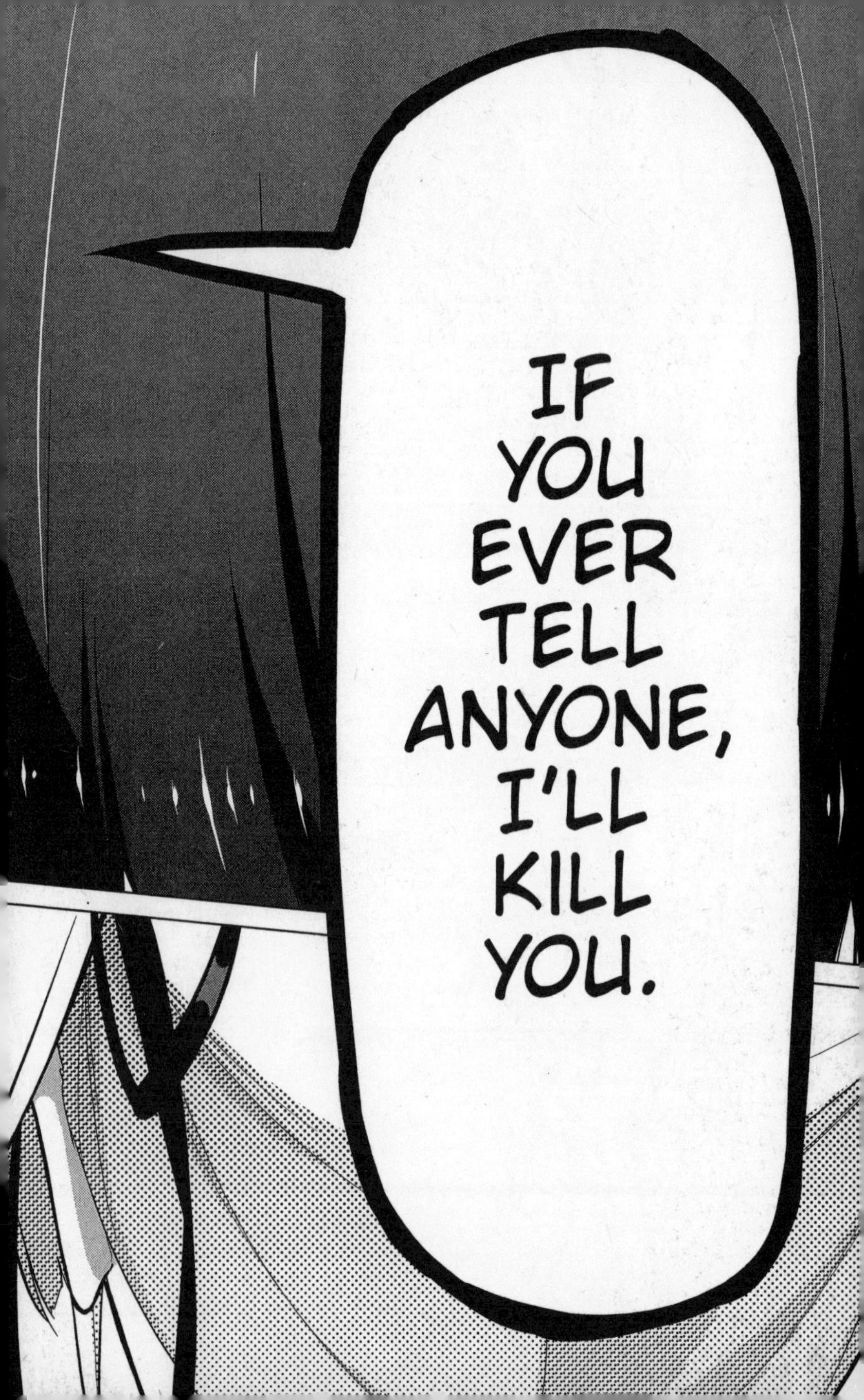
IF YOU EVER TELL ANYONE, I'LL KILL YOU.

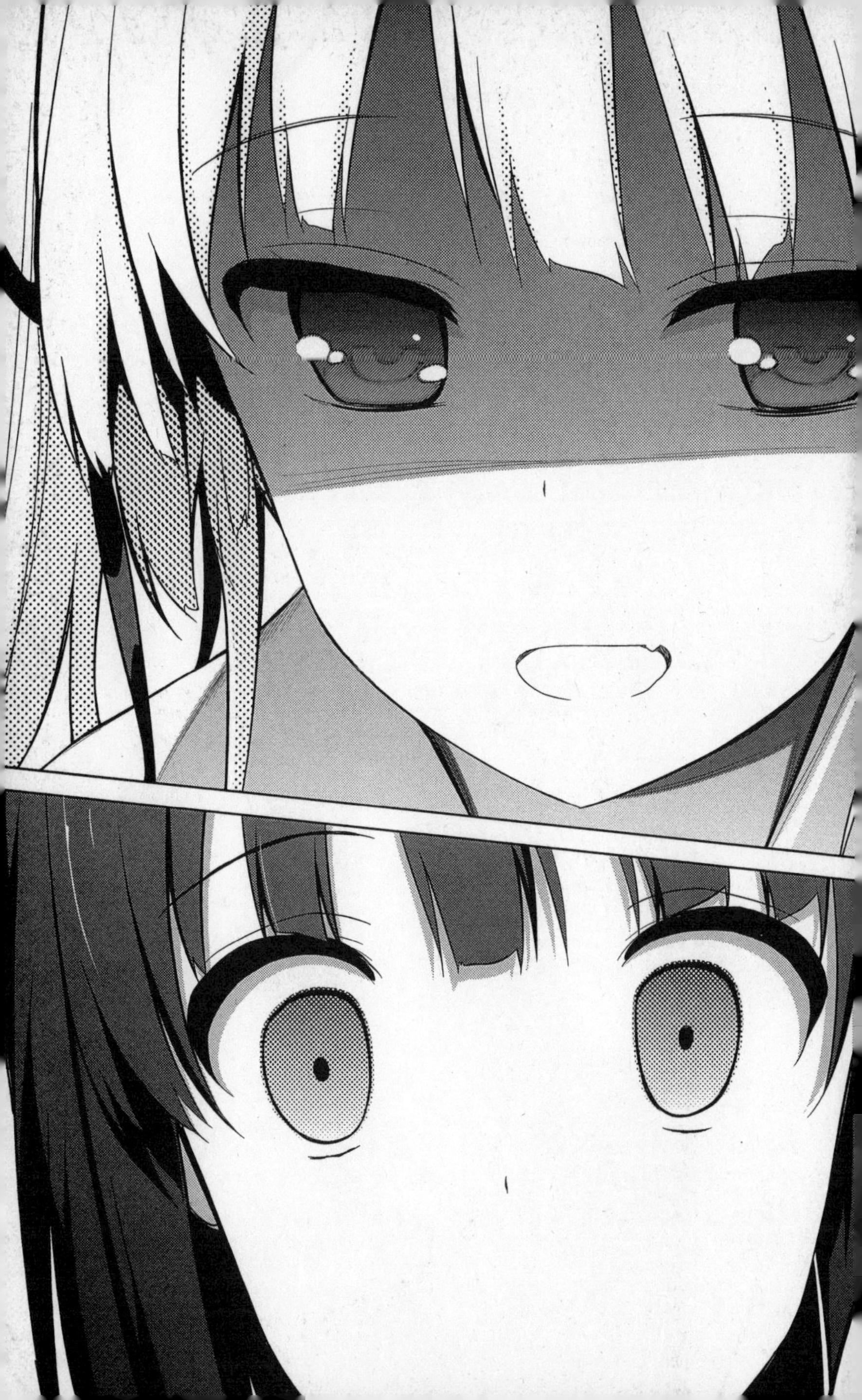

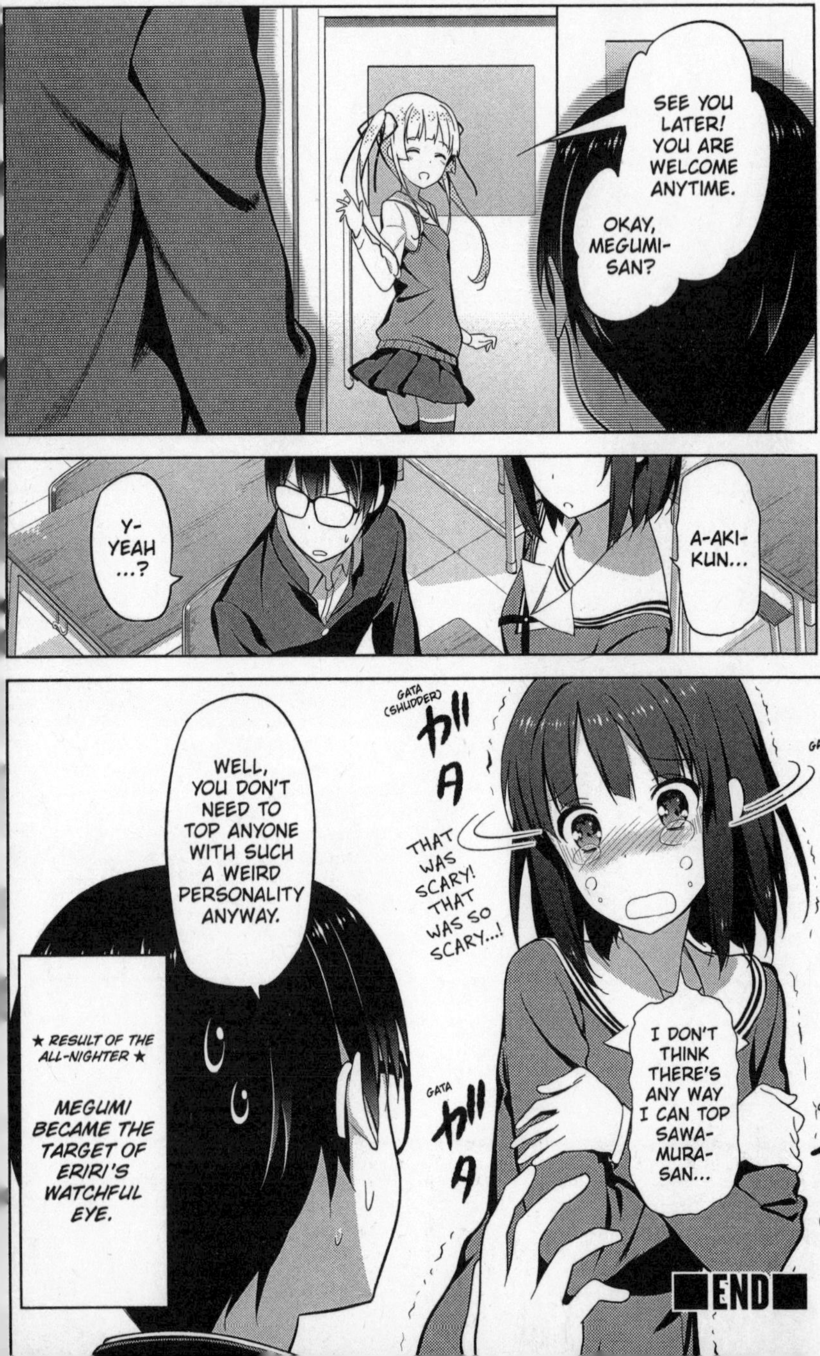
SEE YOU LATER! YOU ARE WELCOME ANYTIME.
OKAY, MEGUMI-SAN?
A-AKI-KUN...
Y-YEAH ...?
GATA
GATA (SHUDDER)
THAT WAS SCARY! THAT WAS SO SCARY...!
WELL, YOU DON'T NEED TO TOP ANYONE WITH SUCH A WEIRD PERSONALITY ANYWAY.
I DON'T THINK THERE'S ANY WAY I CAN TOP SAWA-MURA-SAN...
GATA
GATA
★ RESULT OF THE ALL-NIGHTER ★
MEGUMI BECAME THE TARGET OF ERIRI'S WATCHFUL EYE.
END

How to Raise a Boring Girlfriend

How to Raise a Boring Girlfriend

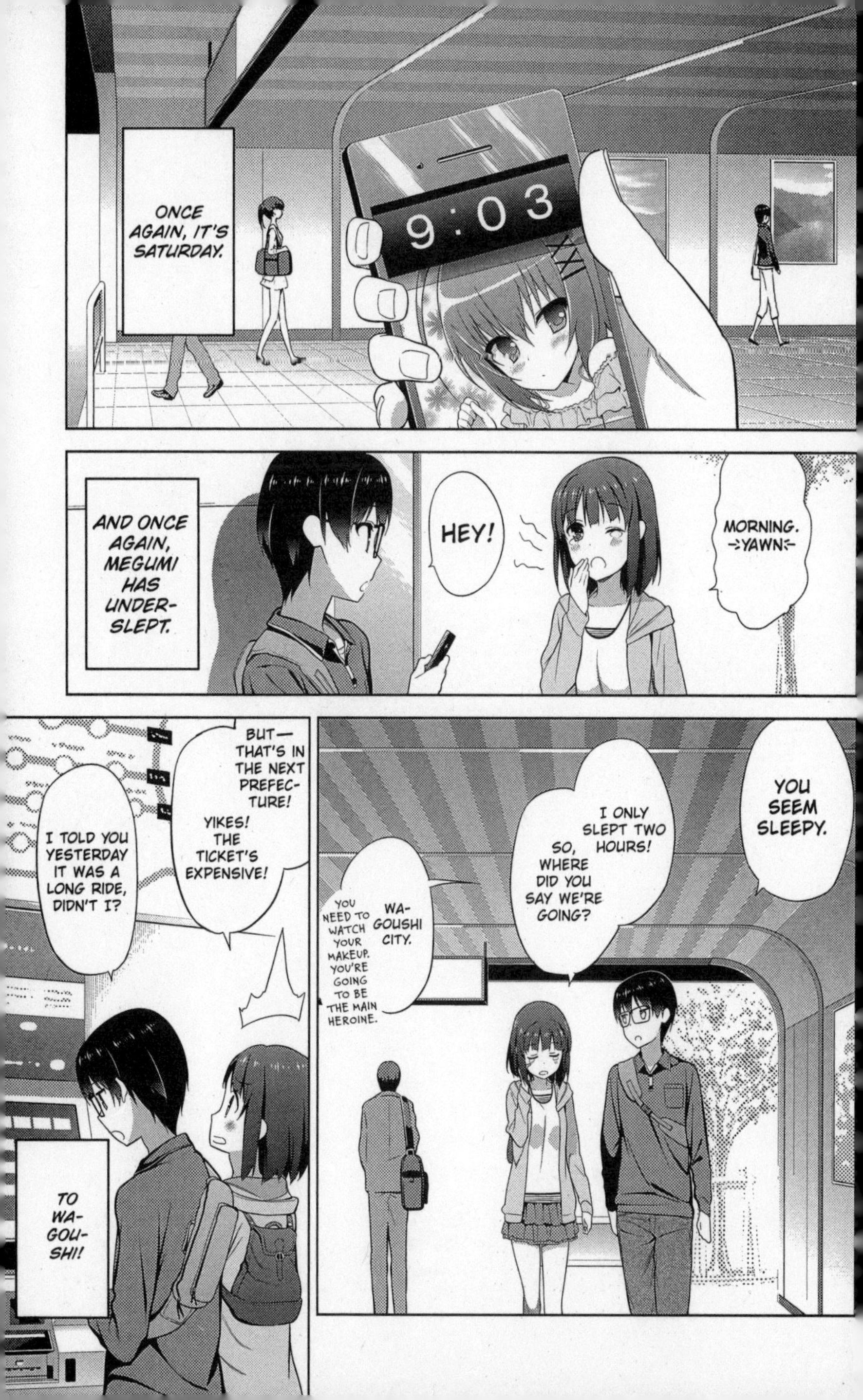
ONCE AGAIN, IT'S SATURDAY.
9:03
MORNING. ~YAWN~
HEY!
AND ONCE AGAIN, MEGUMI HAS UNDER-SLEPT.
YOU SEEM SLEEPY.
I ONLY SLEPT TWO HOURS!
SO, WHERE DID YOU SAY WE'RE GOING?
WA-GOUSHI CITY.
YOU NEED TO WATCH YOUR MAKEUP. YOU'RE GOING TO BE THE MAIN HEROINE.
BUT— THAT'S IN THE NEXT PREFEC-TURE!
YIKES! THE TICKET'S EXPENSIVE!
I TOLD YOU YESTERDAY IT WAS A LONG RIDE, DIDN'T I?
TO WA-GOU-SHI!

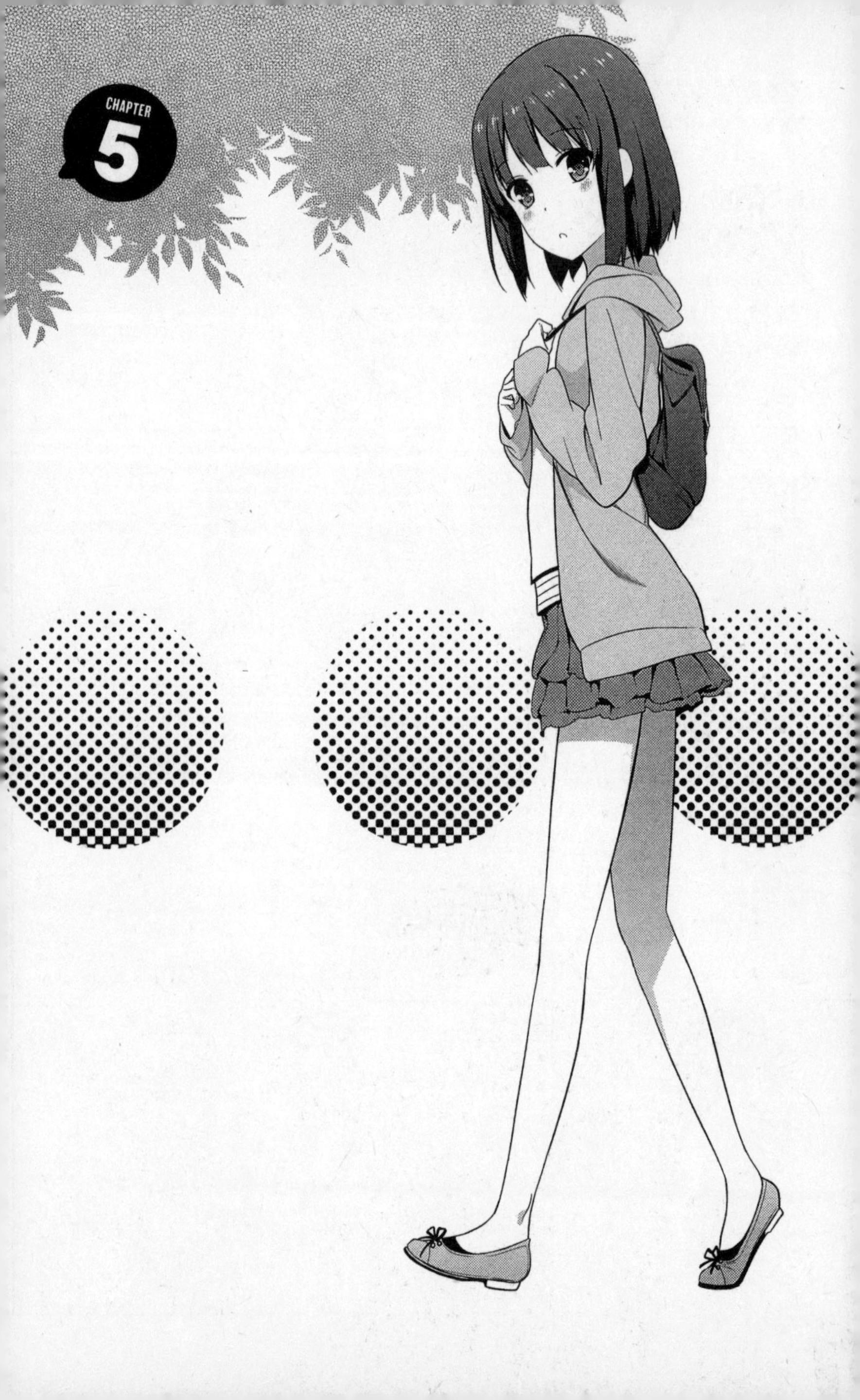
CHAPTER
5

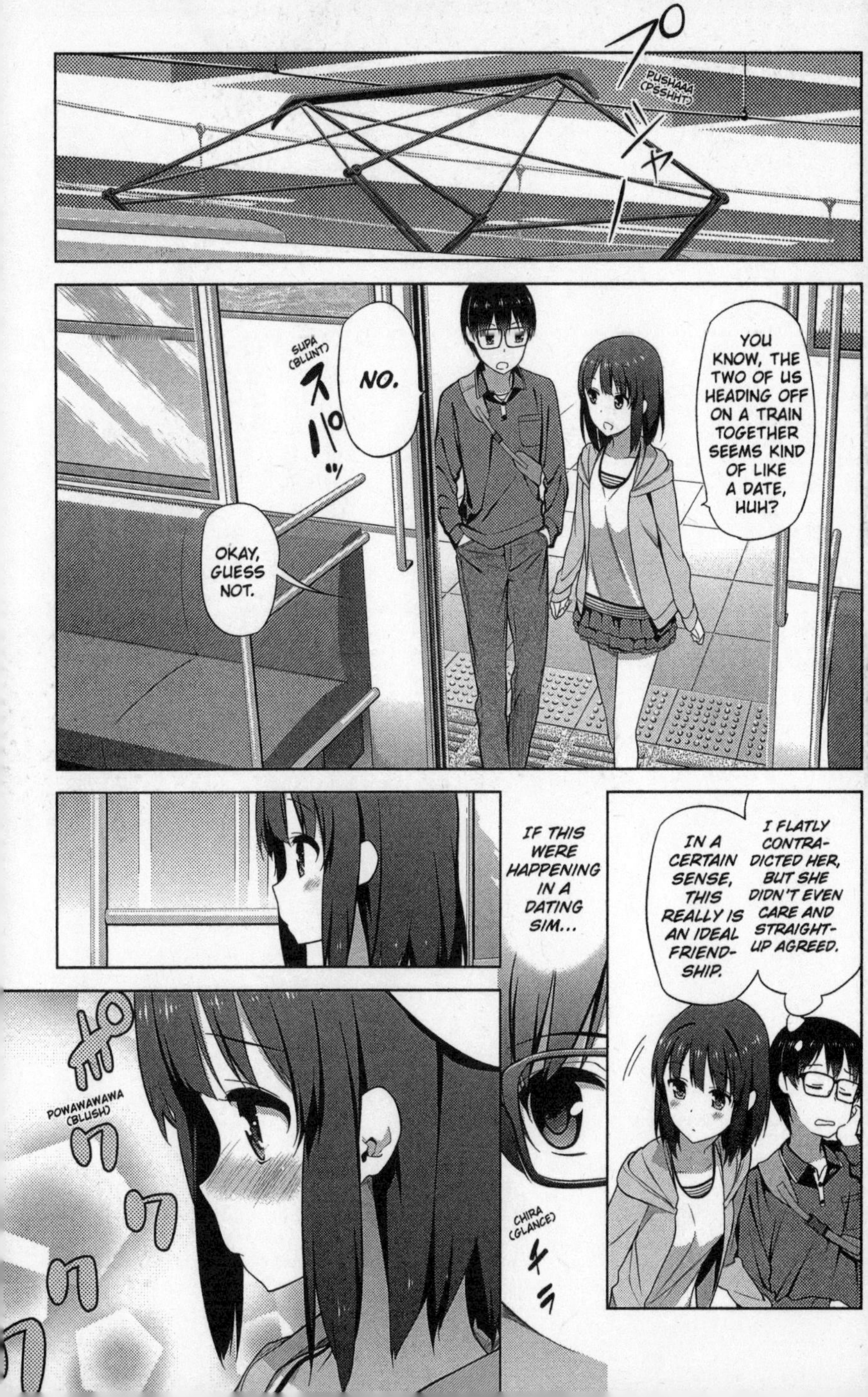
PUSHAA (PSSHHT)
YOU KNOW, THE TWO OF US HEADING OFF ON A TRAIN TOGETHER SEEMS KIND OF LIKE A DATE, HUH?
SUPA (BLUNT)
NO.
OKAY, GUESS NOT.
I FLATLY CONTRADICTED HER, BUT SHE DIDN'T EVEN CARE AND STRAIGHT-UP AGREED.
IN A CERTAIN SENSE, THIS REALLY IS AN IDEAL FRIENDSHIP.
IF THIS WERE HAPPENING IN A DATING SIM...
CHIRA (GLANCE)
POWAWAWAWA (BLUSH)

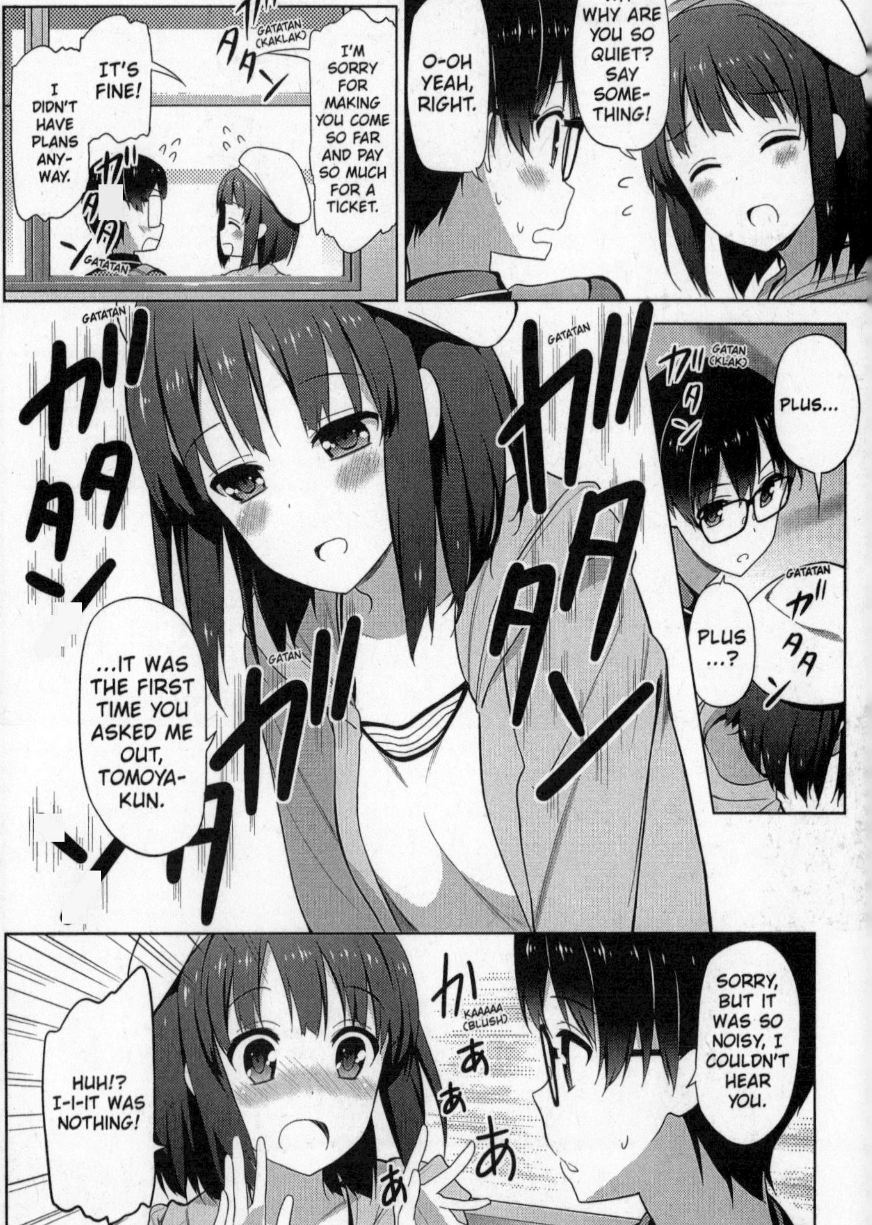
WH- WHY ARE YOU SO QUIET? SAY SOME- THING!
O-OH YEAH, RIGHT.
GATATAN (KAKLAK)
I'M SORRY FOR MAKING YOU COME SO FAR AND PAY SO MUCH FOR A TICKET.
IT'S FINE!
I DIDN'T HAVE PLANS ANY- WAY.
GATATAN
GATAN (KLAK)
PLUS...
GATATAN
PLUS ...?
GATATAN
GATATAN
GATAN
...IT WAS THE FIRST TIME YOU ASKED ME OUT, TOMOYA- KUN.
SORRY, BUT IT WAS SO NOISY, I COULDN'T HEAR YOU.
KAAAAA (BLUSH)
HUH!? I-I-IT WAS NOTHING!

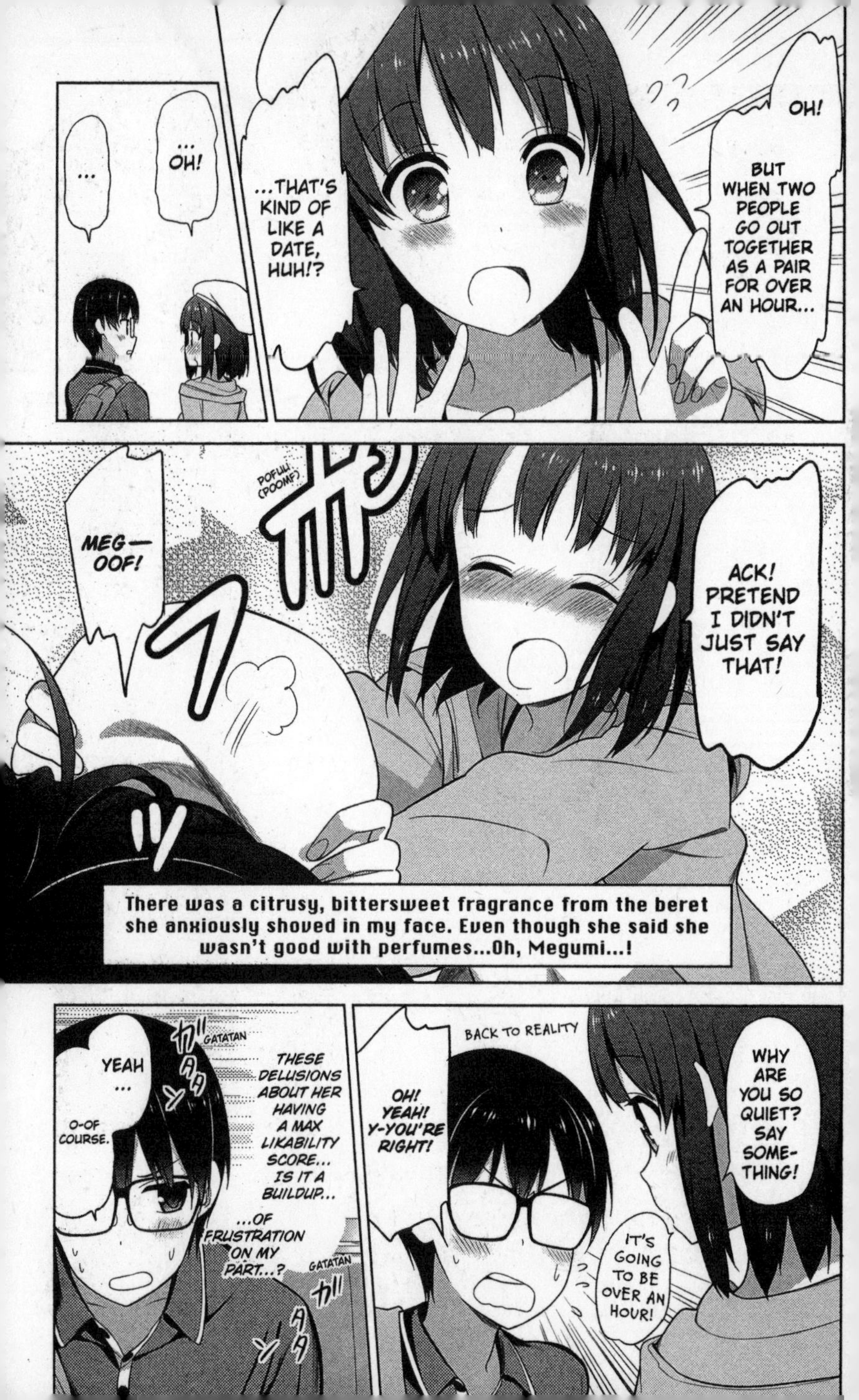
OH!
BUT WHEN TWO PEOPLE GO OUT TOGETHER AS A PAIR FOR OVER AN HOUR...
...THAT'S KIND OF LIKE A DATE, HUH!?
...OH!
...
ACK! PRETEND I DIDN'T JUST SAY THAT!
POFUU (POOMF)
MEG—OOF!
There was a citrusy, bittersweet fragrance from the beret she anxiously shoved in my face. Even though she said she wasn't good with perfumes...Oh, Megumi...!
WHY ARE YOU SO QUIET? SAY SOME-THING!
BACK TO REALITY
OH! YEAH! Y-YOU'RE RIGHT!
IT'S GOING TO BE OVER AN HOUR!
GATATAN
THESE DELUSIONS ABOUT HER HAVING A MAX LIKABILITY SCORE... IS IT A BUILDUP... ...OF FRUSTRATION ON MY PART...?
YEAH...
O-OF COURSE.
GATATAN

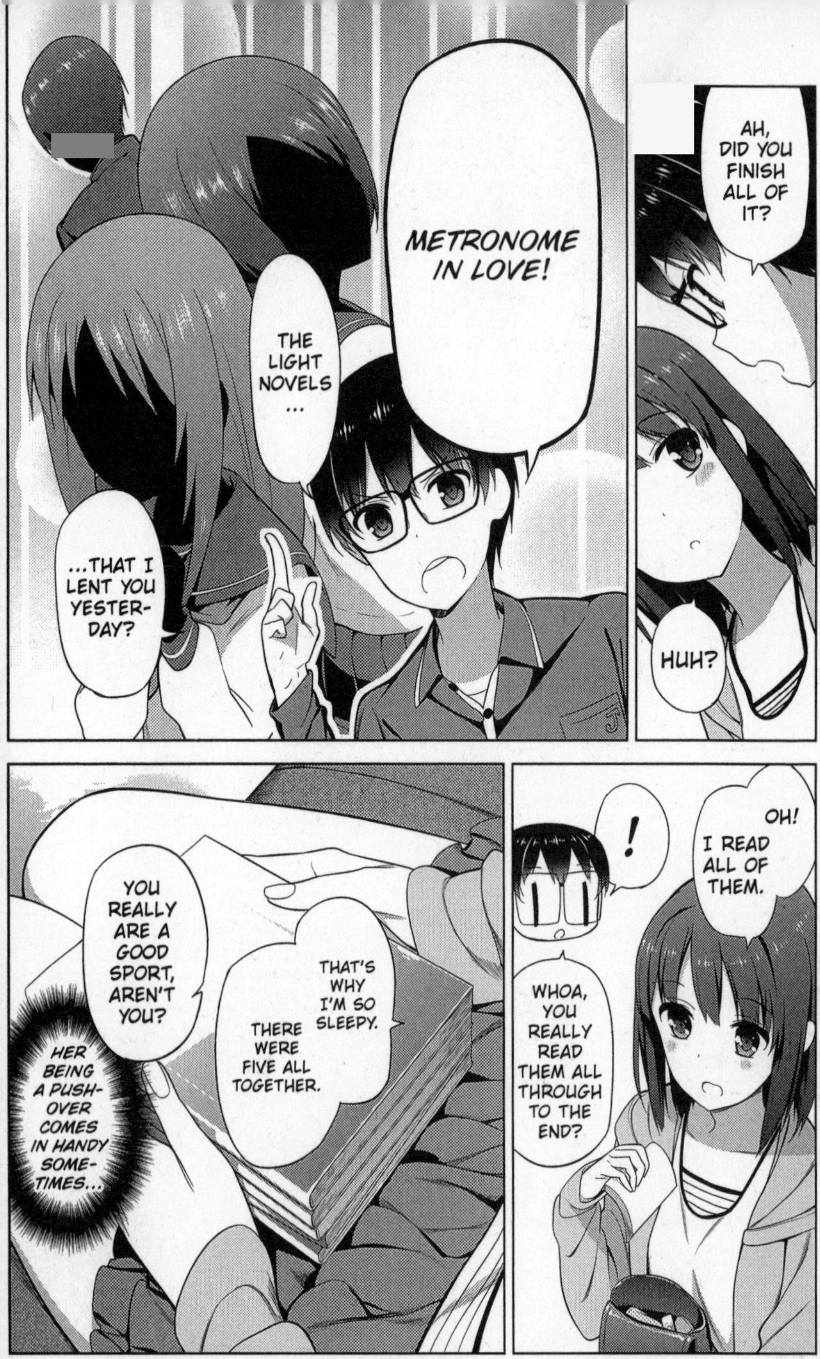
AH, DID YOU FINISH ALL OF IT?
HUH?
METRONOME IN LOVE!
THE LIGHT NOVELS...
...THAT I LENT YOU YESTER-DAY?
OH! I READ ALL OF THEM.
!
WHOA, YOU REALLY READ THEM ALL THROUGH TO THE END?
THAT'S WHY I'M SO SLEEPY.
THERE WERE FIVE ALL TOGETHER.
YOU REALLY ARE A GOOD SPORT, AREN'T YOU?
HER BEING A PUSH-OVER COMES IN HANDY SOME-TIMES...

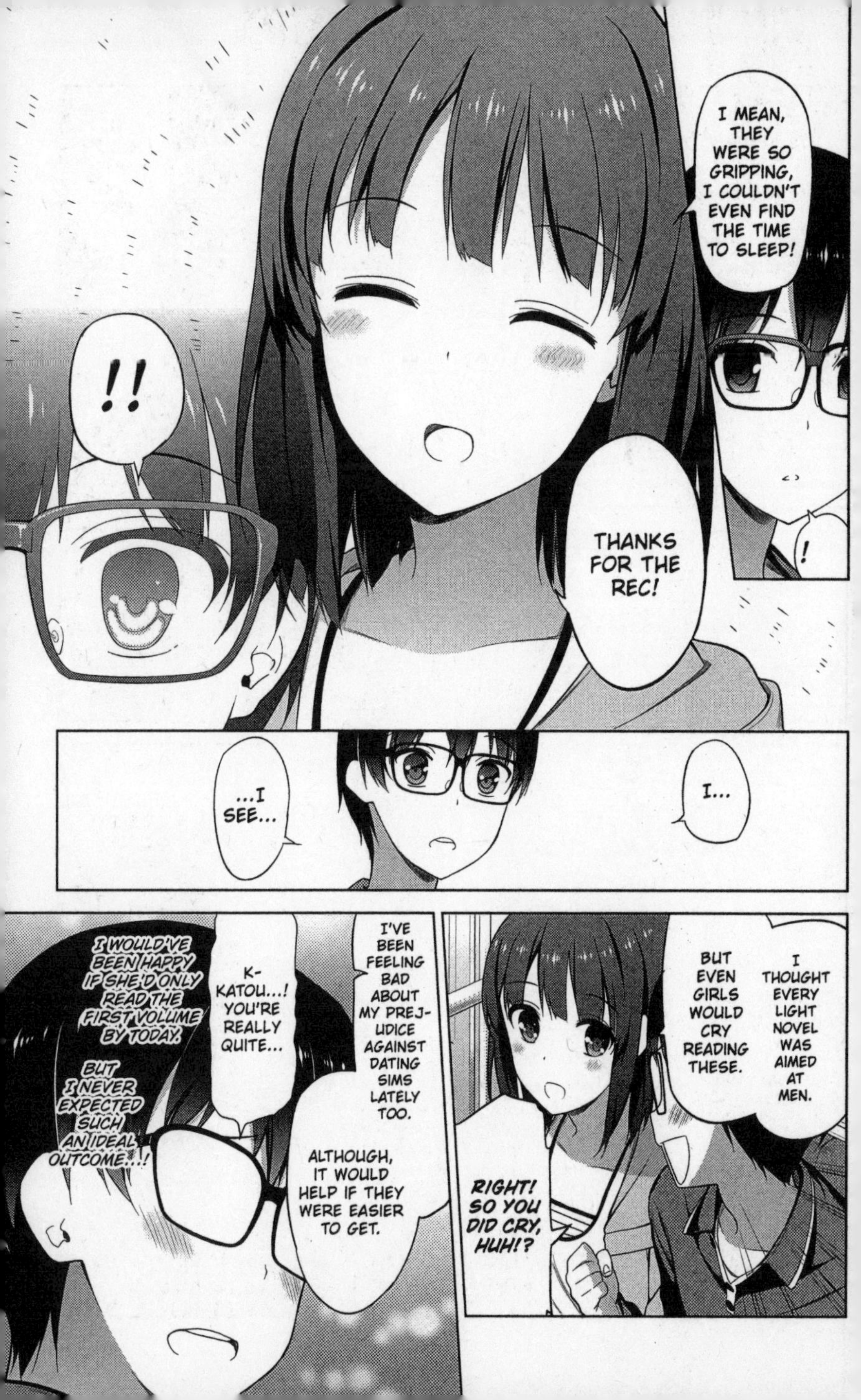
I MEAN, THEY WERE SO GRIPPING, I COULDN'T EVEN FIND THE TIME TO SLEEP!
!
THANKS FOR THE REC!
!!
I...
...I SEE...
I THOUGHT EVERY LIGHT NOVEL WAS AIMED AT MEN.
BUT EVEN GIRLS WOULD CRY READING THESE.
RIGHT! SO YOU DID CRY, HUH!?
I'VE BEEN FEELING BAD ABOUT MY PREJUDICE AGAINST DATING SIMS LATELY TOO.
ALTHOUGH, IT WOULD HELP IF THEY WERE EASIER TO GET.
K-KATOU...! YOU'RE REALLY QUITE...
I WOULD'VE BEEN HAPPY IF SHE'D ONLY READ THE FIRST VOLUME BY TODAY.
BUT I NEVER EXPECTED SUCH AN IDEAL OUTCOME...!

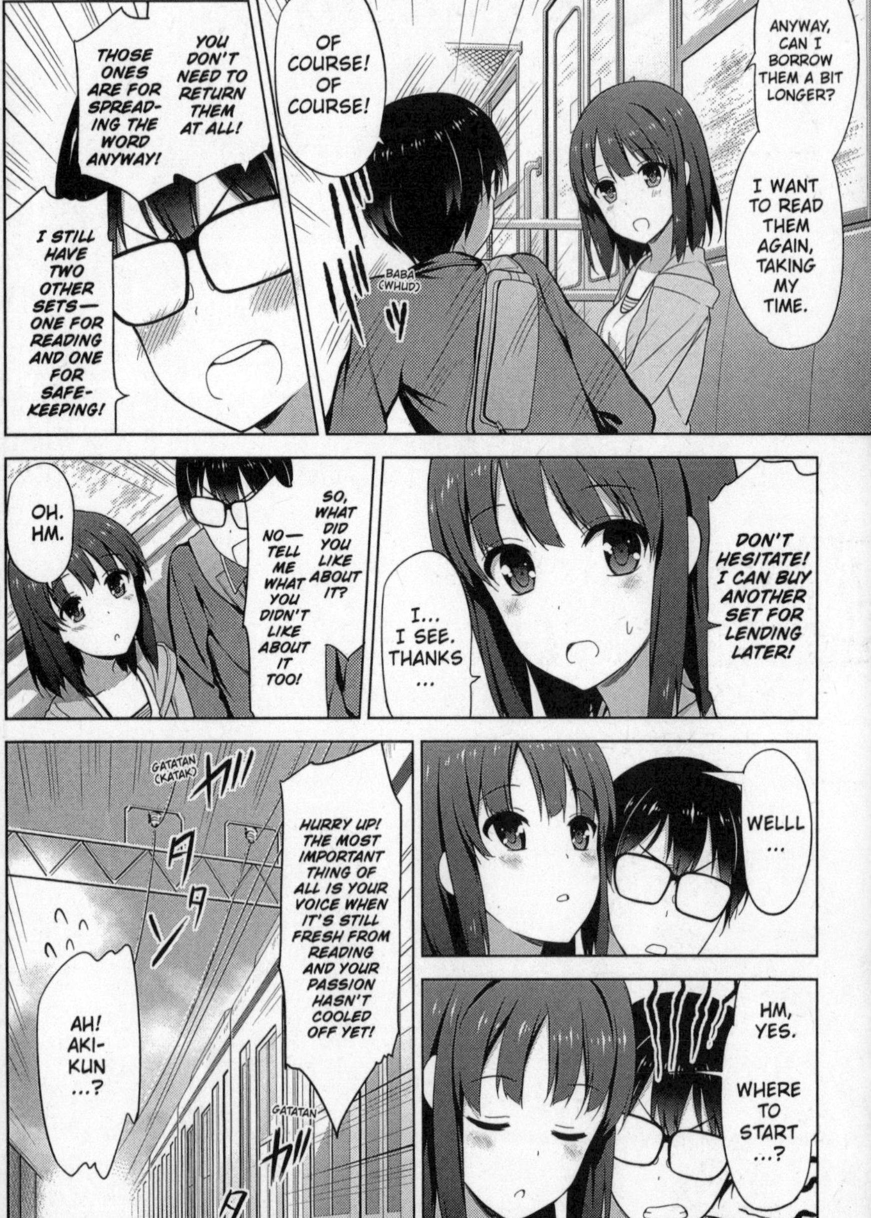
ANYWAY, CAN I BORROW THEM A BIT LONGER?
I WANT TO READ THEM AGAIN, TAKING MY TIME.
OF COURSE! OF COURSE!
BABA (WHUD)
YOU DON'T NEED TO RETURN THEM AT ALL!
THOSE ONES ARE FOR SPREAD-ING THE WORD ANYWAY!
I STILL HAVE TWO OTHER SETS—ONE FOR READING AND ONE FOR SAFE-KEEPING!
DON'T HESITATE! I CAN BUY ANOTHER SET FOR LENDING LATER!
I... I SEE. THANKS...
SO, WHAT DID YOU LIKE ABOUT IT?
NO—TELL ME WHAT YOU DIDN'T LIKE ABOUT IT TOO!
OH. HM.
WELLL...
HM, YES.
WHERE TO START...?
GATATAN (KATAK)
HURRY UP! THE MOST IMPORTANT THING OF ALL IS YOUR VOICE WHEN IT'S STILL FRESH FROM READING AND YOUR PASSION HASN'T COOLED OFF YET!
AH! AKI-KUN...?
GATATAN

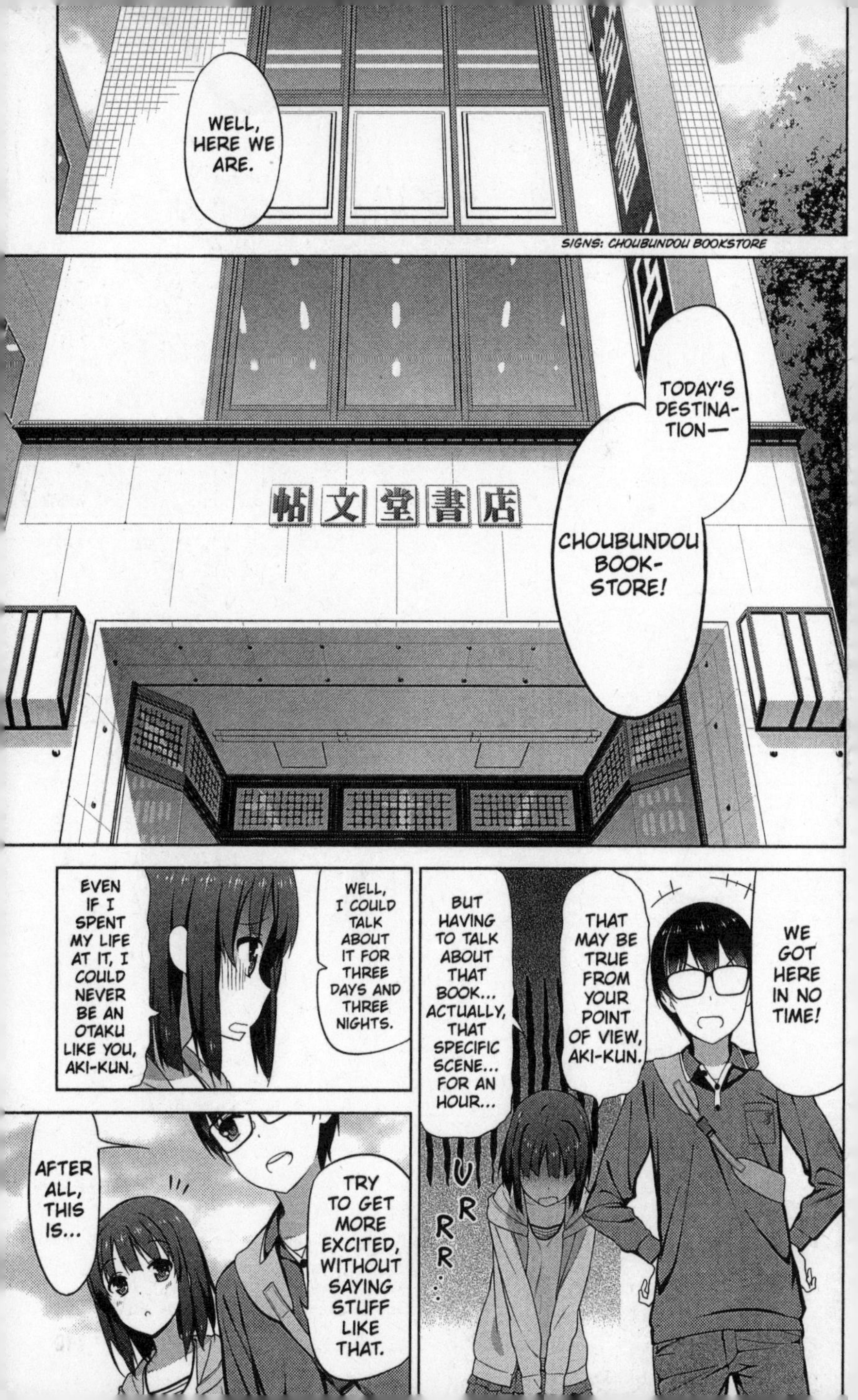
WELL, HERE WE ARE.
帖文堂書店
TODAY'S DESTINATION— CHOUBUNDOU BOOKSTORE!
WE GOT HERE IN NO TIME!
THAT MAY BE TRUE FROM YOUR POINT OF VIEW, AKI-KUN.
BUT HAVING TO TALK ABOUT THAT BOOK... ACTUALLY, THAT SPECIFIC SCENE... FOR AN HOUR...
URRR...
WELL, I COULD TALK ABOUT IT FOR THREE DAYS AND THREE NIGHTS.
EVEN IF I SPENT MY LIFE AT IT, I COULD NEVER BE AN OTAKU LIKE YOU, AKI-KUN.
TRY TO GET MORE EXCITED, WITHOUT SAYING STUFF LIKE THAT.
AFTER ALL, THIS IS...
SIGNS: CHOUBUNDOU BOOKSTORE

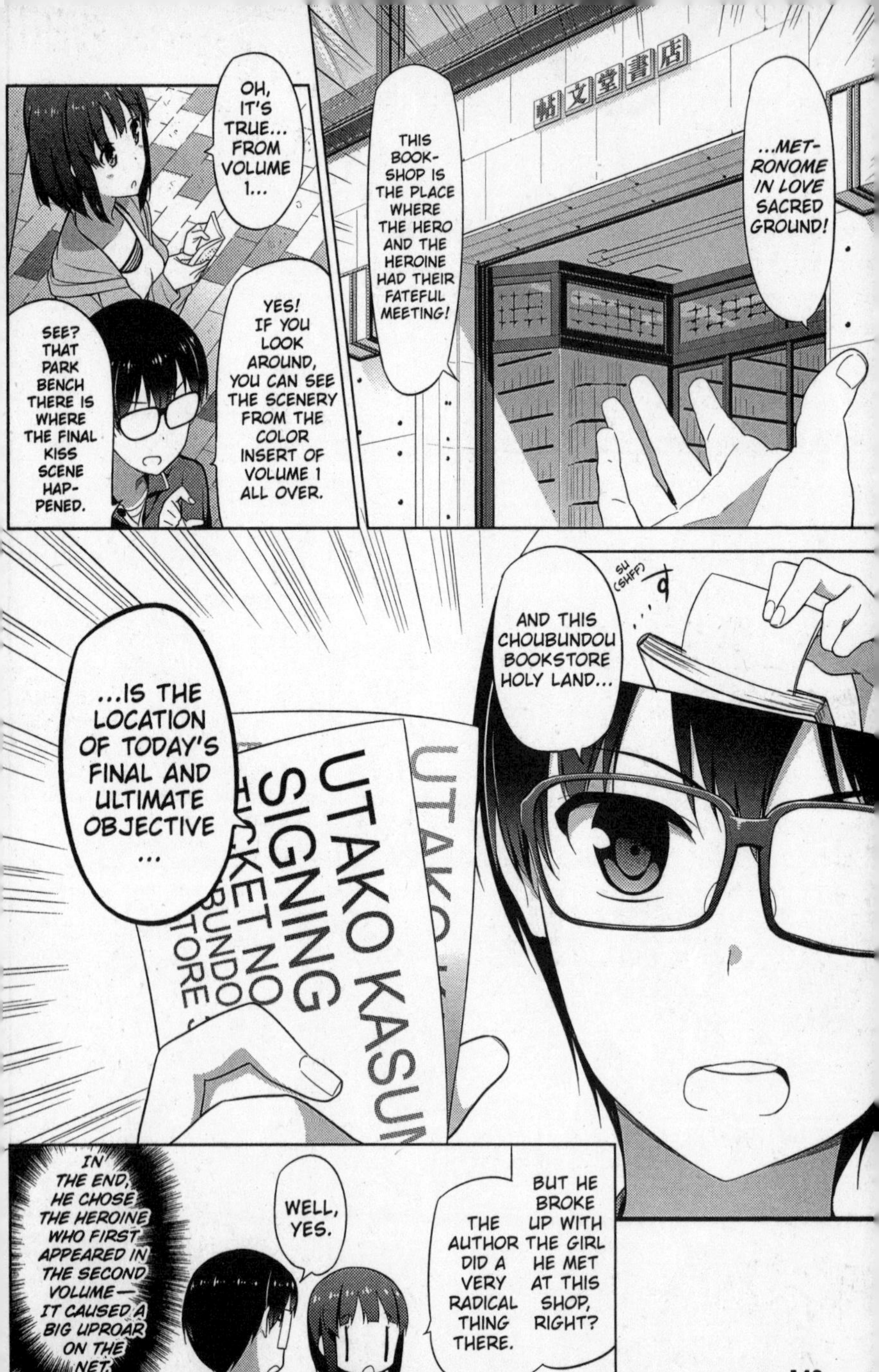

...MET-RONOME IN LOVE SACRED GROUND!
THIS BOOK-SHOP IS THE PLACE WHERE THE HERO AND THE HEROINE HAD THEIR FATEFUL MEETING!
OH, IT'S TRUE... FROM VOLUME 1...
YES! IF YOU LOOK AROUND, YOU CAN SEE THE SCENERY FROM THE COLOR INSERT OF VOLUME 1 ALL OVER.
SEE? THAT PARK BENCH THERE IS WHERE THE FINAL KISS SCENE HAP-PENED.
SU (SHFF)
AND THIS CHOUBUNDOU BOOKSTORE HOLY LAND...
...IS THE LOCATION OF TODAY'S FINAL AND ULTIMATE OBJECTIVE...
UTAKO KASUM
SIGNING
ICKET NO
BUNDO
TORE
BUT HE BROKE UP WITH THE GIRL HE MET AT THIS SHOP, RIGHT?
THE AUTHOR DID A VERY RADICAL THING THERE.
WELL, YES.
IN THE END, HE CHOSE THE HEROINE WHO FIRST APPEARED IN THE SECOND VOLUME—IT CAUSED A BIG UPROAR ON THE NET.

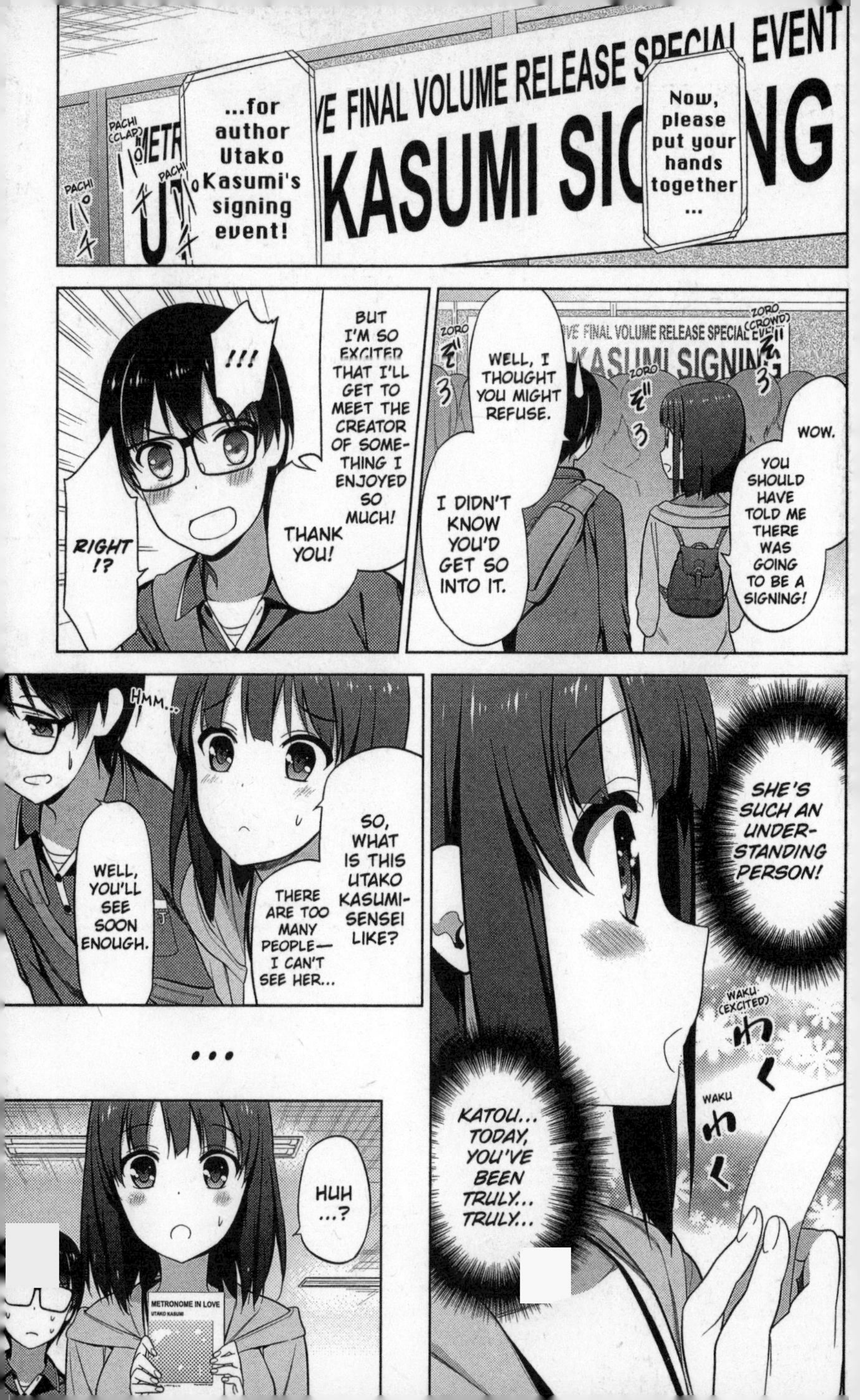
VE FINAL VOLUME RELEASE SPECIAL EVENT
KASUMI SIGNING
Now, please put your hands together...
...for author Utako Kasumi's signing event!
METR
UT
PACHI (CLAP)
PACHI
PACHI
WOW.
YOU SHOULD HAVE TOLD ME THERE WAS GOING TO BE A SIGNING!
ZORO (CROWD)
ZORO
ZORO
WELL, I THOUGHT YOU MIGHT REFUSE.
I DIDN'T KNOW YOU'D GET SO INTO IT.
!!!
BUT I'M SO EXCITED THAT I'LL GET TO MEET THE CREATOR OF SOMETHING I ENJOYED SO MUCH!
THANK YOU!
RIGHT!?
SHE'S SUCH AN UNDER-STANDING PERSON!
WAKU (EXCITED)
WAKU
KATOU... TODAY, YOU'VE BEEN TRULY... TRULY...
SO, WHAT IS THIS UTAKO KASUMI-SENSEI LIKE?
THERE ARE TOO MANY PEOPLE— I CAN'T SEE HER...
HMM...
WELL, YOU'LL SEE SOON ENOUGH.
...
HUH ...?
METRONOME IN LOVE
UTAKO KASUMI

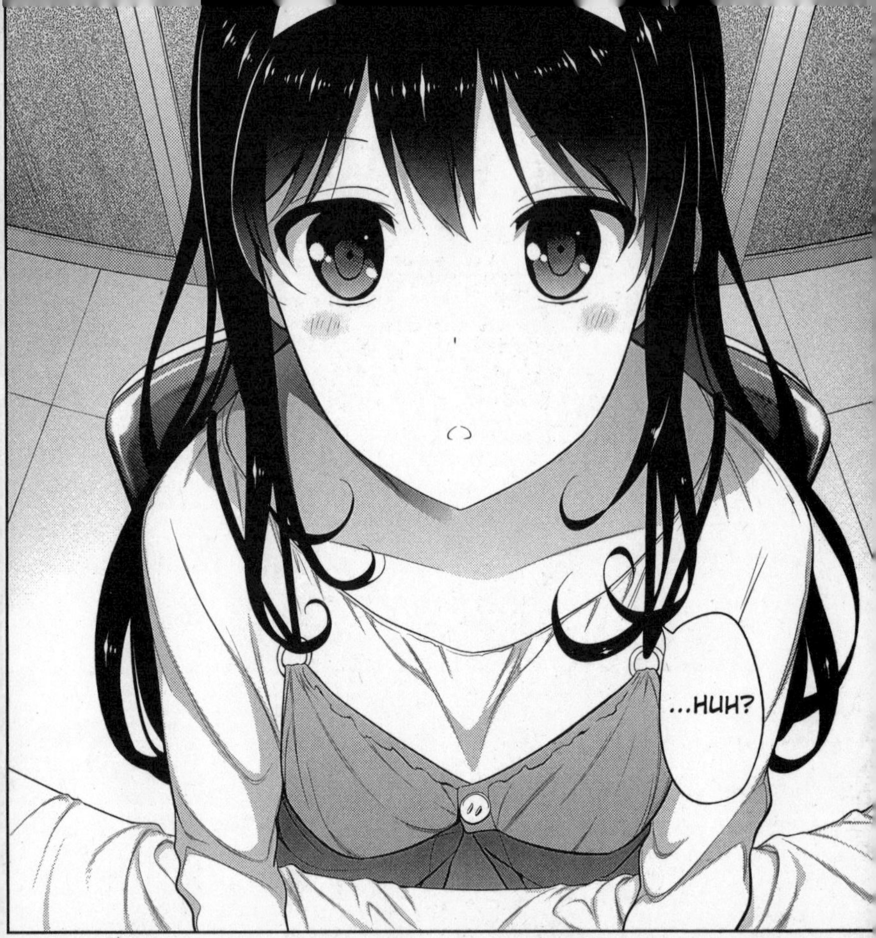
...HUH?

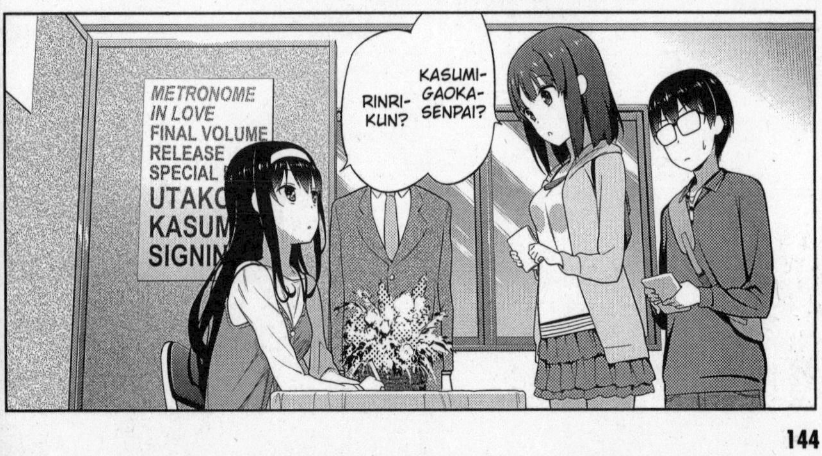
RINRI-KUN? KASUMI-GAOKA-SENPAI?
METRONOME IN LOVE FINAL VOLUME RELEASE SPECIAL
UTAKO
KASUM
SIGNIN

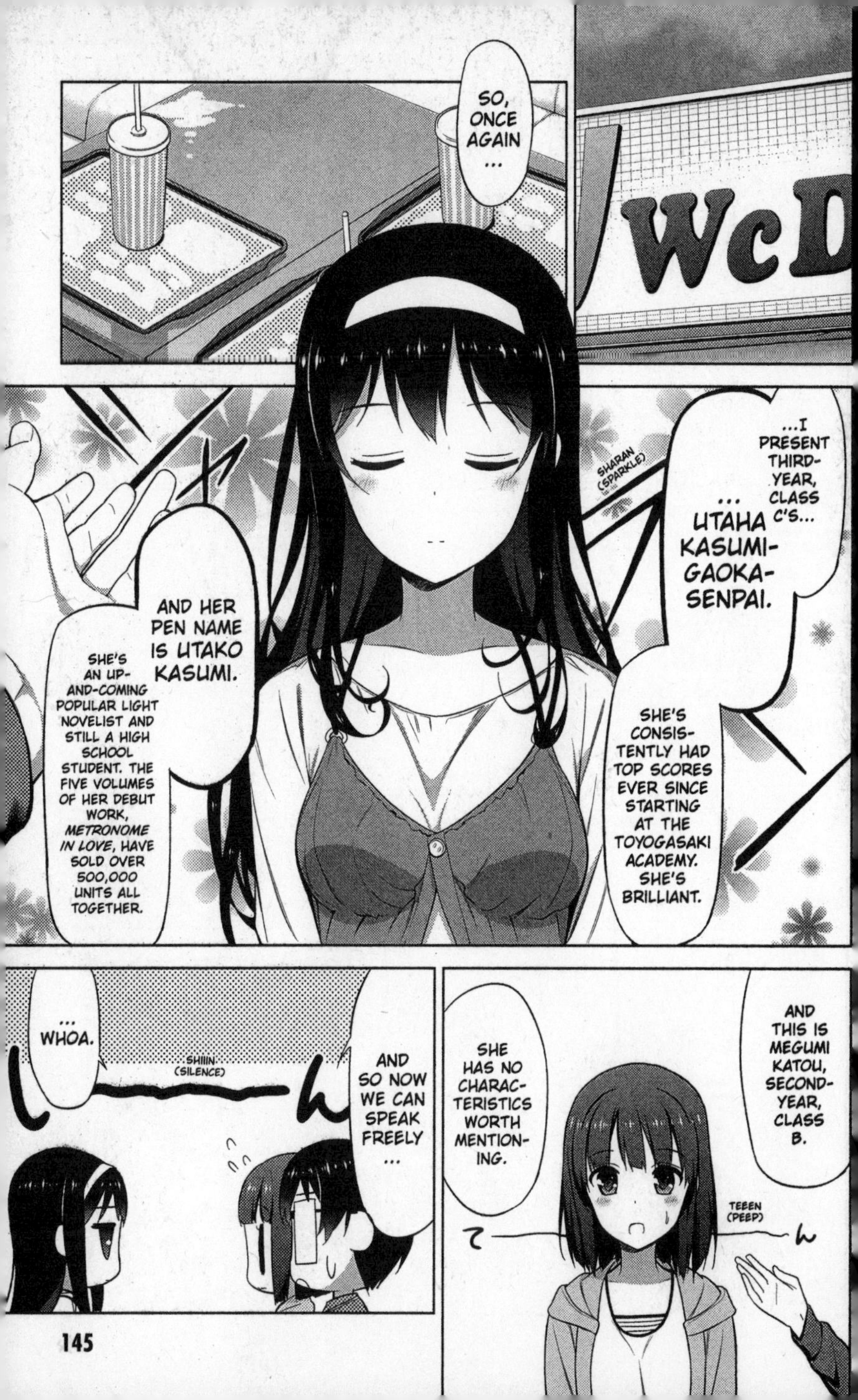
WcD
SO, ONCE AGAIN...
...I PRESENT THIRD-YEAR, CLASS C'S...
...UTAHA KASUMI-GAOKA-SENPAI.
SHARAN (SPARKLE)
SHE'S CONSIS-TENTLY HAD TOP SCORES EVER SINCE STARTING AT THE TOYOGASAKI ACADEMY. SHE'S BRILLIANT.
AND HER PEN NAME IS UTAKO KASUMI.
SHE'S AN UP-AND-COMING POPULAR LIGHT NOVELIST AND STILL A HIGH SCHOOL STUDENT. THE FIVE VOLUMES OF HER DEBUT WORK, *METRONOME IN LOVE*, HAVE SOLD OVER 500,000 UNITS ALL TOGETHER.
AND THIS IS MEGUMI KATOU, SECOND-YEAR, CLASS B.
TEEEN (PEEP)
SHE HAS NO CHARAC-TERISTICS WORTH MENTION-ING.
AND SO NOW WE CAN SPEAK FREELY...
SHIIIN (SILENCE)
...WHOA.

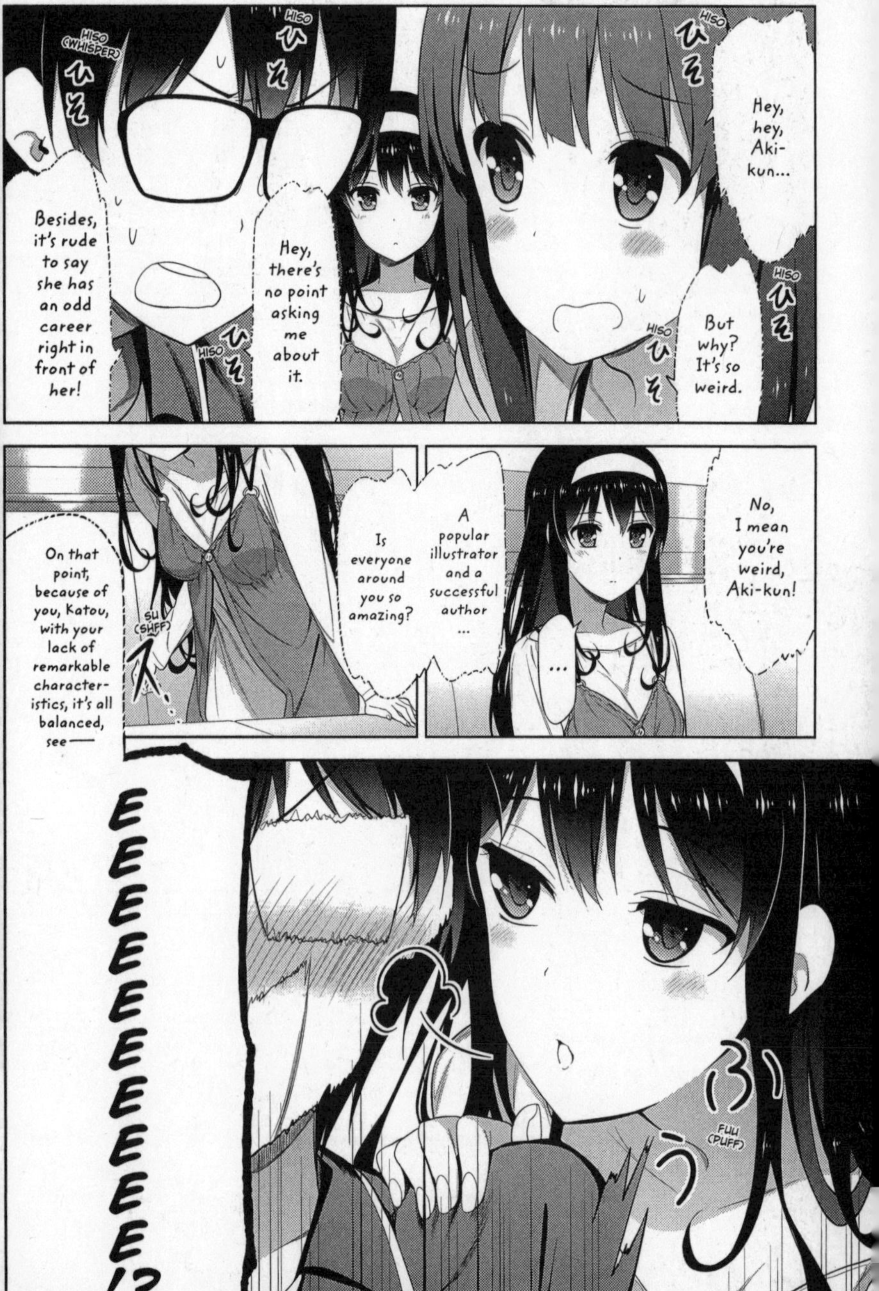
HISO
ひそ
Hey, hey, Aki-kun...
HISO
ひそ
HISO
ひそ
But why? It's so weird.
Hey, there's no point asking me about it.
HISO
ひそ
HISO (WHISPER)
ひそ
Besides, it's rude to say she has an odd career right in front of her!
HISO
ひそ
No, I mean you're weird, Aki-kun!
A popular illustrator and a successful author ...
Is everyone around you so amazing?
...
SU (SHFF)
ス
On that point, because of you, Katou, with your lack of remarkable character-istics, it's all balanced, see—
ふぅ
FUU (PUFF)
EEEEEEEEEEEEEE!?

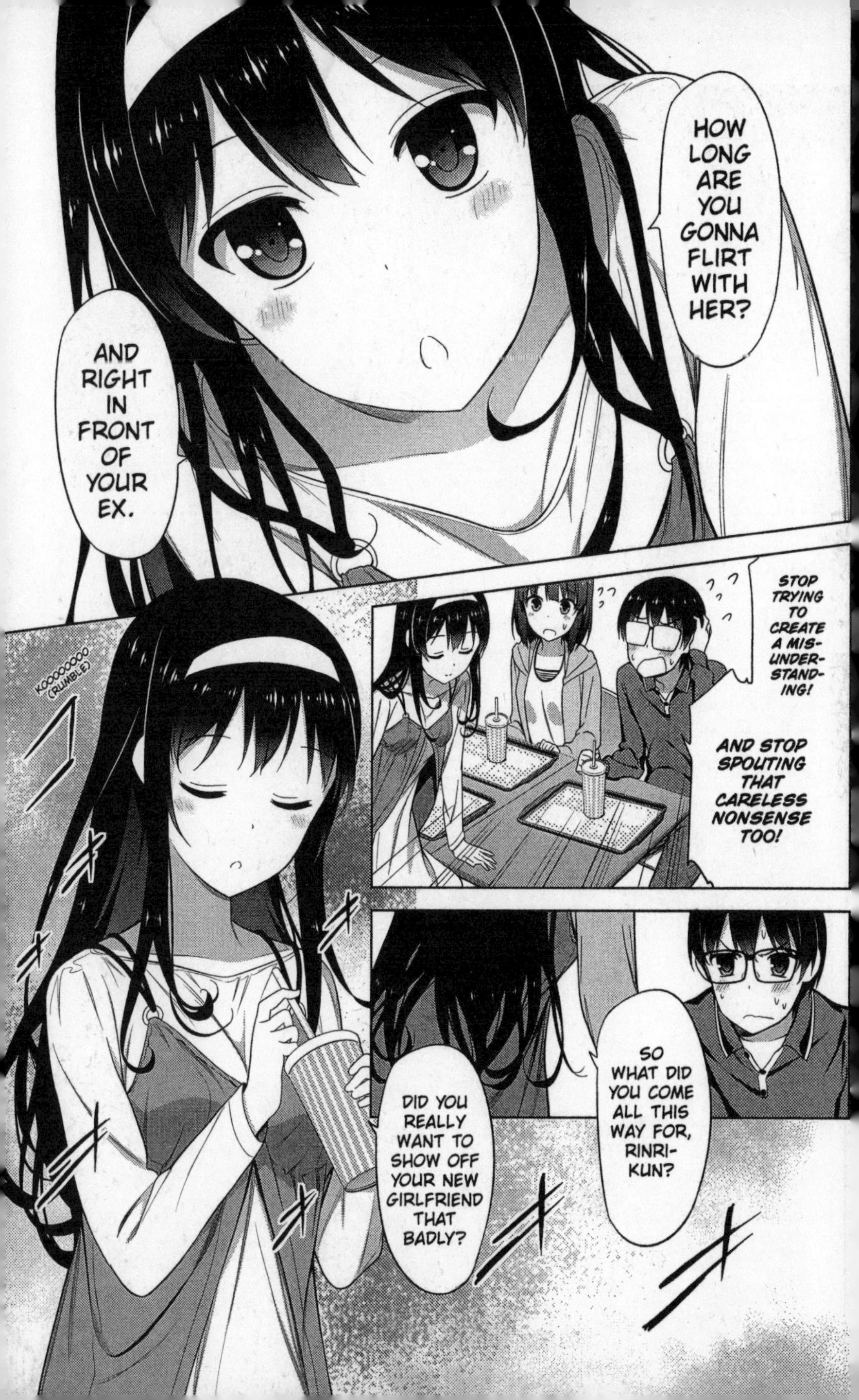
HOW LONG ARE YOU GONNA FLIRT WITH HER?
AND RIGHT IN FRONT OF YOUR EX.
STOP TRYING TO CREATE A MIS-UNDER-STAND-ING!
AND STOP SPOUTING THAT CARELESS NONSENSE TOO!
SO WHAT DID YOU COME ALL THIS WAY FOR, RINRI-KUN?
KOOOOOOOO (RUMBLE)
DID YOU REALLY WANT TO SHOW OFF YOUR NEW GIRLFRIEND THAT BADLY?

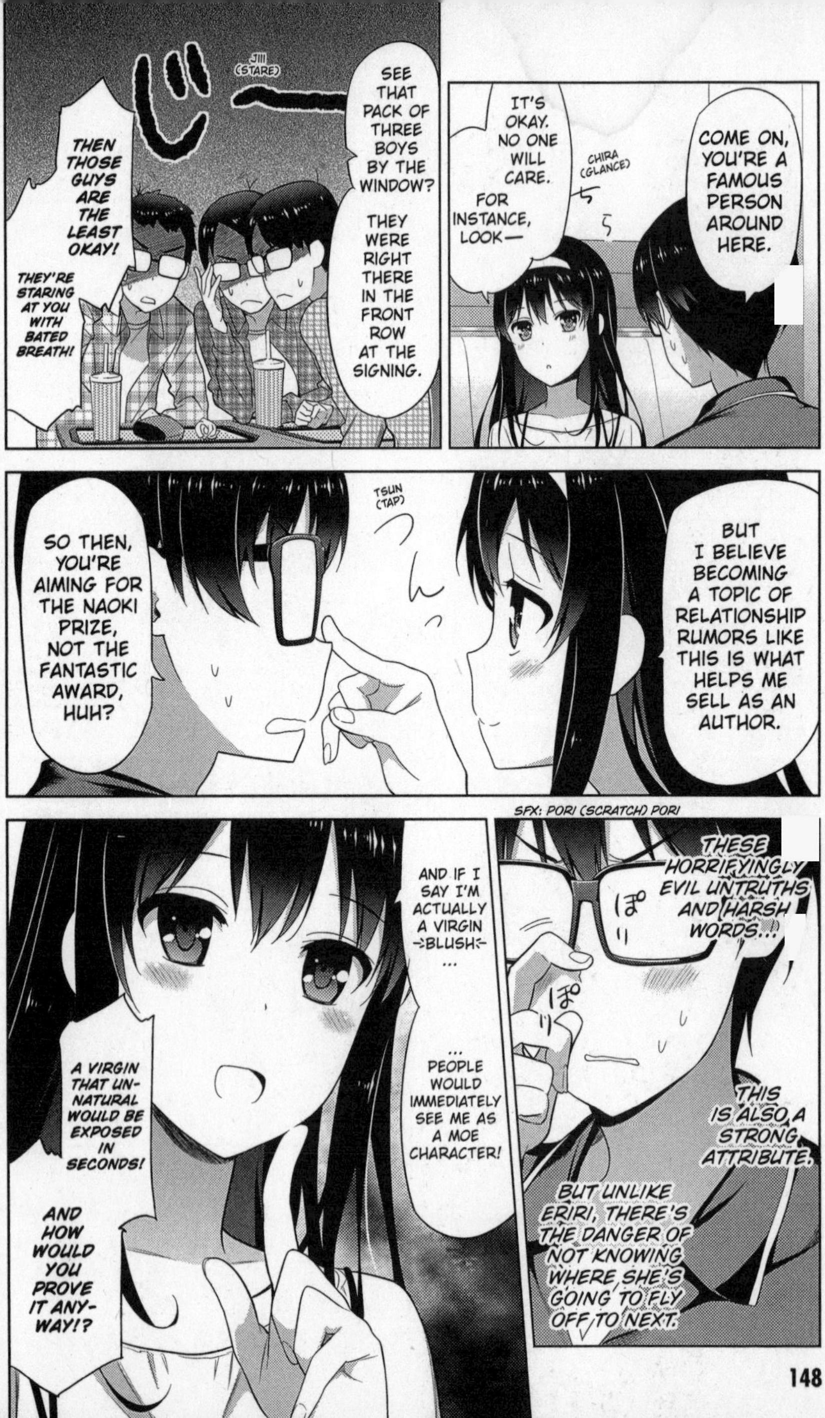
COME ON, YOU'RE A FAMOUS PERSON AROUND HERE.
IT'S OKAY. NO ONE WILL CARE.
FOR INSTANCE, LOOK—
CHIRA (GLANCE)
SEE THAT PACK OF THREE BOYS BY THE WINDOW?
THEY WERE RIGHT THERE IN THE FRONT ROW AT THE SIGNING.
JIII (STARE)
THEN THOSE GUYS ARE THE LEAST OKAY!
THEY'RE STARING AT YOU WITH BATED BREATH!
BUT I BELIEVE BECOMING A TOPIC OF RELATIONSHIP RUMORS LIKE THIS IS WHAT HELPS ME SELL AS AN AUTHOR.
TSUN (TAP)
SO THEN, YOU'RE AIMING FOR THE NAOKI PRIZE, NOT THE FANTASTIC AWARD, HUH?
SFX: PORI (SCRATCH) PORI
THESE HORRIFYINGLY EVIL UNTRUTHS AND HARSH WORDS...!
THIS IS ALSO A STRONG ATTRIBUTE.
BUT UNLIKE ERIRI, THERE'S THE DANGER OF NOT KNOWING WHERE SHE'S GOING TO FLY OFF TO NEXT.
AND IF I SAY I'M ACTUALLY A VIRGIN -BLUSH- ...
... PEOPLE WOULD IMMEDIATELY SEE ME AS A MOE CHARACTER!
A VIRGIN THAT UN-NATURAL WOULD BE EXPOSED IN SECONDS!
AND HOW WOULD YOU PROVE IT ANY-WAY!?

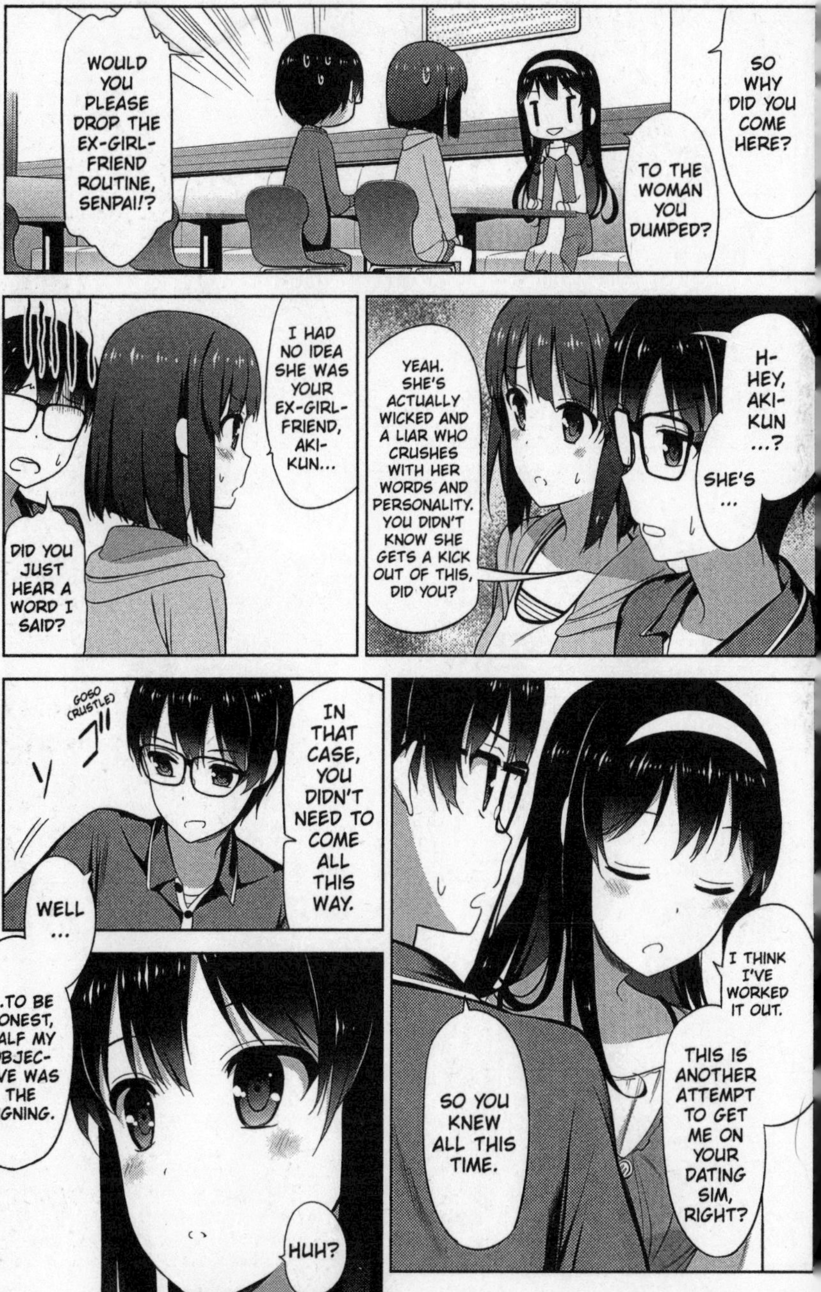
SO WHY DID YOU COME HERE?
TO THE WOMAN YOU DUMPED?
WOULD YOU PLEASE DROP THE EX-GIRL-FRIEND ROUTINE, SENPAI!?
H-HEY, AKI-KUN...?
SHE'S...
YEAH. SHE'S ACTUALLY WICKED AND A LIAR WHO CRUSHES WITH HER WORDS AND PERSONALITY. YOU DIDN'T KNOW SHE GETS A KICK OUT OF THIS, DID YOU?
I HAD NO IDEA SHE WAS YOUR EX-GIRL-FRIEND, AKI-KUN...
DID YOU JUST HEAR A WORD I SAID?
I THINK I'VE WORKED IT OUT.
THIS IS ANOTHER ATTEMPT TO GET ME ON YOUR DATING SIM, RIGHT?
SO YOU KNEW ALL THIS TIME.
GOSO (RUSTLE)
IN THAT CASE, YOU DIDN'T NEED TO COME ALL THIS WAY.
WELL...
...TO BE HONEST, HALF MY OBJEC-TIVE WAS THE SIGNING.
HUH?

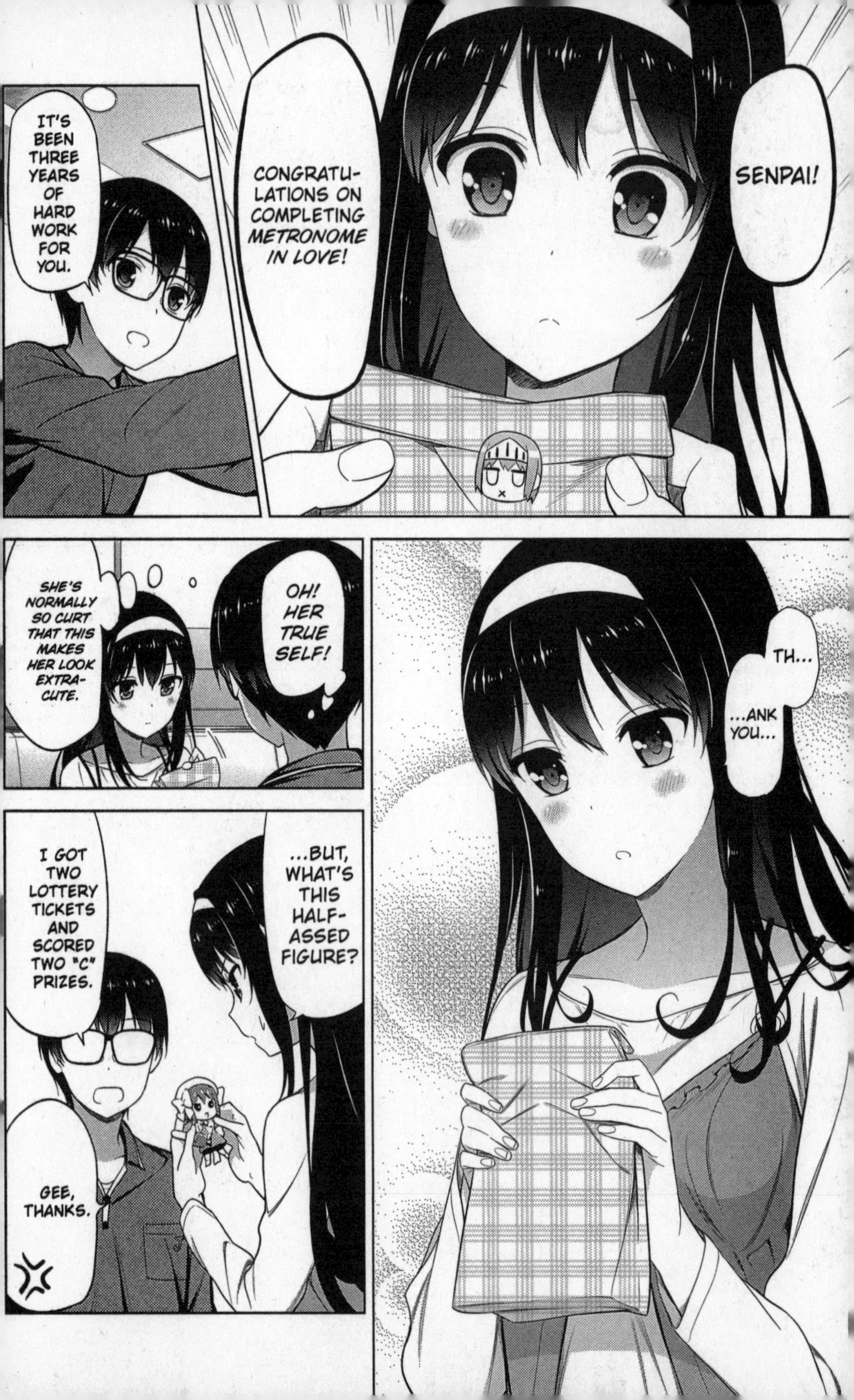
SENPAI!
CONGRATULATIONS ON COMPLETING METRONOME IN LOVE!
IT'S BEEN THREE YEARS OF HARD WORK FOR YOU.
TH...
...ANK YOU...
OH! HER TRUE SELF!
SHE'S NORMALLY SO CURT THAT THIS MAKES HER LOOK EXTRA-CUTE.
...BUT, WHAT'S THIS HALF-ASSED FIGURE?
I GOT TWO LOTTERY TICKETS AND SCORED TWO "C" PRIZES.
GEE, THANKS.

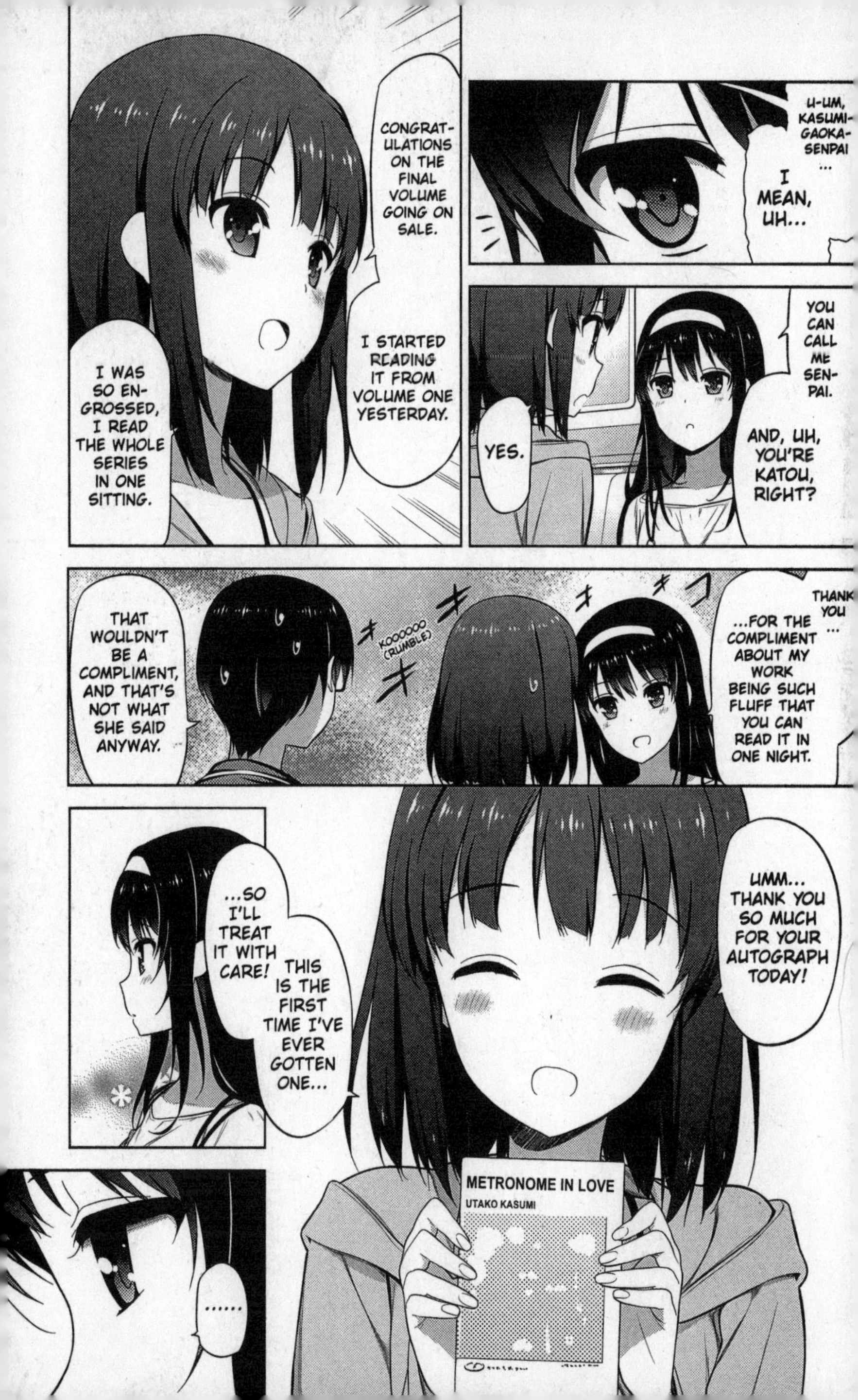
U-UM, KASUMIGAOKA-SENPAI...
I MEAN, UH...
YOU CAN CALL ME SENPAI.
AND, UH, YOU'RE KATOU, RIGHT?
YES.
CONGRATULATIONS ON THE FINAL VOLUME GOING ON SALE.
I STARTED READING IT FROM VOLUME ONE YESTERDAY.
I WAS SO ENGROSSED, I READ THE WHOLE SERIES IN ONE SITTING.
THANK YOU...
...FOR THE COMPLIMENT ABOUT MY WORK BEING SUCH FLUFF THAT YOU CAN READ IT IN ONE NIGHT.
KOOOOOO (RUMBLE)
THAT WOULDN'T BE A COMPLIMENT, AND THAT'S NOT WHAT SHE SAID ANYWAY.
UMM... THANK YOU SO MUCH FOR YOUR AUTOGRAPH TODAY!
METRONOME IN LOVE
UTAKO KASUMI
...SO I'LL TREAT IT WITH CARE!
THIS IS THE FIRST TIME I'VE EVER GOTTEN ONE...
......

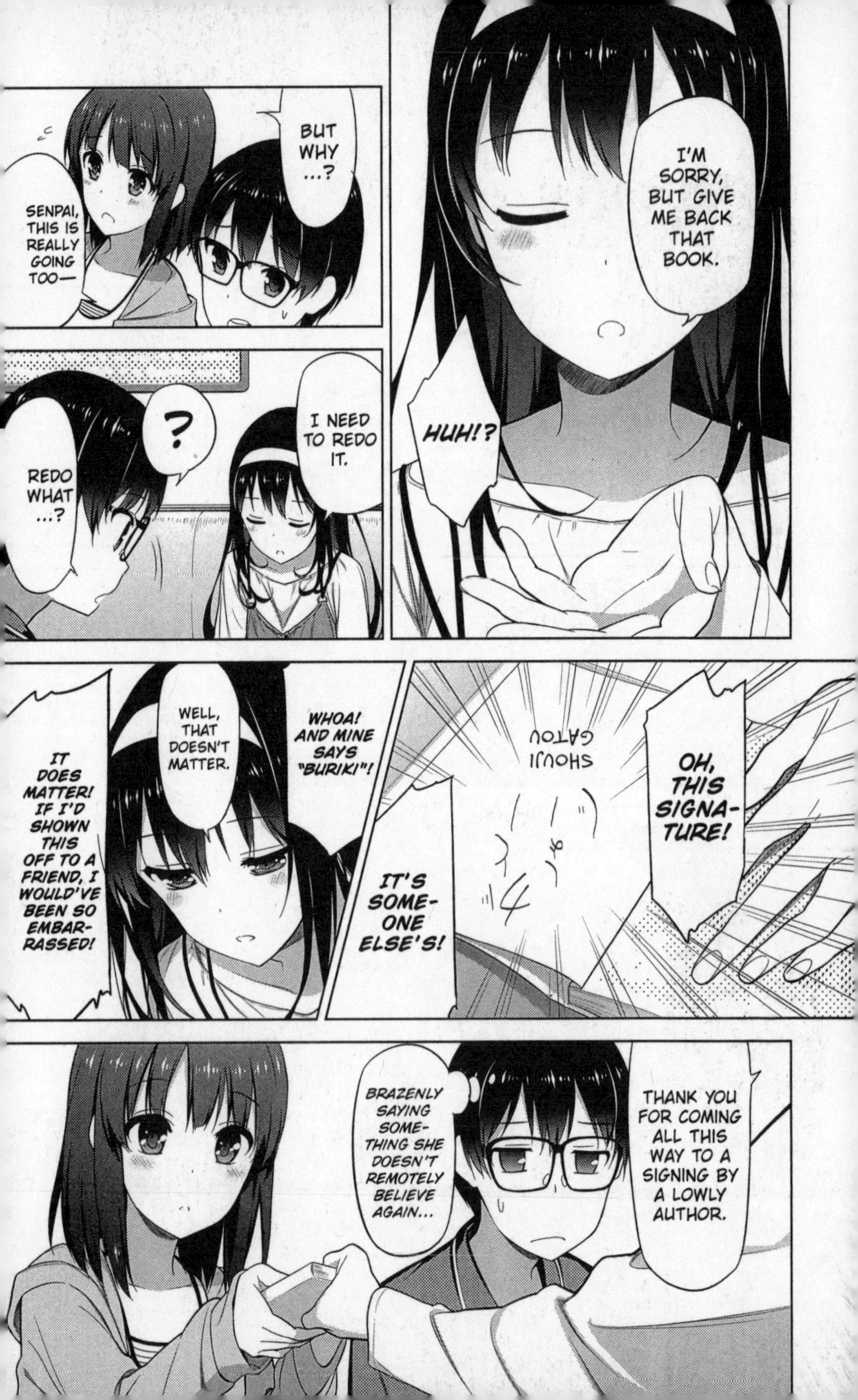
I'M SORRY, BUT GIVE ME BACK THAT BOOK.
HUH!?
BUT WHY ...?
SENPAI, THIS IS REALLY GOING TOO—
I NEED TO REDO IT.
?
REDO WHAT ...?
OH, THIS SIGNATURE!
SHOUJI GATOU
IT'S SOMEONE ELSE'S!
WHOA! AND MINE SAYS "BURIKI"!
WELL, THAT DOESN'T MATTER.
IT DOES MATTER! IF I'D SHOWN THIS OFF TO A FRIEND, I WOULD'VE BEEN SO EMBARRASSED!
THANK YOU FOR COMING ALL THIS WAY TO A SIGNING BY A LOWLY AUTHOR.
BRAZENLY SAYING SOMETHING SHE DOESN'T REMOTELY BELIEVE AGAIN...

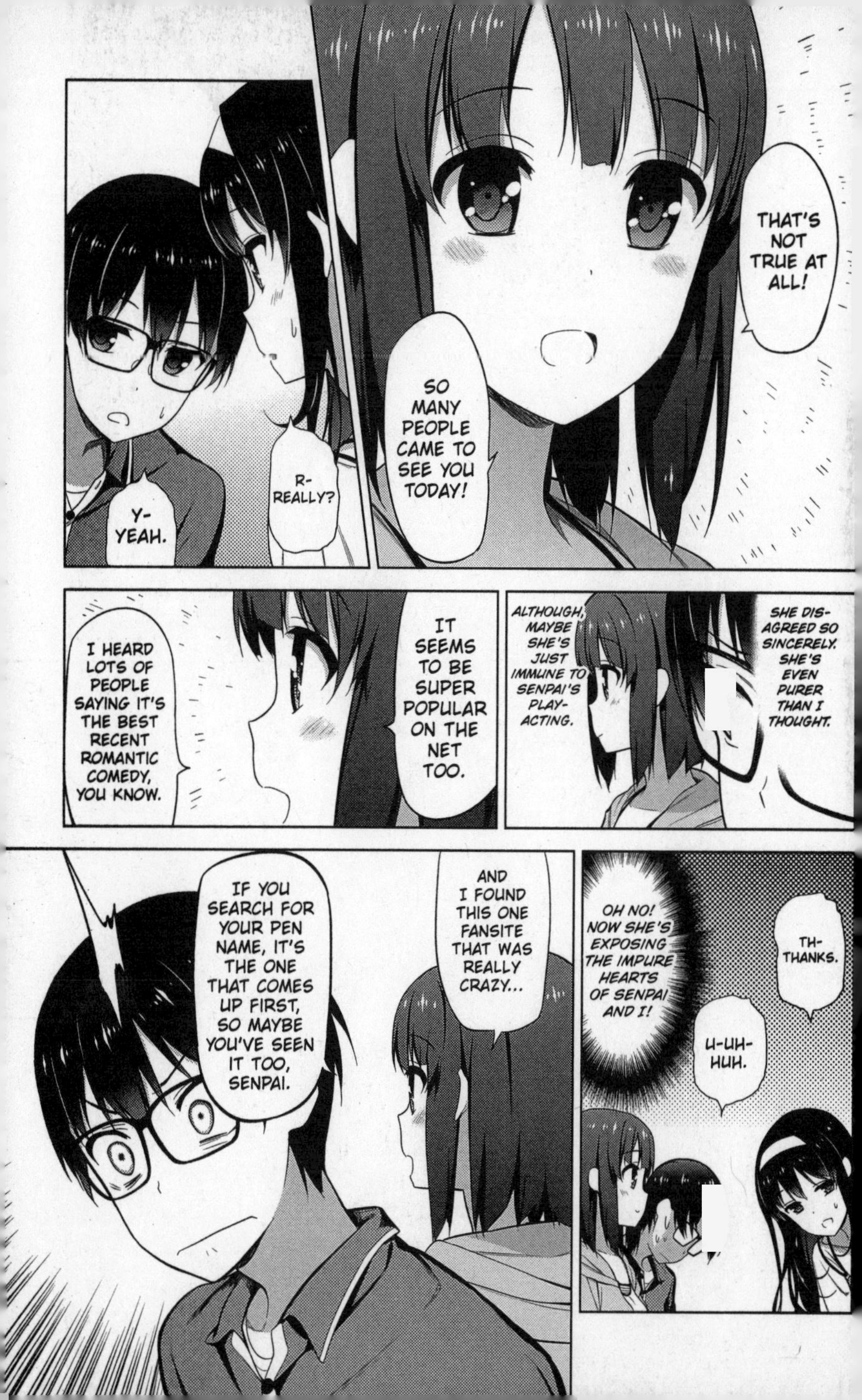
THAT'S NOT TRUE AT ALL!
SO MANY PEOPLE CAME TO SEE YOU TODAY!
R-REALLY?
Y-YEAH.
SHE DIS-AGREED SO SINCERELY. SHE'S EVEN PURER THAN I THOUGHT.
ALTHOUGH, MAYBE SHE'S JUST IMMUNE TO SENPAI'S PLAY-ACTING.
IT SEEMS TO BE SUPER POPULAR ON THE NET TOO.
I HEARD LOTS OF PEOPLE SAYING IT'S THE BEST RECENT ROMANTIC COMEDY, YOU KNOW.
TH-THANKS.
OH NO! NOW SHE'S EXPOSING THE IMPURE HEARTS OF SENPAI AND I!
U-UH-HUH.
AND I FOUND THIS ONE FANSITE THAT WAS REALLY CRAZY...
IF YOU SEARCH FOR YOUR PEN NAME, IT'S THE ONE THAT COMES UP FIRST, SO MAYBE YOU'VE SEEN IT TOO, SENPAI.

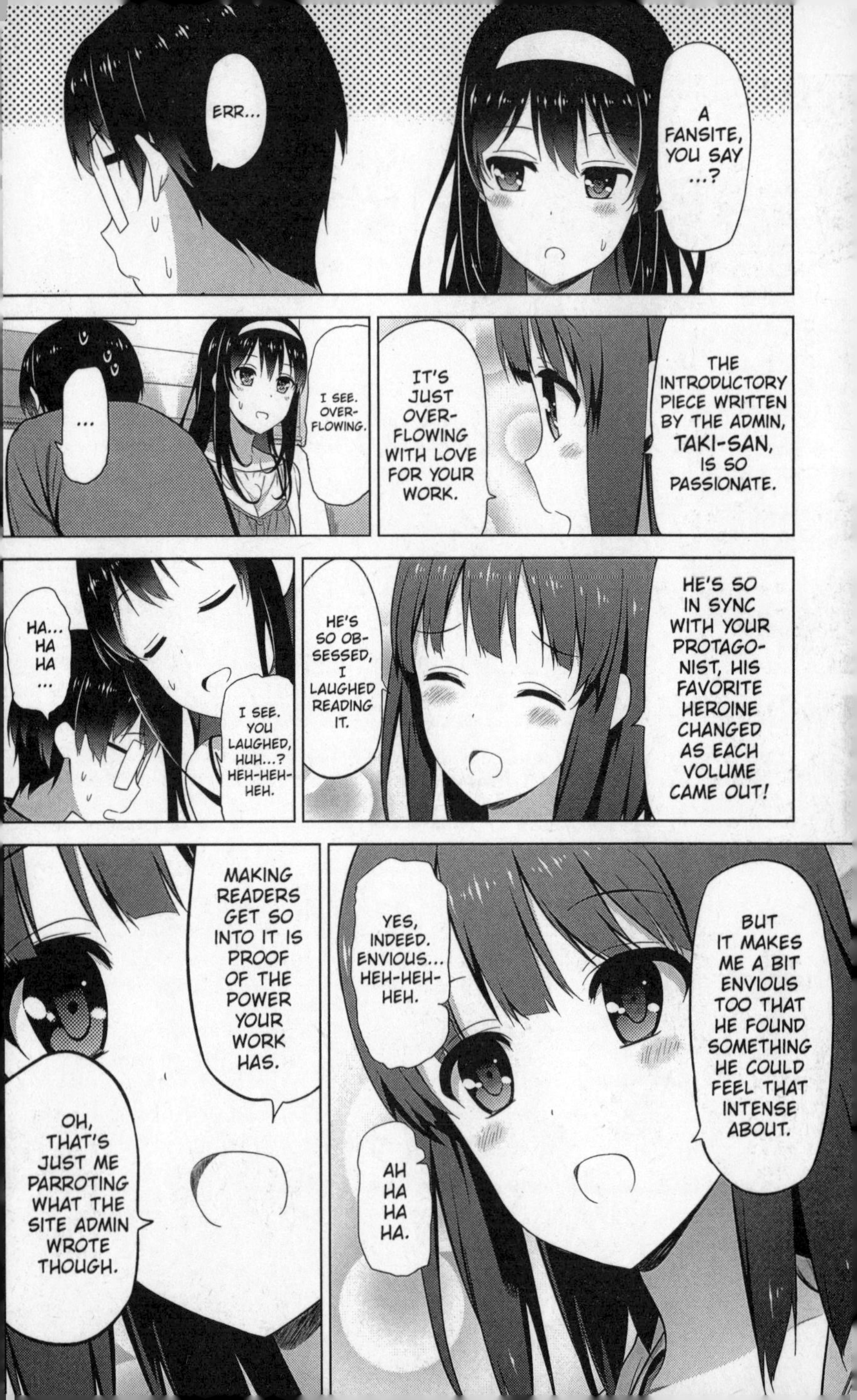

A FANSITE, YOU SAY ...?
ERR...
THE INTRODUCTORY PIECE WRITTEN BY THE ADMIN, TAKI-SAN, IS SO PASSIONATE.
IT'S JUST OVER-FLOWING WITH LOVE FOR YOUR WORK.
I SEE. OVER-FLOWING.
...
HE'S SO IN SYNC WITH YOUR PROTAGO-NIST, HIS FAVORITE HEROINE CHANGED AS EACH VOLUME CAME OUT!
HE'S SO OB-SESSED, I LAUGHED READING IT.
I SEE. YOU LAUGHED, HUH...? HEH-HEH-HEH.
HA... HA HA ...
BUT IT MAKES ME A BIT ENVIOUS TOO THAT HE FOUND SOMETHING HE COULD FEEL THAT INTENSE ABOUT.
YES, INDEED. ENVIOUS... HEH-HEH-HEH.
AH HA HA HA.
MAKING READERS GET SO INTO IT IS PROOF OF THE POWER YOUR WORK HAS.
OH, THAT'S JUST ME PARROTING WHAT THE SITE ADMIN WROTE THOUGH.

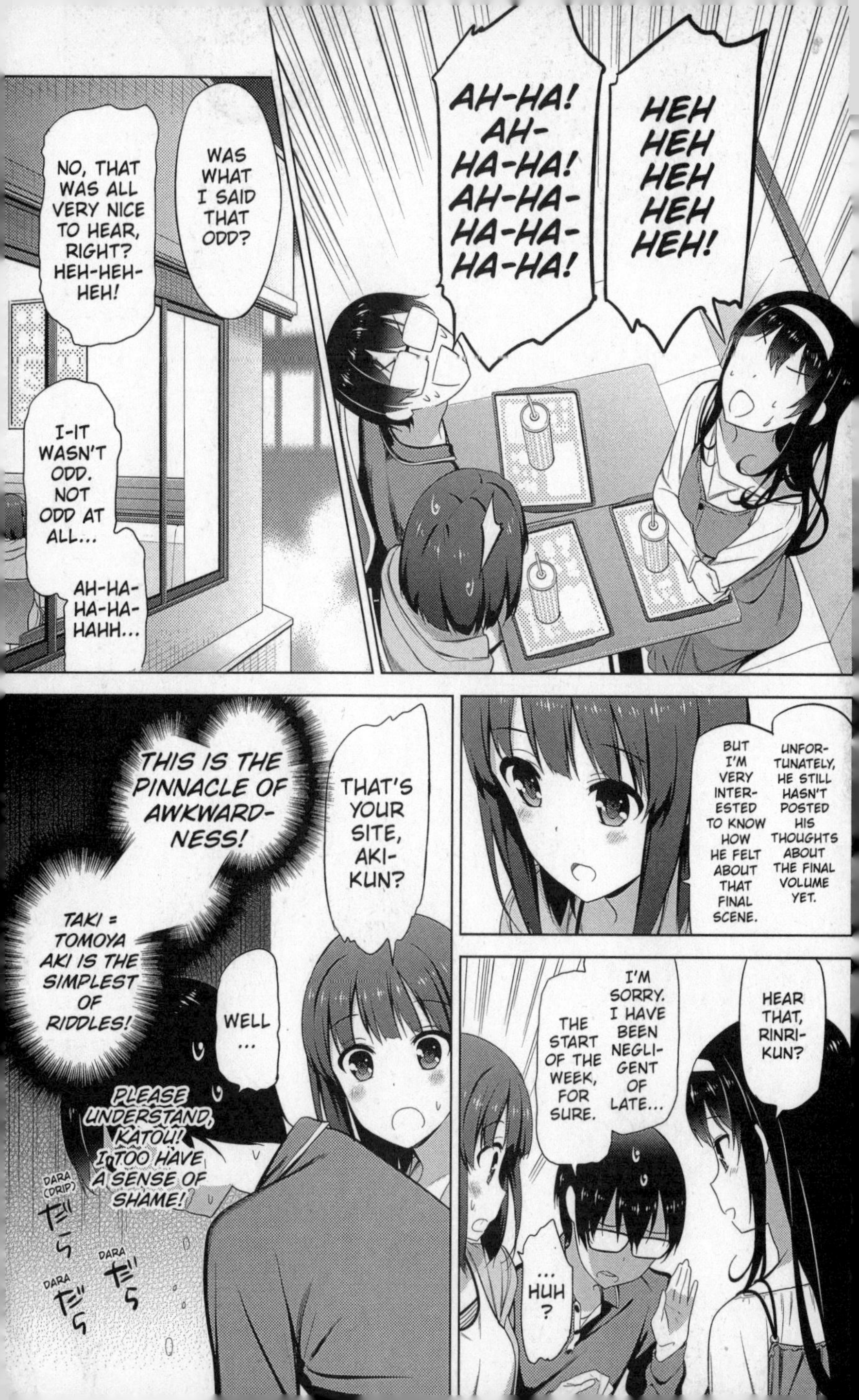
HEH HEH HEH HEH HEH!
AH-HA! AH-HA-HA! AH-HA-HA-HA-HA-HA!
WAS WHAT I SAID THAT ODD?
NO, THAT WAS ALL VERY NICE TO HEAR, RIGHT? HEH-HEH-HEH!
I-IT WASN'T ODD. NOT ODD AT ALL...
AH-HA-HA-HA-HAHH...
UNFORTUNATELY, HE STILL HASN'T POSTED HIS THOUGHTS ABOUT THE FINAL VOLUME YET.
BUT I'M VERY INTERESTED TO KNOW HOW HE FELT ABOUT THAT FINAL SCENE.
HEAR THAT, RINRI-KUN?
I'M SORRY. I HAVE BEEN NEGLIGENT OF LATE...
THE START OF THE WEEK, FOR SURE.
...HUH?
THAT'S YOUR SITE, AKI-KUN?
THIS IS THE PINNACLE OF AWKWARDNESS!
WELL...
TAKI = TOMOYA AKI IS THE SIMPLEST OF RIDDLES!
PLEASE UNDERSTAND, KATOU! I TOO HAVE A SENSE OF SHAME!
DARA (DRIP) だら
DARA だら
DARA だら

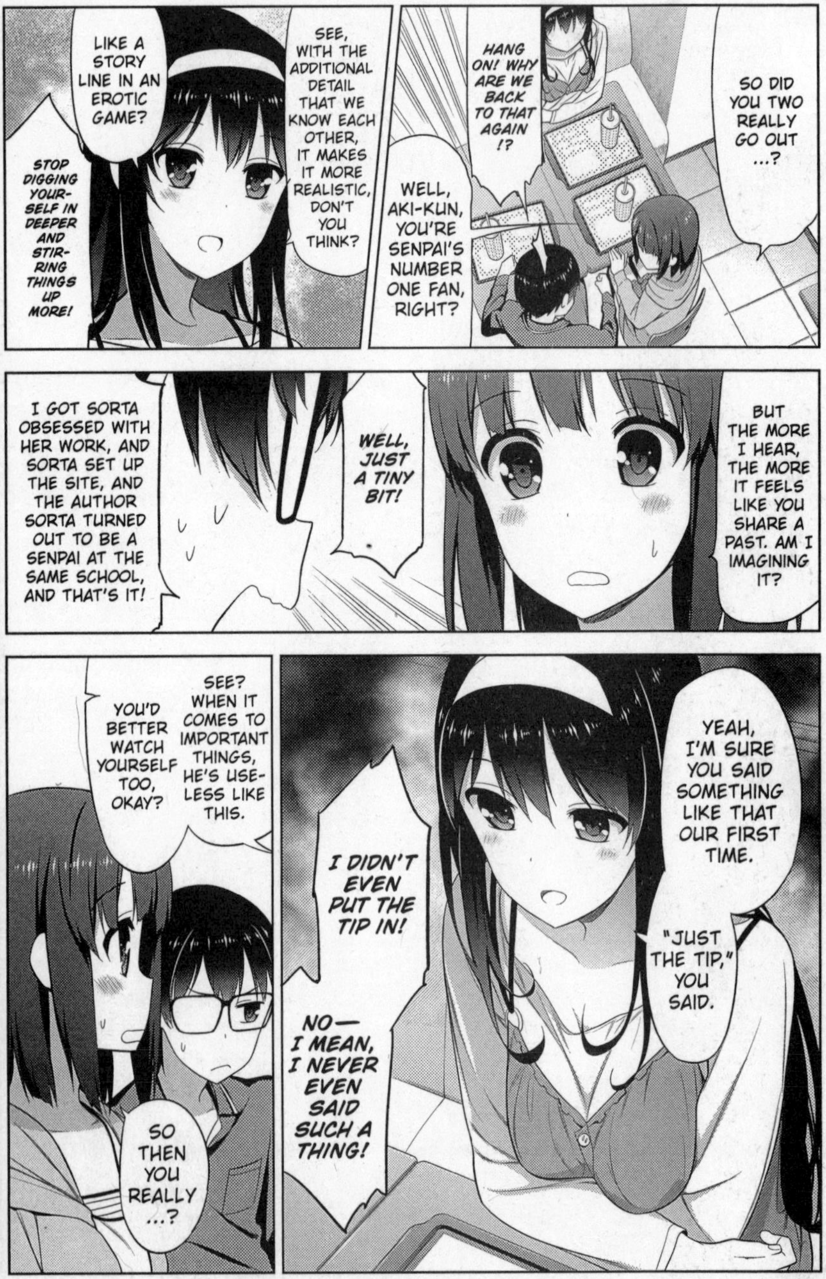
SO DID YOU TWO REALLY GO OUT ...?
HANG ON! WHY ARE WE BACK TO THAT AGAIN !?
WELL, AKI-KUN, YOU'RE SENPAI'S NUMBER ONE FAN, RIGHT?
SEE, WITH THE ADDITIONAL DETAIL THAT WE KNOW EACH OTHER, IT MAKES IT MORE REALISTIC, DON'T YOU THINK?
LIKE A STORY LINE IN AN EROTIC GAME?
STOP DIGGING YOUR-SELF IN DEEPER AND STIR-RING THINGS UP MORE!
BUT THE MORE I HEAR, THE MORE IT FEELS LIKE YOU SHARE A PAST. AM I IMAGINING IT?
WELL, JUST A TINY BIT!
I GOT SORTA OBSESSED WITH HER WORK, AND SORTA SET UP THE SITE, AND THE AUTHOR SORTA TURNED OUT TO BE A SENPAI AT THE SAME SCHOOL, AND THAT'S IT!
YEAH, I'M SURE YOU SAID SOMETHING LIKE THAT OUR FIRST TIME.
"JUST THE TIP," YOU SAID.
I DIDN'T EVEN PUT THE TIP IN!
NO— I MEAN, I NEVER EVEN SAID SUCH A THING!
SEE? WHEN IT COMES TO IMPORTANT THINGS, HE'S USE-LESS LIKE THIS.
YOU'D BETTER WATCH YOURSELF TOO, OKAY?
SO THEN YOU REALLY ...?

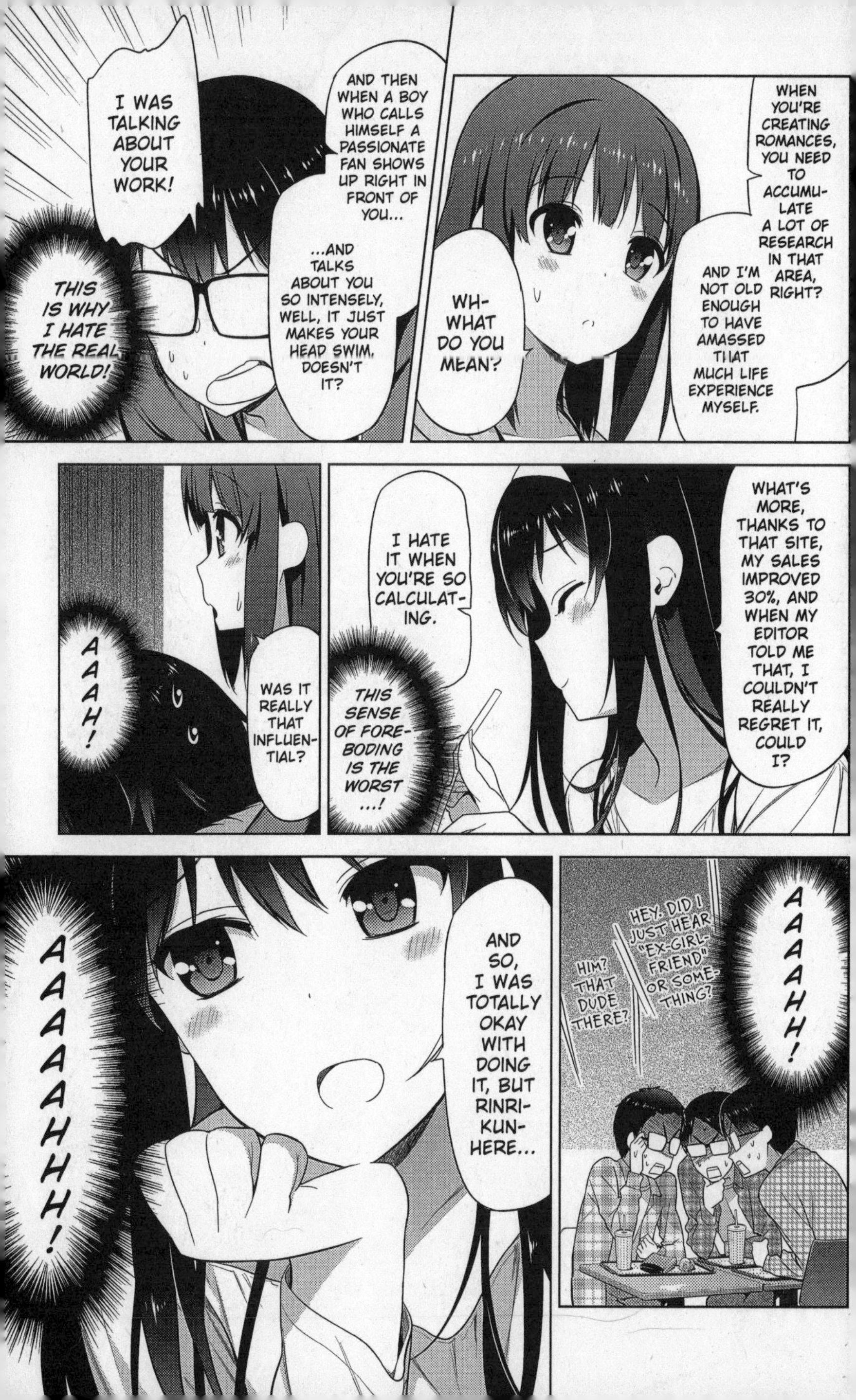
WHEN YOU'RE CREATING ROMANCES, YOU NEED TO ACCUMULATE A LOT OF RESEARCH IN THAT AREA, RIGHT?
AND I'M NOT OLD ENOUGH TO HAVE AMASSED THAT MUCH LIFE EXPERIENCE MYSELF.
WH-WHAT DO YOU MEAN?
AND THEN WHEN A BOY WHO CALLS HIMSELF A PASSIONATE FAN SHOWS UP RIGHT IN FRONT OF YOU...
...AND TALKS ABOUT YOU SO INTENSELY, WELL, IT JUST MAKES YOUR HEAD SWIM, DOESN'T IT?
I WAS TALKING ABOUT YOUR WORK!
THIS IS WHY I HATE THE REAL WORLD!
WHAT'S MORE, THANKS TO THAT SITE, MY SALES IMPROVED 30%, AND WHEN MY EDITOR TOLD ME THAT, I COULDN'T REALLY REGRET IT, COULD I?
I HATE IT WHEN YOU'RE SO CALCULATING.
THIS SENSE OF FOREBODING IS THE WORST...!
WAS IT REALLY THAT INFLUENTIAL?
AAAH!
AAAAHH!
HEY. DID I JUST HEAR "EX-GIRLFRIEND" OR SOMETHING?
HIM? THAT DUDE THERE?
AND SO, I WAS TOTALLY OKAY WITH DOING IT, BUT RINRI-KUN HERE...
AAAAAHHH!

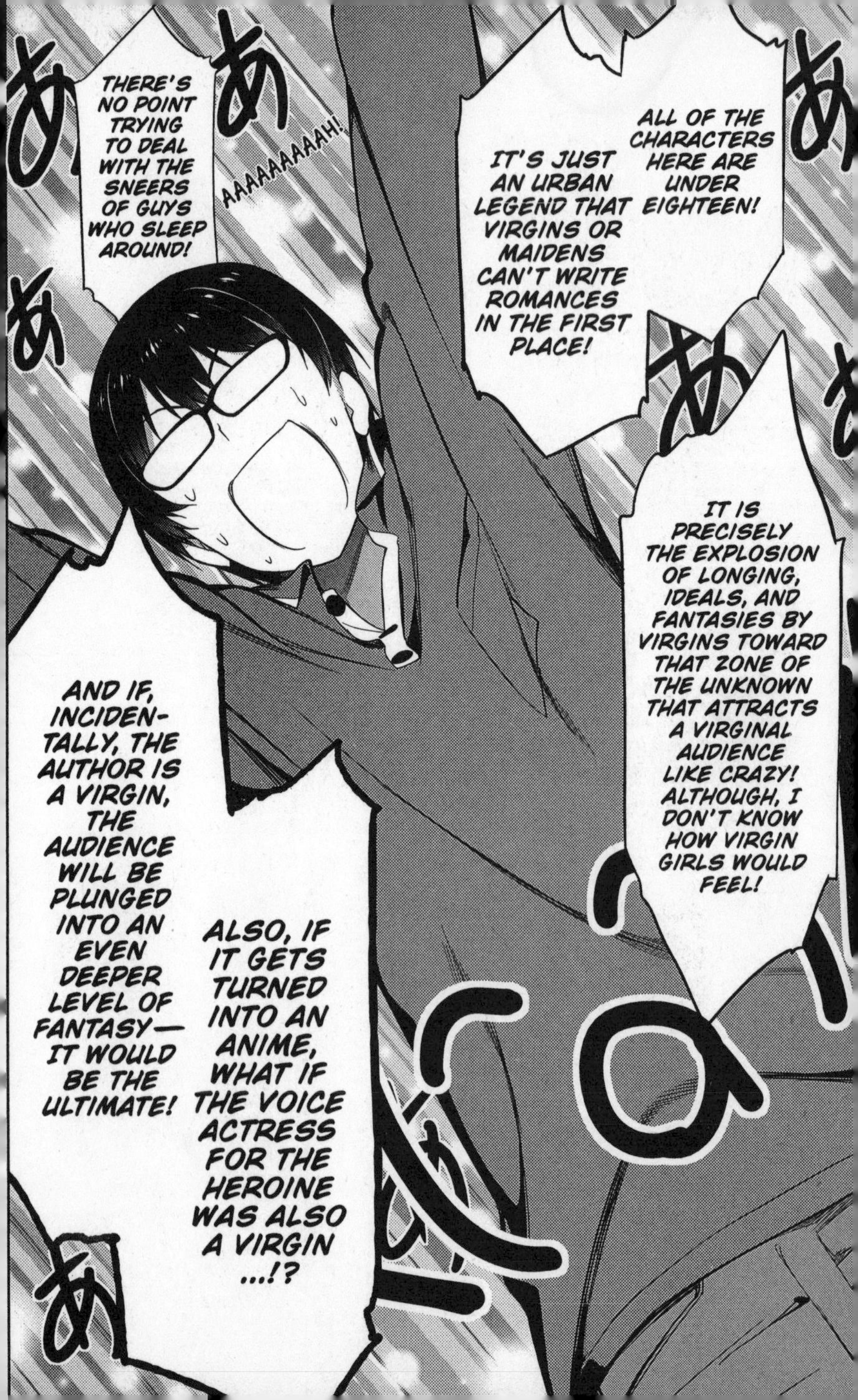
ALL OF THE CHARACTERS HERE ARE UNDER EIGHTEEN!
IT'S JUST AN URBAN LEGEND THAT VIRGINS OR MAIDENS CAN'T WRITE ROMANCES IN THE FIRST PLACE!
AAAAAAAAAH!
THERE'S NO POINT TRYING TO DEAL WITH THE SNEERS OF GUYS WHO SLEEP AROUND!
IT IS PRECISELY THE EXPLOSION OF LONGING, IDEALS, AND FANTASIES BY VIRGINS TOWARD THAT ZONE OF THE UNKNOWN THAT ATTRACTS A VIRGINAL AUDIENCE LIKE CRAZY! ALTHOUGH, I DON'T KNOW HOW VIRGIN GIRLS WOULD FEEL!
AND IF, INCIDENTALLY, THE AUTHOR IS A VIRGIN, THE AUDIENCE WILL BE PLUNGED INTO AN EVEN DEEPER LEVEL OF FANTASY—IT WOULD BE THE ULTIMATE!
ALSO, IF IT GETS TURNED INTO AN ANIME, WHAT IF THE VOICE ACTRESS FOR THE HEROINE WAS ALSO A VIRGIN ...!?

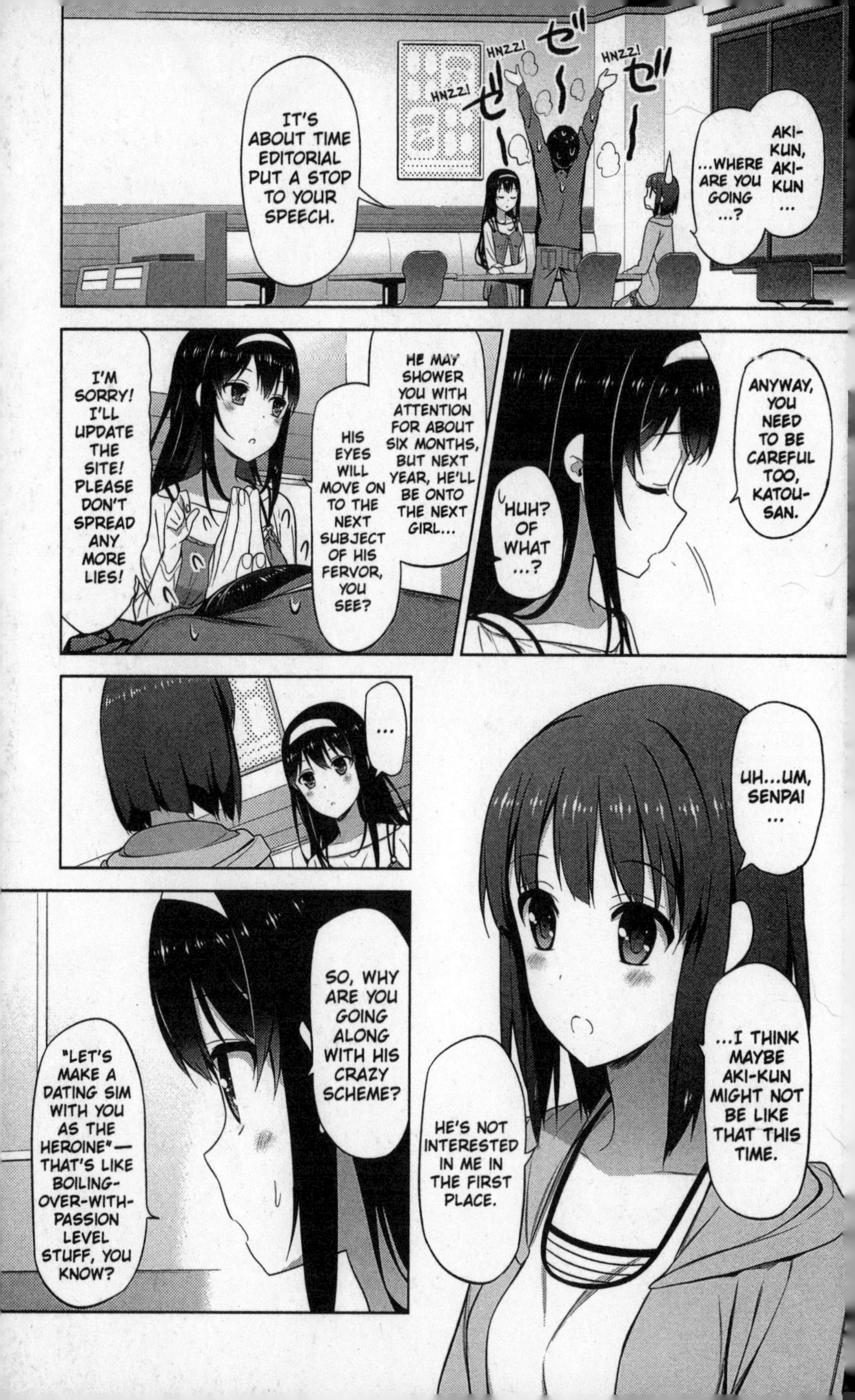
AKI-KUN, AKI-KUN ...
...WHERE ARE YOU GOING ...?
HNZZ!
ゼーゼー
HNZZ!
ゼーゼー
HNZZ!
IT'S ABOUT TIME EDITORIAL PUT A STOP TO YOUR SPEECH.
ANYWAY, YOU NEED TO BE CAREFUL TOO, KATOU-SAN.
HUH? OF WHAT ...?
HE MAY SHOWER YOU WITH ATTENTION FOR ABOUT SIX MONTHS, BUT NEXT YEAR, HE'LL BE ONTO THE NEXT GIRL...
HIS EYES WILL MOVE ON TO THE NEXT SUBJECT OF HIS FERVOR, YOU SEE?
I'M SORRY! I'LL UPDATE THE SITE! PLEASE DON'T SPREAD ANY MORE LIES!
UH...UM, SENPAI ...
...I THINK MAYBE AKI-KUN MIGHT NOT BE LIKE THAT THIS TIME.
HE'S NOT INTERESTED IN ME IN THE FIRST PLACE.
...
SO, WHY ARE YOU GOING ALONG WITH HIS CRAZY SCHEME?
"LET'S MAKE A DATING SIM WITH YOU AS THE HEROINE"—THAT'S LIKE BOILING-OVER-WITH-PASSION LEVEL STUFF, YOU KNOW?

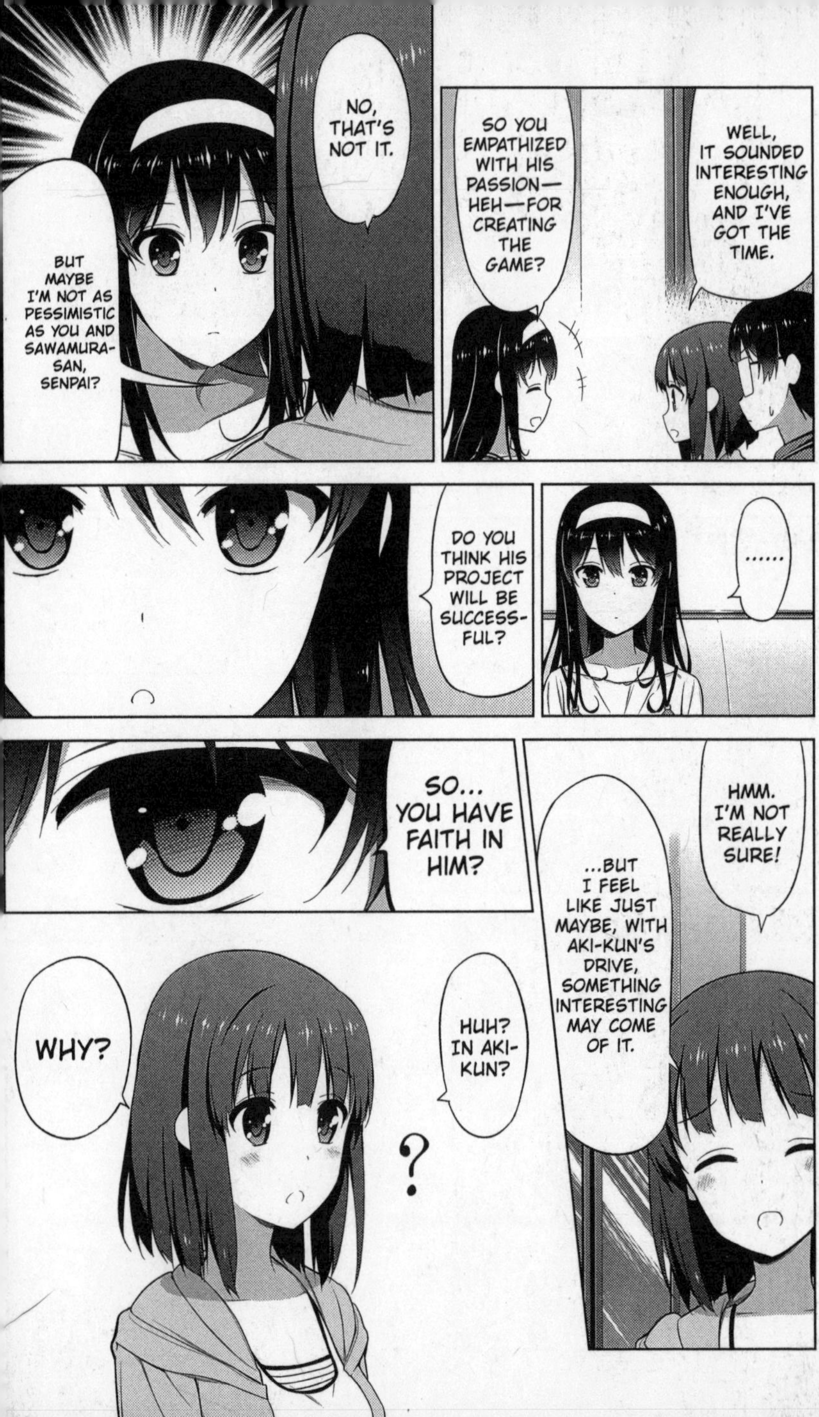
WELL, IT SOUNDED INTERESTING ENOUGH, AND I'VE GOT THE TIME.
SO YOU EMPATHIZED WITH HIS PASSION—HEH—FOR CREATING THE GAME?
NO, THAT'S NOT IT.
BUT MAYBE I'M NOT AS PESSIMISTIC AS YOU AND SAWAMURA-SAN, SENPAI?
......
DO YOU THINK HIS PROJECT WILL BE SUCCESSFUL?
HMM. I'M NOT REALLY SURE!
...BUT I FEEL LIKE JUST MAYBE, WITH AKI-KUN'S DRIVE, SOMETHING INTERESTING MAY COME OF IT.
SO... YOU HAVE FAITH IN HIM?
HUH? IN AKI-KUN?
?
WHY?

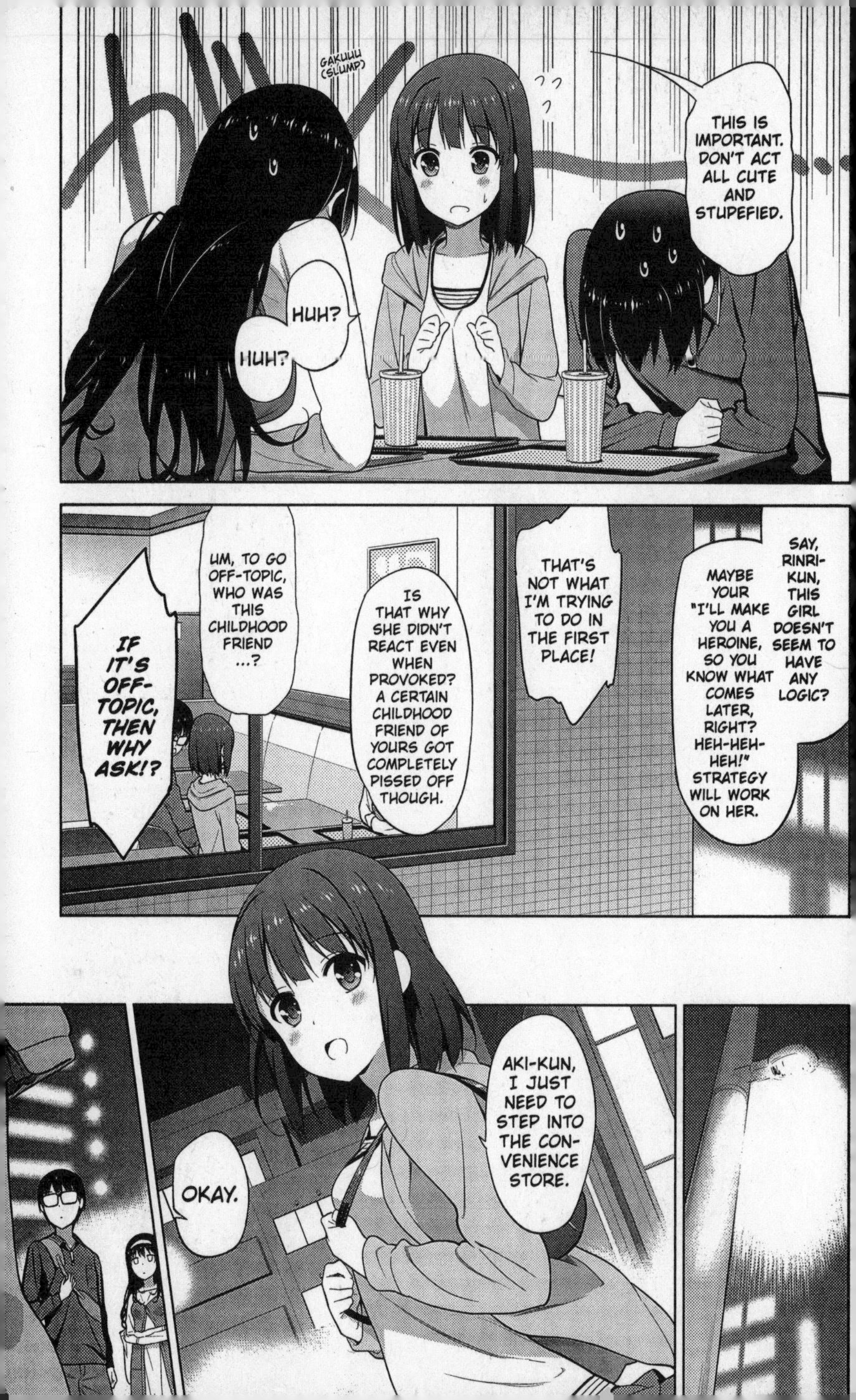
THIS IS IMPORTANT. DON'T ACT ALL CUTE AND STUPEFIED.
GAKUUU (SLUMP)
HUH?
HUH?
SAY, RINRI-KUN, THIS GIRL DOESN'T SEEM TO HAVE ANY LOGIC?
MAYBE YOUR "I'LL MAKE YOU A HEROINE, SO YOU KNOW WHAT COMES LATER, RIGHT? HEH-HEH-HEH!" STRATEGY WILL WORK ON HER.
THAT'S NOT WHAT I'M TRYING TO DO IN THE FIRST PLACE!
IS THAT WHY SHE DIDN'T REACT EVEN WHEN PROVOKED? A CERTAIN CHILDHOOD FRIEND OF YOURS GOT COMPLETELY PISSED OFF THOUGH.
UM, TO GO OFF-TOPIC, WHO WAS THIS CHILDHOOD FRIEND ...?
IF IT'S OFF-TOPIC, THEN WHY ASK!?
AKI-KUN, I JUST NEED TO STEP INTO THE CON-VENIENCE STORE.
OKAY.

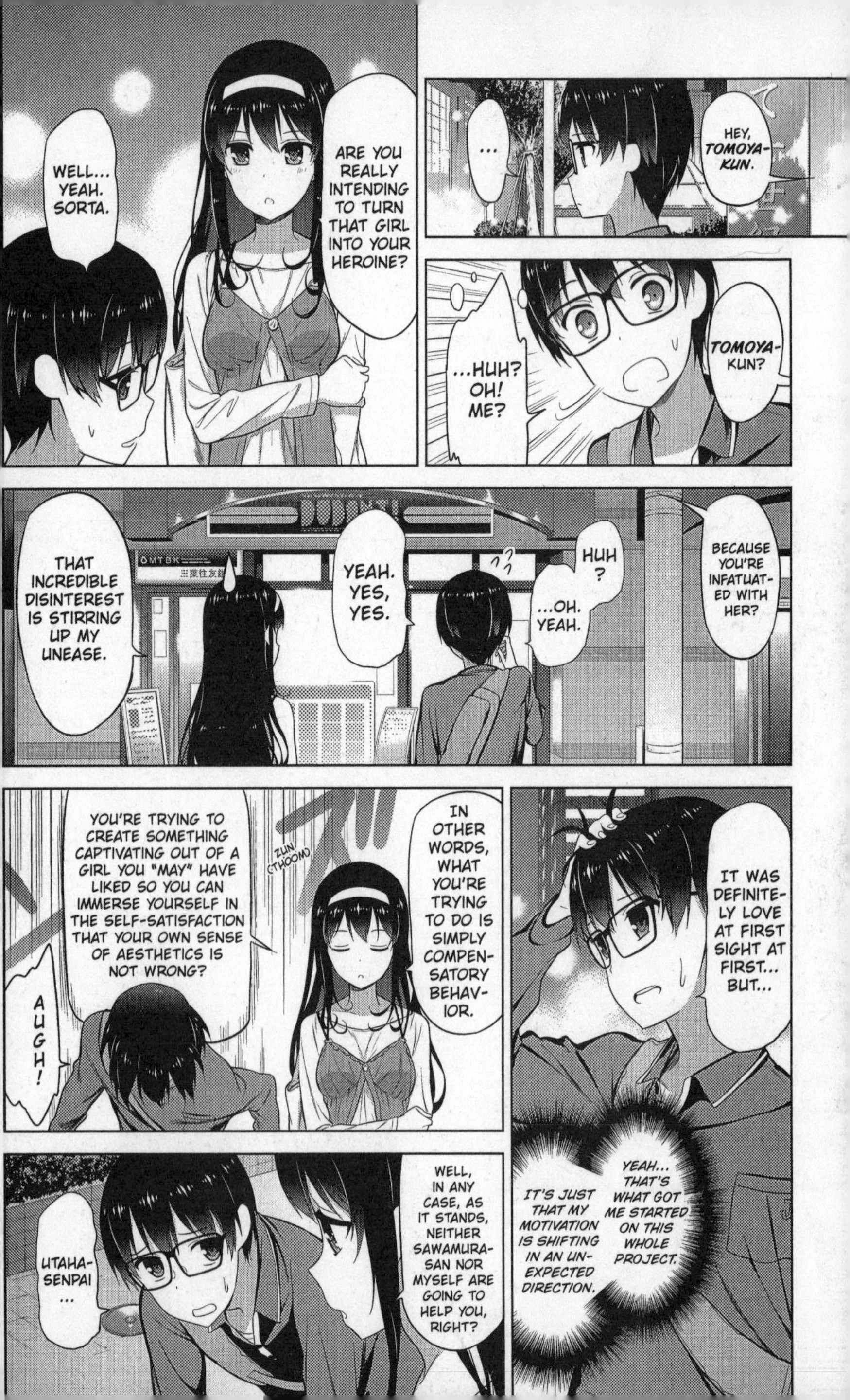
HEY, TOMOYA-KUN.
...
TOMOYA-KUN?
...HUH? OH! ME?
ARE YOU REALLY INTENDING TO TURN THAT GIRL INTO YOUR HEROINE?
WELL... YEAH. SORTA.
BECAUSE YOU'RE INFATUATED WITH HER?
HUH?
...OH. YEAH.
YEAH. YES, YES.
THAT INCREDIBLE DISINTEREST IS STIRRING UP MY UNEASE.
IT WAS DEFINITELY LOVE AT FIRST SIGHT AT FIRST... BUT...
YEAH... THAT'S WHAT GOT ME STARTED ON THIS WHOLE PROJECT.
IT'S JUST THAT MY MOTIVATION IS SHIFTING IN AN UNEXPECTED DIRECTION.
IN OTHER WORDS, WHAT YOU'RE TRYING TO DO IS SIMPLY COMPENSATORY BEHAVIOR.
YOU'RE TRYING TO CREATE SOMETHING CAPTIVATING OUT OF A GIRL YOU "MAY" HAVE LIKED SO YOU CAN IMMERSE YOURSELF IN THE SELF-SATISFACTION THAT YOUR OWN SENSE OF AESTHETICS IS NOT WRONG?
ZUN (THOOM)
AUGH!
WELL, IN ANY CASE, AS IT STANDS, NEITHER SAWAMURA-SAN NOR MYSELF ARE GOING TO HELP YOU, RIGHT?
UTAHA-SENPAI...

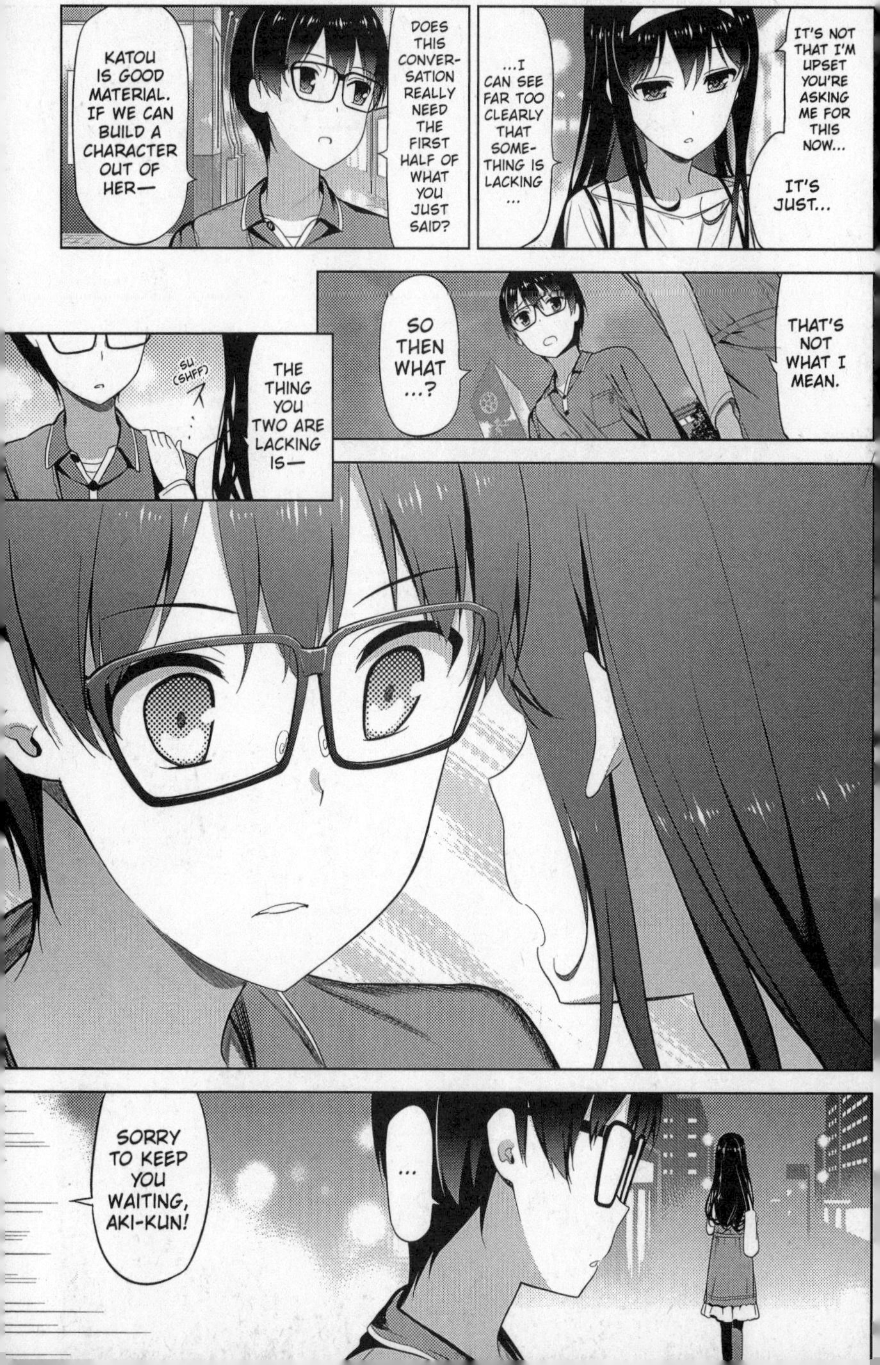
IT'S NOT THAT I'M UPSET YOU'RE ASKING ME FOR THIS NOW...
IT'S JUST...
...I CAN SEE FAR TOO CLEARLY THAT SOMETHING IS LACKING...
DOES THIS CONVERSATION REALLY NEED THE FIRST HALF OF WHAT YOU JUST SAID?
KATOU IS GOOD MATERIAL. IF WE CAN BUILD A CHARACTER OUT OF HER—
THAT'S NOT WHAT I MEAN.
SO THEN WHAT...?
THE THING YOU TWO ARE LACKING IS—
SU (SHFF)
...
SORRY TO KEEP YOU WAITING, AKI-KUN!

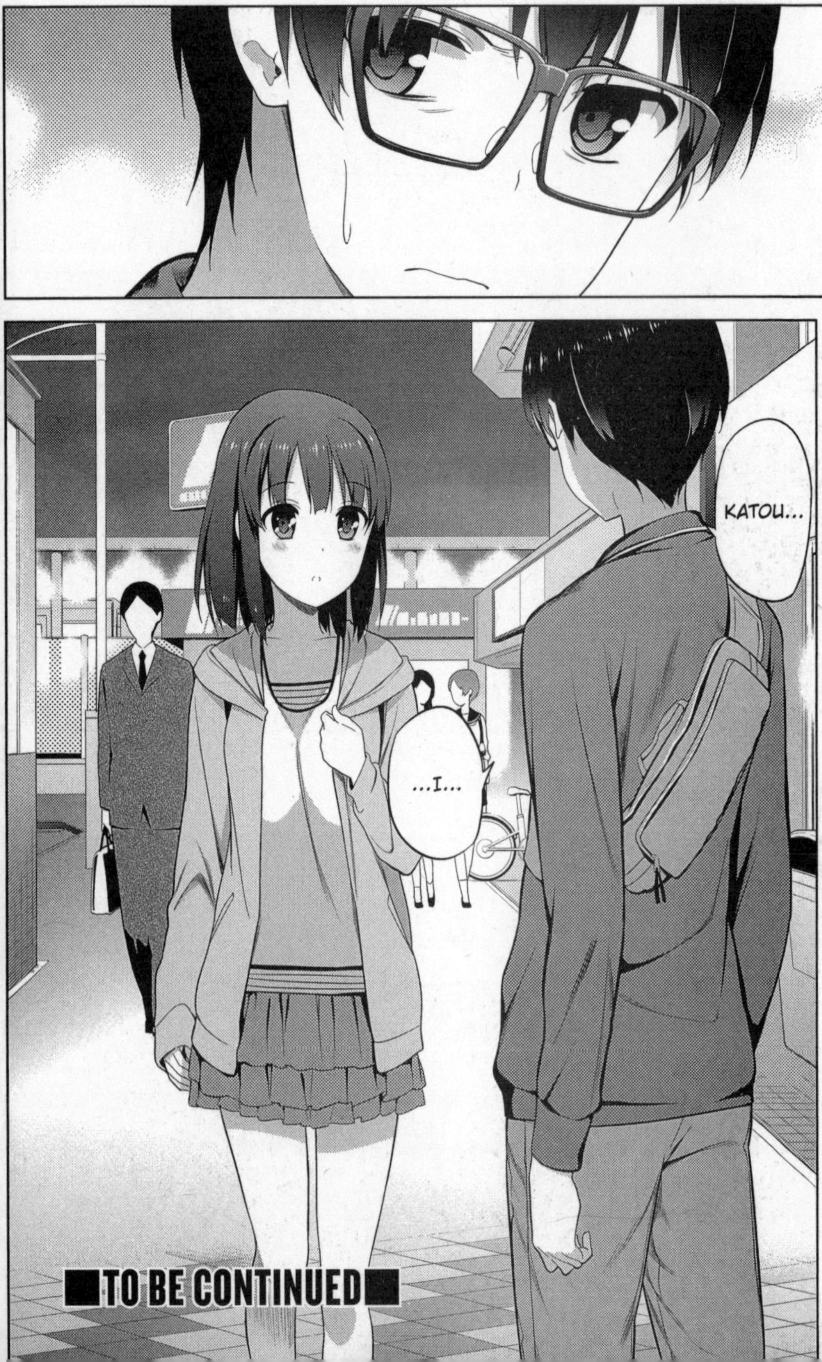
KATOU...
...I...
TO BE CONTINUED

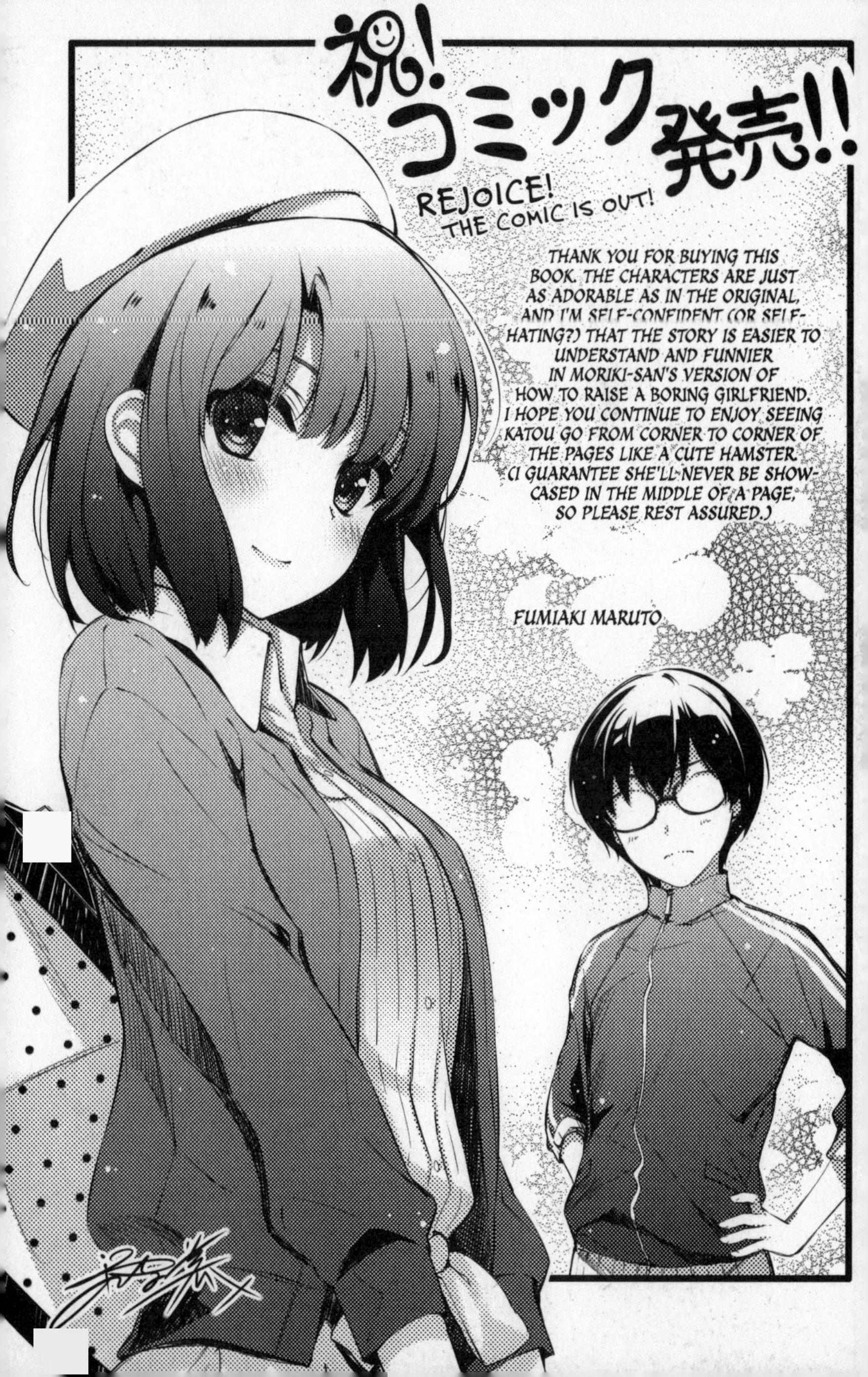
祝！コミック発売！！
REJOICE! THE COMIC IS OUT!
THANK YOU FOR BUYING THIS BOOK. THE CHARACTERS ARE JUST AS ADORABLE AS IN THE ORIGINAL, AND I'M SELF-CONFIDENT (OR SELF-HATING?) THAT THE STORY IS EASIER TO UNDERSTAND AND FUNNIER IN MORIKI-SAN'S VERSION OF HOW TO RAISE A BORING GIRLFRIEND. I HOPE YOU CONTINUE TO ENJOY SEEING KATOU GO FROM CORNER TO CORNER OF THE PAGES LIKE A CUTE HAMSTER. (I GUARANTEE SHE'LL NEVER BE SHOWCASED IN THE MIDDLE OF A PAGE, SO PLEASE REST ASSURED.)
FUMIAKI MARUTO

HOW TO RAISE A BORING GIRLFRIEND ①

WE HOPE YOU ENJOYED IT!
AND THANK YOU!

SPECIAL THANKS
MR. ENDO
EDITOR K-SAMA

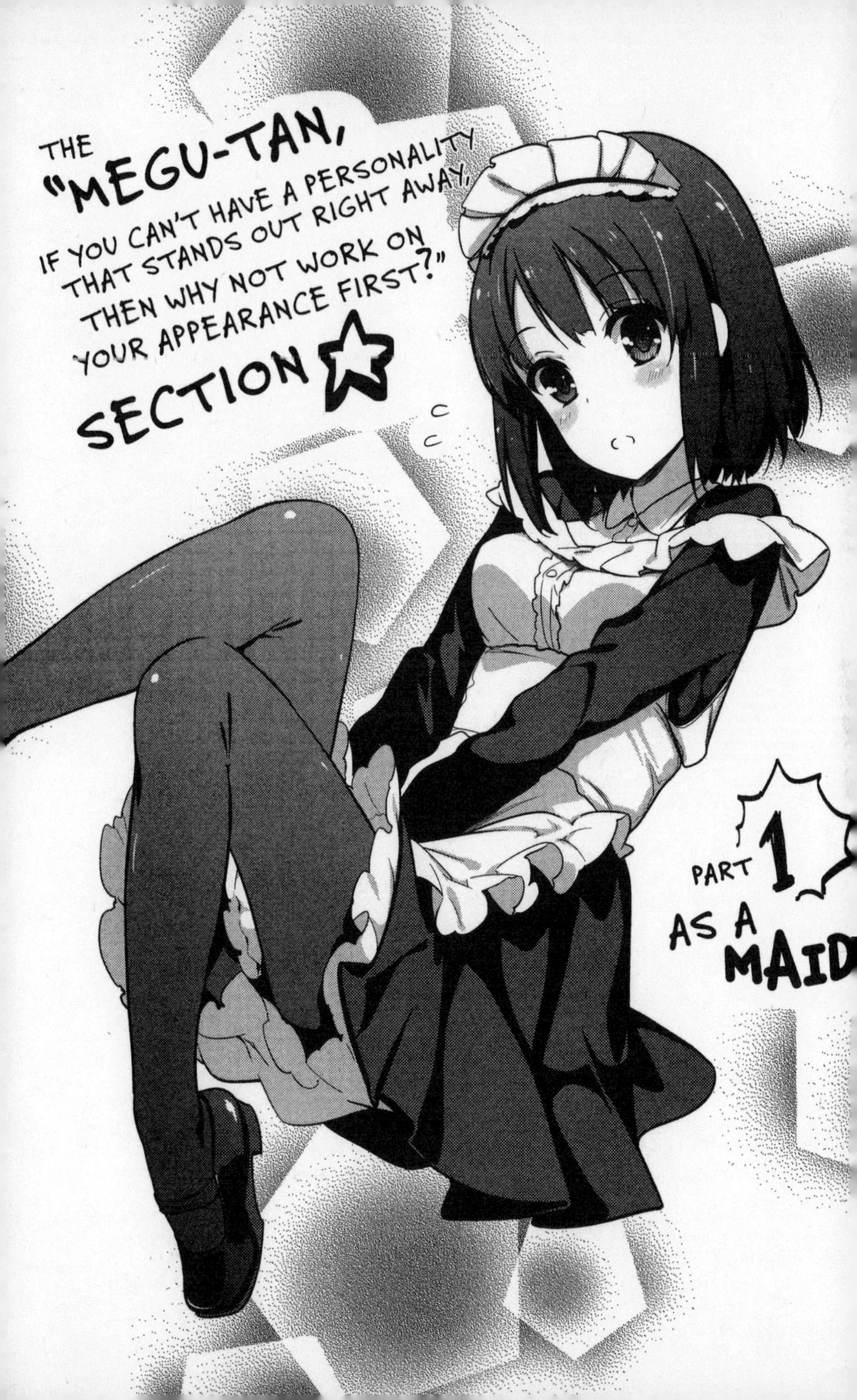
THE "MEGU-TAN, IF YOU CAN'T HAVE A PERSONALITY THAT STANDS OUT RIGHT AWAY, THEN WHY NOT WORK ON YOUR APPEARANCE FIRST?" SECTION ☆
PART 1
AS A MAID

COMMON HONORIFICS

no honorific: Indicates familiarity or closeness; if used without permission or reason, addressing someone in this manner would constitute an insult.

-san: The Japanese equivalent of Mr./Mrs./Miss. If a situation calls for politeness, this is the fail-safe honorific.

-sama: Conveys great respect; may also indicate that the social status of the speaker is lower than that of the addressee.

-kun: Used most often when referring to boys, this indicates affection or familiarity. Occasionally used by older men among their peers, but it may also be used by anyone referring to a person of lower standing.

-chan (also *-tan*): An affectionate honorific indicating familiarity used mostly in reference to girls; also used in reference to cute persons or animals of either gender.

-senpai: An honorific used to address upperclassmen or more experienced coworkers.

-sensei: A respectful honorific for teachers, artists, or high-level professionals.

PAGE 9

Doujinshi (often shortened to *doujin*) is self-published art, comics, video games, or novels produced (usually) by amateurs and often derived from existing properties. The *doujin* market in Japan is massive, despite the fact that derivative *doujin* is technically in violation of copyright and, therefore, illegal.

PAGE 11

Neighborhood Council's Decisions is a play on *Student Council's Discretion* (*Seitokai no Ichizon*), a light novel—shorter pop fiction aimed at the young adult market—series by Aoi Sekina. The plot features an academy where the student council is chosen via popularity contest.

PAGE 15
Rinri in **Rinri-kun**, Utaha's nickname for Aki, means "ethics, morals." The kanji for *tomo* in Tomoya can also be read as *rin*.

PAGE 19
Aki might not be able to **count the negatives**, but there are six total, so ultimately, Utaha does feel a modicum of sympathy for him.

PAGE 35
Imperial GoLion is a play on the anime series, *Beast King GoLion* (*Hyakujuuou GoRaion*), which achieved considerable popularity in the West under the title *Voltron*. Aki is letting his hardcore *otaku* shine by collecting this box set, as the series isn't particularly popular in Japan anymore.

PAGE 35
Nen●●roid stands for Nendoroid, a line of plastic figures with overly large heads produced by the Good Smile Company.

PAGE 59
Moe is a word that describes feelings of attraction or affection, usually toward anime, manga, or video game characters. It is also used to describe a genre of manga, anime, and games specifically intended to inspire such feelings.

PAGE 72
Twintails is the Japanese term for pigtails. Twintails are a characteristic common to *moe* characters and are beloved by fans of *moe*. There's even an official twintail appreciation society called the Japan Twintail Association.

PAGE 81
Yorimeki Memorial is a play on the classic, popular Japanese dating sim series *Tokimeki Memorial*. The game has gone on to spawn a host of sequels and spinoffs. *Tokimeki* is the Japanese word for "heartthrob."

PAGE 86
Katou's idea of a stereotypical *otaku* in the original volume includes the assumption on her part that all *otaku* use the honorific *-dono* ("lord") when addressing other people. This is typically *-shi* ("sir, mister"). Also, she assumes that otaku end their sentences in *dao*, which is portmanteau of *da yo* (a typical colloquial sentence ending).

PAGE 94
Koshien, short for Hanshin Koshien Stadium, is a baseball stadium where the national high school baseball championships are held. Making it to Koshien is kind of like the holy grail for a high school athlete.

PAGE 99
The anime series that Aki loans Eriri is supposed to be **Is This a Zombie?** (*Kore wa Zonbi Desu Ka?*), an anime adaptation of a light novel series by Shinichi Kimura about a zombie boy who unwittingly steals a magical girl's powers and is made to transform into a magical girl himself.

PAGE 99
Aki's addition to the *Is This a Zombie?* DVD case of **"Yes, it's George A. Romero's masterpiece"** indicates that he has replaced the contents with the classic zombie apocalypse horror film, *Night of the Living Dead*, directed by Romero.

PAGE 105
fi●ma stands for figma, a line of action figures with posable joints produced by the Max Factory company. The particular figure being tossed around here is of Haruna, one of the main characters in Kimura's *Is This a Zombie?* series, whose powers end up transferring to the series protagonist.

PAGE 105
Tsundere is a compound term derived from the words *tsuntsun* ("disdainful, prickly") and *de-redere* ("affectionate, fawning") that refers to a person who is initially abrasive or combative but softens over time or reveals a warm inner nature.

PAGE 110
A **circle** is a club or group (or sometimes a single person with their own brand/handle) producing *doujinshi*.

PAGE 110
Comiket, a portmanteau of Comic Market, is the world's largest *doujinshi* fair. Founded in 1975, it is now held twice a year (August and December) in Tokyo and draws crowds exceeding 500,000 heads per show.

PAGE 114
The **mosaicked art** here is common in Japanese anime, manga, and even pornography, where genitals and the like are blurred over to conform to Japan's obscenity laws.

PAGE 116

The **series** shown here include *Rabu★Kira*, *Is This a Zombie?*, and a *Monthly Dragon Age* magazine with *Triage X* on the cover. *Rabu★Kira* may be a play on *Love Hina*, Ken Akamatsu's manga series about a boy's attempt to rekindle romance with his childhood friend. *Monthly Dragon Age* is a manga anthology magazine edited by Fujimi Shobo and published by Kadokawa Corporation, in which *Triage X*, a manga series by Shouji Sato about a vigilante organization at a general hospital, is serialized. The final book in the panel reads *Pai-otsu*, with *pai* being a pun on the Japanese word for "breasts" (*oppai*) and *otsu*, which means "girl, woman."

PAGE 117

The *otaku* here are mumbling the names of popular manga and anime characters, among which are **Azu-meow** (Azusa Nakano) from *K-On!*, a manga series by kakifly about a high school band, and **Haruna** from *Is This a Zombie?*

PAGE 119

Kata●●●●-san probably refers to Ayako Katagiri one of the potential love interests and an art student from the dating sim *Tokimeki Memorial*.

PAGE 122

A **virtual idol** is, as the term implies, a digitally created humanoid singer/persona. The most famous among these is Miku Hatsune, who has even appeared on the *Late Show with David Letterman*. **Vocaloid** is a singing voice synthesizer developed by Yamaha, often used to give voice to virtual idols. The term is also used to refer to the virtual idols themselves. **3D Cu●●●m Girl** stands for "3D Custom Girl," a "game" developed by TechArts3D for designing 3-D models of female characters.

PAGE 123
The **National Stadium** was located in Shinjuku, Tokyo, and served as the venue for both national and international sporting events, including the 1964 Olympic Games. It was also used as home ground by the Japanese national soccer team. It was demolished in 2015 to make way for a new stadium to house the 2020 Summer Olympics.

PAGE 148
Established in 1935, the **Naoki Prize** is an award for popular literature that is presented twice annually. It was named in memory of novelist Sanjuugo Naoki.

PAGE 152
Utaha's faked signatures belong to actual creators. **Shouji Gatou** is the creator of the *Full Metal Panic!* series of light novels and manga. **Buriki** is an illustrator of light novels, including *Haganai: I Don't Have Many Friends* (*Boku wa Tomodachi ga Sukunai*).

How to Raise a Boring Girlfriend

HAVE YOU BEEN TURNED ON TO LIGHT NOVELS YET?

SWORD ART ONLINE, VOL. 1-6
SWORD ART ONLINE, PROGRESSIVE 1-3

The chart-topping light novel series that spawned the explosively popular anime and manga adaptations!

MANGA ADAPTATION AVAILABLE NOW!

SWORD ART ONLINE © REKI KAWAHARA ILLUSTRATION: abec
KADOKAWA CORPORATION ASCII MEDIA WORKS

ACCEL WORLD, VOL. 1-5

Prepare to accelerate with an action-packed cyber-thriller from the bestselling author of *Sword Art Online*.

MANGA ADAPTATION AVAILABLE NOW!

ACCEL WORLD © REKI KAWAHARA ILLUSTRATION: HIMA
KADOKAWA CORPORATION ASCII MEDIA WORKS

SPICE AND WOLF, VOL. 1-16

A disgruntled goddess joins a traveling merchant in this light novel series that inspired the *New York Times* bestselling manga.

MANGA ADAPTATION AVAILABLE NOW!

SPICE AND WOLF © ISUNA HASEKURA ILLUSTRATION: JYUU AYAKURA
KADOKAWA CORPORATION ASCII MEDIA WORKS

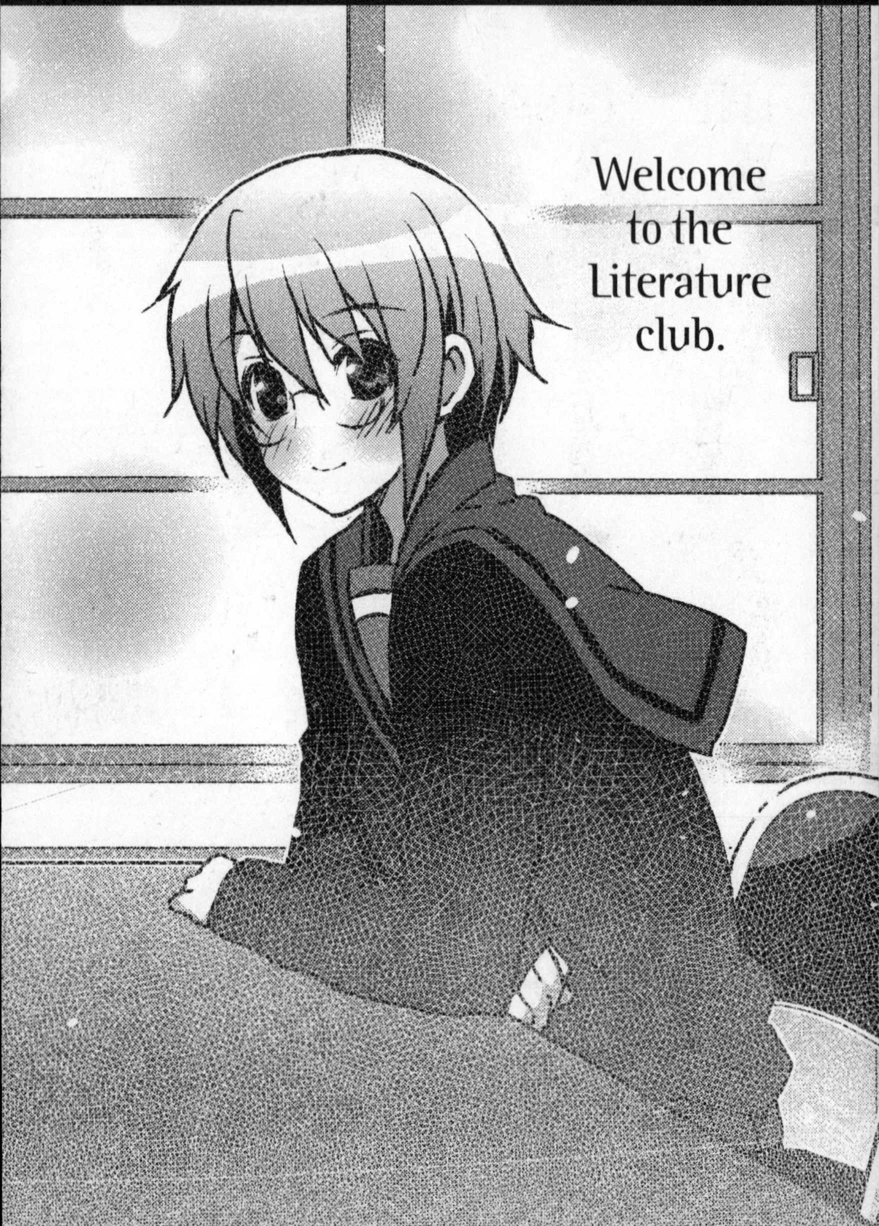
Welcome to the Literature club.

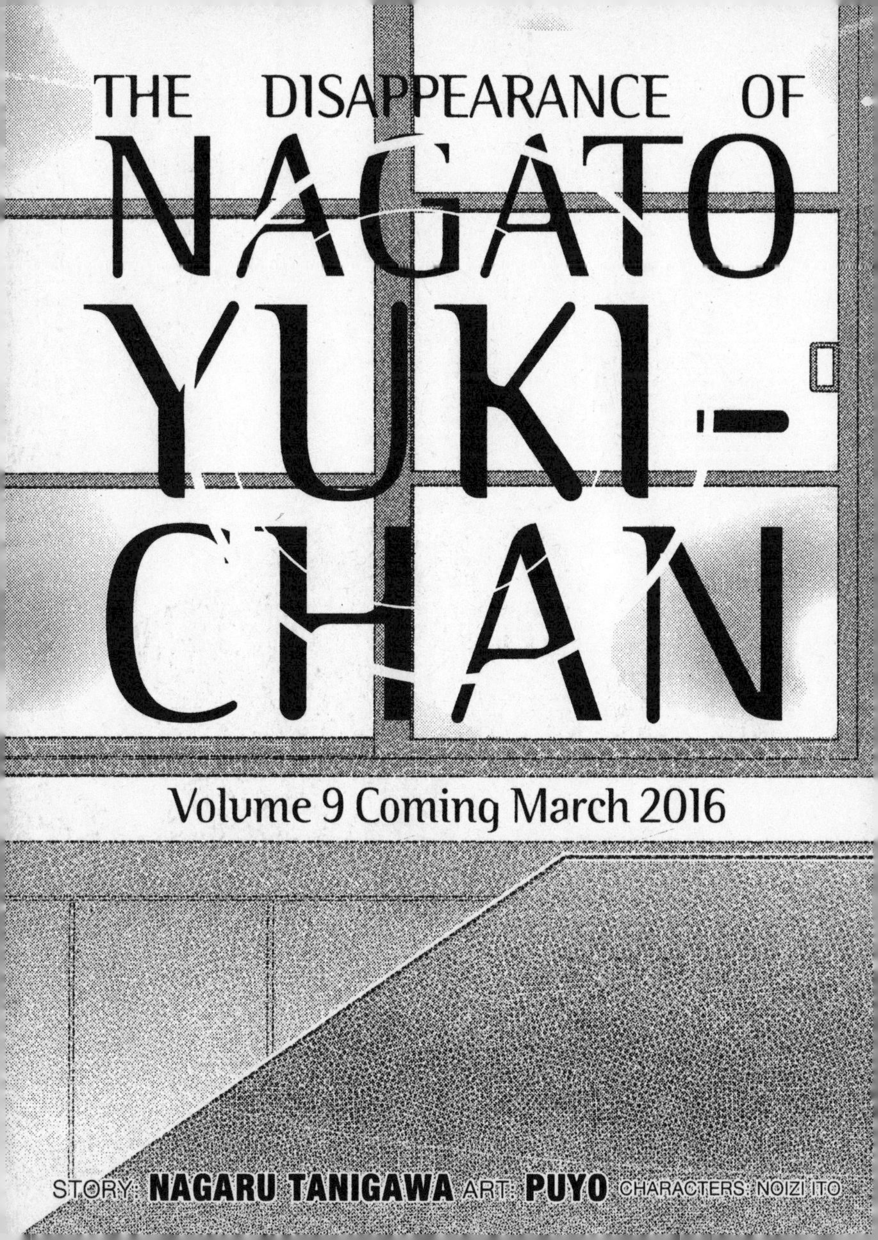
THE DISAPPEARANCE OF
NAGATO YUKI-CHAN
Volume 9 Coming March 2016
STORY: NAGARU TANIGAWA ART: PUYO CHARACTERS: NOIZI ITO

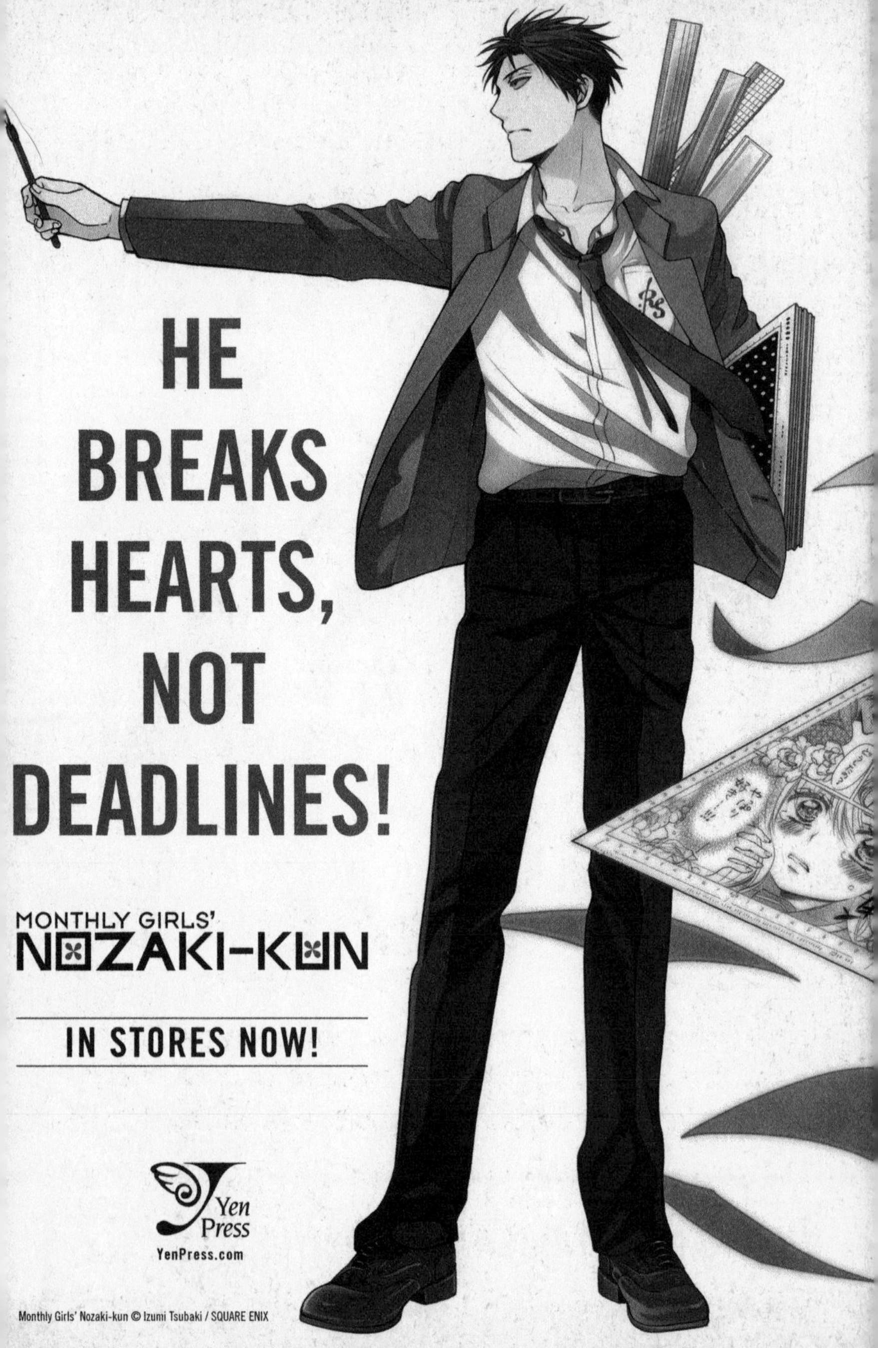
HE
BREAKS
HEARTS,
NOT
DEADLINES!
MONTHLY GIRLS'
NOZAKI-KUN
IN STORES NOW!
Yen Press
YenPress.com
Monthly Girls' Nozaki-kun © Izumi Tsubaki / SQUARE ENIX

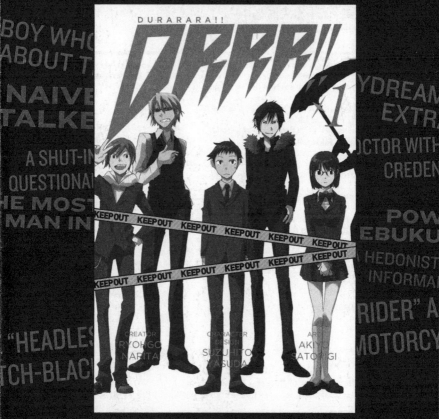

HOW TO RAISE A BORING GIRLFRIEND ❶

TAKESHI MORIKI
Original Story: **FUMIAKI MARUTO**
Character Design: **KUREHITO MISAKI**

Translation: Kumar Sivasubramanian
Translation Consultant: Chitoku Teshima
Lettering: Phil Christie

SAENAI HEROINE NO SODATE-KATA Volume 1
©TAKESHI MORIKI 2013
©FUMIAKI MARUTO, KUREHITO MISAKI 2013
Edited by FUJIMISHOBO
First published in Japan in 2013 by KADOKAWA CORPORATION, Tokyo.
English translation rights arranged with KADOKAWA CORPORATION, Tokyo
through Tuttle-Mori Agency, Inc., Tokyo.

Translation © 2016 by Hachette Book Group, Inc.

Yen Press
Hachette Book Group
1290 Avenue of the Americas
New York, NY 10104

www.hachettebookgroup.com
www.yenpress.com

Yen Press is an imprint of Hachette Book Group, Inc.
The Yen Press name and logo are trademarks of Hachette Book Group, Inc.

The publisher is not responsible for websites (or their content) that are not owned by the publisher.

Library of Congress Control Number: 2015952583

First Yen Press Edition: January 2016

ISBN: 978-0-316-26919-3

10 9 8 7 6 5 4 3 2 1

BVG

Printed in the United States of America